IRISH IDENTITY AND THE LITERARY REVIVAL

SYNGE, YEATS, JOYCE AND O'CASEY

G. J. Watson

CROOM HELM LONDON

BARNES & NOBLE BOOKS · NEW YORK
(a division of Harper & Row Publishers, Inc.)

© 1979 George Watson
Croom Helm Ltd, 2-10 St John's Road, London SW11

British Library Cataloguing in Publication Data

Watson, George Joseph
    Irish identity and the literary revival.
    1. English literature — Irish authors — History
and criticism 2. English literature — 19th
century — History and criticism. 3. English
literature — 20th century — History and
criticism 4. Literature and society — Ireland
I. Title
820'.9'9415   PR8750

ISBN 0-85664-330-0

Published in the USA 1979 by
Harper & Row Publishers, Inc.
Barnes & Noble Import Division

ISBN 0-06-497495-2

Printed and bound in Great Britain by
REDWOOD BURN LIMITED
Trowbridge & Esher

CONTENTS

TO JO, ANNA AND CONOR

PREFACE

My first debt in this study is to previous critics of these four artists, perhaps especially to Richard Ellmann, Conor Cruise O'Brien and Denis Donoghue. But there are many others whose insights I have drawn upon consciously or unconsciously — I trust mostly consciously.

I am also grateful to the British Council for a grant which enabled me to visit Dublin at a crucial point in my research; and to the editors of *The Maynooth Review* for permission to include in Chapter 3 of this book a revised version of an article on Yeats's view of history which first appeared in that journal in 1977.

I should like also to thank Brian Farrington of the University of Aberdeen for some stimulating discussions and for his generous permission to use his poem on J.M. Synge. Cairns Craig and David Fuller of my own Department of English patiently listened as I bored them with my obsessions, and I would like to thank them for their help and encouragement. I am especially grateful to Len Hunt and to Robin Gilmour, who read much of my manuscript and saved me from some major blunders. The blunders that remain are entirely my own work.

Finally, Mrs Margaret Bruce helped me in more ways than she can imagine. My greatest debt of gratitude I can only express, inadequately, through the dedication.

G.J. Watson
Aberdeen
December 1978

LIST OF TEXTS AND EDITIONS CITED FREQUENTLY

The following is a list of the texts used for each author, with (where appropriate) the abbreviations I have employed in the book.

JOYCE

Dubliners, the corrected text with an explanatory note by Robert Scholes (Jonathan Cape, London, 1967).

Stephen Hero, edited with an introduction by Theodore Spencer, revised edition with additional material and a foreword by John J. Slocum and Herbert Cahoon (Jonathan Cape, London, 1956).

A Portrait of the Artist as a Young Man, the definitive text corrected from the Dublin holograph by Chester G. Anderson and edited by Richard Ellmann (Jonathan Cape, London, 1968).

Ulysses (John Lane, The Bodley Head, London 1937, reprinted 1941).

O'CASEY

Collected Plays, vol. 1 (Macmillan, London, 1949).

SYNGE

Collected Works [*CW*] , 4 vols. (Oxford University Press, London). *Poems* (vol. 1), ed. Robin Skelton, 1962. *Prose* (vol. 2), ed. Alan Price, 1966. *Plays* (vols. 3 and 4), ed. Ann Saddlemyer, 1968.

YEATS

Autobiographies (Macmillan, London, 1955).

Collected Poems [*CP*] (Macmillan, London, 1950).

Collected Plays (Macmillan, London, 1952).

Essays and Introductions (Macmillan, London, 1961).

Explorations (Macmillan, London, 1962).

Memoirs, ed. Denis Donoghue (Macmillan, London, 1973).

Mythologies (Macmillan, London, 1959).

Uncollected Prose by W. B. Yeats, 2 vols. (Macmillan, London). First Reviews and Articles 1886-96 (vol. 1), ed. John P. Frayne, 1970. Reviews, Articles and Other Miscellaneous Prose 1897-1939 (vol. 2), eds. John P. Frayne and Colton Johnson.

The Variorum Edition of the Poems of W. B. Yeats [*Variorum Poems*], eds. Peter Allt and Russell K. Alspach (Macmillan, New York, 1966).

A Vision (Macmillan, London, 2nd edn. 1937, reissued with corrections 1962).

1 INTRODUCTION: THE CRACKED LOOKING-GLASS

The last ten years of the nineteenth century and the first thirty or so years of the twentieth saw the shaping and making of modern Ireland. As always, there is a certain vulnerable arbitrariness about this selection of dates. Nevertheless, few, surely, would wish to contest the crucial significance of the forty years that saw the fall of Parnell at the height of his political fame, the decline of the appeal of the parliamentary approach to Home Rule, the increasing allure of extremist politics in north and south, the growth in national self-consciousness and self-awareness as a result of the activities of such diverse groups as the Gaelic Athletic Association, the Gaelic League and what is called the Literary Revival, the rise of militant socialism under Jim Larkin and James Connolly (and its eclipse in the years that followed the foundation of the new state), the Easter Rising of 1916, the guerrilla war of independence, the civil war which followed the signing of the treaty with Britain, and the uneasy settling-down of the Catholic 'Free State' and the Protestant statelet in the North. For good or ill, the events of those years crucially informed and still affect Ireland as we know it today.

W. B. Yeats, James Joyce, J.M. Synge and Sean O'Casey are the most prominent writers of this period; and, taken together, they and their work cover and represent the whole complex spectrum of political, social and religious pressures moulding Ireland during the most dramatic years of her transition from an inert and — in Joyce's word — 'paralysed' colony to a new and frequently violent nation.

The aim of this book is to study these four writers in relation to their common context in those crucial years. The main focus is therefore on the relationship between the literature and its society; the unifying theme is each writer's attempt to grapple with, or define, the nature or meaning of Irish identity, and the resultant effects on the content and form of their art. Subsidiary themes, closely connected, recur — attitudes to the peasantry and the problem of backward Ireland's position in the modern world, to political nationalism seen as both dynamic and destructive, varying attitudes to the hero and the concept of heroism, to the meaning of Ireland's history and the validity of her cultural traditions; and the recurring tension between the writer's

13

desire to identify with his community and his feelings of marginality. I have not attempted to survey completely each writer's total *oeuvre*, but have selected, in order to highlight the issues and themes which seem to me of major importance in understanding the writers against their cultural background. Central to this is the question of identity – Irish identity, each writer's identity, the meaning of 'Irishness': it is *the* theme of Irish writing at the beginning of this century, for obvious and very good reasons. Since 'identity' is such a slippery and multi-faceted concept, such an approach may seem more clumsy and imprecise than an approach to these writers through more restricted and hence manageable themes or topics. There have been useful studies of the various writers through such topics, as for example in relation to the fall of Parnell and the cult of the lost leader, in relation to the rise of the Abbey theatre, in relation to the Easter Rising, in relation to Irish nationalism in general, and so on.[1] But I would hope that my own approach, a study of these four writers in terms of a variety of separate but interrelated themes focused on the problem of the meaning of 'Irishness', would allow of a greater flexibility and a wider sense of the artists' achievements without, on the other hand, becoming simply a series of disparate jottings.

Now, all these writers are important, even 'great' – the case for Yeats and Joyce, especially, verified by the daunting annual flood of critical studies. Yet one often encounters in critical writing (there are, of course, major exceptions) and in readers' responses, an unease about or an indifference to what is felt to be the intrusive Irishness. The Irishness of the subject-matter of the art, that is, is frequently perceived or presented as a limiting 'background', which is complicated, rather boring, and to be got out of the way fast. 'Mad Ireland', in Auden's representative phrase, may have 'hurt' all of them into writing, but the sooner it can be pushed aside, for critical purposes, the better. For then the critic or reader may turn, with an almost audible sigh of relief, to the consideration of Yeats and Joyce as 'fabulous artificers', to the formal complexities or 'universal themes' in their art, or to the consideration of the symbolic and archetypal in the works of Synge and O'Casey; is *A Vision* Yeats's central text? is *Dubliners* a version of *The Pilgrim's Progress*? is Christy Mahon in Synge's *Playboy* a type of Christ? how far is O'Casey's work to be understood in terms of the popular morality plays? – and so on. Clearly one does not wish to dismiss such criticism, which is frequently illuminating and which has done much to make the work of the Irish writers known. But to underplay the Irish cultural and political context, or to treat it as peripheral, is especially damaging since, as this study will try to show, for the writers themselves 'Irishness' and their feelings about it is a major, even obsessive, concern.

Further, to study these writers in their context is, of course, to discover more about that context, about a deeply divided society in change and upheaval. As I write (December 1978), the Provisional IRA has just launched its 'winter offensive' on the cities of mainland Britain; for ten years the part of Ireland in which I was born has been convulsed by violence on a much greater scale. In other words, contemporary events in Ireland, still profoundly affected by those earlier divisions and upheavals, and contemporary attitudes to Ireland, suggest that there may be some profit in examining further that 'felt history' which literature uniquely provides.

The relationship of a literature to a society, always complex, throws up problems in particularly luxuriant profusion in the case of Ireland, where in the period in question at least three different sets of cultural assumptions and values jostle together — English, Irish, and Anglo-Irish. Each of these is united by a common language, but in most other ways co-exist only with considerable tension and strain. And the tensions and strains have powerful shaping effects on the nature and kind of literature written from within this confused and confusing period and country. But I do not propose in this introduction to attempt an inevitably self-defeating survey of Irish history.[2] This is not solely due to an awareness of the difficulty of the task, and of my own incompetence to undertake it. Since I believe strongly that the Irish 'background' should become 'foreground' in the study of these writers, I have preferred to let the themes and issues with which I will be concerned emerge from direct and close study of the works of the writers themselves. To proceed thus is simultaneously to argue my case that the nature of Irishness and problems of identity are indeed at the heart of each artist's work, and to pay due attention to the distinctions between literature on the one hand and sociology, economics and history on the other. However, some preliminary ground may be cleared; or, if that is an overly ambitious way of phrasing it, we may at least begin by having a look at the nature of the terrain.

One must, as in so much to do with Irish questions, begin with English attitudes. For England, Ireland had always been a problem; but, as was only natural for a powerful and imperial nation, only one of many problems. For Ireland, however, England had been for many centuries *the* problem. Consequently, what England or the English thought of Ireland and the Irish had effects on Irish consciousness which may seem disproportionate to the Englishman who, secure in his sense of the continuity, validity and power of his own cultural and political institutions, simply does not worry very much about what other, 'inferior' races may think of him. Quite apart from the actual facts of the overwhelming impact, politically, economically, culturally, of England on Ireland, though of course as a result of that impact, there grew up on each side something more intractable than mere facts – a mythology, a set of images, which perpetuated themselves and begot in their turn equally powerful opposing images. The culture-clash between Ireland England has been so enduring because it has expressed itself mainly through opposing images. And images, as well as being the raw material of the artist, are always more powerful than rational arguments.

The origins of the English desire to impose an unflattering image on the Irish probably lie in part in a sort of imperialist defensive reaction. One might say that Prospero needs to invent his Caliban. Or, as Patrick O'Farrell says more soberly in his recent history:

> The portrayal of Celtic society as savage, with attendant poverty, indolence and brutality, became entrenched in English imagery from medieval times, and provided a moral justification for continued English efforts to dominate or destroy the Celts.[3]

One does not want to appear too much like Evelyn Waugh's Irishman, 'dragging everywhere with him his ancient rancours and the melancholy of the bogs', so perhaps it is sufficient to cite some comments by intelligent – and influential – Englishmen of the nineteenth century, whose tone illustrates that sense of the Irish as primitive savages with a nasty violent streak. Here is Disraeli in a letter to *The Times* in 1836:

> The Irish hate our free and fertile isle. They hate our order, our civilization, our enterprising industry, our sustained courage, our decorous liberty, our pure religion. This wild, reckless, indolent, uncertain and superstitious race have no sympathy with the English character. Their fair ideal of human felicity is an alternation of clannish broils and coarse idolatry. Their history describes an unbroken circle of bigotry and blood.[4]

Here is the historian J. A. Froude, a disciple of Carlyle, in 1841:

> The inhabitants, except where they had been taken in hand and metamorphosed into police, seemed more like tribes of squalid apes

than human beings.[5]

Here is the novelist and historian Charles Kingsley in 1860 in a letter to his wife from Ireland (a letter which in one of its phrases allows us a glimpse of the normally well-suppressed guilt):

> I am haunted by the human chimpanzees I saw along that hundred miles of horrible country. I don't believe they are our fault. I believe there are not only many more of them than of old, but that they are happier, better and more comfortably fed and lodged under our rule than they ever were. But to see white chimpanzees is dreadful; if they were black, one would not feel it so much, but their skins, except where tanned by exposure, are as white as ours.[6]

And here is Lord Salisbury, in a speech of May 1886:

> The confidence you repose in people will depend something upon the habits they have acquired. Well, the habits the Irish have acquired are very bad. They have become habituated to the use of knives and slugs which is wholly inconsistent with the placing of unlimited confidence in them.[7]

Even more favourably disposed Englishmen found it difficult not to think in terms of racial stereotypes, for example, Matthew Arnold in his famous *On the Study of Celtic Literature* (1865-6). Arnold sees a racial basis in the achievements of Celtic literature. To attribute, as Arnold does, the imaginative qualities of that literature to something in the 'Celtic soul' defined as a 'readiness to revolt against the despotism of fact' is to pay an ambiguous and doubled-edged compliment. It is significant that Arnold had no trouble in opposing the Home Rule Bill in 1886.

The Anglo-Saxon stereotypical image of the Irishman, then, is that of Paddy the Ape, violent, drunken, poor, superstitious. The emphasis on Irish violence and also on the gross, pig-in-the-kitchen poverty of Irish peasant life, both highly significant in the context of certain stresses in the work of Yeats and Synge, achieve classic visual form – and wide distribution – in the great cartoons of Tenniel in *Punch*.[8] At a slightly more refined level the Victorian Englishman's image of the Irishman was hardly more flattering and in some ways even more troublesome – the Irishman was childish, unstable, emotional, all blather and no solidity. As L. P. Curtis says:

Of the many pejorative adjectives applied by educated Englishmen to the Irish perhaps the most damaging, certainly the most persistent were those which had to do with their alleged unreliability, emotional instability, mental disequilibrium.[9]

All in all, and despite the existence of more enlightened views, a fairly dismal picture, in which the only alternative to contempt seemed often to be merely condescension.

Next, we must consider the nature of the Irish response to this English view, and their feelings about their own history. These took two contradictory shapes. But I have begged the question. Who are 'the Irish'? The difficulty of giving a straight and simple answer to this will, I hope, become apparent in the course of this book. Nevertheless, if one changes the question slightly to 'Whom did the majority of the people in Ireland consider the Irish to be?', one can establish certain bases from which to work. Conor Cruise O'Brien answers that altered question as follows:

By 'the Irish race' is meant, as far as Ireland is concerned: Primarily, people of native Irish stock, descended from Gaelic speakers, professing the Catholic religion, and holding some form of the general political opinions held by most people of this origin and religion.
Secondarily, people of settler stock in Ireland, and Protestant religion: to the extent that these cast in their lot with people in the first category, culturally or politically, or preferably both.[10]

The largeness of that proviso affecting the second category suggests that here we can concentrate on those in the first category.

The 'native' response to the unflattering English view described above was, as one would expect from a thoroughly colonialised people, mixed. In the first place, clearly, the long history of defeat and loss, linked with the effortless English assumption of superiority and rounded out by an awareness of the denigratory images, could only produce in the Irish mind deep feelings of inferiority, whether conscious or unconscious. Engels noted this, and wrote in a letter of 1856 to Marx, which interestingly dismisses 'nationalist fanaticism' as the comparatively minor phenomenon it undoubtedly was in the aftermath of the Great Famine:

Ireland may be regarded as the first English colony and as one which

because of its proximity is still governed exactly in the old way . . .
The people itself has got its peculiar character from this, and despite
all their Irish nationalist fanaticism the fellows feel that they are no
longer at home in their own country. Ireland for the Saxon! That is
now being realised. The Irishman knows he cannot compete with the
Englishman, who comes with means in every respect superior; emigration will go on until the predominantly, indeed almost exclusively,
Celtic character of the population is all to hell . . . By consistent
oppression they have been artificially converted into an utterly
demoralised nation and now fulfil the notorious function of supplying England, America, Australia, etc., with prostitutes, casual labourers, pimps, thieves, swindlers, beggars and other rabble.[11]

This is the standard picture of a 'demoralised' nation. But feelings of
inferiority may take subtler, less overt and in some ways more difficult
forms. It is arguable that more painful, even, than the awareness of political subjugation, was the knowledge of how thoroughly Irish culture
and life had been anglicised; of just how comprehensively the old Celtic
and Gaelic culture, and especially the language, had been routed. For
this was the knowledge of an irretrievably lost identity. Hence the
phenomenon of the Gaelic League founded in 1893 by Douglas Hyde
to encourage the speaking and dissemination of the Irish language.[12] In
his lecture of 1892, 'The Necessity for De-Anglicising Ireland', Hyde
stated:

. . . this failure of the Irish people in recent times has been largely
brought about by the race diverging during this century from the
right path, and ceasing to be Irish without becoming English.[13]

The sense of cultural dispossession marked here also characterises the
tone and themes of the writings of D. P. Moran, editor of *The Leader*.
Moran argued in an eassy of 1900 called 'The Battle of Two Civilisations':

. . . a distinct nation is a distinct civilisation, and if England went
down to the bottom of the sea tomorrow, that distinct civilisation
which we have turned our backs upon, that woof of national tradition which we have cast from us, would not be restored.[14]

In both these passages, there is a bleak recognition of loss and an
accompanying self-critical note. This ties in, in a powerful and lacerat-

ing way, with the feeling (or with the fact, let it even be said) of cultural inferiority to the great neighbour nation. As Dr O'Brien observes of the anglicising of the Irish mind during the nineteenth century:

> This did not entirely eliminate the old hate [of England], but turned it into one element in a more complex system. So far as hate survived, it had now to include self-hate and self-contempt: quite important components in the psychology of some Irishmen as of other 'colonized peoples'.[15]

The point deserves stressing, since so much emphasis is usually placed (not least by Irish writers) on the Irish love of nation and on the Irish consciousness of its historical identity as a positive phenomenon. In fact, for all the Irishman's notoriously long memory, for all his sense of separate identity ('the ultimate criterion of nationality', says Joseph Lee[16]), for all his comforting sense that his views are shared by the majority of his fellow-islanders, for all his sometimes aggressive proclamation of his nationality, which can — and does — grate on those (usually English) who feel no comparable assertive urges — for all these (which may indeed precisely direct our attention to the point), always lurking somewhere near the surface is a painful sense of insecurity deriving ultimately from the sense of a lost identity, a broken tradition, and the knowledge that an alien identity has been, however reluctantly, more than half embraced. The modern Irish poet Thomas Kinsella may be quoted at some length here, in part because his own citation of Daniel Corkery sends us back to the period in which we are mainly interested:

> The death of a language . . . it is a calamity. And its effects are at work everywhere in the present, reducing energies of every kind, undermining individual confidence, lessening the quality of thought. Daniel Corkery has written very well, I think, about this in his book *Synge and Anglo-Irish Literature*. We know that he has some special convictions about nationality and literature — a strident pessimism that frequently amounts to distortion — but in this passage his emotion seems very much in place:
>
> 'Everywhere in the mentality of the Irish people are flux and uncertainty. Our national consciousness may be described in a native phrase, as a quaking sod. It gives no footing. It is not English, nor Irish, nor Anglo-Irish; as will be understood if one think awhile on the thwarting it undergoes in each individual child of the race as he

grows to manhood . . . For practically all that he reads is English; what he reads in Irish is not yet worth taking account of. It does not therefore focus the mind of his own people, teaching him the better to look about him, to understand both himself and his surroundings. It focuses instead the life of another people. Instead of sharpening his gaze on his own neighbourhood, his reading distracts it, for he cannot find in these surroundings what his reading has taught him is the matter worth coming upon. His surroundings begin to seem un-vital . . . At the least his education sets up a dispute between his intellect and his emotions . . . What happens in the neighbourhood of an Irish boy's home — the fair, the hurling match, the land grabbing, the *priesting*, the mission, the Mass — he never comes on in literature, that is, in such literature as he is told to respect and learn . . . In his riper years he may come to see the crassness of his own upbringing . . . but of course the damage is done' . . .

Corkery is not writing about Dublin, where the hurling match and the land grabbing and the priesting are all foreign games. But to have been born in Dublin, as I was, of people whose families came from the country a hundred years ago, is not to escape the deprivation, nor even to feel it less sharply once the process of self-search has begun.[17]

It seems to me that James Joyce, though not in the least interested in the Irish language, fully understands the generalised feelings of deprivation and inferiority in the Irish psyche and, as I shall argue, his art originates in an attempt to face them with honesty: his greatness is his ability to come to tolerant terms with a fractured culture. By contrast, the Anglo-Irish Yeats and Synge have no such sense of cultural inferiority, and can pick and choose among the fragments to create each his own idealised version of Ireland.

Of course, a vivid sense of cultural inferiority and a haunting sense of lost identity was not the only effect on Irish consciousness of its anglicisation. The Irish are human, after all, despite some arguments to the contrary. So the second kind of response to the unflattering English image of the Irish was resentment — a resentment which produced powerful compensatory counter-images. We will look at one of these counter-images, that of the peasant, since it will enable us to view from another angle 'native' ambivalence or confusion about identity, giving another perspective on what Corkery called the 'quaking sod' of national consciousness; and will also enable us to introduce our third set of cultural assumptions and values, those of the Anglo-Irish.

In 1879 Michael Davitt founded the Land League, which was probably the most important, and certainly one of the most effective, Irish
attempts to mythologise the past. It politicised the peasantry, giving
them an ideology, and prepared the way for the transmogrification of
the peasant by the writers of the literary revival. Briefly, what the Land
League did was to pioneer 'on a mass basis a technique destined to
become indispensable in nationalist agitation, the appeal to spurious
historic rights'.[18] The myth was that the native Catholic peasantry had
once owned their own land in Celtic Ireland, and had been dispossessed
by the (English) settlers. (In fact, it is most unlikely that the leading
families of Celtic Ireland paid much, if any, attention to their tenants'
'rights'.) The League thus asserted an 'ancient' claim, arising from the
invention of the dignified, independent peasant of olden times. It was a
characteristic Irish effort — you look back to create the future you
want. As Joseph Lee, who sees the League as one of the greatest modern-
ising forces in nineteenth-century Ireland, sums up the political and
psychological impact of the Land League on Irish consciousness:

> In 1881 the bulk of the people were still satisfied with rent reduc-
> tions and relative security of tenure, their original aims, though no
> longer as the ultimate goal but merely as a step on the road to pea-
> sant proprietorship. The Land League not merely articulated, but
> largely created, that aspiration, legitimised it with an immaculate
> pedigree by which the tenants acquired retrospective private shares
> in a mythical Gaelic garden of Eden, and pushed it through to with-
> in sight of ultimate victory. It was a virtuoso performance.[19]

Thus, the Irish peasant, who summed up in his poverty, superstition,
ignorance and vulgarity everything that many English minds considered to be wrong with Ireland, could now, thanks to the Land
League's propaganda, be claimed by many Irishmen in a spirit of
defiant contradiction, to embody everything that was good about
Ireland, and to constitute in his way of life its essence. In particular,
Irishmen could measure scornfully England's materialism by the yard-
stick of the peasant's poverty, suddenly become a badge of spiritual
worth. The Catholic magazine *The Lyceum* said in a review in 1890
of Gavan Duffy's life of Thomas Davis:

> While our peasants say their beads and meditate on the mysteries
> of the Rosary, they can never come wholly under the sway of the
> doctrine that men were sent into the world to be happy and to make

money . . . Thomas Davis saw in the factory system a monster that destroyed this ideal life, and he was its foe. He would have Ireland a nation of peasant owners.[20]

The power and persistence of this idealised image of a nation of peasant owners, and the political mileage to be got from it among a land-hungry electorate, may be indicated by the fact that it was the constant theme of Eamon De Valera, who left such an imprint on the new Free State:

> The Ireland we have dreamed of would be the home of a people who valued material wealth only as a basis of right living, of a people who were satisfied with frugal comfort and devoted their leisure to the things of the spirit; a land whose countryside would be bright with cosy homesteads, whose villages would be joyous with the romping of sturdy children, the contests of athletic youths, the laughter of comely maidens; whose fireside would be the forums of the wisdom of old age.[21]

Behind the sugariness of the picture, which is deceptive, shrewd political calculation is going on — as it had been going on right back in the early heady days of the Land League.

For the writers of the literary revival, Yeats, Synge, Lady Gregory and others, the image of a peasant, rather archaic Ireland also held much appeal, and they reinforced it while extending and strengthening its literary (and literate) basis. Their treatment of the peasant naturally did not run much on the mysteries of the Rosary, but there is an obvious overlap with the Catholic native idealisation. And equally clearly, the writers are reacting against the English stereotype. The revival's idealisation of the peasant grew naturally from its hatred of progress, modernity, centralisation, commercialism and industrialised materialism, all of which were embodied and given definitive shape in England. To the vulgarity of all this could be opposed the values embodied in — or projected on — the Irish peasant, the values of the traditional, the archaic, the picturesque and the organic. The importance of this opposition for Irish psychology in terms of a compensation for political impotence and failure can hardly be overstated. The power and success of the mighty imperial neighbour became more tolerable when seen as a badge of 'spiritual' incapacity or grossness. What did it profit a nation to rule the waves if its 'soul' was mass-produced in Birmingham? Thus George Russell (known always as AE) speaks with distaste of 'the shout of the cockney tourist' sounding 'in the cyclopean crypts and mounds once sanctified by druid mysteries, and divine visitations'; and inveighs against England's sordid commercialism which he contrasts most unfavourably with this archaic and druid Ireland.[22] Even George Moore, who, earlier, had written a fairly savage diatribe on Ireland in general, and the idiocy of Irish rural life in particular,[23] could now write in 1900:

> Those who believe that dreams, beauty, and divine ecstasy are essential must pray that all the empires may perish and the world be given back to the small peasant states, whose seas and forests and mountains shall create national aspirations and new gods. Otherwise the world will fall into gross naturalism, with scientific barbarism more terrible than the torch and the sword of the Hun . . . The commercial platitude which has risen up in England, which is extending over the whole world, is horrible to contemplate. Its flag, which Mr Rhodes has declared to be 'the most valuable commercial asset in the world', is everywhere. England has imposed her idea upon all nations, and to girdle the world with Brixton seems to be her ultimate destiny. And we, sitting on the last verge, see into the universal suburb, in which a lean man with glasses on his nose and a black bag in his hand is always running after his bus.[24]

To see even this normally cynical man, usually more at home in Paris than in Mayo, thus caught up in the cultural primitivism of the literary revival is to understand better just how widely and strongly diffused at the turn of the century was the tendency to view the peasant and peasant life as the repository of Irish virtue and genius. It is a major tendency in the work of Yeats and, especially, of Synge, and is discussed more fully below.

If the 'native' Catholic Irish and the writers of the literary revival, especially Synge and Yeats, co-operated in this way to create a Celticist image of the peasant in opposition to the Anglo-Saxonist portrait of Paddy with his Pig, why then did Yeats and Synge encounter so much hostility from the natives, notoriously in the case of *The Playboy of the Western World*, for their portrayal of Irish life? There are two answers to this, one long and one short.

The long answer is to do with the actualities of peasant life. The pattern of Irish rural life changed markedly between 1840 and 1880, mainly as a result of the Great Famine, which was chiefly responsible for instituting a tradition of emigration and for making small farmers extremely reluctant to subdivide their holdings among their sons. One son inherited – the others usually emigrated, or moved to the towns. The heir generally could not marry until he took over the land from his father, and this central event in the cycle of a rural family usually did not occur until the son was well into his thirties. It is easy to understand how a kind of self-perpetuating gerontocracy came into being in these circumstances; if one had not taken over a farm until one was thirty-five or thirty-six, one did not feel very much like handing it over to one's own son when one was merely sixty years old. These conditions alone, quite apart from the skilful propaganda of the Land League, were sufficient to produce a strong land-hunger among the peasantry; and with the emigration of all but those who stood a chance of inheriting land, what had been before the Famine a rural proletariat became what might best be called a rural bourgeoisie.[25] And the native embrace of the Land League's propaganda was designed to ensure the extension and consolidation of that rural bourgeoisie, to turn Ireland into a nation of peasant *owners*, as the *Lyceum* put it. In other words, and despite appearances, there was nothing romantic about the native attitude to the peasant; or if there was, it was on a very different scale to the full-blown romantic primitivism to be found in Synge and Yeats, who both valued the peasant precisely to the extent that he was untainted by anything smacking of the bourgeois.

Further, and here we are back again on the quaking sod of the native consciousness, many Irishmen felt deeply ambivalent about the very concept of 'the peasant'. As we have seen, the Land League could give it an honorific sense, and employ it with great skill for practical political purposes. Against that, the English picture of Paddy with his Pig *had* bitten deeply into the native consciousness, which could and did frequently feel the term 'peasant' to be insulting,[26] a foreign jibe at poverty and a basic inferiority. In a sense, the relationship between landlord and peasant was uncomfortably analogous – so many Irishmen felt – to the larger relationship between England and Ireland. Therefore, despite the ability of the native Irish to beat the big drum of peasant virtue when it suited them, it should not be forgotten, when considering the storms raised by Yeats's *The Countess Cathleen* and most of Synge's works, that many natives did not *like* being reminded that Ireland was an overwhelmingly rural or peasant society. This applied even when the reminder was offered as a source of pride and self-belief, the more so when it was offered by Anglo-Irish 'gentlemen'. The point was that the natural audience for this drama was urban, Dublin-dwellers who felt they had made good by leaving the land, as many of them had in the

recent past. The Famine had produced not merely a tradition of emigration, but an inexorable drift to the towns.[27] The last thing that many
of these new town-dwellers wanted was to be reminded of the poverty
and narrowness of the life they had left behind them in Ireland's lonely
countryside. As Frank O'Connor says:

> The Irish were becoming a nation of town-dwellers without even the
> excuse of industry and high wages. To this day you will still not find
> what you find in almost every European country — the town-dweller
> who pines for a little place where he can garden and keep hens. In
> Ireland the country represents poverty and ignorance — 'beyond the
> lamps' as they said in my youth.[28]

The most famous of Ireland's town-dwellers illustrates the wide gap
between the idealisation of rural Ireland to be found in Synge and
Yeats and Catholic urban feelings about 'the country'. Joyce's Stephen
Dedalus writes in his diary:

> John Alphonsus Mulrennan has just returned from the west of
> Ireland. (European and Asiatic papers please copy.) He told us he
> met an old man there in a mountain cabin. Old man had red eyes
> and short pipe. Old man spoke Irish. Mulrennan spoke Irish. Then
> old man and Mulrennan spoke English. Mulrennan spoke to him
> about universe and stars. Old man sat, listened, smoked, spat.
> Then said:
> — Ah, there must be terrible queer creatures at the latter end of
> the world.
>
> (*Portrait of the Artist*, p. 256)

The short answer to the question of the tensions between Yeats and
Synge and their audiences or readers is that Yeats and Synge were
Anglo-Irish, and the Anglo-Irish were suspect in the eyes of the natives.

Conor Cruise O'Brien's second category of 'the Irish race', it may be
remembered, comprised people of settler stock and of the Protestant
faith. But the natives would not regard such people as Irish in the way
they (the natives) were, unless the settlers cast in their lot, culturally
or politically, with the natives. And even in such cases, there was always
likely to be still a question mark. In other words, birth did not guarantee 'Irishness'. One qualified only on the grounds of descent, religion or
politics, and usually needed the combination of all three for native

acceptance. This is not fair, and it certainly put in an awkward position the Anglo-Irishman whose family might have lived in Ireland for several generations. But it is how the Catholic natives felt, and how many of them still feel. Brendan Behan defined an Anglo-Irishman as 'a Protestant with a horse'. This captures succinctly the native malice and native sense of difference, compounded as it is of the factors of class and caste, economics and religion. The shaky native sense of identity could consolidate itself around at least this assurance, that it was sure what it was not, and what it was not was 'Anglo-Irish'.

'Anglo-Irish', in ordinary and historical usage, 'denotes the Protestant community that dominated Ireland in the eighteenth century and those who inherited and maintained its tradition in the changed and changing circumstances of a later age', says J. C. Beckett.[29] The 'Anglo' component might refer to English parentage or descent, to an education in England, to acting politically in England's interest in Ireland, to allegiance to the religion which English attempts to impose on the recalcitrant Papists of Ireland had made such a decisive badge of difference, or to all of these. This community was numerically small, even insignificant, in relation to the majority population, but very powerful. The Penal Laws enacted between 1695 and 1727 had barred Catholic 'natives' from Parliament, from carrying arms, and from owning a horse worth more than £5 (probably the remote origin of Behan's crack), and a series of 'no education' acts made it illegal for Catholics to go for education abroad or to run proper schools at home. They were of course barred from taking degrees at Trinity College, Dublin. Thus, 'a whole code was passed to bar Catholics from the land, the army, the electorate, commerce and the law.'[30] These laws were not rescinded until the Catholic Emancipation Act of 1829. Hence, for a century and more, the Protestant community controlled Parliament, had a total stranglehold on the professions, and in the case of the aristocrats were often enormously wealthy and extensive land-owners.

It was inevitable in such circumstances, and especially after the Act of Union, that these Irish Protestants should be seen by the natives as the allies and agents of the hated English government, as, in J. C. Beckett's words, 'the means whereby an alien power held down an oppressed and discontented people – in short, as an "English Garrison" in a conquered country'.[31] The Anglo-Irishman, like Yeats or Synge, who wished to relate to, even identify with, that other 'native' Ireland, had thus a very wide chasm to cross, a great ravine of suspicion and mistrust and sometimes downright hatred. One can only admire their courage and the generosity of spirit which impelled them to make the

effort. To point to that chasm is not to minimise the apparently paradoxical fact that some Protestant Anglo-Irishmen throughout the
nineteenth century had not only abandoned the traditional Unionism
of their caste but had become political or moral leaders of the other
Catholic Ireland — one need mention only Thomas Davis and Charles
Stewart Parnell. However, though such Anglo-Irishmen made great
contributions towards raising the level of political consciousness of the
native Irish, they did little or nothing to change the exclusivist or
Catholic nature of that consciousness.

Even as the power of the Anglo-Irish declined, as it did steadily
throughout the nineteenth century,[32] their sense of caste-superiority,
bred into them by history, remained strong. This is where that other
term often applied to the Anglo-Irish, the Protestant Ascendancy, is
useful, since it suggests something ever present in the general Anglo-
Irish consciousness. 'No petty people', 'one of the great stocks of
Europe', 'the people of Burke and of Grattan' as Yeats described his
'stock' in 1925 — the people of Burke and of Grattan could not help
looking down on the natives, particularly if and when the natives
showed signs of getting uppity. Even in Yeats and Synge, who were in
many ways unusual Anglo-Irishmen, the impulse to denigrate the
natives is sometimes present and at war with the impulse to identity
with them, adding a fascinating tension and drama to their work. A
classic illustration of the Anglo-Irish sense of caste-superiority is provided by J. P. Mahaffy (1839-1919), classics don and later Provost of
Trinity College, Dublin, a bastion of English and Anglo-Irish values.
Mahaffy, who referred to himself proudly as an example of 'that
splendid breed of mongrel, the Anglo-Irishman', remarked in his later
life:

> James Joyce is a living argument in favour of my contention that it
> was a mistake to establish a separate university for the aborigines of
> this island — for the corner-boys who spit into the Liffey.[33]

That 'aborigines' is beautiful. If the Anglo-Irish were regarded by the
natives then as a 'different' race, a good part of the reason lay in the
Anglo-Irishry's own very high opinion of itself as indeed a different
race, as naturally, socially, and racially superior.

But as the exclusivist aggressiveness of native self-consciousness
probably originates in the sense of a lost identity, similarly one detects
again and again an underlying sense of insecurity behind Anglo-Irish
confidence. Cut off by religion, by social class, history and their own

tradition from the majority of their countrymen, the Anglo-Irish felt themselves isolated, even aliens, in their own land. Elizabeth Bowen, for example, describes brilliantly how as a child in Dublin she came to an awareness of there being two Irelands, and of the chasm between them:

> It was not until after the end of those seven winters that I under- stood that we Protestants were a minority, and that the unques- tioned rules of our being came, in fact, from the closeness of a minority world. Roman Catholics were spoken of by my father and mother with a courteous detachment that gave them, even, no myth. I took the existence of Roman Catholics for granted but met few and was not interested in them. They were, simply, 'the others', whose world lay alongside ours but never touched. As to the dif- ference between the two religions, I was too discreet to ask ques- tions – if I wanted to know. This appeared to share a delicate, awk- ward aura with those two other differences – of sex, of class . . . I walked with hurried step and averted cheek past porticos of churches that were 'not ours', uncomfortably registering in my nostrils the pungent, unlikely smell that came round curtains, through swinging doors . . . This predisposition to frequent prayer bespoke, to me, some incontinence of the soul.[34]

Frequently the Anglo-Irish simply did not know anything about what Elizabeth Bowen calls 'the others'. Lily Yeats, the sister of the poet, recorded her reactions to her first reading of Joyce's *Dubliners*:

> I saw the elderly women coming out and slipping into the city chapels for mouthfuls of prayer, seedy men coming out and slipping into greasy public houses for mouthfuls of porter – but of their lives I knew nothing. Since I read *Dubliners* I feel I know something of their lives.[35]

This sense of ignorance served to increase the Anglo-Irish consciousness of marginality. Even when the Anglo-Irishman did not feel victim of a crisis of identity, he had to encounter the spoken or unspoken view that, whether he liked it or not, he was different. Thus Stephen Gwynn records:

> I was brought up to think myself Irish without question or qualifi- cation; but the new nationalism prefers to describe me and the like of me as Anglo-Irish. A E has even set me down in print as being

the Anglo-Irishman *par excellence* — or, to put it more modestly, the typical Anglo-Irishman. So all my life I have been spiritually hyphenated without knowing it.[36]

Such an attitude is unusual. More commonly that special, difficult awareness of apartness — what Yeats called 'Anglo-Irish solitude' — is inborn and inescapable. The distinguished Anglo-Irish critic Vivian Mercier has written:

> The typical Anglo-Irish boy . . . learns that he is not quite Irish almost before he can talk; later he learns that he is far from being English either. The pressure on him to become either wholly English or wholly Irish can erase segments of his individuality for good and all. 'Who am I?' is the question that every Anglo-Irishman must answer, even if it takes him a lifetime, as it did Yeats.[37]

And in attempting to understand how Samuel Beckett — unlike Yeats or Synge — seems never to have felt the need to avoid alienation by 'impatriating' or 'Gaelicising' himself, he offers a neat vignette of the Anglo-Irish problem in its ordinary everyday manifestation, as he describes growing up in Ireland in the twenties:

> . . . unlike myself, Beckett had never lived in or perhaps even visited any part of Ireland where he was unpleasantly conscious of minority or alien status . . . I assume that Beckett never underwent the minor ordeal that I endured daily when at home in Clara, Offaly, of walking past a row of half-doors over which stared ironic Irish eyes — not those of romanticizable peasants but of sharp-tongued women, girls and boys, the wives and children of factory-workers, who knew more about me and my family than I would ever know about them. I never could decide whether I hated them or longed to be accepted by them: as I went to a one-teacher Protestant school while they went to big schools taught by nuns and monks, there really was no common ground for us to meet on.[38]

The Anglo-Irishman's relationship with England placed him in a position equally difficult. It is true that Bishop Berkeley, who was to figure in Yeats's later poetry as a type of Anglo-Irish excellence, could enquire in the *Querist* in 1735 'Whether the upper part of this people are not truly English by blood, language, religion, manners, inclination and interest? Whether we are not as much Englishmen as the children of old Romans, born in Britain, were still Romans?'[39] But history, and the rise of a separatist national and cultural consciousness during the nineteenth century, in the fostering of which consciousness he had played such a part, made it extremely difficult for a man like W. B. Yeats to reconcile within himself his 'Anglo' and his Irish selves. In a powerful passage from his 'General Introduction' to his work, written in 1937, Yeats points up the dilemma. He speaks of English 'wars of extermination' during the sixteenth and seventeenth century, and of the persecution of the Irish 'up to our own day', and goes on:

No people hate as we do in whom that past is always alive, there are moments when hatred poisons my life and I accuse myself of effeminacy because I have not given it adequate expression. It is not enough to have put it into the mouth of a rambling peasant poet. Then I remind myself that though mine is the first English marriage I know of in the direct line, all my family names are English, and that I owe my soul to Shakespeare, to Spenser and to Blake, perhaps to William Morris, and to the English language in which I think, speak, and write, that everything I love has come to me through English; my hatred tortures me with love, my love with hate. I am like the Tibetan monk who dreams at his initiation that he is eaten by a wild beast and learns on waking that he himself is eater and eaten. This is Irish hatred and solitude, the hatred of human life that made Swift write *Gulliver* and the epitaph upon his tomb, that can still make us wag between extremes and doubt our sanity.[40]

Perhaps the artist is, almost by definition, a marginal figure in any society, and one should not labour this clichéd question of identity so much. One thinks, after all, of another great modern artist untouched by anything to do with 'mad Ireland'. T. S. Eliot wrote to Herbert Read in 1928:

I want to write an essay about the point of view of an American who wasn't an American, because he was born in the South and went to school in New England as a small boy with a nigger drawl, but who wasn't a southerner in the South because his people were northerners in a border state and looked down on all southerners and Virginians, and who so was never anything anywhere and who therefore felt himself to be more a Frenchman than an American and more an Englishman than a Frenchman and yet felt that the U.S.A. up to a hundred years ago was a family extension. It is almost too difficult even for H.J. who for that matter wasn't an American at all, in that sense.[41]

Nevertheless, even granting the artist's 'natural' marginality, I think that the situation of the Irish writers raises the issue in a particularly acute and problematic form. For each of them has to face not just the question of his own particular identity and affiliations within the culture. This can be extremely urgent, as that last quotation from Yeats surely illustrates; and many passages from Synge and Joyce have a comparable urgency. The really great difficulty is, however, as I hope this introduction has shown, that the identity of the very culture itself is in question. Ireland was (still is?) such a deeply divided country that for each writer there must have seemed no stable point of reference, a total lack of a relatively steady tradition, like that of the English or French. The political upheavals from 1913 through till 1923 can only have added to the sense of fragmentation — what finer symbol of this, after all, than partition and a civil war? Particularly disturbing for the artist, because so difficult to measure, were the distortions produced by the propinquity of England, which might be called the sleeping partner of every Irish artist's dreams — or nightmares. Take the work of Yeats, Synge and Joyce. Yeats and Synge clearly begin by trying to reject their 'English' aspects, attempting to break with the strict affiliations of their Anglo-Irish status. For them, then, the 'real Ireland', initially at any rate, is the 'native', peasant Ireland, and they each make, in their art, a brave effort to cross that chasm that has been described, and in Mercier's word, to 'impatriate' themselves. But first, they are each locked outside the inner recesses of the native's consciousness, which itself is not quite sure of its own identity anyway, and second, as a result, they are regarded with suspicion and hostility. Almost inevitably, Yeats and Synge end up asserting their Anglo-Irish separateness, Yeats explicitly, Synge more obliquely through his valuation of the outsider figures in his plays. James Joyce struggles against his 'native' sense of Ireland's cultural inferiority, a product in large part of the denigratory English stereotype view. But for Joyce there is an extra problem; he also struggles against what he sees as false stereotypes of Irish virtue embodied in the works of writers like Yeats and Synge, which again are partly a reaction against the English view of Irishness. In the opening episode of *Ulysses*, Buck Mulligan invites Stephen Dedalus to inspect himself in a cracked shaving-mirror:

- Look at yourself, he said, you dreadful bard . . .
  Laughing again, he brought the mirror away from
  Stephen's peering eyes.
- The rage of Caliban at not seeing his face in a
  mirror, he said. If Wilde were only alive to see you.[42]
  Drawing back and pointing, Stephen said with bitterness:
- It is a symbol of Irish art. The cracked looking-glass
  of a servant.

               (*Ulysses*, pp. 4-5)

It is a finely symbolic moment. For *Ulysses* is set in 1904, by which time the literary revival, and especially the Abbey theatre, was in full spate; so that Stephen has in mind not just obviously servile Irish art of the kind that had for long produced stage-Irishmen and similar stereotypes created for the English market, but also the archaic 'Cuchulanoid' Ireland and the Ireland of the noble peasant created by the genius of Yeats and Synge. In either case, that ever-present consciousness of the power and dignity of the English cultural tradition produces, in Joyce's eyes as in Stephen's, the distortions of Irish art; whether the Irish artist assents to the English view of Ireland, or attempts to confute it in constructing powerful and idealised counter-images of Ireland, in either case English cultural hegemony is confirmed. The looking-glass, cracked, is not telling the truth.

This is the true significance of Joyce's 'dispassionateness', the excellence of his art: that he can look at unlovely Ireland, see all its faults yet preserve a humorous tolerance of attitude, a willingness to accept the realities of a gapped culture, a broken tradition and the irreparableness of the loss of the old Gaelic identity. In so doing, Joyce in his art offers a way out of the 'nightmare of history', as Stephen calls it. By accepting the broken Irish tradition, he contributes, paradoxically, to our sense of its continuity, seeing it as 'continuous, or healed — or healing — from its mutilation'.[43] That is why Joyce is the 'hero', if there is one, of this book. To quote Thomas Kinsella again:

His stomach, unlike Yeats's, is not turned by what he sees shaping the new Ireland: the shamrock lumpenproletariat, the eloquent and conniving and mean-spirited tribe of Daniel O'Connell or De Valera or Paudeen do not deter him from his work; they are his subjects. He is the first major Irish voice to speak for Irish reality since the death of the Irish language.[44]

One may dispute this, of course. Perhaps nobody can give a whole picture of a society so deeply divided as that of Ireland, and the models of Yeats and of Synge have their own kind of authenticity, as they certainly have their compelling and imaginative eloquence. At least one thing is clear. However painful the question of identity may be for the Irish in real life, it has functioned, deeply embedded as it is in the Irish political and literary situation, as a superb catalyst to the production of some of the great art of the century, reaching out of Ireland to the world.

A final brief word on Sean O'Casey, who has been somewhat neglected in this introduction. In part this neglect is deliberate, because O'Casey's main concern in his Dublin plays is with the nature of political nationalism, an aspect of Irish identity which has been copiously commented on by literary critics as well as historians, not to mention journalists. But also I see O'Casey as the least significant of these four writers. In another way, he is the most problematic, since, given his subject-matter, and because of the contemporary situation in Ireland, at first sight O'Casey's work seems charged with a relevance possessed by none of the other writers in this study. For this reason alone, it seems worthwhile to take a close critical look at his art. Does O'Casey offer useful insights which might be helpful in extending our comprehension of the present tragedy? As I shall argue, plays which on the surface tell us so much about Ireland's political upheavals earlier in the century, in reality tell us very little; and, with their damaging and sentimental oversimplification of the relationship of nationalist politics to Irish life, O'Casey's plays offer even less insight into the complexities of the present situation in the North.

2   J. M. SYNGE: THE WATCHER FROM THE SHADOWS

Synge presents us with the paradox, or seeming paradox, of a lonely and isolated man who is concerned constantly in his plays and his quasi-documentary writings with images of community and community life. His life and work may therefore be seen as in many ways paradigmatic of the situation and problems of the Ascendancy writer in Ireland, torn between the desire to identify and merge with a community and the desire to assert the distinguishing and defining values of the individual self.

The roots of that powerful sense of isolation, which receives such commanding expression in the language of 'lonesomeness' in the plays, lie in Synge's childhood and its background. He was born in 1871, in the highly respectable Dublin suburb of Rathfarnham, into a family whose Ascendancy credentials were much more authentic than those of the Yeats family, being untainted by 'trade' or by the even more disreputable bohemianism which Synge's family throughout his life (and even after his death) consistently associated with art and artists. It should be remembered that to be of the Ascendancy did not necessarily mean to be an aristocrat — one might paraphrase a remark of Yeats about the middle class and say that it was an attitude of mind. Nevertheless, the Synges had produced five bishops since their arrival in Ireland in the seventeenth century, which in Irish terms certainly gave them a certain aristocratic *bouquet*; more significantly, perhaps, Synge's father (a barrister who died in 1872, not long after young John's birth) owned land in Co. Galway as well as estates in Co. Wicklow, and his brother Edward was land agent for the family estates in Wicklow, and later for Lord Gormanstown. In 1875 Edward was evicting tenants in Cavan, Mayo and Wicklow, and in 1887 at the height of Parnellism and the Land War, he evicted one Hugh Carey, the sole support of two sisters, from the Synge estate in Glanmore — an incident reported in some detail in the *Freeman's Journal*, which may be part of the explanation for that paper's subsequent hostility to the plays of Edward's brother.[1] T.R. Henn reminds us that one of Synge's uncles had 'ironically enough gone to the Aran Islands as a Protestant missionary in an attempt to convert the people.'[2] And his mother, the daughter of a Rector in Co. Cork, was a strict and narrowly orthodox evangelical

Protestant who brought up her children to 'fear God and honour the King', or Queen as the case might be. She might well have been one of those whom D. P. Moran, the vitriolic editor of *The Leader*, had in mind when he invented the bigoted and sectarian — but apt — expression, 'sour-face'. Certainly her famous son spoke feelingly of the terrors inspired in him by her insistence during childhood on the more punitive aspects of Christianity.[3]

Bishops and proselytizing, landlords, absenteeism, evictions and an innate sense of caste superiority — Synge's background constitutes almost an anthology of Ascendancy attributes. He seems to have sensed at an early age this first badge of isolation from the lives of the majority of his fellow countrymen. As he tells us of his boyhood in an impressive passage from a fragment of autobiography written in 1898:

> I studied the arabs of the streets . . . I remember coming out of St Patrick's [the Cathedral in Dublin where Swift had been Dean], Sunday after Sunday, strained almost to torture by the music, and walking out through the slums of Harold's Cross as the lamps were being lit. Hordes of wild children used to play around the cathedral of St Patrick and I remember there was something appalling — a proximity of emotions as conflicting as the perversions of the Black Mass — in coming out suddenly from the white harmonies of the Passion according to St Matthew among this blasphemy of childhood. The boys and girls were always in groups by themselves, for the utterly wild boy seems to regard a woman with the instinct of barbarians. I often stood for hours in a shadow to watch their manoeuvres and extraordinarily passionate quarrels . . .
>
> (*CW*, vol. 2, pp. 5-6)

By temperament also, Synge was a solitary and isolated child and youth. Always delicate, he was educated at home and at private schools. Early on, he conceived a passion for natural history which led him to spend much time among the lonely hills and mountains of Wicklow, and as he tells us in that same autobiographical fragment:

> When I recovered [from one of his frequent illnesses] I began to collect moths and butterflies and other insects, a pursuit which kept me engrossed for several years. It gave me a great fondness for the eerie and night and encouraged a lonely temperament which was beginning to take possession of me.
>
> (*CW*, vol. 2, p. 9)

The 'lonely temperament' can only have been further fostered by an
unhappy adolescent love-affair, but the major isolating crisis of his
youth came with his rejection, at the age of sixteen or seventeen, of
Christianity which followed on his discovery of Darwin. In a family
like Synge's, this was indeed an earthquake:

> This story is easily told, but it was a terrible experience. By it I laid
> a chasm between my present and my past and between myself and
> my kindred and friends. Till I was twenty-three I never met or at
> least knew a man or woman who shared my opinions.
>
> (*CW*, vol. 2, p. 11)

Thus began Synge's withdrawal from his own class and background.
This alienation was to affect profoundly the direction of his creative
life, which might be described without too much exaggeration as an
attempt to assuage, imaginatively, his sense of isolation, to find a feeling
of belonging. The rejection of the religion led fairly rapidly to a ques-
tioning of the whole Ascendancy ethos. Synge's mother and the family
in general were firmly Unionist in politics, of course; now John began
to compound his guilt. As he says:

> Soon after I had relinquished the Kingdom of God I began to take
> a real interest in the kingdom of Ireland. My politics went round
> from a vigorous and unreasoning loyalty to a temperate Nationalism.
>
> (*CW*, vol. 2, p. 13)

The word 'temperate' there is most judicious. Synge's spiritual crisis
and the rift with his family and all that this entailed coincided with the
years of Parnell's greatest power and influence, but it is probable that
Synge was much less interested in the politics and implications of Home
Rule than in the symbolic spectacle of somebody else at odds with his
own class and also — when the scandal broke — at odds with the puri-
tanical taboos common to both major religious persuasions in the land.[4]
It is true that Synge's friend Stephen MacKenna argues a different case,
and with vehemence:

> As regards political interest, I would die for the theory that Synge
> was most intensely Nationalist; he habitually spoke with rage and
> bitter baleful eyes of the English in Ireland, though he was proud of
> his own remote Englishry.[5]

However he spoke, Synge left remarkably little written evidence of such feelings and we must not confuse, in any case, radical republican nationalism with the familiar Celticist identification of England with materialism, industrialisation and, in general, lack of 'spirituality'. Further, we have the testimony of Yeats as to Synge's lack of involvement in politics,[6] testimony which is slightly misleading in some ways that we shall go on to examine, but which tends to buttress the notion of a 'temperate' Synge rather than a 'bitter' and 'baleful' Synge.

The point is that though Synge might struggle to free himself from Ascendancy attitudes, he could find no compensatory haven in the various 'nationalist' movements of the time (using 'nationalist' in a wide sense). For 'nationalist' Ireland was, and increasingly so, overwhelmingly Catholic Ireland. Yeats had found a metaphor for his involvement with that Ireland which conveys brilliantly his almost Eastern sense of caste-pollution – he called it 'the baptism of the gutter' (*Autobiographies*, p. 410). Synge did not reach quite that conciseness, but there is plenty of evidence that shows that residue of quasi-aristocratic contempt for 'the natives' which Synge derived from his background and which he was never able to expunge totally. Sometimes he gives himself away almost unaware, as in an article in *The Academy and Literature* of 1902 where he is discussing the role of the Gaelic League, here seen as offering fairly harmless fodder to darkened minds while the Anglo-Irish writers create the way of true light:

> If, however, the Gaelic League can keep the cruder powers of the Irish mind occupied in a healthy and national way till the influence of Irish literature, written in English, is more definite in Irish life, the half-cultured classes may come over to the side of the others, and give an intellectual unity to the country of the highest order.
>
> (*CW*, vol. 2, p. 386)

Later, his view of the Gaelic League – a predominantly middle-class and Catholic organisation, though Douglas Hyde, its founder, was of Synge's own kind of background – was expressed more virulently. He wrote in 1907, in a letter he decided not to publish:

> I believe the nation that has made a place in history by seventeen centuries of manhood, a nation that has begotten Grattan and Emmet and Parnell [all three of impeccable Ascendancy pedigree] will not be brought to complete insanity in these last days by what is senile and slobbering in the doctrine of the Gaelic League. There was

never till this time a movement in Ireland that was gushing, cowardly
and maudlin, yet now we are passing England in the hysteria of old
women's talk . . . there is more in heaven and earth than the weekly
bellow of the Brazen Bull-calf and all his sweaty gobs, or the snivelling booklets that are going through Ireland like the scab on sheep.

(*CW*, vol. 2, pp. 399-400)

The emotion here is clearly in excess of the object, which is Synge's
rejection both of the optimism of the Gaelic League that Ireland might
become Irish-speaking and of the kind of Irish it inculcated. The violence of the epithets suggests, as Nicholas Grene argues, Synge's resentment at the ever-increasing drift of power away from the Ascendancy
and towards the Catholic middle classes.[7] Caste-contempt, amounting
almost to physical revulsion, may be seen even more clearly in Synge's
well-known letter to MacKenna after the riots over *The Playboy of the
Western World* in 1907:

I sometimes wish I had never left my garret in the rue d'Assas . . .
the scurrility and ignorance and treachery of some of the attacks
upon me have rather disgusted me with the middle-class Irish Catholic. As you know I have the wildest admiration for the Irish Peasants,
and for Irish men of known or unknown genius – do you bow? –
but between the two there's an ungodly ruck of fat-faced, sweaty-
headed swine.

(*CW*, vol. 2, p. 283)

Given *The Playboy* riots, one might well feel that Synge was entitled to
his view of the sweaty-heads; but this is not simply a moment of angry
retaliation. Two years earlier, after his tour of Connemara with Jack B.
Yeats to write articles for the *Manchester Guardian*, Synge had written
to MacKenna:

There are sides of all that western life, the groggy-patriot-publican-
general-shop-man who is married to the priest's half-sister and is
second cousin once-removed of the dispensary doctor, that are
horrible and awful . . . All that side of the matter of course I left
untouched in my stuff [the articles]. I sometimes wish to God I
hadn't a soul and then I could give myself up to putting those lads
on the stage. God, wouldn't they hop! In a way it is all heart rending,
in one place the people are starving but wonderfully attractive and
charming, and in another place where things are going well, one has a

rampant, double-chinned vulgarity I haven't seen the like of.

(*CW*, vol. 2, p. 283)

The sociological objectivity of Synge's viewpoint is not at issue here. What is revealing is the tone ('double-chinned', 'slobbering', 'sweaty', 'fat-faced') which indicates so clearly in these passages — and there are more[8] — that Anglo-Irish hauteur and social animus out of which Yeats created some of his great poetry of contempt. This is more significant than the fact that Synge wrote only once with sympathy, in an essay called 'A Landlord's Garden in County Wicklow', directly about 'the tragedy of the landlord class' and of 'the innumerable old families that are quickly dwindling away' (*CW*, vol. 2, pp. 230-1).

Thus, while Synge's Anglo-Irish attitudes seem less obvious than, for example, is the case with Yeats, who frequently delights in proclaiming defiantly those attitudes in the teeth of the 'base-born products of base beds', they were always operative and especially liable to surface in stressful situations. They were certainly strong enough to make it impossible for him, having moved away from his own class, to feel at home in the ethos of Catholic nationalist Ireland, especially as that manifested itself in Dublin. Yet despite — or because of — his isolation, he felt the more keenly the need to belong to, or give expression to, some kind of communal consciousness. So he writes in a notebook, probably in 1898:

Goethe's weakness [is] due to his having no national and intellectual mood to interpret. The individual mood is often trivial, perverse, fleeting, [but the] national mood [is] broad, serious, provisionally permanent.

(*CW*, vol. 2, p. 349)

Hence Synge turns away from both Protestant gentry and Catholic bourgeois to attempt to find his imaginative sense of community in the peasant — perhaps one should say The Peasant.[9]

Synge's idealisation of the peasantry was in large measure a creative act of the imagination. For as I have pointed out in the introduction, changes in the pattern of Irish rural life consequent upon the Great Famine had tended to produce a highly conservative peasantry with a strong hunger to own land. The rural community was characterised by the dominance of old men who clung rigidly to their small-holdings, and by the drift of the young away from the land either to the towns, especially Dublin, or abroad, to England or the United States. It is at this time, roughly between 1850 and 1880, that the phenomenon of the late — and usually loveless — marriage made its appearance. 'The average Irish peasant' it was observed, 'takes unto himself a mate with as clear a head, as placid a heart and as steady a nerve as if he were buying a cow at Ballinasloe Fair'.[10]

It was doubtless the effects of these kinds of pressures on rural character which led Joyce to observe that the peasants of Ireland as he knew them were 'a hard, crafty and matter-of-fact lot'.[11] While Synge would not have agreed with this sweeping generalisation, he was familiar with the type — one need think only of such characters in the plays as Dan Burke, Michael Dara, and Shawn Keogh. What Synge wanted to satisfy his imaginative need to relate to a community was a peasantry untainted by any marks of the 'bourgeois', or prosperity (for in Synge's mind, as in Yeats's, the two concepts are always closely linked). We have already seen, in Synge's letter to MacKenna after his Connemara tour, the emergence of a typical kind of equation and opposition — an equation of poverty with being 'attractive and charming', which is opposed by another equation, that of prosperity with 'rampant, double-chinned vulgarity'. This becomes even more explicit in the first of the published articles on Connemara in the *Manchester Guardian*:

> One's first feeling as one comes back among these people and takes a place, so to speak, in this noisy procession of fishermen, farmers, and women, where nearly everyone is interesting and attractive, is a dread of any reform that would tend to lessen their individuality rather than any very real hope of improving their well-being. One feels then . . . that it is part of the misfortune of Ireland that nearly all the characteristics which give colour and attractiveness to Irish life are bound up with a social condition that is near to penury.
>
> (*CW*, vol. 4, p. 286)

Synge found his ideal peasant society, of course, on the Aran Islands, and perhaps we may see more clearly now why Yeats's famous advice of 1896[12] fell on such receptive ears. *Déclassé*, and in the words of his favourite, Villon, 'in my own country . . . in a far-off land', Synge found the longed-for consciousness of community on Aran and even at times could feel he had healed the split in the Anglo-Irish psyche:

> I told them [the islanders]I was going back to Paris in a few days to sell my books and my bed, and that then I was coming back to grow as strong and simple as they were among the islands of the west.
>
> (*CW*, vol. 2, p. 142)

But a poignant and moving sense of his isolation keeps cutting across the sense of identity, and Synge's honesty keeps his cultural primitivism in check. He knows that fundamentally he is still, as he had been as a boy, the watcher from the shadows:[13]

> In some ways these men and women seem strangely far away from me. They have the same emotions that I have, and the animals have, yet I cannot talk to them when there is much to say, more than to the dog that whines beside me in a mountain fog. There is hardly an hour I am with them that I do not feel the shock of some inconceivable idea, and then again the shock of some vague emotion that is familiar to them and to me. On some days I feel this island as a perfect home and resting place; on other days I feel that I am a waif among the people. I can feel more with them than they can feel with me, and while I wander among them, they like me sometimes, and laugh at me sometimes, yet never know what I am doing.
>
> (*CW*, vol. 2, p. 113)

Robin Skelton is clearly right, in speaking of Synge's Aran experiences and of the book he made from them, when he says that 'it is the value-system created in this book that gives us an indication of the attitude we must have in reading the later drama.'[14] What I wish to draw attention to, before we go on to examine this value-system in more detail, is how Synge's metaphoric move from Ascendancy house to Aran cabin, his desire to find a sense of community yet his failure to achieve — except imaginatively and briefly — such a sense, illustrate the problems of the Anglo-Irish writer in his attempt 'to interpret the national and intellectual mood', to paraphrase Synge on Goethe. Such a situation, crammed as it is with problems about identity and tradition can be, of course, and indeed was, extremely fruitful creatively. But one must also register, though not with the virulent hostility of Synge's nationalist critics, the probable narrowness of the 'value-system' that it is possible to erect on such a restricted basis. Synge's innerness with the 'psychic locality' of Aran is not self-evidently the ideal starting point for the creation of a drama to interpret the national mood of Ireland in the early twentieth century.

Apart from the particular shape given by these aspects of Synge's background to what Corkery calls 'his quest for a fatherland, a spiritual home',[15] there were other literary and cultural factors at work to make the Aran islanders exemplars to Synge of a romantic, heroic and elemental life-style which he found extremely congenial. Wordsworth was

perhaps Synge's favourite poet, and those aspects of the *Preface* to the
Lyrical Ballads and the poetry which assert the harmonising and ennobling of grand and elemental landscapes on those who live and work
among them, struck a deep chord in Synge. One may remark in passing
that the approach to a sense of belonging through an attempt to immerse
oneself in, or define the elusive quality of, the Irish landscape is an
obvious way for the Anglo-Irish writer to compensate for the lack of a
sense of any strong social bonding. For example, even the normally
clear-headed George Bernard Shaw seems to identify 'Irishness' with
landscape and climate in a rare moment of intensity — or sentimentality
— in *John Bull's Other Island* (written in 1904). 'No, no,' says his Larry
Doyle, rebuking the fatuous Broadbent's attempt to suggest similarities
between England and Ireland,

> . . . the climate is different. Here, if the life is dull, you can be dull
> too, and no great harm done [*Going off into a passionate dream*].
> But your wits can't thicken in that soft moist air, on those white
> springy roads, in those misty rushes and brown bogs, on those hill-
> sides of granite rocks and magenta heather. You've no such colours
> in the sky, no such lure in the distances, no such sadness in the
> evenings.

Synge is more overtly Wordsworthian. Describing a funeral amid the
harsh grandeur of the rocks and seas of the island, he writes:

> In Inishmaan one is forced to believe in a sympathy between man
> and nature, and at this moment when the thunder sounded a death-
> peel of extraordinary grandeur above the voices of the women, I
> could see the faces near me stiff and drawn with emotion.
>
> (*CW*, vol. 2, p. 75)

And in a notebook written in 1899 we find:

> I cannot say it too often, the supreme interest of the island lies in
> the strange concord that exists between the people and the im-
> personal limited but powerful impulses of the nature that is round
> them.
>
> (*Ibid.*)

As with Wordsworth, this not only gives the artist a compelling theme,
but simultaneously offers an antidote to what Wordsworth called in

'Resolution and Independence' the 'despondency and madness' attendant upon the melancholy isolation of the artist. Synge spells it out:

> On the low sheets of rock to the east I can see a number of red and
> grey figures hurrying about their work. The continual passing in this
> island between the misery of last night and the splendour of today,
> seems to create an affinity between the moods of these people and
> the moods of varying rapture and dismay that are frequent in
> artists, and in certain forms of alienation.
>
> *(CW*, vol. 2, p. 74)

A more pervasive general influence on Synge's vision of Aran was,
of course, the cultural primitivism at the heart of the Celtic — and
Celticist — revival, a primitivism which became the more marked as the
revival came more and more under Yeats's influence.[16] We have seen in
the introduction how even a sophisticated cosmopolitan like George
Moore could pray that 'all the empires may perish and the world be
given back to the small peasant states.'
fore responds with alacrity to aspects of life on Aran which seems to
support the romantic primitivist viewpoint. He speaks admiringly of the
wide range of skills of the Aran man which enable him to turn his hand
to a variety of tasks 'in the absence of any division of labour' (the
spectre of Birmingham lurks behind the phrase). He praises the simplicity and unity of the dress of the islander, and even evokes the very
Yeatsian value-combination of archaic individuality for the curraghs,
churns, baskets and other household utensils the islanders use:

> Every article on these islands has an almost personal character,
> which gives this simple life, where all art is unknown, something of
> the artistic beauty of medieval life.
>
> *(CW*, vol. 2, pp. 58-9)

Perhaps most importantly of all in terms of the complexities of Synge's
class orientation is the absence on Aran of any trace or taint of the
bourgeois, or indeed of any class one might find in an urban context; a
situation which enables 'peasant' and 'aristocrat' to become identical. A
passage like the following shows, among other things, just why Synge's
work was so important to and so valued by Yeats:

> The absence of the heavy boot of Europe has preserved to these
> people the agile walk of the wild animal, while the general simplicity

of their lives has given them many other points of physical perfection. Their way of life has never been acted on by anything much
more artificial than the nests and burrows of the creatures that live
round them, and they seem in a certain sense to approach more
nearly to the finer types of our aristocracies — who are bred artificially to a natural ideal — than to the labourer or citizen, as the wild
horse resembles the thoroughbred rather than the hack or cart-horse.

(*CW*, vol. 2, p. 66)

Here romantic primitivism and Ascendancy attitudes are inextricably
entwined in what might be called an Irish version of pastoral. Yeats's
'dream of the noble and the beggar-man'[17] was fleshed out, as it were,
and given a quasi-documentary corroboration by Synge's vision of Aran.
'Quasi-documentary', for it should be obvious that Synge read as much
into Aran as he actually found there, despite his disclaimer in the introduction to *The Aran Islands*: 'In the pages that follow I have given a
direct account of my life on the islands, and of what I met with among
them, inventing nothing, and changing nothing that is essential' (*CW*,
vol. 2, p. 47).[18]

Further, critics have pointed out how Synge plays down, almost to
the point of suppression, the Catholic aspects of the spiritual life of the
islanders. As Corkery says:

He drenched himself in all the features of the physical world they
moved in, but he made choice among the features of their mental
environment. Of their spiritual environment he did not even do that
same.[19]

It is understandable, in the light of our discussion of Synge so far, why
he should have preferred to separate off, in every possible way, this
ideal community from the especially despised middle-class and lower
middle-class Irishmen of the mainland. Even so, one must admire the
sleight of hand with which Synge transmutes unpalatable aspects of
island life into his primitivist vision. For example, the conclusion to his
description of the islanders at the funeral mentioned above reads:

They are usually silent, but in the presence of death all outward
show of indifference or patience is forgotten, and they shriek with
pitiable despair before the horror of the fate to which they all are
doomed. Before they covered the coffin an old man kneeled down
by the grave and repeated a simple prayer for the dead.

There was an irony in these words of atonement and Catholic belief spoken by voices that were still hoarse with the cries of pagan desperation.

(CW, vol. 2, p. 75)

And in *Riders to the Sea* — the only one of Synge's plays, interestingly, to be actually set on Aran — while the islanders' Catholicism is admitted into the play in various ways, its significance is offset by the power of Maurya's climactic vision of her dead son on the grey pony, which owes nothing to any orthodox religion, and by her exchange with Nora:

> *Nora.* Didn't the young priest say the Almighty God won't leave her destitute with no son living?
> *Maurya.* [in a low voice but clearly] . It's little the likes of him knows of the sea . . .

(CW, vol. 3, p. 21)

Thus Synge in his presentation of Aran manages to convey that its orthodox Catholicism is the thinnest of veneers laid over a basically deeply pagan sensibility. This imaginative procedure is hardly a result of anti-Catholicism or bigotry on Synge's part; it can best be understood in terms of that complex area of Irish life where social class and religious affiliation intermingle.

Two last favourable touches in Synge's admiring portrait of Aran should be mentioned. Firstly, throughout his account is evident his delight in the lack of emotional inhibition in the islanders, whether this expresses itself in the passionate keenings of grief or in the elaborate maledictions of anger and dispute, in the 'exquisite bright frankness' of the girls or the 'chatty, cheerful and inquisitive' loquacity of the old men. They all have the 'healthy animal blood of a peasant and delight in broad jests and deeds' (*CW*, vol. 2, p. 102). Vitality or energy or 'wildness' was to be a cardinal virtue in all of Synge's plays.

Secondly, the Eden-like status of the islands is validated in Synge's imagination by his awareness of the fragility of their life-style, of impending irrecoverable loss. It would not be permissible to say that what we have here is a sort of projection on to the Aran Islands of Synge's sense of the decline and withering of his own class, but what is obvious is that Synge found in contemplating the life of the islands that powerful elegiac tone which is such a marked feature of the great poetry of Yeats. Married as it is to his own personal sense of mortality, this elegiac sense becomes one of the strongest features of Synge's sensibility and a firm base for his critique of the Ireland developing around him. As he writes at the end of his first visit to Aran:

> The thought that this island will gradually yield to the ruthlessness of 'progress' is as the certainty that decaying age is moving always nearer the cheeks it is your ecstasy to kiss. How much of Ireland was formerly like this and how much of Ireland is today Anglicized and civilized and brutalized . . .
>
> (*CW*, vol. 2, p. 103)

If Aran is Eden, then the rest of Ireland is fallen.[20] In a remarkable passage, again describing the end of his first visit to the islands, Synge shows how his primitivism and his class attitudes reinforce one another:

> I have come out of an hotel full of tourists and commercial travellers, to stroll along the edge of Galway bay, and look out in the direction of the islands. The sort of yearning I feel towards those lonely rocks is indescribably acute. This town [Galway], that is usually so full of wild human interest, seems in my present mood a tawdry medley of all that is crudest in modern life. The nullity of the rich and the squalor of the poor give me the same pang of wondering disgust; yet the islands are fading already and I can hardly realise that the smell of the seaweed and the drone of the Atlantic are still moving round them.
>
> (*CW*, vol. 2, pp. 102-3)

The islands never did 'fade away' from Synge's imagination, yet it is a curious fact that he chose to set only one play, *Riders to the Sea*, in that background. This is despite the fact that it was on Aran that he picked up the stories or anecdotes — one of them admittedly a folk-tale — which were to form the basis of *The Shadow of the Glen* and *The Playboy of the Western World*. The first he transplanted to Wicklow, and the second to Mayo. I would like to suggest that a possible reason for this, which brings us close to the heart of Synge's dramatic strengths, is that while he did indeed find on Aran all the essential elements of his value system, the very perfection of that world as he saw it did not allow him, in depicting it, to explore creatively and in sufficient depth the tensions he felt within himself arising from his total cultural situation. *Riders to the Sea* is indeed a great play, but a play which, as the many critical accounts of it seem to me to demonstrate, needs little critical explication. Dignified, moving, even tragic, it has a kind of

inevitable rightness about it down to the authenticity of the smallest
prop and of the sparest detail:

> *Nora.* It's the second one of the third pair I knitted, and I put up
> three-score stitches, and I dropped four of them.
>   (*CW*, vol. 3, p. 15)

Yet it is lacking in dramatic tension or conflict, however strong it is on
inevitability, atmosphere and simple eloquence. This has less to do, I
feel, with the fact that the play's main antagonist is impersonal and
inhuman, because Synge's words do bring the ocean vividly before our
imaginative eyes, but more that Synge's very success in effacing himself, in disappearing totally into the dramatic world created, gives
Riders to the Sea the static self-enclosed quality of a lovingly constructed genre painting. Though obviously heavily dependent on Synge's
'first serious piece of work', *The Aran Islands*, the most obvious difference between play and prose-work is the absence from the former of
the opposing or alien consciousness, that of the narrator, which makes
the prose-work such a fascinating and ultimately more dramatic creation. This is unlikely to be a generally accepted view, especially to those
for whom *Riders to the Sea* is (as it was for Daniel Corkery) Synge's
quintessential work; nevertheless, the fact remains that after *Riders to
the Sea* Synge turned to quite a different style of drama where the
values absorbed on Aran are held in tension — whether bitterly, ironically or exuberantly — with different values and different contexts.
Tension or conflict in themselves are no marks of literary value. My
point is that for a man like Synge in the Ireland of his time they were
an inevitable part of his sensibility.

   It may seem odd to have made no reference thus far, except tangen-
tially, to Synge's association of the peasantry with a highly coloured
imaginative speech, since this, it may be argued, was for him the most
valuable and precious contribution of all.

> In a good play every speech should be as fully flavoured as a nut or
> apple, and such speeches cannot be written by any one who works
> among people who have shut their lips on poetry. In Ireland, for a
> few years more, we have a popular imagination that is fiery, and
> magnificent and tender . . .
> (From the Preface to *The Playboy of the Western World CW*, vol.4,
>   p. 54)

And Synge himself asserted the close connection between the speech of the people and his own dramatic language, stating in a letter of 1907:

> I look on *The Aran Islands* as my first serious piece of work — it
> was written before any of my plays. In writing out the talk of the
> people and their stories in this book, and in a certain number of
> articles on the Wicklow peasantry which I have not yet collected, I
> learned to write the peasant dialect and dialogue which I use in my
> plays.
>
> (*CW*, vol. 2, p. 47)

The aside here is important — I think it likely that it was in Wicklow,
and in Kerry, which Synge first visited in 1903, where the people were
much more naturally bilingual than in Aran, that he found the elements
of the highly figurative speech of his plays. One might say, with some
simplification, that while Synge learned his syntax on Aran, much of
the 'fully-flavoured' vocabulary and idiom of his plays he derived from
the more English-speaking areas of the mainland.[21]

There is a more important reason for giving separate discussion to
Synge's language and its relation to his ideal peasantry. It is 'the language problem' which has above all bedevilled and complicated the question of Synge's 'authenticity', or fidelity to the life he attempted to
portray, since clearly in any literary work of art the life described can
only be mediated through words. And Synge's idiom is highly personal,
even idiosyncratic. There would be no problem if Synge himself had
not raised the 'authenticity' bogey with remarks like those in the introduction to *The Aran Isles*, in the letter cited above, and most famously
and misleadingly of all, in the preface to *The Playboy*:

> In writing *The Playboy of the Western World*, as in my other plays,
> I have used one or two words only that I have not heard among the
> country people of Ireland . . . Any one who has lived in real
> intimacy with the Irish peasantry will know that the wildest sayings
> and ideas in this play are tame indeed, compared with the fancies
> one may hear in any little hillside cabin in Geesala, or Carraroe, or
> Dingle Bay . . . When I was writing *The Shadow of the Glen*, some
> years ago, I got more aid than any learning could have given me from
> a chink in the floor of the old Wicklow house where I was staying,
> that let me hear what was being said by the servant girls in the
> kitchen.
>
> (*CW*, vol. 4, p. 53)

Critics irritated by Irish obtuseness in what they see as a failure to

distinguish between 'real life' and the shaping selectivity of art, the sort
of obtuseness that leads to a dismissal of Synge in some such remark as
'No Irishman ever spoke like that', should remember that Synge must
himself bear some of the responsibility for the confusion.[22] While
accepting all the evidence supplied by linguistic analyses[23] as to the
basis of Synge's dramatic language in a syntax considerably affected
by Irish Gaelic and a vocabulary often archaic or 'Elizabethan', which
are obvious features of the English spoken in Ireland, it is surely best
and most profitable to agree that no Irishman ever spoke with as full
a 'flavour' as any of Synge's characters. This leaves us free to examine
the more interesting and critical question as to what Synge's deliberately shaped and even artificial language tells us of his sensibility and of
his stance in relation to the language and the culture he describes. In
other words instead of attacking or defending Synge on the realism of
his dramatic language, we shall be trying to see what features in English-
Irish speech he found particularly congenial for the expression of his
own vision.

That it is 'his own vision' emerges from a paradoxical fact. Synge's
characters are not marked off one from another by any noticeable
linguistic devices or tics, though it is true that Christy Mahon and
Martin Doul, for example, have more linguistic *awareness* than those
around them. The point needs little illustration — compare any of the
speeches of the sensitive and imaginative Nora in *The Shadow of the
Glen* with these words of the dour and harsh Dan:

> It's lonesome roads she'll be going and hiding herself away till the
> end will come, and they find her stretched like a dead sheep with the
> frost on her, or the big spiders maybe, and they putting their webs
> on her, in the butt of a ditch.
>
> (*CW*, vol. 3, p. 55)

This could be Nora herself describing the end of Peggy Cavanagh. The
same point could be made about Timmy the smith in *The Well of the
Saints* or even Shawn Keogh of *The Playboy*, who function dramatically as dull and timid foils to the heroes of their respective plays, yet
whose language has the same volubility and, at times, the same beauty
of cadence, as in these words of Timmy's:

> . . . for he's brought a sup of the water slung at his side, and, with
> the like of him, any little drop is enough to cure the dying, or to
> make the blind see as clear as the grey hawks do be high up, on a still

day, sailing the sky.

(CW, vol. 3, p. 81)

And Synge imposed the same kind of distinctive uniformity of speech-patterning as we find in the 'peasant' plays even on the heroic/aristocratic saga-world of *Deirdre.*

It is easy to see one important reason why Synge imposes linguistic uniformity of this kind even at the dramatic risk of possible monotony: he can thus create that sense of community which he responded to so strongly and for which, as we have seen, he had a powerful emotional need. Yet the paradox is that the artistic effect of the procedure is to direct attention at the controlling sensibility behind this use of language, a sensibility which imposes itself on the characters it creates in a more obvious way than in most drama.[24]

Synge's syntax is marked most prominently by his fondness for paratactic constructions in long, balanced sentences, and by a strong rhetorical rhythm manifesting itself most clearly in his much-noted concluding cadence ('in the dews of night', 'the grace of God', 'in the year that's gone', etc.). Here is part of Martin Doul's wooing of Molly Byrne:

> You'd do right not to marry a man is after looking out a long while on the bad days of the world; for what way would the like of him have fit eyes to look on yourself, when you rise up in the morning and come out of the little door you have above in the lane, the time it'd be a fine thing if a man would be seeing, and losing his sight, the way he'd have your two eyes facing him, and he going the roads, and shining above him, and he looking in the sky, and springing up from the earth, the time he'd lower his head, in place of the muck that seeing men do meet all roads spread on the world.

(CW, vol. 3, p. 117)

Trapped, like Molly herself, in what the stage-direction calls the 'mesmeric' rhythm, and in the apparently endless self-generating heaping up of clauses, the audience or reader begins to lose the normal sense of time. The syntax enables Synge to modulate from a future conditional state ('what way would be like of him . . .') into a sort of timeless continuance ('the time . . .' 'the way . . .' 'the time . . .' 'and he going . . .' 'and he looking . . .'). It is a common effect in Synge's plays, and can be seen again in the tramp's words to Nora near the end of *The Shadow of the Glen:*

> We'll be going now, I'm telling you, and the time you'll be feeling
> the cold, and the frost, and the great rain, and the sun again, and the
> south wind blowing in the glens, you'll not be sitting up on a wet
> ditch, the way you're after sitting in this place, making yourself old
> with looking on each day, and it passing you by. You'll be saying
> one time: 'It's a grand evening, by the grace of God,' and another
> time, 'It's a wild night, Gold help us; but it'll pass, surely.' You'll
> be saying . . .
>
> (*CW*, vol. 3, p. 57)

Especially clear here is another major aspect of Synge's syntax, his
fondness for the continuous form of the verb[25] — 'It's a long time I'm
keeping that stick' rather than standard English 'I've kept that stick'.
The tense of the verb tends to be immaterial, whether present, or as in
the tramp's speech, future: 'We'll be going . . . you'll be feeling . . .
you'll not be sitting up . . . You'll be saying . . .' It may be related to
the similar use of the continuous form in the frequent interjections —
'I'm thinking', 'I'm saying' — which Synge's characters employ, an
example of which occurs in the tramp's speech ('I'm telling you').

To these omnipresent features may be added a third, the heavy use
of syntactic parallelism, which makes Synge's prose so patterned. In a
speech of the Widow Quin's we can see all these elements at work:[26]

> You'll be doing like myself, I'm thinking, when I did destroy my
> man, for I'm above many's the day, odd times in great spirits,
> abroad in the sunshine, darning a stocking or stitching a shift; and
> odd times again looking out on the schooners, hookers, trawlers is
> sailing the sea, and I thinking on the gallant hairy fellows are drifting
> beyond, and myself long years living alone.
>
> (*CW*, vol. 4, p. 127)

It is no accident that the patterning, the progressive or continuous
verbal forms and the parataxis should be employed so frequently in
contexts where, as in the three examples cited, the temporal reference
is strong. Synge's syntax largely creates what may be called the time-
sense of his dramatic universe: that of a static continuum. The process
of time is frequently alluded to in his plays and is no doubt in part
derived from Synge's personal and powerful intimations of mortality
which are scattered everywhere through his letters, prose and poems.
Confronting the temporal allusions of the plays, however, and giving
them some of the imaginative tension which makes Synge so interesting,

is his deeper and more fundamental sense of his world as static. Synge's world is static not only in its locations, whether insulated in the remoteness of the past (*Deirdre*), or in the isolation of his islands and glens, but also in the elaborately wrought artifices of its syntax, endlessly circling round upon itself.

This aspect is derived partly from direct observation. Synge comments on the Aran islanders' freedom from 'clock-time':

> Few of the people, however, are sufficiently used to modern time to understand in more than a vague way the convention of the hours, and when I tell them what o'clock it is by my watch they are not satisfied, and ask how long is left them before the twilight . . . the shadow of the door-post moving across the kitchen floor indicates the hour . . .
>
> (*CW*, vol. 2, p. 66)

Partly it is a linguistic *donnée* of both Irish and English-Irish speech, which does emphasise condition and general state above any very meticulous use of tense.[27] But this does not explain why Synge chose from a range of options those aspects of Anglo-Irish syntax which *highlight* the feeling of continuum or stasis even where, as I have tried to illustrate, the context is one of temporality or process. This again is, I believe, to be explained in relation to aspects of Synge's Ascendancy sensibility, and in particular to the hostility to the idea of change, the romantic primitivist rejection of modernisation and the modern world which is such a feature of the Anglo-Irish literary revival. Synge's 'dread of any reform' that would 'lessen the individuality' of his peasant world can thus be seen as operative in however displaced or unconscious a fashion in the very syntax of his plays.

This elaborate syntax enabled Synge therefore to create a sense of community and to imbue the representation of that sense with a feeling of continuity. Further, of course, as Alan Price among many others has pointed out,[28] it was such a syntax that enabled Synge to escape the restrictions of a naturalistic prose medium and to employ consistently such a 'rich and copious' diction – to use his own epithets from *The Playboy* preface. Again, rather than attempting to give a comprehensive analysis of Synge's rhetoric, it will be most useful to concentrate on an important aspect of it which helps to illustrate the complex nature of the relationship between Synge and Irish culture in general.

I refer to the powerful stress in Synge's similes, images, and passages of invective as well as of grotesque fantasy, on violence, or 'wildness',

harshness or brutality. It is clear that for Synge these qualities are
almost synonomous with the vitality whether of speech or deed which
he saw as a prime virtue in peasant life; and it is as if Synge stresses
them the more in order to imbue his dramatic universe with a principle
of energy to offset, in a compensatory way, the feeling of stasis mediated through the syntax.[29]

Something of Synge's delight in the 'healthy animal blood' of his
peasants, in their 'broad jests and deeds' has already been indicated (see
above p. 46). Peasant life undoubtedly was harsh and even brutal in
ways, and there is plenty of evidence that the violence or 'wildness'
which Synge documents in his prose was not just a subjective imposition on his part.[30] But two points need to be stressed: first, that Synge
gives surprising, even disproportionate, prominence to violence in his
prose and especially in his plays; second — and the points can't be
separated — his attitude to the violence of peasant life is still that of
the romantic primitivist. As Robin Skelton says:

> In their wildness and savagery [Synge] saw the vitality that civiliza-
> tion had minimized with its moral codifications.[31]

What I wish to do is to establish just how pervasive is the rhetoric of
violence in Synge's plays. The term 'violence' in this context is admittedly a slippery one, but words like Synge's favourite 'wildness', or
'energy', are just as imprecise. It is hoped that the illustrations will eke
out the imperfections of the general critical label. To begin, then, many
of Synge's similes connect the processes of physical decay, aging and
death with the harsh indifferent naturalism of the small farmer's life or
of nature itself. Here is a group fortuitously linked by common reference to loss or paucity of hair:

(a) *Nora* . . . . and there she is now walking round on the roads, or
   sitting in a dirty old house, with no teeth in her mouth, and no
   sense, and no more hair than you'd see on a bit of a hill and they
   after burning the furze from it.

   (*CW*, vol. 3, p. 51)

(b) *Martin Doul*. . . . I'm telling you there isn't a wisp on any grey
   mare on the ridge of the world isn't finer than the dirty twist on
   your head. There isn't two eyes in any starving sow, isn't finer
   than the eyes you were calling blue like the sea.

   (*CW*, vol. 3, p. 97)

(c) *Mary Doul*. It's them that's fat and flabby do be wrinkled young,
and that whitish yellowy hair she has does be soon turning the
like of a handful of thin grass you'd see rotting, where the wet
lies, at the north of a sty.

(*CW*, vol. 3, p. 121)

(d) *Mary Doul*. In a short while you'll have a head on you as bald
as an old turnip you'd see rolling round in the muck.

(*CW*, vol. 3, p. 129)

There is no special significance for Synge in hair, or balding, of course,
and the same kind of tone is found in many other similes of an un-hairy
kind, as in the rural/natural

(e) *Dan*. . . . and they find her stretched like a dead sheep with the
frost on her . . . in the butt of a ditch.

(*CW*, vol. 3, p. 55)

(f) *Pegeen*. . . . it's sooner on a bullock's liver you'd put a poor girl
thinking than on the lily or the rose.

(*CW*, vol. 4, p. 155)

There is no need to dwell on how, in these examples, the human is
associated, in a consistent way, with images of rural life which connote,
not the traditional pastoral, but rather the poverty, the harshness, the
squalor, the 'unaccommodated' life. The sow is 'starving', the grass is
'thin'. What gives the examples that edge of violence is that in their
contexts they are all, with the exception of (a), verbal assaults made by
one character on another. The harshness of reality is rammed aggressively at the 'victim' — and, it may be added, at the audience too —
with a detail and a visual immediacy which makes Synge's characters so
frequently great masters of vituperation.

The energy of Synge's language of vituperation and invective is self-
evident and has been justly admired:

(a) *Mary Doul*. I wouldn't rear a crumped whelp the like of you.

(*CW*, vol. 3, p. 99)

(b) *Christy*. To be letting on he was dead, and coming back to
his life, and following me like an old weasel tracing a rat . . .
and he a kind of carcase that you'd fling upon the sea . . . May

I meet him with one tooth and it aching, and one eye to be seeing seven and seventy devils in the twists of the road, and one old timber leg on him to limp into the scalding grave. [Looking out] . There he is now crossing the strands, and that the Lord God would send a high wave to wash him from the world.

(CW, vol. 4, p. 125)

The quality of baroque elaboration in Christy's curse enables us to relate invective and vituperation to all those passages of grotesque fantasy of which Synge is fond and which again evidence an exuberant lack of imaginative restraint, or 'wildness'. These passages are typical, and typical also in their reference to drunkenness, death, violence, and even cannibalism. Significantly, they are all from *The Playboy of the Western World*.

(a) *Pegeen*. Doesn't the world know you reared a black ram at your own breast, so that the Lord Bishop of Connaught felt the elements of a Christian, and he eating it after in a kidney stew?

(CW, vol. 4, p. 89)

(b) *Philly*. . . . when I was a young lad, there was a graveyard beyond the house with the remnants of a man who had thighs as long as your arm. He was a horrid man, I'm telling you, and there was many a fine Sunday I'd put him together for fun, and he with shiny bones you wouldn't meet the like of these days in the cities of the world.

(CW, vol. 4, p. 135)

(c) *Jimmy*. . . . I knew a party was kicked in the head by a red mare, and he went killing horses a great while, till he eat the insides of a clock and died after.

(CW, vol. 4, p. 137)

(d) *Old Mahon*. There was one time I seen ten scarlet divils letting on they'd cork my spirit in a gallon can; and one time I seen rats as big as badgers sucking the lifeblood from the butt of my lug.

(CW, vol. 4, p. 143)

These rhetorical features coalesce to form a drama whose verbal 'atmosphere' is almost aggressively energetic and lively. It becomes difficult, in fact, as the quotations show, to separate the energy from a sense of violence, whether linguistic or actual. Another way of putting this might be to say that frequently Synge's characters are stimulated to their energetic outpourings by feelings of hostility, anger, scorn, competitiveness, self-aggrandisement, which then receive expression in the appropriate vivid, violent, or even brutal language. This distinctive and, in my view, definitive, tone in Synge is reinforced by another use of language, which is to extend the image of violence beyond the immediate dramatic context, suggesting thus a world where it is normal, habitual, taken for granted or even admired. I am trying to distinguish between the 'violence' of a plot or dramatic action and the 'violence' conveyed through verbal accounts whether of deeds in the past, or to come. Hence:

(a) *Mary Doul.* Maybe they're hanging a thief, above at the bit of a tree? I'm told it's a great sight to see a man hanging by his neck . . .

(*CW*, vol. 3, p. 77)

(b) *Martin Doul.* . . . there isn't the like of you for plucking your living ducks, the short days, and leaving them running round in their skins, in the great rains and the cold.

(*CW*, vol. 3, p. 105)

(c) *Pegeen.* . . . Where now will you meet the like of Daneen Sullivan knocked the eye from a peeler, or Marcus Quin, God rest him, got six months for maiming ewes . . .

(*CW*, vol. 4, p. 59)

(d) *Pegeen.* You never hanged him, the way Jimmy Farrell hanged his dog from the licence and had it screeching and wriggling three hours at the butt of a string, and himself swearing it was a dead dog, and the peelers swearing it had life?

(*CW*, vol. 4, p. 73)

(e) *Susan.* You'd have a right so to follow after him, Sara Tansey, and you the one yoked the ass-cart and drove ten miles to set your eyes on the man bit the yellow lady's nostril on the northern shore.

(*CW*, vol. 4, p. 97)

(f) *Widow Quin.* . . . you'd best be hasty, for them lads caught a maniac one time and pelted the poor creature till he ran out

raving and foaming and was drowned in the sea.
                                               (*CW*, vol. 4, p. 145)

All these illustrations may be taken as Synge's means of thickening the
'local colour'; they very obviously help to create what Synge called the
'psychic state of the locality' of his plays,[32] and in doing so make
credible the harshness, the cruelty and the violence which make up a
good deal of the action of the drama. (One thinks at once of Dan's
banishment of Nora and his relishing of it, of the tinkers' treatment of
the priest in *The Tinkers' Wedding* when, as Vivian Mercier argues
persuasively, Synge's zest for violence is so forced as to distort the
aesthetic balance of the play,[33] of the jeering laughter of their communities at both Martin Doul and Christy in their predicaments, of
Martin Doul's threat to strike out Mary's 'little handful of brains', of
the slipping of the hangman's noose over Christy's head and of Pegeen's
burning of his shin with a lighted sod — and of course of much else in
The Playboy).

I have illustrated this point at such length in an attempt to show the
centrality of Synge's 'rhetoric of violence' in creating the overall effect
of his plays.[34] When one speaks of Synge's language being 'poetic' then
much of one's evidence for the assertion must rest on passages like
those I have quoted, which have a superb force and vividness. By contrast, and despite Seamus Deane's assertion that Synge's language is to
be 'understood as a merging of his own idiom of erotic joy and pagan
ecstasy with the Gaelic tongue's long-learned capacity to embody such
experiences',[35] Synge's more obviously and conventionally 'lyrical'
passages of joy or ecstasy seem often to be straining for effects which
do not come off, and to ring hollow in their self-consciousness. Martin
Doul's wooing of Molly Byrne, cited above (p. 51), seems to be trying
to make up in amplitude for what it lacks in force; and we may put
beside the impact of Mary Doul's 'I wouldn't rear a crumpled whelp the
like of you' such typical 'lyrical' extravagances from Christy as

Amn't I after seeing the love-light of the star of knowledge shining
from her brow, and hearing words would put you thinking on the
holy Brigid speaking to the infant saints . . .
                                               (*CW*, vol. 4, pp. 125-7)

and the pseudo-Elizabethan 'rapture of

If the mitred bishops seen you that time, they'd be the like of the

holy prophets, I'm thinking, do be straining the bars of Paradise to
lay eyes on the Lady Helen of Troy, and she abroad pacing back and
forward with a nosegay in her golden shawl.

(*CW*, vol. 4, p. 149)

Surely T. R. Henn is right in finding this sort of thing false and indulgent.[36] W. B. Yeats, at any rate, is in no doubt as to the real essence of
Synge. In an address delivered in the United States in 1932 he spoke of
the strength of Synge's influence on those

. . . who in reaction, a reaction Synge himself began, either against
our tendency at the beginning [of the literary revival] to select too
obviously what was noble, or against popular Catholic idealism,
select for the themes of their art brutality or violence. The medieval
[*sic*] speech of the peasant is as well fitted for violence as for beauty.

and he goes on to deprecate that influence on lesser talents:

Play after play is sent to the Abbey directors where speech or action,
more often speech . . . have a violence that seems mere convention.[37]

Synge's delight in contemplating and creating a Rabelaisian robust-
ness and wild energy in the diction of his characters stems both from
psychological factors and from conscious aesthetic choices. In part it
is clearly a reaction away from the cramped repressiveness of his evangelical upbringing, from the genteel chit-chat, in an atmosphere of
gloom and antimacassars, of his mother's drawing-room, which was of
its nature hostile to 'wild sayings'. Synge's nephew Edward Stephens
tells us that the mother taught Synge

. . . that to refer to God in any but a strictly religious manner was a
sinful taking in vain of the Holy Name, that to use oaths or exple-
tives was a breach of St James's injunctions (James 5:2), and that to
exaggerate was to lie.[38]

Further, there was the imaginative compensation involved in the exultation in peasant vitality, especially of speech, for a man suffering
during all his creative life from the disease which killed him – as
Yeats movingly expresses it, Synge 'dying, chose the living world for
text'. The sickness, and the narrow scope of Synge's immediate linguistic
background, are focused together in the well-known anecdote about

j

Synge's reaction on coming round after one of his operations:

> Damn the bloody Anglo-Saxon language that a man can't swear in without being vulgar![39]

But Synge's cult of a 'brutal' diction is also a deliberate artistic decision. It grew in the first place, as the comment of Yeats cited above suggests, from his rejection of the ethereal, twilight, fey elements in the literary revival which Joyce too lambasted fiercely in his comic broadside 'The Holy Office'. This extended to a rejection of Yeats's belief in the cultivation of the legendary and heroic past of the Old Irish sagas for dramatic purposes. In an exchange of letters with Mackenna, Synge wrote in 1904:

> I do not believe in the possibility of 'a purely fantastic unmodern, ideal, breezy, springdayish, Cuchulanoid National Theatre'. We had *The Shadowy Waters* on the stage last week, and it was the most *distressing* failure the mind can imagine – a half-empty room with growling men and tittering females.[40]

He was even more explicit in a poem, 'The Passing of the Shee' (subtitled 'After looking at one of AE's pictures', AE being notoriously 'ethereal'), which could be seen as a sort of manifesto for his own drama:

> Adieu, sweet Angus, Maeve, and Fand,
> Ye plumed yet skinny Shee,
> That poets played with hand in hand
> To learn their ecstasy.
>
> We'll stretch in Red Dan Sally's ditch,
> And drink in Tubber fair,
> Or poach with Red Dan Philly's bitch
> The badger and the hare.
>
> <div align="right">(<i>CW</i>, vol. 1, p. 38)</div>

Deirdre of the Sorrows is only apparently an exception to Synge's preference for the 'reality' of Tubber fair in his drama. As many critics have pointed out, either with regret or with admiration, Synge makes the legendary characters of his last play speak, to quote the High King Conchubor himself, 'like the common lot scattered in the glens.' The old woman at the beginning of the play strikes the 'homely' note right away, as the rural marriage-views of late nineteenth-century Ireland are anachronistically foisted on the Ireland of the sagas:

> Shouldn't she be well pleased getting the like of Conchubor, and he middling settled in his years itself?
>
> (*CW*, vol. 4, p. 183)

That is very much from the world of Dan and Nora Burke. Synge confessed that he had difficulties in the conception of his *Deirdre*, writing in 1907 'I am a little afraid that the "Saga" people might loosen my grip on reality'; and in another letter of 1908 he said:

> These saga people, when one comes to deal with them, seem very remote; one does not know what they thought or what they are or where they went to sleep, so one is apt to fall into rhetoric.
>
> (*CW*, vol. 4, pp. xxvi-xxvii)

Hence it is interesting that this play too is so full of verbal violence, especially in the somewhat grotesque role of Owen.[41] Grene comments on the 'gratuitous brutality' in some of Lavarcham's phrases, and relates it to Synge's struggle to avoid remoteness and to keep a tight grip on reality — 'At times Synge appears to be trying to convince us and himself that his characters are really real.'[42] Again we find that Synge tends to see 'the real' in terms of the violent or wild; and believes that to produce the appropriate aesthetic response (defined as 'joy' in the Preface to *The Playboy*) to the presentation of 'what is superb and wild in reality' requires a certain kind of language. Synge's conscious and deliberate emphasis on a harsh, 'strong' diction is made explicit in the Preface to his poems, written in 1908:

> I have often thought that at the side of the poetic diction, which every one condemns, modern verse contains a great deal of poetic material, using poetic in the same special sense . . . In these days poetry is usually a flower of evil or good; but it is the timber of poetry that wears most surely, and there is no timber that has not strong roots among the clay and worms. Even if we grant that exalted poetry can be kept successful by itself, the strong things of life are needed in poetry also, to show that what is exalted or tender is not made by feeble blood. It may almost be said that before verse can be human again it must learn to be brutal.
>
> (*CW*, vol. 1, p. xxxvi)[43]

So a theory of language and certain psychological factors combine with observation of the actual harshness of life in the poorer parts of Ireland to produce that intensely powerful atmosphere of violent energy in Synge's drama. The 'realism' becomes almost synonymous with the violence, which is its guarantor – and guarantor also of linguistic health. The similes, curses, flytings, grotesque arabesques and so forth – these are even more important than the actions of the plots in creating the sense of violence in Synge's work, because they are so pervasive. And they show the bias of Synge's mind. Clearly, as much of the evidence in Synge's own critical writing (in his letters and prefaces) suggests, 'violence' is not to be deplored, but rather admired as cause or effect of energy. The cult of 'wildness' enables the artist to reject the Celtic twilight and 'Cuchulanoid' idealism as unreal, yet tied in as it is with a primitivist stance, to avoid any danger of confusion between his realism and the realism to be found in the 'joyless and pallid' works of Ibsen and Zola.

Like Yeats, Synge too is one of 'the last romantics' though it can hardly be said of him that he chose to highlight 'traditional sanctity and loveliness' in making his 'book of the people'.[44] Yet the emphasis in his work which I have argued as so prominent is easily compatible with a literary allegiance to the Romantic stance. As Mark Roberts has argued,[45] the morality of Romanticism is essentially a morality of *energy*, and its central text is Blake's *Marriage of Heaven and Hell*, with its famous proposition 'Energy is eternal delight' – a phrase that could stand as appropriate epigraph to all Synge's work. In the peasant life of Ireland, Synge felt he had found the perfect 'objective correlative' for the expression of this energy, this Dionysiac vitality, and he gave it most perfect form in his masterpiece, *The Playboy of the Western World*.

Synge is not a simple primitivist, and *The Playboy* is a very complex play. But although Synge could see and present the peasant as Caliban, the context I have outlined helps to indicate that, for all its comedy, *The Playboy* was intended as a warm tribute to the vitality of Irish peasant life and not as a sardonic critique. Even Daniel Corkery, always on the alert to detect any sign of an 'alien Ascendancy's callous caperings', agrees:

> Not for a moment do we think he intended *The Playboy* as a satire on the people of the West. Rather it is his tribute to them, his thank offering that, among them, the daemonic had liberty to strike out, to caper on the sands, to tumble about, even outrageously. This

was for him the real spirit of the place, its psychic state.[46]

How and why, then, did this play produce such protest and anger, beyond anything that Joyce's seemingly far more offensive obscenity was to produce?

To answer this is to see from another angle the problem of the gapped culture, the difficulties and failures of communication between artist and audience, both subject to the psychological and cultural malformations induced by a colonial situation. But first we must look sceptically at a common critical view of the controversy Synge's plays aroused, a received idea which derives much of its weight from the imposing authority of Yeats.

Yeats's view of Synge's relationship with his audience, which went from bad to worse between *The Shadow of The Glen* and *The Playboy*, is consistent and simple. For him it was purely a case of casting artistic pearls before political swine. Since literature is supreme, works of art can only be understood and judged according to laws of their own creating, by aesthetic standards; political and social criteria are irrelevant. (While in one way this is true, it is surely difficult to understand fully the art of a man like Synge without examining that admixture of biographical, social or political 'impurities' which, as this essay attempts to show, so shapes the direction of the creative impulse). Thus, defending *The Shadow of the Glen* from nationalist attacks, Yeats wrote in 1903, with a finely contemptuous stroke at the Irish audiences:

> Literature must take the responsibility of its power, and keep all its freedom; it must be like the spirit and like the wind that blows where it listeth; it must claim its right to pierce through every crevice of human nature . . . Aristophanes held up the people of Athens to ridicule, and even prouder of that spirit than of themselves, they invited the foreign ambassadors to the spectacle.
>
> (*Explorations*, p. 117)

The people of Ireland, by contrast, were blinkered by the sacred stereotypes of an intolerably narrow nationalism, which prevented them taking the rich imaginative nourishment offered them by the autonomous art of the Irish stage, of which Synge's plays were the crowning glory. For Yeats this audience comes to seem more and more like the imaginative eunuchs of his poem 'On Those that Hated "The Playboy" ', or like the mean-spirited and ignoble Biddys and Paudeens whom he lashes without mercy in his middle-period poems.

Yeats is very persuasive, and literary critics have tended to adopt his
model for the conflict, which they see in his terms as a clash between
an autonomous art and a biased nationalism of the most philistine kind.
Thus, as a representative example, Robert O'Driscoll, editor of a recent
anthology of critical essays on the Irish theatre and nationalism:

> . . . they [Yeats and Synge and O'Casey] upset their countrymen's
> preconceptions and propaganda, for they presented Ireland, not as
> her political apologists would wish her to be seen, but as she was.[47]

The last three words show a touching faith in the artist's objectivity, in
his ability to keep his work free of those personal 'impurities', stemming from background or social context, which might cloud the otherwise beautifully transparent glass. The situation is more complex than
this. It may be doubted that any art is free of all political 'preconceptions'. It is certainly highly dubious that the Irish national drama,
arising when and how it did, was ever anything other than highly political. The argument then is not between a free and somehow 'neutral'
art on the one hand and a narrow and aesthetically obtuse nationalism
on the other (though the nationalists were frequently narrow and
obtuse); properly it is a clash between two different kinds of cultural
and political consciousnesses.

I have discussed more fully in the introduction the general nature
of the culture-clash between Ireland and England and the way in which
that clash tended to express itself through conflicting and deeply
embedded images. Given the stress in the Anglo-Saxonist stereotype on
the simian crudity of Irish life, the chief stress in Celticist thought
naturally is placed on the spirituality (in the widest sense) of the
Irishman; he is presented as the romantic and heroic bearer of the
torch of idealism in a grossly materialist modern commercial world,
as the repository of traditional and archaic virtues. The details of the
Celtic image need not be rehearsed again; Synge's own treatment of the
Aran Islanders gives a pretty comprehensive picture. More immediately
relevant here is the statement of aim contained in the manifesto of the
Irish Literary Theatre, founded in 1899 by Yeats, Lady Gregory and
Edward Martyn:

> We will show that Ireland is not the home of buffoonery and easy
> sentiment, as it has been represented, but the home of an ancient
> idealism. We are confident of the support of all Irish people, who are
> weary of misrepresentation.[48]

We might first note that the statement implies a very vivid conscious-ness of the master-culture ('show' − to whom?); more importantly, in the context I have sketched out, however briefly, it should be clear that such an aim is inescapably part of that battle of images, Anglo-Saxon *v.* Celtic, hence fundamentally and inescapably 'political', whatever Yeats may have thought of such a dirty word. By Yeats's own proclamation, the plays of the Irish National Theatre inevitably become part of a larger political and social drama. When the Irish audiences objected to the plays of Yeats and Synge, it was not simply a matter of the irrele-vant importation of political and social criteria into purely aesthetic spheres − as Yeats disingenuously claimed − but, more basically, a collision between Ascendancy and 'native' views of Ireland, with their inescapable social and political concomitants.

In one of his earliest reviews, written in 1886, Yeats had said:

Irish singers who are genuinely Irish in thought, subject and style must, whether they will or no, nourish the forces that make for the political liberties of Ireland.[49]

Obviously this begs several questions. What does 'genuinely Irish' mean? The problem of the gap between the Ascendancy and the 'native' Irish, in terms of religion, class and cultural inheritance, is vividly present in the consciousness of both Synge and Yeats. No matter how sympathe-tic they personally feel to that other Ireland, they feel themselves to be locked outside the deepest structures of its racial memories and culture. They know themselves to be victims of the colonial situation, and that the bridging of the gap requires, at very least, strenuous efforts. As Yeats wrote in 1901:

All Irish writers have to choose whether they will write as the upper classes have done, not to express but to exploit this country; or join the intellectual movement which has raised the cry that was heard in Russia in the seventies, 'To the people'. Moses was little good to his people until he had killed an Egyptian; and for the most part a writer or public man of the upper classes is useless to this country till he has done something that separates him from his class.

(*Explorations*, p. 83)

Just how difficult it was for Yeats and Synge to separate themselves from their 'class' may be illustrated from the first production of the Irish Literary Theatre in 1899, Yeat's *The Countess Cathleen*, and from the reactions to it. It caused riot and protest and required, like *The Playboy*, police protection. In one scene, the peasant Seamus kicks to pieces the little shrine of the Virgin Mary in his cabin, because in his words, 'The Mother of God has dropped asleep and cannot hear the poor'. Yeats said in 1935 of this: 'In using what I considered traditional symbols I forgot that in Ireland they are not symbols but realities' (*Autobiographies*, p. 416). At a superficial level the play did fall foul of the more inflamed Irish religious sensibilities,[50] just as *The Playboy*'s 'shift' irritated Irish prudishness. But at a more interesting and fundamental level, *The Countess Cathleen* expresses a consciousness in many ways alien to that of its audience. A brief examination may serve as a kind of prolegomenon or guide to the more spectacular case of *The Playboy*, where again artist and audience are on different cultural wavelengths.

Although Yeats revised *The Countess Cathleen* extensively, the main outline of the simple plot remains clear in all versions.[51] In Ireland, 'in the old times' as the Celtic twilight stage direction tells us, famine rages. The peasants are starving to death, until two devils disguised as merchants (note the typical Celticist hatred of commerce) comes among them, offering them gold which will enable them to buy food. In exchange they must give the devil-merchants their souls. When the Countess Cathleen, a beautiful and tender-hearted aristocrat of much piety, hears of this terrible trade, she decides to redeem the souls of her peasants by offering her own soul in exchange for theirs. The devil-merchants accept with alacrity; the peasants are redeemed; but on Cathleen's swiftly ensuing death it is made clear that she too is saved, because God 'looks always on the motive, not the deed'.

This little play was clearly not intended as in any way a satire on the Irish, yet that gap between 'Ascendancy' and 'native' ensured its hostile reception. For example, Yeats offers in the play, innocently but tactlessly, a particularly cringing and servile peasantry – when the starving Seamus hears that ladies and gentlemen are near his cottage, he instructs his son in the methodology of begging, thus:

> Sit on the creepy stool
> And call up a whey face and a crying voice,
> And let your head be bowed upon your knees . . .

Innocent – but the overall cultural context makes this tone, from an Ascendancy writer, potentially deeply offensive to his audience. That audience, further, would not have been enchanted with the image of

what one might call landlordly merit at the heart of the play's action.
The peasants' souls are rated at one hundred crowns apiece, Cathleen's
at five hundred thousand. These going rates seem entirely appropriate
to Yeats's peasants, who beg Cathleen not to go ahead with her self-
sacrificing bargain:

> Do not, do not; the souls of us poor folk
> Are not precious to God as your soul is.

There is, underlying these aspects (and underlining them), an explosive
gap between Yeats's version of famine and the myth of the Great
Famine implicitly believed and accepted by most Irishmen. While some
landlords did try to alleviate the miseries of starvation, many — especially the absentee landlords — looked on what was happening in Ireland
in the late 1840s with the comforting knowledge of the inexorability of
the economic laws defined by Malthus and Ricardo. Others, among
whom were numbered the Persses of Galway, Lady Gregory's family,
displayed a concern very unlike the simple altruism of the Countess
Cathleen; the starving tenant might be given his bowl of soup on condition that he renounced his Romish superstitions and practices.
Surprisingly few of a desperate population became 'soupers', but the
repellent blackmail was fiercely remembered. By contrast, Yeats's
peasants cheerfully sell their souls, and would rather they stay sold
than have their noble landlord endanger hers. The play, as Conor Cruise
O'Brien says, 'did shock people who saw it; it shocked not for theological, but for social and tribal reasons'.[52]

The Countess Cathleen therefore does imply a social and class analysis of a certain phase of the Irish experience, but a very different one
from that to which its audience would have subscribed. Further, it even
includes the thesis that 'the aesthetic life' may be worth more than the
involvement with the realities of history, which is exactly the defensive
position that Yeats was to adopt in reaction to attacks on this and
other Abbey plays. The function of Oona, Cathleen's foster mother,
and Aleel, a poet (and clearly a surrogate for Yeats, especially as
Cathleen owes something to Yeats's idealisation of Maud Gonne), is to
advance the idea that Cathleen's real salvation lies in turning away from
immediate and pressing ugly reality to find health and rejuvenation in
old legends — one might say in the poetic world which Yeats himself
was trying so hard to create in this and the other works of his early
years. As Oona says to Cathleen:

Dear heart, make a soft cradle of old tales,
And songs, and music: wherefore should you sadden
For wrongs you cannot hinder?

So not only does the play seem to offer an Ascendancy interpretation
of the Famine, but adds fuel to the flames with the evasive implication
that all politics and historical facts matter less anyway than the presumably apolitical 'old tales and songs and music'. (Even when politics
and history *do* matter for Yeats, what they produce is — inevitably —
'a terrible *beauty*'). Of course, this Irish reaction was a biased one; there
was no malice on Yeats's part, his inversion of tribal and racial myths
being made with the innocence of somebody essentially outside those
myths. The problem was that bias and the suspicion of bias were built
in to a highly politicised cultural context, which Yeats could not —
despite vigorous efforts — simply negate.

The cultural clash between England and Ireland, the awkward role
of the Ascendancy writer caught between two cultures within Ireland,
the claims of pure art versus the claims of a nationalist drama in a
national theatre — all these issues are focused in *The Playboy of the
Western World* and the reactions to it — reactions which have in a sense
become part of the 'meaning' of the play. As we have seen, despite
Synge's great admiration for the life-style and values of the Aran Islanders, he was fully aware of less pleasant aspects of 'peasant' life in the
rest of Ireland, as he saw them. In fact he used the Aran values either
explicitly or implicitly to criticise aspects of those other 'peasants'.
Therefore it is significant that he should have transferred the story of
the man who killed his father, heard on Aran,[53] to Mayo, where the
action of *The Playboy* is located. This enabled Synge to express and to
explore, more fully than the monolithic unity of *Riders to the Sea* had
allowed him to do, a wider and more ambiguous range of feelings about
Irish rural life. In the character of Shawn Keogh, for instance, and in
Shawn's relation to Pegeen, Synge highlights a particularly unappealing
side to that life, the rural loveless match made solely for economic
considerations. For Shawn, and for Michael James, Pegeen's father,
this match is clearly a 'good bargain', and only that. His 'drift of heifers'
and his 'blue bull from Sneem' are sufficient to outweigh the universal
contempt felt by the community for Shawn on all other grounds.
Shawn is a moral and emotional imbecile, no more than what a stage-
direction tells us, Pegeen's 'property'. He can only compete with
Christy in terms of his comparative wealth, the bribes of a ticket to the
United States and the new clothes. Pegeen's judgement on him is

crushingly final — 'a middling kind of a scarecrow', reminiscent of a 'bullock's liver' — yet the conditions of the life are such that at the end of the play we see that not only has Pegeen lost Christy, but is now almost certainly fated to Shawn. The situation had been treated before in Synge's plays, of course;[54] the wedding of Timmy the smith and Molly Byrne in *The Well of the Saints* is certainly not a love-match, and Nora Burke in *The Shadow of the Glen* spells out the desperate realities of many a woman's situation in rural Ireland:

> What way would I live and I an old woman if I didn't marry a man with a bit of a farm, and cows on it, and sheep on the back hills?
>
> (*CW*, vol. 3, p. 49)

This play, in fact, is particularly bleak in its presentation of the emotional poverty of rural life, for both Dan Burke and Michael Dara, despite the difference in their age and temperaments, are clearly two of a kind, as their sitting down to a complacent drink together at the end indicates. In terms of dramatic convention we expect to see Michael as the young rival to the aged husband; however, as he steadfastly and singlemindedly counts over the money during Nora's great evocation of the loneliness of life, we realise, as Dan does, that he is indeed 'a quiet man', and that there is more than a touch of the 'bullock's liver' about him, too. Nora's only future lies, significantly, with an outsider, the tramp. Michael Dara's puling impotence is heightened and reinforced in the case of Shawn Keogh by the snivelling servility of his attitude to authority, particularly the authority of the Church — on being asked to keep Pegeen company overnight, he reacts with 'horrified confusion':

> I'm afeard of Father Reilly, and what at all would the Holy Father and the Cardinals of Rome be saying if they heard I did the like of that?
>
> (*CW*, vol. 4, p. 63)

Shawn in this respect is a recognisable Irish type, called to this day in Ireland — and the phrase applies to both sexes — a holy-water hen. A brilliant comic creation, Shawn Keogh gives Synge a chance to get some of his own back, dramatically, on the 'horrible and awful sides of all that western life' to which he referred in his letter to MacKenna in 1905 (see above, p. 39). He is a very long way removed from the noble savages of Aran.

The Playboy contains quite a few other glimpses of Irish life not at all like the Celticist stereotypical images. The authoritarian brutality which goes along with a patriarchal gerontocracy, which Synge had first shown us in Dan Burke, is developed even further in Old Mahon, whose climactic battle with Christy, we may note incidentally, yet again originates from the attempt to impose a 'good bargain' of a marriage:

> 'You squinting idiot,' says he, 'let you walk down now and tell the priest you'll wed the Widow Casey in a score of days' . . . He was letting on I was wanting a protector from the harshness of the world, and he without a thought the whole while but how he'd have her hut to live in and her gold to drink.
>
> (CW, vol. 4, pp. 101-3)

Then, the emphasis on the monotony and boredom of rural Irish life is pervasive in all Synge's plays, especially *The Shadow of the Glen* and *The Playboy*, and he clearly dramatises the connections between the monotonous loneliness and the prevalence of heavy drinking and even insanity, as well as a sort of compensatory relish for violent deeds.

Switching the locale of the source-story from Aran to Mayo enabled Synge, then, to infuse his portrait of peasant life in *The Playboy* with a more critical realism. While there may have been a certain amount of provocative coat-trailing in some details of that portrait,[55] especially in the fairly regular invocation of a grotesquely large squadron of saints, undoubtedly Synge's darker colours come from direct observation (admittedly through Aran-tinted spectacles, of course) and from a deliberate rejection of the 'breezy, springdayish Cuchulanoid' emphasis in the literary revival. And these astringent modifications of the romantic primitivist side of the revival in general, and of Synge's own work in particular, add immeasurably to the quality of the drama. Naturally, Synge's refusal to idealise without qualification the peasant life he depicted would have been — and was — offensive to those reared solely on a sickly diet of undiluted Celticist pap. To adapt the words cited from the *Lyceum* (see above, p. 22), 'while our peasants say their beads and meditate on the mysteries of the Rosary and gradually all move towards the peasant-owner Utopia dreamed of by Thomas Davis, they can surely *never* be like Shawn Keogh or Christy Mahon or Old Mahon.' Such an outlook need not detain us — had the objections to *The Playboy* (and to Synge's work in general) been based solely on this gross sentimentalism and pious naivete, then clearly they would have merited an even more brusque dismissal than the majority of commentators, from Yeats onwards, have given them.

But surely it is difficult to credit that Irish attitudes to Synge's work were quite so banal. At the very least we may say they were more interestingly prejudiced. For a start, though Synge's audience was predominantly middle-class and lower middle-class Dubliners, many of these, if not all, would have been the sons or grandsons of country-dwellers or peasants, or at any rate have had a lively awareness of the essentially rural nature of Ireland. The Irish, as I point out in my introduction, have and had a very uneasy relation with their rural roots, for the reasons I have there explored. Therefore an Anglo-Irish writer like Synge would have had particular difficulties in treating peasant life without controversy, quite apart from the prominence he gives it in his work and from the fact that that work is cast mainly in the mode of comedy. Thus in the very choice of subject-matter itself, the Yeats-Synge stress on the peasant, on the 'sole test' of the soil, as Yeats called it, was disconcerting to an audience painfully insecure about its own cultural values. It is a familiar paradox of cultural primitivism: Yeats and Synge, unsmeared by the soil, and educated, can celebrate the virtues of peasant life far more confidently than those who are, or whose parents or grandparents were, 'living in the bogs' as we say in Ireland. Their idealisation is itself a measure of their 'outsider' status.[56]

One might say, therefore, that the great irony of Synge's work is that he encountered hostility not so much because of his dislike of aspects of Irish life, but more because of what he chose to celebrate in that life. He idealised the Irish in ways which they could not feel to be ideal. This applies particularly to that primary emphasis in Synge, illustrated above and strongly marked in *The Playboy*, wildness and exuberant savagery of both deed and word, which for him exemplified an emotional and imaginative vitality dying or dead in more 'civilised' communities. Christy's slaying of his da, with its action replay, Pegeen's lament for that violent enemy of policemen, Daneen Sullivan, Jimmy Farrell's hanging of his dog, the spectator-sports of the village girls (hoping that another man will turn up to bite the yellow lady's nostril), the Widow Quin's suckling of a black ram and the cannibalistic consequences experienced by the Lord Bishop of Connaught, Michael James's epic account of the epic drunk at the wake, Pegeen's burning of Christy's leg, Christy's biting of Shawn's leg, and much more in the same joyously violent vein — all this represents Synge's celebration of his artistic commitment to 'daemonic' (the epithet is Corkery's) energy. But where Synge intended glorification, the Irish audience found something else — inevitably.

Inevitably, because what the Anglo-Irishman chooses to celebrate —

'wildness', 'savagery' – is so close to what the Englishman had for centuries chosen as the major denigratory feature in his image of the Irish – violence, and another kind of savagery. This heady mixture of English stereotypical images of Irish violence, of Irish resentment of those images, and of Synge's stress on violence, which for him is almost synonymous with vitality, is, far more than the word 'shift', what made *The Playboy* so explosive. George Moore felt, he says in *Vale*, that 'there could be no doubt that it was the bloody bandage that caused the row in the Abbey Theatre', and Padraic Colum likewise reports: 'That scene [where Old Mahon enters] was too representational. There stood a man with a horribly-bloodied bandage upon his head, making a figure that took the whole thing out of the atmosphere of high comedy.'[57] But, as I have tried to show, the sense of violence is more pervasive in Synge's work than these comments imply, being built-in to his rhetoric.[58] It was a particularly unfortunate quality to highlight, even admiringly. Patrick Kenny, in the *Irish Times* of 30 January 1907, wrote: 'It is as if we looked in a mirror for the first time, and found ourselves hideous'.[59] The Irish mostly denied the reliability of the mirror. For them it was cracked, and like Christy's 'divil's own mirror' in the play, 'would twist a squint across an angel's brow'. From the Irish point of view, what could Synge's wild, violent, poverty-stricken, drunken, blathering Irishman be except Paddy the Ape of *Punch* come back to life, on – unkindest cut of all – the stage of a supposedly national theatre? How would this representation 'nourish', in Yeats's words, 'the forces that make for the political liberties of Ireland?'[60] While it is true that the literary revival and its plays made Ireland seem more culturally respectable in England, such a question was a perfectably understandable one on Irish lips – a thoroughly colonised people dread the reactions of ridicule and condescension on the part of the dominant culture. The Irish could only feel that in many ways Synge's *Playboy* would confirm the pejorative English stereotype image. That sense of a watching alien audience is illustrated neatly in the *Freeman's Journal*'s comment, with its interesting colonial reference, 'This hideous caricature would be slanderous of a Kaffir kraal', and in the shouts of the rioters as reported in the Dublin papers, 'Take your miserable effort to England at once.'[61]

That Synge should have been surprised at this reaction is itself further evidence of the gap in cultural consciousness between Ascendancy man and native. Certainly some of the actions of Yeats during the week of first production tended to validate the nationalist assumption that the Ascendancy directors and writers of the Abbey were at

last showing themselves in their true (English) colours. For the third
night of the play, Yeats gave free tickets to a claque of students from
Trinity College (Protestant, Unionist, and Anglophile), who came
along to wave Union Jacks and sing 'God Save the King' during the
performance. As Conor Cruise O'Brien says suavely:

> The exact point of their demonstration remains a little obscure:
> that it was a counter-demonstration to the native one is clear.
> Presumably they agreed with the natives that the play represented
> the natives as savages, but denied that the natives had a right to ob-
> ject to such a representation, since savages was what the natives
> were. Politically, the natives were unfit for self-government, and the
> play, and the natives' reaction to the play, both proved it.[62]

And in his famous speech at the debate on the riots, Yeats cited the
case of a priest in Liverpool who had written a play only to withdraw
it because of protests and who had apologised to his audience. He went
on: 'We have not such pliant bones, and did not learn in the houses that
bred us a so suppliant knee' (*Explorations*, pp. 226-7). There speaks the
authentic voice of Ascendancy Ireland, proud, and contemptuous of an
inferior caste (the rest of Ireland). Certainly the effect of *The Playboy*
fracas was to polarise even more sharply the antagonisms between
Ascendancy and native Irishman. While Synge's early death leaves us
only speculation about the possible development of his attitudes, it is
clear that after this point Yeats retired firmly into the Ascendancy
House that did not breed suppliant knees.

It has seemed worthwhile to try to convey something of the complexity of the cultural situation out of which *The Playboy* came and
with which it interacted, even at the expense of the 'close reading'
approach. The old New Critical emphasis on the study of 'the words on
the page' seems especially inappropriate to drama, the most social of
the arts, which is best understood in as wide a social context as one can
create for it.[63] But if we turn from this general consideration of the
overall rhetorical and emotional implications of *The Playboy* to examine the relations of its basic story or fable to the Irish cultural context, we will find again that Synge, consciously or unconsciously, invites the hostile reaction which he got.

The story of Christy Mahon's mutation from timid poltroon ('the
loony of Mahon's', as Synge titled the work in early drafts) to swag-
gering and confident playboy is clearly another — if highly individual —
contribution to the Irish store of heroic myths. In this case, one might

say that Christy exemplifies the heroism of the imagination as he
struggles to become the image he has of himself, and succeeds — a
success highlighted the more by its solitariness, as even Pegeen defects
at precisely the moment when her empirical doubtings have become
irrelevant in relation to the new Christy. In part, as Una Ellis-Fermor
says, *The Playboy* 'takes for its theme a mind's exploration and discovery of itself.'[64] But Synge, unlike Yeats with his long line of 'Olym-
pians' from Cuchulain to Parnell to Maud Gonne to himself, chooses to
treat his hero-myth in the comic mode. In stressing the readiness of the
Mayo community to see a superman in this unlikely victor of a
squabble in a potato patch, and their susceptibility to his 'blather' ('it's
a grand story, and he tells it lovely', as Susan and Honor say), in which
lies the initial impetus in the creation of the hero, Synge could be felt
to be debunking the mythologising or hero-worshipping tendency itself.
This is deeply rooted in Irish life, and especially in Irish nationalism,
functioning fairly obviously as a powerful compensatory agent in the
psyche of a subject nation. (One may remark, in passing, that the
mythologising machinery is still in good working order, despite changed
circumstances; many Provisionals in the North in the last few years have
been 'changed, changed utterly' in the popular imagination. The force
of Yeats's rhetorical question in the poem 'Sixteen Dead Men' is still
powerfully operative: 'And is their logic to outweigh/MacDonagh's
bony thumb?') Further, nationalist mythology is deeply imbued with
what may be called the idea of *sudden* or *miraculous* transformation or
transfiguration. Long centuries of disillusion and failure had given
nationalist Irishmen a distaste for the slow processes of steady working
towards a goal. The hero, or the heroic moment, or a transfigured
Ireland would emerge like a bolt from the blue. This is part of the
secret of the great success of Yeats's *Cathleen ni Houlihan*, which is
itself a sort of short miracle play.

    — Did you see an old woman going down the path?
    — I did not, but I saw a young girl, and she had the walk of a queen.

The revolutionary commitment produces *instantaneous* changes; and,
rather disconcertingly, life seemed to imitate art at Easter, 1916. Hence,
apart altogether from the materials on which Synge based his version of
heroism, the very fact that he concentrated, as it were, on the machinery, or the process, of myth-making, emphasising Christy's frequent
set-backs and the fortuitous comedy and lying involved in his shaky
road to self-affirmation, was almost certainly offensive to the mythic

version of instant transfiguration subscribed to by the nationalist theo-
reticians of the heroic.

But, as Synge himself said, 'there are, it may be hinted, several sides
to *The Playboy*'.[65] If the emphasis on the peasant, and on violence,
made most Irishmen uneasy, and if the emphasis on the haphazard
process or machinery of hero-making offended romantic nationalists,
there may be a yet more ironic implication in the fable or action of
The Playboy. Synge himself may not have been aware consciously of
the political reverberations of an action which showed the successful
liberation, by violence (and repeated violence, at that), of an oppressed
victim from the domination of a paternalistic tyranny. Yet the play
does invoke, in however shadowy a way, in the starkness of its fable, an
intense and revolutionary analogy of Ireland's relations with England.
There is evidence that this aspect of the play, allusive and understated
as it is, manifested itself in a confused and half-formulated way in the
minds of the contemporary audiences of that first confusing week.
Thus the reviewer of the *Evening Mail* of 28 January 1907, after a few
ritual slashes at Synge's decadent cosmopolitanism, fumbles his way
towards a real insight only to back off into nervous frivolity; *The
Playboy*

> . . . is absurd and un-Irish, and smacks of the decadent ideas of the
> literary flaneurs of Paris rather than of simple Connaught; or, per-
> haps, it is an allegory, and the parricide represents some kind of
> nation-killer, whom Irishmen and Irish women hasten to lionize.
> If it is an allegory it is too obscure for me. I cannot stalk this alliga-
> tor on the banks of the Liffey.[66]

If Synge's play does embody this political 'allegory', we must qualify,
or complicate the common account that it simply offended 'nationalist
feelings' — a conveniently vague term. On the thesis I have been advan-
cing, at least part of the hostile reaction of the audience is to be explained in terms of bourgeois timidity, or middle-class anger at the
suggestion, whether conscious or not, of the efficacy of violent revolution at a time when all but a small minority of Irishmen still believed
in the constitutional path to Home Rule. The efficacy of violence was
at the heart of the play's action, and complemented the general tone of
'ferocity' created by the rhetoric; middle-class Irishmen glanced uneasily over their shoulders to see how the English master might respond,
at this delicate juncture, to a work of art which seemed to confirm the
English view of the Irishman's incorrigible tendency to seek violent

solutions to political problems. These relatively neglected aspects of
The Playboy's 'meaning' have been explored deftly and wittily in Brian
Farrington's poem 'Homage to J. M. Synge':

> There was always the imperial Parent, looking on,
> Time-honoured know-all, brooking no answer back,
> Responsible, deprecating, self-appointed
> Author of our achievements,
> Always there, the strict correct paternal
> Umpire that his sons would never set on.
>
> You couldn't have understood what you were doing,
> And if you had you'd likely have suppressed it;
> Your brother evicting tenants in Mayo
> Maintained the family income that you lived on.
> You tried to opt out, only half-succeeded,
> Broke, not poor, you never looked for a job:
> Art for art's sake on a private pittance.
> And yet, tenebrous mollycoddle with the silver tongue,
> It came from you, or through you, it was yours,
> The stark triumphant image, faked out in prancing words,
> The bootstrap myth that made of us the first
> New Nation. No wonder they couldn't take it,
> The Independent readers in their pit,
> No wonder they tried to chase you from the stage
> When you reached for the loy to split that meddler's crown.[67]

The Playboy, then, cuts across and disturbs many prejudices, con-
ceptions and ideals in the total Irish context in a way that was only
possible given Synge's distance from its cultural, social and political
presuppositions. But all of Synge's plays (except *Riders to the Sea*)
have the ability to disturb and disconcert, and to do this not merely
to Irish audiences. There is, in other words, a complexity in Synge
which may be explained in more orthodox literary terms, and which
combined with the problems of the cultural consciousness gap we have
examined to make him such a puzzling figure in and for the Ireland of
his time.

Every writer on Synge acknowledges the difficult of trying to
classify his plays in any of the conventional generic terms applied to
drama — comedy, farce, tragi-comedy, satiric drama. Characteristically
Synge draws his source material from folk-tale, farcical anecdote or

fable, but then proceeds to treat his dramatic elaboration of the source-matter with a disconcertingly unexpected naturalism, which gives a considerable observed vividness to character and setting. However, naturalism is not the object — it is itself subject to a highly formal awareness and use of the conventions of dramatic comedy. The interplay between the very different sets of expectations raised by the folk or 'shanachie' base material ('shanachie' is Robin Skelton's preferred label for the genre of Synge's plays),[68] by the naturalistic mode of the handling, and by the patterns of comic convention, is what gives Synge's work its aesthetic complexity, its ability to upset the tendency to confident dramatic classification in audience or reader.

The Shadow of the Glen, for example, is based on an international folk-tale which Synge heard in a localised setting and in all its vigorous, amoral simplicity from the old shanachie, Pat Dirane, on Aran.[69] The basic outline of the story, with its Chaucerian overtones of January and May, and its allusion to the story of the Widow of Ephesus, sets up expectations which are confounded by the play which Synge made out of it. The folk-device of the husband's trick of shamming death in order to catch out the flighty wife and her young and virile lover is completely transmuted by Synge's development of Nora Burke into a complex fully-rounded character. This produces the bafflement so clearly recorded by, and evidenced in, Daniel Corkery:

> In his elaboration of the character of the woman, Nora Burke, Synge introduced so many elements that were contrary to the spirit of the comedy that one scarcely knows whether to call his play tragic or comic. Neither did Synge himself; neither does the audience . . . [The] story he deprived to some degree of its elemental folk flavour when he elaborated the humanity of the young wife, changing it from personality to character, from the Old Man's Wife to Nora Burke.[70]

Corkery is right in all but the most important of the essentials. Many things in the play, especially the character of Dan Burke and his tetchy inability to lie still when Nora is out of the house because of his consuming thirst, are the broadest folk-comedy; equally clearly, the 'humanity' of Nora is emphasised in words which suggest an intense loneliness and sense of mortality:

> Isn't it a long while I am sitting here in the winter, and the summer, and the fine spring, with the young growing behind me and the old

passing . . . It's a pitiful thing to be getting old, but it's a queer thing
surely . . . God forgive me, Michael Dara, we'll all be getting old, but
it's a queer thing surely.

(*CW*, Vol. 3, pp. 49-53)

What Corkery does not see is that, far from being evidence of Synge's
lacking 'certainty of touch', the clash of dramatic registers is deliberately engineered by Synge to enable him to explore more deeply the
ambiguities and confusions of life itself, and to purge the 'film of
familiarity' which may insulate his audience from reality. Corkery
himself, Skelton, and Grene, among many other critics, have illustrated
sufficiently just how deeply Synge understands Nora Burke and her
situation, trapped inside the loveless rural Irish marriage, with no easy
way out; one might stress here, to emphasise how deliberate is Synge's
transformation of the folk-ethos of his source into something more
complex, his extension and modification of the role of the young rival
in his final version. In earlier drafts, Michael Dara is a 'fine handsome
man', with a strong personality. Synge actually has him threaten the
tramp physically: 'If he gives any jaw, I'll walk him out through [that
door] as I'd walk any bloody god-damned know-nothing like him.'[71]
By the finished version, however, Michael has become the week-kneed
fore-runner of Shawn Keogh that I have already commented on (see
above, p. 69), a change which adds incidental touches of humour, but
which overall greatly darkens the tone of the play by emphasising the
more strongly the emotional sterility of rural Irish life, and Nora's
predicament. This, rather than the ruthless cunning of the husband in
Pat Dirane's tale, becomes the major issue in *The Shadow of the Glen*,
and it becomes so not least because Synge's inclusion of the folk-ele-
ments directs our attention to quite different possibilities in the
method of treatment. As Grene sums it up, 'Folk-tale and farce, peasant
naturalism and poetic drama all coexist in *The Shadow of the Glen*, and
it is the balance and ironic contrast between these several modes which
go to make up the play's meaning.'[72]

There is a very similar pattern of clashing expectations underlying
the dramatic strategy of *The Well of the Saints*. The well which could
cure blindness Synge had heard about on Aran, but the folk or shanachie
element is probably less marked than its origins in the medieval French
fable of Andrieu de la Vigne, *Moralité de l'aveugle et du boiteux*, which
Synge had first encountered in Paris at de Jubainville's lectures in
1895-6, and which he noted down more fully from his lecturer's book
in 1903.[73] The tone of the medieval fable is purely ironic, as Greene

and Stephens in their summary make clear:

> A blind man agrees to carry a crippled man on his back so that each
> can compensate for the other. The arrangement is completely success-
> ful until they are both cured by passing a procession in which the
> remains of St Martin are displayed. The blind man is delighted, but
> the cripple curses the saint for destroying an easy life on the back of
> his companion.[74]

The bare bones of Synge's plot paraphrased might suggest something of
the same cheerful irony: two blind beggars are cured by a saint, but
when they discover they are not as handsome as they had been led to
believe by their community, thankfully re-accept the state of blindness,
and deliberately run away from the saint's second attempt to cure
them. There is what Grene calls 'the diagrammatic lucidity of the
parable'[75] about this; certainly nothing in it prepares us for the emotional intensity with which Synge invests the ending of Act I, where a
newly sighted couple grope round desperately to find the allegedly
handsome partner each thinks to see. Here is real cruelty, in the mocking
communal laughter (which anticipates the same sort of thing in *The
Playboy*):

> *People* [jeeringly]. Try again, Martin, try again, you'll find her yet.
> (*CW*, vol. 3, p. 97)

Here is real pain, in the anguished humiliation and suffering of Martin
and Mary — indeed Synge in his plan has marked this scene as 'tragic':

> *Mary Doul* [beginning to realise herself.] If I'm not so fine as some of
>   them said, I have my hair, and my big eyes, and my white skin —
> *Martin Doul* [breaking out into a passionate cry.] Your hair and your
>   big eyes, is it? . . . I'm telling you there isn't a wisp on any grey
>   mare on the ridge of the world isn't finer than the dirty twist on
>   your head. There isn't two eyes in any starving sow, isn't fairer
>   than the eyes you were calling blue like the sea.
> (*CW*, vol. 3, p. 97)

Yet immediately afterwards, at the beginning of Act II, Synge is able to
exploit the broad comedy inherent in the idea of the fable story as he
presents Martin grumbling to Timmy the smith, with all the ingenuity
of the naturally lazy, at the curse of work which has fallen on him with

his sight. Comic convention modulates into serious, even intense emotion; the passages of intensity themselves modulate in turn into the detached and anaesthetised gratification of comic or even farcical expectations.

As in *The Shadow of the Glen* and *The Well of the Saints*, so in *The Playboy of the Western World* does Synge create 'a pattern of unstable and fluctuating convention, so that uncertainty and confusion is built into his dramatic strategy'.[76] Synge's initial decision was to treat the story he had heard on Aran as a farce, and the titles of his first draft show clearly how Christy's role was to be subordinated to the exigencies of farce: 'The Murderer (A Farce)', 'Murder Will Out', 'The Fool of the Family', 'The Fool of Farnham'. Dr Saddlemyer's presentation of much of the extensive draft material for the play[77] enables us to see how strong was Synge's initial intention to end the play with the farcical exposure of Christy and his reversion to his father's cowed slave again; this would have been a good rollicking comedy of a traditional kind – the deflation of the braggart. But as Synge worked on the play, this base pattern is overlaid by – perhaps even dislocated by – something quite different; the elaboration of Christy into a dynamic character capable of change and growth, who is able eventually to confront the farcical bathos of the ending prepared for him (as it were) and rise superior to it, on to a different dramatic plane altogether. Christy's real achievement, yet the farcical substratum of the whole play, are held in superb tension in the wonderfully complex ending of *The Playboy*, a tension illustrated finely in an exchange like this:

> *Shawn* [shrieking.] My leg's bit on me! He's the like of a mad dog, I'm thinking, the way that I will surely die.
> *Christy* [delighted with himself.] You will, then, the way you can shake out hell's flags of welcome for my coming in two weeks or three, for I'm thinking Satan hasn't many have killed their da in Kerry and in Mayo too.
>
> (*CW*, vol. 4, p. 171)

The Playboy is Synge's greatest work because in fact in it he finds most scope for this juggling with the intriguing gap between material or content, which raises one set of expectations, and a form or convention which raises a very different set of expectations – a dramatic strategy that, as illustrated, he had polished in *The Shadow of the Glen* and *The Well of the Saints*. *The Playboy* is the more disconcerting, and especially to Irishmen, as we have seen, because at the heart of its action there is a deed of violence. This violence is itself subjected to Synge's chameleon perspective; we are lulled into easy acceptance by the clever farcical elements in its introduction:

> Is it killed your father?
> With the help of God I did surely, and that the Holy
> Immaculate Mother may intercede for his soul.
>
> (*CW*, vol. 4, p. 73)

— and then, as Old Mahon reveals his spectacularly bloody bandage, and as Christy seizes the loy to strike him again, we are forced to confront the violence as painfully real. Pegeen's words measure not just her own journey, but the distance that all readers or audiences of the play are forced to travel by Synge's manipulation of perspective:

> I'll say a strange man is a marvel with his mighty talk; but what's a squabble in your back-yard and the blow of a loy, have taught me that there's a great gap between a gallous story and a dirty deed.
>
> (*CW*, vol. 4, p. 169)

And even then, of course, we are not at the end of the journey. The last few minutes of *The Playboy* are justly celebrated as one of the most elaborate exercises of almost dizzying audience manipulation in the history of the stage,[78] where the current of our expectations and sympathies is set flowing in different directions almost from moment to moment up to Pegeen's final 'wild lamentation'. Again, the 'shock ending', as we may call it, is the inevitable product of the interplay between shanachie elements, naturalism and dramatic convention; and again, Synge's assurance in the control of this interplay in *The Playboy* is due to his polished use of it in *The Shadow of the Glen* and *The Well of the Saints*. In the first of these, the effect is the more obvious because of the compression inherent in what is a very economical piece. The Tramp's lyrical invitation to Nora to share his life follows without a break on his hardheaded suggestion that she lives with Michael for the sake of the 'half of a dry bed', Nora's acceptance of the offer qualifies the romance with realism ('it's myself will be wheezing that time with lying down under the heavens when the night is cold') and, above all, there is the final reversal when Dan and Michael are left alone, and 'the about-to-be-wronged husband sits down to drink with his would-be betrayer.'[79] At the end of *The Well of the Saints*, the pact established between Martin and Mary to reject the saint's cure is broken by Mary's giving in, the cruelty of the people to Martin is a paradoxical offshoot of their desire to be kind to him by restoring his sight, Martin's 'plausible whine' as he asks to be cured himself, after all, seems a major change of heart, but then he strikes the miraculous water from the saint's hand, and, as Christy is to do in the later play, triumphantly defies the outraged crowd. The triumph is undercut, however, by Mary's last despondent words, and Timmy's suggestion that on their dangerous journey to the south they may well both be drowned.

Right to the ends of his plays, an audience does not know which way to 'have' Synge. The continuity of the dramatic strategy we have examined, from *The Shadow of the Glen* to *The Playboy*, does more than show basic technical links between his plays; it points to an attitude of mind clearly deeply rooted in Synge's sensibility.

The point may be approached by seeing that comedy as a form generally or traditionally has involved some kind of affirmation of a social order. This is especially obvious in satiric comedy which commonly attacks the disorders of society by making ridiculous the violators of its standards of morals or manners; as Sidney put it in *The Defence of Poesie*: 'The comic writer represents the common errors of our life . . . in the most ridiculous and scornefull sort that may be; so as it is impossible that any beholder can be content to be such a one.' But at a more fundamental level, as the primitive origins of comedy indicate,[80] comedy involves a representation of a renewal of society symbolised by the common dance or wedding festivity qf its conclusion. One thinks of the quadruple wedding at the end of *As You Like It*, or the triple wedding at the end of *A Midsummer Night's Dream*, or the prenuptial dance at the end of *Much Ado About Nothing* – Benedick's

Come, come, we are friends. Let's have a dance ere we are married that we may lighten our own hearts and our wives' heels.

In this atmosphere of festivity and celebration, the predominant emotion will be social, and the spirit of tolerance and reconciliation will be marked. The tendency of much comedy – certainly Shakespeare's – is to include as many people as possible in its final society. Crabbed parents, stern uncles, rigid dukes, misers and melancholics are more often reconciled or converted than repudiated. As for the villainous Don Johns of the world – as Benedick says, 'Think not on him till tomorrow!' The basic commitment of comedy is, then, towards society, society somehow purged or renewed by the comic action. As Northrop

Frye describes the pattern of Shakespearean comedy:

> The action of the comedy begins in a world represented as a normal
> world, moves into the green world [the wood outside Athens, the
> Forest of Arden, Belmont, Bohemia], goes into a metamorphosis
> there in which the comic resolution is achieved, and returns to the
> normal world.[81]

Clearly, these aspects of the comic convention depend on a fundamental acceptance of society. In the case of Synge, that consistent thwarting
or complication of the straightforward comic pattern which we have
seen in his work may be understood in terms of his divided sensibility.
That is, Synge's experience and valuation of Irish folk life, and especially of Aran, shows us a man deeply committed to the idea of finding a
community with which to identify imaginatively and emotionally. At
the same time, the isolation of his class background prevents a full and
easy identification with the society he depicts, especially when he
moves imaginatively away from Aran. Instead, Synge asserts again and
again the value of the individual who projects himself above and
beyond his society, who rejects it or is rejected by it. This is essentially
a Romantic, individualistic position and is opposed to the comic convention's assertion of community values. In *The Shadow of the Glen,
The Well of the Saints, The Tinker's Wedding* and *The Playboy*, the
values of tramps, blind beggars, tinkers and criminals are shown to be
worth more than the values of established society. They have more
spirit, more imagination, more 'fine talk'; they have what Yeats called
the 'wasteful virtues' that 'earn the sun'. As Vivian Mercier sums up
these plays:

> In each of Synge's mock-pastoral plays the comic hero (or heroine)
> is an anti-hero, owing no allegiance to any but the anti-society. He
> and/or she is banished from the stage before the final curtain, and
> established society in effect says 'Good riddance', but our hearts
> go with the Tramp and Nora, with Martin and Mary Doul, with
> Christy Mahon, and we have nothing but mocking laughter for the
> solid folk who remain behind. Pegeen's last wild cry tells us that her
> heart too has gone with 'the only playboy of the western world.'[82]

Synge's high valuation of the solitary outcast is consistent with that
hatred of the bourgeoisie and of middle-classness in general which he
shared with Yeats, a middle-classness he saw as a creeping disease

spreading over Ireland. Also, the tramp-figure or social reject is his version of the isolated artist type, the more so as Synge always endows him (the Tramp and Nora, Martin Doul, Christy) with the artist's imagination and heightened eloquence. In his essay, written about 1901, 'The Vagrants of Wicklow' Synge spells out his sense of affinity with the vagrant which is to be fully illustrated in the plays to come:

> Their abundance has often been regretted; yet in one sense it is an interesting sign, for wherever the labourer of a country has preserved his vitality, and begets an occasional temperament of distinction, a certain number of vagrants are to be looked for. In the middle classes the gifted son of a family is always the poorest — usually a writer or artist with no sense for speculation — and in a family of peasants, where the average comfort is just over penury, the gifted son sinks also, and is soon a tramp on the roadside.
> (*CW*, vol. 2, p. 202)

The pattern of Synge's plays, then, describes the movement towards fulfilment and liberation of poetic and anarchic solitaries, a liberation achieved in the teeth of and at the expense of the society inside which the action is located. In fact *The Tinker's Wedding* fails in part at least because Synge is trying to describe the counter-movement of the already liberated towards conventional conformity, and clearly his heart is not in the job. And yet, as is seen most clearly in *The Playboy* but is implied in all the plays (in so far as all Synge's communities are at the very least tinged with that 'popular imagination that is fiery, and magnificent, and tender'), the solitary is given some sort of nurture by his community; his special qualities can, after all, only achieve their definition in relation to it.

To sum up, Synge remained obsessed by the *idea* of community as he saw it on Aran and on the Blaskets. Yet he tends to create the community in his dramas mainly in terms of its rejection by the familiar romantic solitary or outcast. The valuation of community remains theoretical, but again and again isolation or alienation tends to be the hallmark of individual quality. Two general points may be made about this. Firstly, we can see how admirably that dramatic strategy described above, the manipulation of a pattern of fluctuating conventions, is adapted to expressing the division in Synge's sensibility, the tension between the pull towards community and towards individualism. We may also see, secondly, that this is not just a matter of a conscious aesthetic choice, a deliberate expression of a sense of ironic detachment as the repetition of the pattern from play to play would seem to indicate, but that the ambiguous resultant tone is an 'unconscious' reflection of Synge's relation to his total cultural context. We are back again to the special difficulties and problems of the Ascendancy artist, wishing to be fully integrated in Irish society, unable to be so integrated, knowing he will always be in some sense, like the young Synge gazing at the children of the Dublin slums, a watcher from the shadows. As with Yeats, so with Synge, therefore; he begins with the idea of bridging the gap in the Irish cultural tradition, and attempts to create in his writing compelling images of community, yet what his plays (with the exception of *Riders to the Sea*) really celebrate is the victory of the 'occasional temperament of distinction', the individualist, the tramp-artist. In the end, as his background made almost inevitable, Synge found it more congenial to imagine not the typical Irishman, but the unusual, isolated Irishman.

Yet it is only out of such radical conflict and tension and inner contradiction, surely, that drama of such quality as Synge's can spring. One must disagree with Sean O'Tuama's verdict:

> For Joyce and Yeats, the conflict arising from the problem of whether to identify or not to identify with facets of Irish culture was clearly one of the most dynamic and productive factors in their whole work. For Synge, a much more monolithic character, the effort to identify never assumed the proportions of a problem: he merely went through the process simply, rigorously and successfully.[83]

On the contrary, Synge's work is deeply instinct with the problems of identity and identification, problems only slightly masked in his case by his choice of the dramatic mode; and clearly for him, too, as for his two more famous contemporaries, such problems proved extremely 'dynamic and productive'. Daniel Corkery, attempting to illustrate what he thinks is the ideal relationship between the artist and the society to which he addresses himself, cited a quotation from Rozanov which appeals to him:

> You look at a Russian with a shrewd eye ... He looks at you with a shrewd eye ... And all is said. And no words wanted. That is just the thing that is impossible with a foreigner.[84]

For 'foreigner', read Ascendancy writer — though Corkery concedes

that Synge 'stands apart from all his fellow Ascendancy writers' because
he 'went into the huts of the people and lived with them', and 'ceased
almost to be an outsider'.[85] Perhaps we should be glad that Synge
never attained, and could never attain, the full cultural assimilation of
Corkery's Russians. 'And no words wanted' — if the price of Synge's
drama is his sense of difference, of cultural isolation, it seems a price
worth paying.

It would be equally misguided to lament that Synge may have mis-
represented Ireland in his work. Synge's plays are not, and are not
intended as, documentary studies of Irish life. The 'truths' they offer
about Ireland are, as this essay has tried to show, interesting and compelling precisely because so illustrative of the relation of artist to
society in a context of cultural fission, of the gapped tradition, of the
colonial legacy. And finally, though it is not a hypothesis subject to
proof by the tools of the critic, even the most tendentious element in
Synge's representation of Ireland — what I have called his cult of violence, or energy — may have been of more benefit to Irishmen than
they thought at the time. As Yeats wrote in one of his frequent defen-
ces of Synge, two years before *The Playboy*:

> The misrepresentation of the average life of a nation that follows
> of necessity from an imaginative delight in energetic characters and
> extreme types, enlarges the energy of a people by the spectacle of
> energy.
>
> (*Explorations*, p. 191)

Perhaps. It is hoped, at any rate, that the reader may now be in a
slightly better position to understand some of the reasons for Synge's
creative 'misrepresentation' of Irish life.

3 W. B. YEATS: FROM 'UNITY OF CULTURE' TO 'ANGLO-IRISH SOLITUDE'

From an early age Yeats was conscious of the anomalous status of the Protestant middle and professional class of Ireland into which he had been born. Of his childhood he wrote:

> Everyone I knew well in Sligo despised Nationalists and Catholics, but all disliked England with a prejudice that had come down perhaps from the days of the Irish Parliament.
>
> (*Autobiographies*, pp. 33-4)

There was a double aspect to this sense of not quite belonging anywhere in Yeats's case, since he goes on to record how, as a young man, he felt ill at ease even inside his own background:

> I had noticed that Irish Catholics among whom had been born so many political martyrs had not the good taste, the household courtesy and decency of the Protestant Ireland I had known, yet Protestant Ireland seemed to think of nothing but getting on in the world.
>
> (*Autobiographies*, pp. 101-2)

Here lay the seeds of that 'Anglo-Irish solitude', as he was later to call it,[1] which moulded and shaped both his whole life and his art.

How did the man brought up in that nationalist-despising Sligo come to write *Cathleen ni Houlihan* for the Irish National Theatre Society, which first performed the little play in 1902 (and regularly afterwards)? For, with the possible exceptions of the poem 'September, 1913' and some of the late ballads on Parnell and Casement, this is the most intensely and narrowly nationalist of all Yeats's writings. It was of this play that Yeats was thinking when he wrote, near the end of his life:

> All that I have said and done,
> Now that I am old and ill,
> Turns into a question till
> I lie awake night after night
> And never get the answers right.

Did that play of mine send out
Certain men the English shot?

('The Man and the Echo', *CP*, p. 393)

The answer to the poet's question must be 'No', but it is a question he
can ask without fatuity.[2] The play, set in the revolutionary year of
1798 ('Who fears to speak of '98?' is the title of one of Ireland's most
famous republican anthems), tells with ballad-like speed, economy and
force, of the arrival in a peasant cottage in the west of a Poor Old
Woman (one of the many personifications in tradition for Ireland herself). Sustained by hopes of getting her 'four beautiful green fields'
back, and 'putting the strangers out of my house', she contemptuously
rejects the peasants' offer of money — 'If any one would give me help
he must give me himself, he must give me all', and goes off to join the
friends who are gathering to help her ('If they are put down today they
will get the upper hand to-morrow'), with these ringing words:

It is a hard service they take that help me. Many that are red-cheeked
now will be pale-cheeked; many that have been free to walk the hills
and the bogs and the rushes will be sent to walk hard streets in far
countries; many a good plan will be broken; many that have gathered
money will not stay to spend it; many a child will be born and there
will be no father at its christening to give it a name. They that have
red cheeks will have pale cheeks for my sake, and for all that, they
will think they are well paid.

[She goes out; her voice is heard outside singing.]
They shall be remembered for ever,
They shall be alive for ever,
They shall be speaking for ever,
The people shall hear them for ever.

(*Collected Plays*, p. 86)

Responding to the latent symbolism and the appeal of the Old Woman's
words, Michael, the elder son of the cottage, rushes out after her voice
away from his family and the girl he is to marry the following day.
When the younger son comes in, his father asks him 'Did you see an old
woman going down the path?', and he replies 'I did not, but I saw a
young girl, and she had the walk of a queen.'

In this short play Yeats has embodied and unleashed, in an extra-
ordinarily powerful way, the definitive myths of the republican nationalist movement. There is the binding nature of the call of total sacrifice

of all merely personal ties and interests to the service of Ireland; the emphasis on the need for blood-sacrifice; the emphasis on the glorious-ness of the heroic gesture, a glory which makes failure irrelevant, or indeed can make failure a kind of triumph; the transmutation of the individual caught in history into a legendary being ('They shall be remembered for ever'), made possible by the sacrificial act; the belief in the power of the heroic sacrifice to work its own miraculous, quasi-religious transubstantiation on Ireland herself — the poor old woman becomes, at the moment of commitment to her, a young girl with the walk of a queen. It is historical fact that such emotions and ideas filled the minds and informed the deeds of the leaders of the Rising which took place fourteen years after the first performance of Yeats's play, especially in the case of the romantic Pearse.[3] And such emotions and ideas, further validated, as it were, by the (partial) success of that Rising — itself so much a romatic-heroic gesture — continue to play a large part in the mythology of republican nationalism in Ireland to this very day.

Many factors were at work in the young Yeats's alignment of himself with the nationalist *credo* of which *Cathleen ni Houlihan* is such a passionate expression.[4] In the first place, it is an indication of that cultural or racial loneliness discussed above — Yeats did not feel English, despite the traditional Unionism of his class, and further felt that his membership of that class cut him off from the majority of his fellow countrymen. As he wrote in 1901:

> Moses was little good to his people until he had killed an Egyptian; and for the most part a writer or public man of the upper classes is useless to this country till he has done something that separates him from his class.
>
> > (*Explorations*, p.83)

Cathleen is very much an act of severance, and an attempt to assert a sense of identity with an uncompromised 'Irishness'.

Yeats might have achieved this more simply by becoming a Catholic, of course, the whimsical could argue. But the silly point serves to indicate a special appeal of radical republicanism to him; it had been, from its origins, anti-clerical, a regular recipient of episcopal condemna-tions, and hence — in Yeats's early years, and especially after the fall of Parnell, which did much to fan anti-clericalism in the country — could meet his desire for identity without making him feel swamped by the vulgarity of Catholicism (the lack of 'good taste,' of 'household courtesy and decency').

It would be very wrong to suggest, naturally, that sociological factors alone motivated Yeats's nationalist tendencies. There was a genuine idealism in the romantic republican tradition which meshed with a genuine romantic idealism in Yeats himself. The revulsion from the comic stereotypical Irishman of *Punch* with his 'amusing' tipsiness, unreliability, inability to speak proper English and farcical indifference to tomorrow, underlay much of the idealisation in the writings of the literary revival. Both Yeats and Lady Gregory saw the prime aim of their work at the outset as the necessity to bring back dignity to the image of Ireland, both at home and abroad. The intransigence of the republican tradition, the persistence of the ideal of selfless service to a romantic vision of Ireland through fair times and foul, the self-perpetuating legendary quality of this romantic nationalism which could invest the present and the future with the glamour of a glorious past ('They shall be remembered for ever,' says the Old Woman, and proves it by citing her own litany of the glorious dead) — all of this cerainly suggests and supplies images and symbols of more 'dignity' than anything in the Paddy-with-the-pig-in-his-kitchen-and-the-caubeen-in-his-gob, stage-Irish stereotype. Yeats was to change his mind about the virtues of intransigence, of 'hearts with one purpose alone'; but at this early stage, he found it necessary, as well as congenial, to present Ireland in his art as tragic heroine rather than comic ape.[5]

Also, the record of the extreme nationalist movement, like the record of Irish history at large, is one of failure (on a fairly spectacular scale). This made it profoundly appealing to Yeats. One does not say this cynically, implying that Yeats could quite happily throw in his emotional lot with 'the irreconcilable temper' (as Joyce called it), in the satisfying knowledge that there would be no danger of having to take practical steps to mount, or consolidate, a revolution. Rather, the tradition of heroic defeat stirred something in the deepest sources of Yeats's poetic personality, creating or finding there the emotional and spiritual commitment to lost causes which can be traced through all of Yeats's life,[6] and which gives so much of his art its profound elegiac or even eschatological tone. For Yeats identified failure — the failure of his country politically and economically — with spirituality and a higher kind of power than the merely material, the power of poetry and romance and idealism. Thus he writes in 1897:

It is hardly an exaggeration to say that the spiritual history of the world has been the history of conquered races. Those learned in the traditions of many lands, understand that it is almost always some defeated or perhaps dwindling tribe hidden among the hills or in the forests, that is most famous for the understanding of charms and the reading of dreams, and the seeing of visions. And has not our Christianity come to us from defeated and captive Judea?

(*Uncollected Prose*, vol. 2, p.70)

Failure and poetry went together, then, and Yeats feared success if the price to be paid was prose.[7] Ireland's attainment of her political ends was not worth the loss of her soul. It is a very characteristic Yeatsian stance, in that it casts doubt on the political struggle *as worthy in itself*; but it is not quietist, since the heroic reassertion of nationalism in revolutionary gesture, from generation to generation, is necessary to, and proof of, the vitality of that idealism of those who are only undefeated because they have kept on trying.

For both 'sociological' and idealistic reasons, then, Yeats found the ethos of romantic nationalism congenial. One must also say that the adherence of Maud Gonne and John O'Leary to the republican ideal played a major part in swaying Yeats towards the frame of mind out of which he could create *Cathleen ni Houlihan*. For they were two of his 'beautiful lofty things', and had the power to make him feel, against any personal reservations, the dignity of passionate commitment to a cause. As he says in his *Memoirs* of Maud and O'Leary at this time:

We were seeking different things: she, some memorable action for final consecration of her youth, and I, after all, but to discover and communicate a state of being. Perhaps even in politics it would in the end be enough to have lived and thought passionately and have, like O'Leary, a head worthy of a Roman coin.

Romantic nationalism involves 'passion', then — always a good for Yeats. One can see here, however, the beginnings of that tendency in Yeats to subordinate political and historical reality to the demands of his aesthetic sense. Thus, the aims of nationalist struggle are less important than the motive and the cue it provides for 'passionate' living and thinking, and heroism becomes itself aesthetic, divorced from purposeful action, frozen and static, a head on a coin. Years later, Yeats was to write, characteristically, of the culminating deed in the long saga of nationalist endeavour: 'A terrible *beauty* is born'[8] (my italics).

Nevertheless, it is important to begin a discussion of Yeats by asserting that an idealism in him met and understood an idealism in the romantic nationalism of the republican school, and that this enabled him to express memorably a major aspect of Irish life in those troubled years. Yeats's art, ironically enough, displays more genuine innerness with this powerful force than the art of the Catholic Joyce for whom 'romantic Ireland' does not exist except as a joke, or than the art of O'Casey who was actually a founder-member of the Irish Citizen Army.

Cathleen ni Houlihan is, however, as I hinted earlier, unusual among Yeats's nationalist writings for the directness and uncompromising clarity with which it articulates the mythology which inspired the republican movement. More frequently, Yeats is more oblique, his interest in the occult, in the epic Ireland of ancient myth and legend, and in the folk and 'fairy' Ireland, blurring the stark outline of the simple recurrent drama in which Cathleen calls her sons to heroic martyrdom.

Yeats's interest in occult and theosophical matters is often dismissed as mere crankiness and certainly as unrelated to his nationalist leanings. It should not be so dismissed. Both Yeats and AE (the oracular 'yogibogeybox' of *Ulysses*) had absorbed from Madame Blavatsky's *Secret Doctrine* the idea of the imminence of a new epoch to be ushered in by a Messiah figure, and inaugurated with revolutionary violence and war.[9] The messianic belief, the sense of imminent upheaval, the eager anticipation of apocalypse, was also a part of the emotional make-up of the revolutionary patriots in the Fenian movement. Thus, mysticism and revolutionary dreams could be married most happily. Yeats wrote 'The Valley of the Black Pig' in 1896 (*CP*, p.73):

> The dews drop slowly and dreams gather: unknown spears
> Suddenly hurtle before my dream-awakened eyes,
> And then the clash of fallen horsemen and the cries
> Of unknown perishing armies beat about my ears.
> We who still labour by the cromlech on the shore,
> The grey cairn on the hill, when day sinks drowned in dew,
> Being weary of the world's empires, bow down to you,
> Master of the still stars and of the flaming door.

Yeats's note on the poem, that 'all over Ireland there are prophecies of the coming rout of the enemies of Ireland in a certain Valley of the Black Pig, and these prophecies are, no doubt, now, as they were in the Fenian days, a political force', is far more explicit than the poem itself, which has none of the directness of *Cathleen ni Houlihan*. 'Master of the still stars and of the flaming door' evokes nothing like as definite a response in the Irish reader's imagination as references to 'four beautiful

green fields' and 'putting the strangers out'. The Celtic twilight atmosphere of the poem is marked; the violent clash of armies (who are
'unknown') is perceived in a dream-vision which cleverly confuses
prophecy with retrospect – the poem seems to point forward, but the
spears and horsemen are of an archaic past. And yet, the poem is instinct
with a pattern of feeling – the apocalytic imminence of violent and
decisive action arising from weariness with 'the world's empires' (a nicely
ambiguous phrase) – exactly like that of revolutionary nationalism.
Indeed, precisely by siting his poem, as it were, among the cromlechs
and cairns of antiquity, Yeats associates heroic struggle with a dignified
antiquity which goes back way beyond 1798. The very cloudiness and
imprecision of the poem may be one of its strengths, from a nationalist
angle. Speaking generally of the effect of Yeats's dreamily visionary early
poetry, Nicholas Mansergh says:

> Yeats's vision of Ireland was imprecise, but in one sense it was that
> very imprecision that made it so stirring an inspiration, for it meant
> different things to different men and in so doing filled the minds of
> his countrymen with dreams and clothed in glamour his country's
> past.[10]

Yeats was himself fully aware that his yoking of nationalist themes to a
mystical and occult symbolism represented a departure from the flat
rhetorical simplicities of republican ballads, or of the poets of *The Nation*
school. He writes in 'To Ireland in the Coming Times' (*CP*, pp.56-7):

> Know, that I would accounted be
> True brother of a company
> That sang, to sweeten Ireland's wrong,
> Ballad and story, rann and song;
> Nor be I any less of them,
> Because the red-rose-bordered hem
> Of her, whose history began
> Before God made the angelic clan,
> Trails all about the written page . . .
> Nor may I less be counted one
> With Davis, Mangan, Ferguson,
> Because, to him who ponders well,
> My rhymes more than their rhyming tell
> Of things discovered in the deep . . .

The red-rose-bordered hem that trails about the written page certainly differs from the nationalist thrust of a work like *Cathleen ni Houlihan*, but it also represents the first of the many attempts by Yeats to broaden the basis of the Irishness of national cultural identity. One could not argue that the Irish are or were ever a nation of theosophists, but certain aspects of Catholicism and the strength of folk belief and custom in the countryside made them more susceptible to the semi-mystical appeal in many of Yeats's early poems. At least so he believed and hoped. For if he could familiarise his Irish readers with the Ireland of folk and fairy belief, and of the epic legends of a pre-Christian era, he felt he could go a long way towards the 'de-Davisisation of Irish literature',[11] and create with his emphasis on Celtic themes and the Celtic ethos, a more substantial and enduring basis for that 'unity of culture' which he hoped to see in a country too hagridden with divisive politics and a nightmarish history. The trouble with the past invoked by the republican tradition and even by the mid-nineteenth-century poets of *The Nation*, such as Thomas Davis — a most idealistic and generous-spirited man — was that it was too recent for the long Irish memory, too capable of arousing violent bitterness, a sense of division between the Catholic peasantry and the Protestant land-owners, and sectarian animosity. Yeats saw in the Old Irish myths and legends, discovered by the great nineteenth-century antiquarians and grammarians and popularised in the works of men like Ferguson and Standish O'Grady, a subject that was undoubtedly national, but untinged by modern politics and modern hatreds. Hence it might appeal to a number of writers of different kinds and to a wider audience. The unity of culture desiderated in the future would be sought for first in the remote past. And so Yeats writes *The Wanderings of Oisin*, 'The Madness of King Goll', 'Cuchulain's Fight with the Sea', 'Fergus and the Druid', and many other poems in his early period, which employ Old Irish epic machinery. These poems are remarkable chiefly in the very absence from them of the strident, hectoring tone of militant nationalism. Though they suggest a world of rarefied heroic dignity, Yeats does not try to enforce in them or through them any kind of exemplary moral for the Ireland of his own times.[12] Sometimes, indeed, one feels — and this is what keeps the poems fresh, of course — that the legendary trappings of the heroic world are relatively unimportant in themselves, merely masks for more personal themes, such as the antithesis between the values of action and those of 'dreaming wisdom' which is the subject of 'Fergus and the Druid', and which is one of Yeats's life-long themes.

The dissemination through the culture of the image of an epic, legendary Ireland by Yeats and many other poets, popularisers and antiquarians, did indeed have an effect on the popular imagination. Unfortunately, for all the nobility of conception behind Yeats's belief in the salving power of the remote past, for all his hopes about 'unity of culture', the effect was not of a kind which made him feel any the easier in his Anglo-Irish identity. J. C. Beckett, himself a distinguished member of Yeats's class, points up the irony sympathetically:

> . . . it is not altogether fanciful to suppose that Anglo-Irish writers felt, perhaps subconsciously, that the further back they went the safer they were . . . But this study of Gaelic antiquity proved more potent and more divisive than those who encouraged it could have foreseen. The popular imagination was caught by the picture of a glorious past, of an Ireland with a distinctive culture of its own, untouched by English influence; and the very vagueness of the outline left the imagination free to shape the picture as it would . . . [The Anglo-Irish writers] thus contributed, unwittingly, to the downfall of their own tradition. The ideal of a Gaelic Ireland bred an attitude conducive to cultural, and even to racial, exclusiveness.[13]

Certainly, as time went on, Yeats's own characters from the remote past began to become rather self-consciously 'aristocratic' – the poet's reaction to the militant nationalists' 'exclusivist' use of the heroic sagas and legends.

Concurrently with this epic material Yeats was writing a great deal on another kind of Ireland, the Ireland of folk and fairy. There are the various collections and anthologies of stories – *Fairy and Folk Tales of the Irish Peasantry*, *The Celtic Twilight*, *Stories from Carleton* and *Representative Irish Tales*, all of which he hoped would become source books for Irish poets. There are many poems on the Sidhe, and on men who dream of fairyland or who lose their brides to the fairies, and on children who are stolen away. This most aloof and aristocratic of poets even writes – not very convincingly – a number of ballads about Father O'Hart and Moll Magee and the Foxhunter and Father Gilligan and the Fiddler of Dooney. All of this represents an amazing and sustained effort at an idealisation of the Irish peasantry. Synge's idealisation of peasant society pales by comparison with Yeats's, for Synge at least knew Irish, and lived with the people of the west and the islands in their own cottages; he had more basis in experience for the importance which he assigned to the peasant as a symbol of life's potentialities, and, anyway, his portrait is tempered with realistic observation. Yeats, making forays in his floppy hat from Coole Park to the surrounding cottages, in the comforting and Irish-speaking presence of Lady Gregory, is a different case.

There were several reasons why Yeats idealised the peasantry, why this idealisation was important to him, and why it can be considered as playing a part, in its own way, in 'the cause' of Irish independence. In the first instance, the folk-beliefs and superstitions of the country people enabled him to make a satisfying link with his own theosophical beliefs. The spiritual, the visionary and the occult are fit subjects of concern for Irish writers, because the true Celtic nature, shown in the stories and visions of the peasantry, is in intimate contact with the occult. Thus Blake, Shelley, Swedenborg, the peasant of the west of Ireland, and W. B. Yeats could all be related, in their belief in the 'ancient religion of the world.'[14] What was 'esoteric' in Madame Blavatsky's front room was, after all, popular when one met it among sturdy Connemara men. Yeats could thus naturalise his occult interests, and the peasantry in turn underwrote his conviction of the spirituality of experience. As can be seen easily, Yeats's conception of the peasant was highly specialised, being romantic, not social or political (when he thought of the peasantry as a socio-political reality, it dwindled in his poetry into 'Mean roof-trees'); yet it was of the greatest importance to Yeats's idealisation that he could see the peasant's spirituality in terms of folk-belief, folk-superstition, folk-mythology. Because this meant that he did not have to consider the (for him) awkward fact of the peasant's devout Catholicism. This was most useful to Yeats, as he constructed over the years his ideal, semi-feudal Ireland:

> Sing the peasantry, and then
> Hard-riding country gentlemen . . .

The uninstructed reader of Yeats could be forgiven for thinking that the peasants believed in magic and dreams and visions, while only the hated middle-class urban 'half-educated' type was Catholic. Yeats refuses to consider the spirituality of his ideal peasant on any but his own terms.

But his unremitting assertion of that spirituality represents one of those points in Yeats's writings where an apparently 'unpolitical' point in fact engages with the poet's deepest feelings of nationhood. The image of the peasant was the focal point of a racial and cultural clash of images in the nineteenth century. For many Englishmen, Paddy and his Pig stood for the comic slovenliness of the Irish, a kind of Caliban whose poverty and lack of education was proof positive of Ireland's inability to govern herself. The cartoons of Tenniel in *Punch* make the point with striking visual immediacy. Therefore, in the battle to bring back dignity to Ireland, to prove it to be 'the home of an ancient idealism',[15] the rehabilitation of the peasant was a top priority for many Irish writers. For Yeats, the folklore of the peasants indicated their access to a spirituality markedly superior to the gross philistinism which, taking his cue not only from Arnold but from his own experiences, he saw as dominating the urban culture of materialist Victorian Britain. This opposition — archaic, peasant but spiritual Ireland versus modern, urban and materialist Britain — became an article of faith among the literary revivalists. The Irish countryman could never fall victim to the utilitarian materialism which afflicted the unfortunate Englishman, because his racial memory, imagination, even his very landscape, were saturated with the ethos of an alternative and ancient world. Yeats describes 'The Man Who Dreamed of Faeryland' (*CP*, pp.49-50):

> He wandered by the sands of Lissadell;
> His mind ran all on money cares and fears,
> And he had known at least some prudent years
> Before they heaped his grave under the hill;
> But while he passed before a plashy place,
> A lug-worm with its grey and muddy mouth
> Sang that somewhere to north or west or south
> There dwelt a gay, exulting, gentle race
> Under the golden or the silver skies;
> That if a dancer stayed his hungry foot
> It seemed the sun and moon were in the fruit:
> And at that singing he was no more wise.

Thus Irish culture could hold its head up alongside English culture — indeed, alongside any culture. The imagination of the peasant, steeped in fairy and folk-lore, offered the richest possible basis to the artist; and again Yeats draws an unflattering comparison with the urban culture of Britain which can produce only the limited art of realism or naturalism on the one hand, or on the other, and in reaction to this 'grossness', the literature of decadence — 'the poetry of cigarettes and black coffee, of absinthe and the skirt dance', as Yeats scornfully characterises it.[16] He wrote in the same article of 1893:

> Imagination is God in the world of art, and may well desire to have

us come to an issue with the atheists who would make us naught but 'realists', 'naturalists', or the like.

Folk-lore is at once the Bible, the Thirty-nine Articles, and the Book of Common Prayer, and well-nigh all the great poets have lived by its light. Homer, Aeschylus, Sophocles, Shakespeare and even Dante, Goethe and Keats, were little more than folk-lorists with musical tongues. The root-stories of the Greek poets are told to-day at the cabin fires of Donegal . . .

(Uncollected Prose, vol. 1, p.284)

Therefore, 'the peasantry' features in Yeats's writings almost purely as a literary ideal. Unlike Synge, Yeats is not even interested in their speech patterns, and rarely attempts to embody peasant speech in his work. He does not consider them in social or political terms, but as a romantic phenomenon. Nevertheless, the image he creates in his work of a people dignified by an easy commerce with a mythology and folk-lore alive yet reaching back into antiquity was of powerful national appeal; it gratified the Irish wish to believe that the successful neigh-bour nation was soulless, and that Ireland herself retained in spite, or because, of her history of defeat, a moral and spiritual superiority.[17] Yeats did not create this mood or feeling singlehanded, of course, but his early writings gave it a powerful and eloquent impulse, so that Padraic Pearse, addressing a university debating society, owed as much of this characteristic tone to the literary revivalists as to the Gaelic League:

The Gael is not like other men; the spade, and the loom and the sword are not for him. But a destiny more glorious than that of Rome, more glorious than that of Britain awaits him: to become the saviour of idealism in modern intellectual and social life, the regenerator and rejuvenator of the literature of the world, the instructor of nations, the preacher of the gospel of nature-worship, hero-worship, God-worship — such, Mr. Chairman, is the destiny of the Gael.[18]

At the basis of all this was the idealisation of the peasant. The socio-logical accuracy of the portrait of Irish country life drawn by Yeats is not pertinent, for as he said in connection with the work of Thomas Davis, whose rhetorical narrowness he tried so hard to broaden,

. . . a country which has no national institutions must show its young men images for the affections, although they may be but diagrams of what should be or may be.

(*Essays and Introductions*, pp.312-3)

Finally, the nationalism of the young Yeats found expression in the celebration of the landscape, particularly of his own Sligo and the west of Ireland. 'The Lake Isle of Innisfree' is only the best known example of this poetry of place − all of Yeats's early writing is informed by the spirit of locality. He genuinely loved the west of Ireland for its physical beauty as well as for its associations with folk-lore and legend and myth; further, he saw in the celebration of place a useful corrective to the abstractness of 'conscious patriotism'. Looking back in middle life on his youthful attempts to encompass Ireland in his art, he draws a distinction between the poet of Ballyshannon, William Allingham, and Thomas Davis:

Allingham and Davis are two different kinds of love of Ireland. In Allingham I find the entire emotion for the place one grew up in which I felt as a child and which I sometimes hear of from people of my own class. Davis was possessed on the other hand with ideas of Ireland, with conscious patriotism. His Ireland was artificial, an idea built up in a couple of generations by a few commonplace men. This artificial idea has done me as much harm as the other has helped me.

(*Memoirs*, p.153)

Yet, on the whole, Yeats benefited from his conscious attempt to link himself with the nationalist movement. Clearly it eased the sense of marginality arising from his Anglo-Irish birth, giving him a sense of belonging which in turn lent his art confidence and a sense of direction. He wrote in the *United Irishman* in 1901:

Nobody can write well . . . unless his thought, or some like thought, is moving in other minds than his . . . that which has made John Eglinton turn from all National ideals and see the hope of the world in individual freedom, in 'the individual grown wiser than his institutions', has made me a Nationalist and has made me see the hope of the world in rearrangements of life and thought which make men feel that they are part of a social order, of a tradition, of a movement wiser than themselves.

(*Uncollected Prose*, vol. 2, p.257)

Ironically, Yeats was to adopt Eglinton's views within a few years, as we shall see. But, unquestionably, Yeats's generous embrace of nationalism sustained and confirmed in him a sense of identity. It also saved him from going in the direction of many of his friends in the Rhymers' Club, up the cul-de-sac of aestheticism.[19] Yeats never lost his belief in the value of an audience, of the importance of the artists' relationship to society. He had imbibed this as a young man via John O'Leary and the poets of *The Nation* school. And he paid them handsome tribute right at the end of his life. He writes in 1937, in 'A General Introduction for My Work', that he knew that Davis and the others were not good poets and dismissed their 'dry eighteenth-century rhetoric',

> . . . but they had one quality I admired and admire: they were not separated individual men; they spoke or tried to speak out of a people to a people; behind them stretched the generations.
>
> (*Essays and Introductions*, p.510)

Yeats brought much as well as receiving much. His early poetry, prose and plays represent a considerable effort to purify Irish nationalism from within, to broaden its base from the narrowly political to the wider cultural, to refine its idealism and filter out its rancorous bitterness. If he created an idealised Ireland of his own, an 'artificial idea' as he said of Davis, at least that ideal was less abstract, less of a diagram, than that of the rhetoricians of *The Nation*, and much more generous than the sloganised 'Irish Ireland' of the chauvinists, unmercifully and permanently pinned down in the Citizen of Joyce's *Ulysses*.[20]

But the very success of Yeats's literary movement, alongside the efforts of the Gaelic League, the Gaelic Athletic Association and like organisations, in raising the national consciousness, brought difficulties down on the poet's head, and rammed home to him again his Anglo-Irish predicament. Yeats's 'broadness' was too broad for many of a nationalist persuasion, who wished that he would keep writing more *Cathleen ni Houlihan*s, as it were, urging him to shape his art in conformity with their fairly simple model of an ideal Ireland. Yeats found himself attacked for his 'refusal to preach a doctrine or to consider the seeming necessities of a cause' (*Essays and Introductions*, p.257). His disengagement from the Celticising nationalism of the early years was, as many critics have pointed out, in part a reaction to the devastating blow of the marriage, in 1903, of his great love Maud Gonne (who had played the lead in *Cathleen ni Houlihan*) to Major John MacBride, the 'drunken, vainglorious lout' who was to be 'changed, changed utterly'

in 1916. Her fiery commitment had undoubtedly helped to give impetus
to Yeats's involvement in an active, popular nationalism. The attacks of
the extreme nationalists on the Irish Theatre which Yeats had been
largely instrumental in founding, attacks which had begun with his own
Countess Cathleen in 1899, and continued with increasing virulence as
Synge rose to prominence with *The Shadow of the Glen* in 1903, dis-
illusioned Yeats further with 'the daily spite of this unmannerly town'
(*CP*, p.169). The bitter clash between the idea of a free and autonomous
theatre, held by Yeats, and the propaganda machine desiderated by the
nationalists, which culminated in the furore over *The Playboy of the
Western World* in 1907, is discussed more fully in the chapter on Synge.
Here it is enough to remark that it helped to drive Yeats back into his
Anglo-Irish solitariness, and forced him to abandon his noble ideal of a
'unity of culture' for Ireland.

Conor Cruise O'Brien, in his witty and stimulating discussion of
Yeats's politics, suggests that at about this time (1903-7), Yeats found in
the adversities he encountered an opportunity to re-assert his Protestant
sense of class-superiority. In the years of his more directly political
nationalism (of which the flower is *Cathleen ni Houlihan*), this Irish
Protestant, says O'Brien,

> . . . had necessarily emphasized his Irishness, minimizing or denying
> the separate and distinct tradition which the word Protestant implies.
> The Protestant now re-emerged with an audible sigh of relief. It had
> been stuffy in there, and getting stuffier.[21]

It is certainly true that the excoriation of the Catholic middle-class
Ireland that we find in Yeats's prose and poetry from now on has a class
basis in the Protestant sense of belonging to a superior caste. Looking
back over 'the Irish propaganda', as he calls it, of his earlier years, Yeats
describes the difficulties of his position in terms which bear out O'Brien:

> If I must attack so much that seemed sacred to Irish Nationalist
> tradition, I must, I knew, see to it that no man suspect me of doing
> it to flatter Unionist opinion. Whenever I got the support of some
> man who belonged by birth and education to University or Castle, I
> would say, 'Now you must be baptized of the gutter.'
>
> (*Autobiographies*, p.233)

Nevertheless, despite this kind of remark (which anyway in this particular
case dates from 1922), O'Brien's point must be taken rather cautiously.

It is less than generous to Yeats. For, just as his presentation of the Irish peasantry in his early — indeed, in all his work — is partly an expression of a feudal or archaic class-sense, but also partly an expression of a genuine idealism, similarly his rebuke of the Catholic middle class in the work of his middle and later years is more than simply a class attitude. It cannot be defined in narrowly sociological terms (though as I say this, I can hear the Marxist battle-chariots thunder over my head), because as his version of the peasant demonstrates, Yeats did not think in the objective or descriptive terms of the sociologist. Yeats's emergence as a leading representative of the national renaissance seemed to D.P. Moran, the vitriolic editor of *The Leader*, 'one of the most glaring frauds that the credulous Irish people have ever suffered', as he wrote in 1900.[22] Moran's argument is based on racial and class grounds; and in the course of his defence, Yeats advanced a point of relevance to my argument here, when he said of his expressed hostility to the middle class: 'I use the word to describe an attitude of mind more than an accident of birth' (*Uncollected Prose*, vol. 2, p.241). That there is something more than mere snobbishness involved in Yeats's hostility to the middle class, that he is attacking more an attitude of mind than a social grouping (he was, after all, himself of the middle class, in a sociological sense, as George Moore among others was quick to point out gleefully[23]), can be seen in what is simultaneously one of his most powerful expression of contempt for 'middle Ireland' and one of his finest poems, 'September 1913' (*CP*, p.120). The poem begins:

> What need you, being come to sense,
> But fumble in a greasy till
> And add the halfpence to the pence
> And prayer to shivering prayer, until
> You have dried the marrow from the bone?
> For men were born to pray and save:
> Romantic Ireland's dead and gone,
> It's with O'Leary in the grave.

What is under attack here is a mean-spirited prudential morality, incapable of selfless action or altruism, a morality at once utilitarian, mechanical and servile. Yeats was nurtured from his earliest youth to hate the utilitarian ethos, and tends to define his social position not in hereditary or 'blood' terms, still less in terms of a sense of Protestant hegemony, but — simply — in terms of an opposition to that utilitarianism of the spirit:

My father had brought me up never when at school to think of the
future or of any practical result. I have even known him to say,
'When I was young, the definition of a gentleman was a man not
wholly occupied in getting on.'

(Autobiographies, pp.89-90)

So, in 'September, 1913' the fumblers in the greasy till are measured
against 'Romantic Ireland' − not against the well-bred hauteur of the
great Protestant houses, but against powerful types of a reckless, un-
calculating idealism:

> Was it for this the wild geese spread
> The grey wing upon every tide;
> For this that all that blood was shed,
> For this Edward Fitzgerald died,
> And Robert Emmet and Wolfe Tone,
> All that delirium of the brave?
> Romantic Ireland's dead and gone,
> It's with O'Leary in the grave.

The gap between self-interest and selflessness is dramatised as sharply as
possible in the application of the word 'delirium' to the courageous
activities of the patriots, for so it must seem to the timidity of vision of
merchant and clerk. Two kinds of saving, material and spiritual, are
brought together in a contrast of explosive contempt in the great
punning lines:

> But little time had they to pray
> For whom the hangman's rope was spun,
> And what, God help us, could they save?

Was it worth trying to 'save' an Ireland that has become a mere nation
of 'savers'? Emphatically yes, in Yeats's view; it is the essence of the
anti-utilitarian position adopted here that practical results matter less
than heroic efforts, realities less than idealism. The poem occurs in the
Responsibilities volume of 1914, the introduction to which contains a
line which strikes a tonal chord for the whole volume: 'Only the wasteful virtues earn the sun' (*CP*, p.113). So the highest and culminating
praise of the legendary patriots, what marks them off most from modern
huxtering Irishmen, is the 'wastefulness' of their attitude: 'They weighed
so lightly what they gave.' The vital contrast in the poem, then, *is* one

of 'attitude of mind'. From the perspective of this important poem, it is easier to grasp the Yeatsian flavour of lines like

> Before the merchant and clerk
> Breathed on the world with timid breath
>
>   ('At Galway Races', *CP*, p.108)

where the emphasis is more on the timidity than on the social status, the 'accident of birth'.

One other thing is important about the idealistic patriots celebrated in 'September 1913'. They lost. In the important essay 'Poetry and Tradition' of 1907 (*Essays and Introductions*, pp.246-60), where, in the aftermath of the death of O'Leary and *The Playboy* controversy, Yeats sums up his disillusionment and indicates the new directions of his art, he writes:

> O'Leary had joined the Fenian movement with no hope of success, as we know, but because he believed such a movement good for the moral character of the people.

Yeats almost *identifies* here the improvement of 'moral character' with lack of success; it is a marked feature of his particular kind of romanticism,[24] as the equation of success with moral vulgarity had been endemic in the Irish nationalist sensibility, as a compensatory defence-mechanism, during a good part of the nineteenth century. Now, with the healing of the post-Parnell split in the Irish Parliamentary Party, and with Home Rule a definite policy of the Liberal Party, it seemed that 'all that delirium of the brave' over the centuries was going to issue in a prosaic and constitutional passage to an acceptable (non-republican) measure of Irish freedom. Yeats loved Irish nationalists as heroic losers, but Irish nationalists as potential winners — and politician-winners at that — was a different matter. It must be remembered that Yeats's attitude to history was aesthetic (as we shall see in more general terms later on). An important aspect of this aestheticism was his constant pursuit of images of heroic failure, of those things which, as he says in one of the 'Meditations in Time of Civil War', might

> . . . exalt a lonely mind,
> Befitting emblems of adversity.
>
>   (*CP*, p.227)[25]

Later in his 1907 essay 'Poetry and Tradition', Yeats makes explicit his belief in the aesthetic possibilities of the old nationalism as compared to the new. He says that he did not at first see that

> . . . as belief in the possibility of armed insurrection withered, the old romantic Nationalism would wither too, and that the young would become less ready to find pleasure in whatever they believed to be literature.

It is significant that at the juncture where Irish nationalism seemed at last to have a real possibility of success, Yeats should throw in his poetic lot with an idealised aristocratic class, finding in it an even more powerful metaphor of heroic pride in defeat.

Objecting to a mean-spirited servile utilitarianism, objecting also in a more complicatedly 'aesthetic' way to the possibility of political victory, Yeats also objected to the negative bigotry and emotional sterility which he felt characterised middle-class nationalism, rendering it not only culturally barren in itself but also, in its hate-fuelled narrowness, incapable of tolerating the free creativity of others. This is the basis of Yeats's 1909 poem, 'On Those That Hated "The Playboy of the Western World", 1907':

> Once, when midnight smote the air,
> Eunuchs ran through Hell and met
> On every crowded street to stare
> Upon great Juan riding by:
> Even like these to rail and sweat
> Staring upon his sinewy thigh.

(CP, p.124)

There were many reasons why *The Playboy* caused such a furore, as I attempt to explain above, but one does not need to read very much nationalist rhetoric either of those years or of today to feel that Yeats has a valid point — which, *pace* O'Brien, need not necessarily stem solely from the Protestant in him emerging gratefully from the 'stuffiness' and proclaiming his class superiority. Hatred — of which Yeats himself was no mean exponent — has indeed bedevilled Irish history and culture, and fed the bitterness of the national attempt to find an identity. It is not a good basis on which to build. The diary entry of 1909 out of which Yeats made that poem is more explicit:

The root of it all is that the political class in Ireland — the lower-middle class from whom the patriotic associations have drawn their journalists and their leaders for the last ten years — have suffered through the cultivation of hatred as the one energy of their movement, a deprivation which is the intellectual equivalent to a certain surgical operation. Hence the shrillness of their voices. They contemplate all creative power as the eunuchs contemplate Don Juan as he passes through Hell on the white horse.

(*Autobiographies*, p.486)

Again, although there is a denigratory class-reference here, the 'eunuchs' are attacked not so much for their class affiliation as for an 'attitude of mind'.

It is difficult to get the emphasis right here. I am not denying that Yeats lacked that Protestant sense of caste-superiority of which O'Brien speaks. He tended, however, not to give this full expression until much later in his life,[26] and I would prefer to stress the idealistic and romantic basis of Yeats's excoriation of the Paudeens and the Biddys in his middle period. In one way, Yeats is a bit like Evelyn Waugh's Guy Crouchback — for both of them the real enemy is the modern world. Yeats sees Irish middle classness as part of the hated Modern Age — he keeps referring to it as 'new' in Ireland, and hence as marking a sad falling off from the nobler values of the past: 'the new ill-breeding of Ireland, which may in a few years destroy all that has given Ireland a distinguished name in the world' (*Autobiographies*, p.463). Snobbery is present, and adds its tang, but is subservient to the deployment of a characteristic value-system — a belief in heroic failure, in commitment to arduous and apparently hopeless struggle, in the philosophy of risk; hatred of servility and utilitarianism and prudential morality, which all breed timidity. The whole mixture can be seen working together in the conclusion of the essay 'Poetry and Tradition'. It is a heady brew, but I would give it a more generous reading than O'Brien:

I could not foresee that a new class, which had begun to rise into power under the shadow of Parnell, would change the nature of the Irish movement, which, needing no longer great sacrifices, nor bringing any great risk to individuals, could do without exceptional men, and those activities of the mind that are founded on the exceptional moment ... Power passed to small shopkeepers, to clerks, to that very class who had seemed to John O'Leary so ready to bend to the power of others, to men who had risen above the traditions of the

countryman, without learning those of cultivated life or even educat-
ing themselves, and who because of their poverty, their ignorance,
their superstitious piety, are much subject to all kinds of fear.
Immediate victory, immediate utility, became everything, and the
conviction . . . that life is greater than the cause, withered . . .

(Essays and Introductions, pp.259-60)

The growing hostility between Yeats and the increasingly powerful and
strident voice of 'middle-class' nationalism broke the dream of his early
manhood, 'that a modern nation can return to Unity of Culture'
(*Autobiographies*, p.295). But Yeats's most attractive quality is the
incorruptibility of his idealism, and rather than this disillusionment
leading him to a cynical withdrawal and disengagement from Ireland, he
made from his disappointment two closely related myths, dominant
and powerfully creative themes during the rest of his life; the mythology
of the great individual, the hero, and the mythology of the cultured
aristocracy. Through these themes, he attempted to offer to Ireland
richer and more ideal models for her self-realisation, arising from his
belief that national culture must be based on something larger than
politics — or rather, than the intensely rhetorical and rancorous politics
of his contemporary Ireland, since clearly Yeats's themes carry considerable political overtones of their own. The unpopularity of his
attitudes in that Ireland did not worry him, since as we have seen already
in a variety of connections, success (in this context popular esteem) was
not a condition which he valued highly. As he said in the lines of 1913
addressed 'To A Friend Whose Work Has Come To Nothing':

Bred to a harder thing
Than Triumph, turn away
And like a laughing string
Whereon mad fingers play
Amid a place of stone,
Be secret and exult,
Because of all things known
That is most difficult.

(*CP*, p.122)

Adversity is the condition of great creative achievement — Yeats both
believed this and gave, in his work, proof of the creative efficacy of the
belief.

The importance of the idea of the hero to Yeats has been discussed very fully by Alex Zwerdling,[27] among other critics. Yeats's celebration of individuality, whether in the different types of heroism represented by such diverse types as Parnell, Robert Gregory, Maud Gonne, Mabel Beardsley (celebrated in the sequence 'Upon a Dying Lady'), and the isolated poet himself, is easily seen as a reaction away from the collectivist notions implied by his earlier and disappointed hopes to create 'Unity of Culture'. Yeats could say and believe in 1901 that nobody can write well unless he assents to become a mouthpiece for corporate thoughts, that 'nobody can do more than speak messages from the spirit of his time' (see above, p. 99). After more than six years of dispute over the theatre, he had reversed his thought dramatically. Speaking of the *Playboy* furore in June 1907, he wrote:

> Many are beginning to recognize the right of the individual mind to see the world in its own way, to cherish the thoughts that separate men from one another, and that are the creators of distinguished life, instead of those thoughts that had made one man like another if they could, and have but succeeded in setting hysteria and insincerity in place of confidence and self-possession..
>
> (*Uncollected Prose*, vol. 2, p.353)

A powerful and authoritative intellectual influence behind Yeats's change of position here was Nietzsche, 'that strong enchanter',[28] whom he had read in 1902 for the first time. Naturally enough, Nietzsche's description of a master-morality and a slave-morality appealed to Yeats, since it chimed with his disaffection from what he saw as the debilitating effects of the 'democratisation' and 'commercialisation' of the nationalist movement.

So Yeats's hero defines himself, firstly, by his solitariness, his isolation from or opposition to, the crowd. This is true, as we have seen in discussing 'September 1913', even when the hero is nominally acting for a whole people —

> Yet they were of a different kind,
> The names that stilled your childish play . . .
>
> (*CP*, p.121)

For Yeats, Parnell's quality, too, is guaranteed not so much by his political successes in the struggle for Home Rule, but by the furious opposition of the mob or 'pack', to use Yeats's own term of abuse — 'popular rage,/*Hysterica passio* dragged this quarry down' he says in

'Parnell's Funeral', employing a favourite image of the noble stag at bay; and he goes on to schematise the difference between the politicians of 1933 (De Valera, Cosgrave, O'Duffy) and the purified isolation of Parnell:

> Had even O'Duffy — but I name no more —
> Their school a crowd, his master solitude;
> Through Jonathan Swift's dark grove he passed, and there
> Plucked bitter wisdom that enriched his blood.
>
> (*CP*, p.320)

That opposition recurs again and again in Yeats's poetry. For example, as he itemises his 'Beautiful Lofty Things' (*CP*, p.348):

> My father upon the Abbey stage, before him a raging crowd:
> 'This Land of Saints', and then as the applause died out,
> 'Of plaster Saints'; his beautiful mischievous head thrown back.

The Yeatsian hero, then, even when a patriot or political leader, let alone a private citizen, makes no attempt to serve the people in any of the obvious or usual ways. He simply seeks to express the fullness of his nature. This is closely connected to Yeats's praise of the 'wasteful virtues' that 'earn the sun' (*CP*, p.113) — his hatred of anything that smacks of 'getting on', of the merely practical and utilitarian. The hostility of the group is a kind of guarantee of the purity of the wasteful virtues of the individual, who remains unconcerned in the midst of general betrayal. At the end of the 'heroic farce' of 1910, *The Green Helmet*, the Red Man who is 'Rector of this land' awards the champion's helmet to Cuchulain, saying that he chooses 'the man who hits my fancy':

> And I choose the laughing lip
> That shall not turn from laughing, whatever rise or fall;
> The heart that grows no bitterer although betrayed by all;
> The hand that loves to scatter; the life like a gambler's throw . . .
>
> (*Collected Plays*, p.243)

The life lived like a gambler's throw will necessarily produce defeat, isolation, even death; but it will have both style and intensity, a conscious self-mastery and self-expression which has the power to transmute even necessity and mortality into a dominating assertion of freedom. All of the fundamental lineaments of Yeats's concept of heroism are summed up in the short poem he made out of the death of Major Robert Gregory in air-combat in 1918, 'An Irish Airman Foresees His Death' (*CP*, p.152):

> I know that I shall meet my fate
> Somewhere among the clouds above;
> Those that I fight I do not hate,
> Those that I guard I do not love;
> My country is Kiltartan Cross
> My countrymen Kiltartan's poor,
> No likely end could bring them loss
> Or leave them happier than before.
> Nor law, nor duty bade me fight,
> Nor public men, nor cheering crowds,
> A lonely impulse of delight
> Drove to this tumult in the clouds;
> I balanced all, brought all to mind,
> The years to come seemed waste of breath,
> A waste of breath the years behind
> In balance with this life, this death.

The airman is one of Yeats's most complete symbols of the heroic type, the disengaged free spirit committed only to the lonely extravagant gesture, which is self-realisation in a moment of burning intensity. He has no public 'cause', is constrained by neither 'law nor duty' to fight, is indifferent to the public consequences of his deeds ('No likely end could bring them loss . . .'); the rhetorical strategy of the poem even manages to assert that death may be the definitive expression of free choice ('I balanced all, brought all to mind . . .'). The 'lonely impulse of delight' is the supreme example of the heroic *gesture*, of the extravagance of 'life like a gambler's throw', which produces an intensity into which all life seems rammed. As Yeats puts it more generally in the elegy 'In Memory of Major Robert Gregory':

> Some burn damp faggots, others may consume
> The entire combustible world in one small room
> As though dried straw, and if we turn about
> The bare chimney is gone black out
> Because the work had finished in that flare.[29]

(*CP*, p.151)

Thus the hero fulfils himself, and knows that the business of life is to give expression to his soul's knowledge

> . . . that it is self-delighting,
> Self-appeasing, self-affrighting,
> And that its own sweet will is Heaven's will.
>
> (*CP*, p. 214)

This is the crucial opposition, then, between the Yeatsian hero indifferent to public or social canons and valuations, and the popular hero who embodies merely the stereotyped aspirations of the crowd (say, Irish political nationalists):

> Here in Ireland we have come to think of self-sacrifice, when worthy of public honour, as the act of some man at the moment when he is least himself, most completely the crowd. The heroic act, as it descends through tradition, is an act done because a man is himself, because, being himself, he can ask nothing of other men but room amid remembered tragedies; a sacrifice of himself to himself, almost, so little may he bargain, of the moment to the moment.[30]

Clearly, Yeats has been influenced by Nietzsche.[31] What I want to emphasise particularly, however, is how Yeats's conception of the hero offers him a way out of the predicaments of Irish history and of his own Anglo-Irish roots. That is, the emphasis Yeats places on spontaneity of heroic gesture, the lonely quest of the hero to fulfil a purely personal destiny, means that the hero (and with the hero, the admiring poet) simply stands outside the long slow processes of actual history. Historical realities and the bitterness of cultural, racial and class-based oppositions become not very relevant, and the poet is enabled to displace or transmute the awkwardness of his own immediate relationship to his country into compelling images and symbols of autonomous self-realisation, undetermined by necessity. The Irish airman is presented as totally free of any pressure from beyond the self; analogously, in the poem on his own ancestors ('Pardon, old fathers', *CP*, p. 113), Yeats praises those who were soldiers and who 'gave, whatever die was cast'; reckless men, they too, presumably, did not hate whom they fought or love those they guarded, but acted on impulse, rose above history.[32]

The same opposition between the hero and history can be seen most interestingly and most paradoxically in Yeats's poems about the Easter Rising. In 'Easter 1916' (*CP*, p. 202), the rising is seen as a spontaneous self-contained gesture,[33] a heroic act cutting across history, as it were, rather than as the culmination of a few centuries of insurrectionary thought and tradition. Yeats's tone is carefully designed to convey a note of surprise, a sense of the unexpectedness of the irruption of heroism into a context of utter mundanity:

> I have met them at close of day
> Coming with vivid faces
> From counter or desk . . .
> I have passed with a nod of the head
> Or polite meaningless words . . .
> And thought before I had done
> Of a mocking tale or a gibe
> To please a companion
> Around the fire at the club,
> Being certain that they and I
> But lived where motley is worn . . .

The poem implies that the rising sprang from nothing in one wild blaze of 'terrible beauty', and specifically contrasts to the glorious 'delirium' (to cite the characteristic word applied to the patriots of 'September 1913') of the heroic act, the stone-like, deadening effects of lengthy dedication to a cause:

> Too long a sacrifice
> Can make a stone of the heart.

The poem's tone is shifting and complex, and many critics argue persuasively that there is considerable ambiguity in Yeats's attitude to the 1916 martyrs, that the heroic deed is, though glorious in itself, criticised as being the expression of a narrowing fanaticism of 'Hearts with one purpose alone', which is contrasted unfavourably with the images of life's essentially spontaneous and protean variety through time (the birds that range from cloud to tumbling cloud, the moor-hens, etc.) informing the third stanza. This is certainly a generalising element in the poem's thought, but Yeats's treatment of the actual leaders of the rising presents *them* not so much as dedicated fanatics working steadily towards a goal, but as prosaic partakers in life's comedy who *suddenly* and *unexpectedly* achieve transcendence:

> This other man [MacBride] I had dreamed
> A drunken, vainglorious lout . . .
> Yet I number him in the song;
> He, too, has resigned his part
> In the casual comedy;
> He, too, has been changed in his turn,
> Transformed utterly:
> A terrible beauty is born.

The heroes step, therefore, from history — boring, rancorous, and, for Yeats, full of awkward questions of personal identity and affiliation — into the *largior aether* of legend. Yeats's strategy is to drive a wedge between the realities of politics — for him always a dirty word — and the heroic deed by presenting it as an act leading out of nothing and to nothing. It is self-contained:

> We know their dream; enough
> To know they dreamed and are dead.

In 'The Rose Tree', Yeats presents Pearse and Connolly as actors in an allegory who themselves see history and politics as antagonistic to their efforts to realise a symbol:

> 'O words are lightly spoken',
> Said Pearse to Connolly,
> 'Maybe a breath of politic words
> Has withered our Rose Tree . . .
> O plain as plain can be
> There's nothing but our own red blood
> Can make a right Rose Tree'.
>
> (CP, p. 206)

There is an essentially theatrical aspect to Yeats's conception of the hero, since the hero in his work defines himself again and again in the large *gesture*. This in turn means that history may be altered by being aestheticised. Yeats consistently thinks of Irish history in theatrical images, which emanate from his belief in the individual hero's ability to rise above and deny necessity in the fulfilment of the self. Thus he looks back over the nineteenth century in these terms:

> I had seen Ireland in my own time turn from the bragging rhetoric and gregarious humour of O'Connell's generation and school, and offer herself to the solitary and proud Parnell as to her anti-self, buskin followed hard on sock . . .
>
> (Autobiographies, p. 195)

This idea of a change from buskin to sock underlies the aestheticised treatment of history in 'Easter 1916' — the 'motley' of the 'casual comedy' is transmuted into the dignified tragedy of 'terrible beauty'. The theatrical metaphor is even more overt in one of the 'Three Songs to the One Burden', first published in 1939:

> Come gather round me, players all:
> Come praise Nineteen-Sixteen,
> Those from the pit and gallery
> Or from the painted scene
> That fought in the Post Office
> Or round the City Hall.

(CP, p. 373)

A note appended to this poem shows how far Yeats went in his effort to see nationalist politics as, and translate them into, dramatic art:

> A nation should be like an audience in some great theatre — 'in the theatre', said Victor Hugo, 'the mob becomes a people' — watching the drama of its own history . . . that sacred drama must to all native eyes and ears become the greatest of parables.

(Variorum Poems, p. 837)

The idea of the hero as an individual who can make of his life a work of art, impose the beauty of defining gesture upon accident and contingency, is the basis on which Yeats builds his interpretation of Irish history as drama.

Finally, Yeats subdues history to the demands of the literary imagination by contriving to suggest that heroes exist mainly to provide artists with fitting symbols. As early as 1904, he wrote:

> If one remembers the men who have dominated Ireland for the last one hundred and fifty years, one understands that it is strength of personality, the individualising quality in a man, that stirs Irish imagination most deeply in the end. There is scarcely a man who has led the Irish people, at any time, who may not give some day to a great writer precisely that symbol he may require for the expression of himself.

(Explorations, pp. 147-8)

The hero's life in history is less important than his life in art. The Red Man at the end of *The Green Helmet* praises the archetypal hero Cuchulain for his possession of the wasteful virtues — 'The hand that

loves to scatter; the life like a gambler's throw' — anticipates his ultimate defeat, but significantly ends by proclaiming a kind of ultimate
'justification by art', which renders defeat irrelevant, even ennobling:

> And these things I make prosper, till a day come that I know,
> When heart and mind shall darken that the weak may end the strong,
> And the long-remembering harpers have matter for their song.
>
> *(Collected Plays*, p. 243)

Nietzsche had said that 'only as an aesthetic phenomenon is existence
and the world eternally justified'.[34] Yeats, in his valuation of the hero
who transcends history and hence enables us to see it as drama, is not,
however, simply giving expression to a philosophic and intellectual
influence of a congenial kind. Primarily, he has found a superbly
expressive means of ignoring, or holding at arm's length, the coming
into being of an Ireland in which his own cultural and class inheritances
made him feel profoundly uncomfortable.

The same dismissal of the political realities of Irish history, or their
transmutation into powerful idealised images, underlies Yeats's treatment of aristocracy and the aristocratic society in the work of his
middle and later years. The aristocrat is important to Yeats, not because
he was naive enough to suppose that the Great Houses of the Protestant
Ascendancy represented much in the way of cultural vitality, or believed
in the possibility of their historical continuance; but because in the
idealised aristocrat he found the last link to complete an alternative
poetic world already peopled by an idealised peasantry and by the
artists — who could celebrate both noble and peasant. This world could
simultaneously exclude the hated modern, mechanised, urban mob,
and, merely by being realised in art, provide a damning commentary on
the mean realities which lay outside it. The poet, the peasant and the
aristocrat are indissolubly and organically linked; they have nothing to
do with the 'timid breath' of the commercial-bourgeois world, they
share something of the Yeatsian hero's wasteful virtue, and they have
tradition and antiquity on their side:

> Three types of men have made all beautiful things. Aristocracies
> have made beautiful manners, because their place in the world puts
> them above the fear of life, and the countrymen have made beauti-
> ful stories and beliefs, because they have nothing to lose and so do
> not fear, and the artists have made all the rest, because Providence
> has filled them with recklessness. All these look backward to a long

tradition, for, being without fear, they have held to whatever pleased
them.

('Poetry and Tradition', 1907, *Essays and Introductions*, p. 251)

In part, Yeats saw in the aristocratic style and idea a means of holding
on to his cherished hope for unity of culture, in a scaled-down form
that might be easier of attainment than it had proved to be on the
national level —

> . . . the dream of my early manhood, that a modern nation can
> return to Unity of Culture, is false; though it may be we can achieve
> it for some small circle of men and women, and there leave it till the
> moon bring round its century.

(Autobiographies, p. 295)

There was a basis in reality for Yeats's celebration of the aristocratic
life, in Lady Gregory and her estate at Coole Park with its woods, lake
and swans which are memorialised so superbly in Yeats's poetry. He
valued the long continuity of culture that he found at Coole —

> Beloved books that famous hands have bound,
> Old marble heads, old pictures everywhere . . .

In the same great poem of tribute, 'Coole Park and Ballylee, 1931' (*CP*,
p. 275), Yeats contrasts the rooted stability, the sense of tradition and
permanence which sustains the aristocratic house, no mere pile of
stones but a focus for social cohesion, with the contemptible nomadism
and fragmentation of modernity:

> A spot whereon the founders lived and died
> Seemed once more dear than life; ancestral trees,
> Or gardens rich in memory glorified
> Marriages, alliances and families,
> And every bride's ambition satisfied.
> Where fashion or mere fantasy decrees
> We shift about — all that great glory spent —
> Like some poor Arab tribesman and his tent.

The actuality of Coole gives Yeats's lines their sonorous authority, as
Lady Gregory's friendly relationship with her tenants, and their respect
for her,[35] underpins his belief in the validity of his feudal model of

social organisation, in which peasant and aristocrat live in a harmonious concord celebrated by the necessary third member of the trinity, the artist (himself, by his nature, in love with tradition):

> John Synge, I and Augusta Gregory, thought
> All that we did, all that we said or sang
> Must come from contact with the soil, from that
> Contact everything Antaeus-like grew strong.
> We three alone in modern times had brought
> Everything down to that sole test again,
> Dream of the noble and the beggar-man.
>
> ('The Municipal Gallery Revisited', *CP*, p. 369)

And yet, and despite the existence of Lady Gregory and of Coole, it would be wrong to see Yeats's aristocratic poetry as simply expressive of his endorsement of the Anglo-Irish cultural tradition. Lady Gregory was a special case, and Yeats knew it. The Anglo-Irish aristocracy, the landlords of the Protestant Ascendancy were on the whole much less cultured, much more indifferent to Ireland; and Yeats, like Standish O'Grady, feared that they had become effete, a class withering away into irrelevance through failure to commit itself to any 'service' (the reciprocal duty imposed on the aristocrat by his inherited wealth). The first of the 'Meditations in Time of Civil War', 'Ancestral Houses' (*CP*, p. 225), deals with this idea of aristocratic degeneration, the substitution of passive enjoyment for creative activity. Yeats thinks on the genesis of the great house, and on its inheritors:

> Some violent bitter man, some powerful man
> Called architect and artist in, that they,
> Bitter and violent men, might rear in stone
> The sweetness that all longed for night and day,
> The gentleness none there had ever known;
> But when the master's buried mice can play,
> And maybe the great-grandson of that house,
> For all its bronze and marble, 's but a mouse.

Despite his birth, despite his naturally hierarchical cast of mind, Yeats could not simply appropriate the Ascendancy house and style as 'naturalised' symbols, then. He had to fit them into a nobler mythology, that of the Renaissance. This not only immeasurably enriched the notion of aristocracy in Yeats' work. 'As a personal quest for identity', as Daniel Harris says, 'the mythic sequence [of poems] measures his grave difficulty in grappling with his Anglo-Irish birth.'[36] As with his treatment of the hero, so Yeats's treatment of the aristocracy represents another powerfully creative and ennobling swerve away from the realities of Irish history and society.

In 1907 Lady Gregory took Yeats to Italy. He had read Shakespeare, Spenser, Ben Jonson and Castiglione's *The Courtier* between the years 1901 and 1907. From these and his visits to Ferrara and Urbino, Yeats made the Renaissance court and country-house his symbols of aristocratic excellence, and through these Renaissance spectacles he could both create and criticise the well-born, leisured and wealthy of his own land. He had found that idealising perspective which seems to have been a necessity of his temperament.

The magnanimity, style and love of culture of the Renaissance court is manipulated brilliantly as an evaluative metaphor in the spirited and splendid poem of 1913, 'To a Wealthy Man Who Promised a Second Subscription to the Dublin Municipal Gallery If It Were Proved the People Wanted Pictures' (*CP*, p. 119). The wealthy man is probably Lord Ardilaun; the context of the poem is the controversy over the offer of the collection of Impressionist paintings to Dublin made by Sir Hugh Lane (Lady Gregory's nephew), provided that a suitable gallery was built. Dublin Corporation was unenthusiastic, and patrons of the arts and the Anglo-Irish aristocrats were equally half-hearted. The controversy focuses two burning issues for Yeats; the role of art in elevating the culture, taste and emotional energy of a nation, and the role of the aristocrat as patron and encourager of the arts. In the poem's finely contemptuous first stanza, the Dublin aristocrat is degraded by his sharing of the utilitarian and calculating values of the Paudeens and Biddys, looking for 'evidence', the magnanimous gesture frozen in mid-action ('You gave, but will not give again') and hence devalued. The contrast is with Duke Ercole, indifferent to anything but his own passion for the best, looking to past greatness (Roman Plautus) to ensure present cultural vitality:

> You gave, but will not give again
> Until enough of Paudeen's pence
> By Biddy's halfpennies have lain
> To be 'some sort of evidence',
> Before you'll put your guineas down,
> That things it were a pride to give
> Are what the blind and ignorant town

Imagines best to make it thrive.
What cared Duke Ercole, that bid
His mummers to the market-place,
What th' onion-sellers thought or did
So that his Plautus set the pace
For the Italian comedies?

Guidobaldo, Duke of Urbino, and Cosimo de Medici are also invoked as
exemplars of aristocratic heroes whose lives fuse perfectly the impulse
to serve the community and the impulse to fulfil the self — Yeats writes
of Cosimo's great vision of an Italy stabilised by 'Delight in Art whose
end is peace', through his commissioning of the San Marco library, that
this shows his greatness not just as a patron, but as a man. It is proof of
the 'exultant heart':

Your open hand but shows our loss,
For he knew better how to live.

The whole drive of the poem, therefore, is — as with many of Yeats's
nationalist writings — an attempt to purify an aspect of Irish life from
within by offering it, through his art, higher and more ideal models for
imitation. The Anglo-Irish Ascendancy can only survive, can only retain
any dignity, by imitating an aristocracy greater than itself; just as Irish
nationalism can only retain its soul by imitating an idealism that
weighed so lightly what it gave. The passionate conclusion to the poem,
suggesting that the gifts of art can redeem nature itself ('breed', 'eagle's
nest'), goes beyond satire to the expression of a hope beyond the fling
of the dull historian's hoof:

Let Paudeens play at pitch and toss,
Look up in the sun's eye and give
What the exultant heart calls good
That some new day may breed the best
Because you gave, not what they would,
But the right twigs for an eagle's nest!

The intense humanism of Yeats's belief in the civilising powers of art,
and in the potentialities for 'service' of enlightened aristocratic patrons,
finds shape in proud and 'exultant' images, which transcend historical
reality or sociological analysis.

Even Lady Gregory's Coole, which had a genuine Anglo-Irish culture of its own, Yeats insisted for many years in seeing in Renaissance terms. Thus, in a poem written some years before 'To a Wealthy Man', a poem which originates in one of the thorniest problems of Irish history, the land problem, we find the characteristic Yeatsian transposition:

How should the world be luckier if this house,
Where passion and precision have been one
Time out of mind, became too ruinous
To breed the lidless eye that loves the sun?
And the sweet laughing eagle thoughts that grow
Where wings have memory of wings, and all
That comes of the best knit to the best? Although
Mean roof-trees were the sturdier for its fall,
How should their luck run high enough to reach
The gifts that govern men, and after these
To gradual Time's last gift, a written speech
Wrought of high laughter, loveliness and ease?
('Upon a House Shaken by the Land Agitation', *CP*, p. 106)

Although the Land Act of 1909, which forced large land-holders to sell off parts of their estates to the peasantry, and to reduce the rents of their tenants,[37] lies behind the poem, its imagery transcends the local Irish situation. On 'Urbino's windy hill', Guidobaldo made

That grammar school of courtesies
Where wit and beauty learned their trade . . .

— lines which stress the formal pursuit of, and the hard discipline involved in, the achievement of style and self-possession, at the Renaissance court. So at Coole

Where passion and precision have been one
Time out of mind . . .

the same 'trade' is studied. The natural and the artificial are fused, so that life turns into art, art seems but the over-abundance of life itself —

. . . a written speech
Wrought of high laughter, loveliness and ease.

The poem's central image (the 'lidless eye', 'eagle thoughts', 'wings') is

common to 'To a Wealthy Man', and indicates how the aspiring idealism
of the Renaissance aristocracy is not just a touchstone for Yeats but
also a way of defusing – or attempting to defuse – the difficulties
inherent in the actual historical situation. For this house does not seek
to stamp political power on the 'mean roof-trees', and is uninterested in
the perpetuation of itself in any political or dynastic sense. It does not
seek even to breed children, but rather 'the lidless eye that loves the
sun'. It seeks to breed 'metaphors of visionary aspiration',[38] and is thus
built on that borderland between history and symbolism or legend,
which Yeats found a particularly fascinating – and liberating – terrain.

The Renaissance haunts Yeats's conception of the aristocracy, then,
right into the 20s,[39] when the destruction and burning of the Great
Houses put too much of a strain on the tension between actuality and
ideal images, and Yeats himself shed his Celtic and his Renaissance
courtier-poet masks to embrace his Anglo-Irish identity. For him, until
then, the Renaissance court is almost literally just round the corner:

> I might have lived,
> And you know well how great the longing has been,
> Where every day my footfall should have lit
> In the green shadow of Ferrara wall;
> Or climbed among the images of the past –
> The unperturbed and courtly images –
> Evening and morning, the steep street of Urbino
> To where the Duchess and her people talked
> The stately midnight through until they stood
> In their great window looking at the dawn;
> I might have had no friend that could not mix
> Courtesy and passion into one like those
> That saw the wicks grow yellow in the dawn . . .

This is from 'The People', written in 1915 (*CP*, p. 169), and serves to
show how for Yeats 'images of the past' have a breath-taking physical
and contemporary reality – 'I might have lived' proposes the ducal
courts as *available*, genuine and immediate alternatives to 'the daily
spite of this unmannerly town' (Dublin).

Denis Donoghue comments on Yeats's incorrigible tendency to
idealise and the parallel tendency to ignore what Donoghue calls (in
another context) 'the ordinary universe':

He admired notable people, but his respect for ordinary people as

constituting a particular society and living a certain life at a certain
time was extremely weak; when he looked beyond the chosen few
he saw a fictive race rather than a finite society.[40]

Even the notable and chosen few are 'fictionalised' by the Renaissance
context. I have tried to argue that his Anglo-Irish birth lay at the root
of all Yeats's strategies for encompassing Ireland in his poetry that we
have so far examined — the activation of a legendary and remote past,
the stress on the folkloric 'spirituality' of the peasant rather than on his
Catholicism and probable membership of the Land League, the presentation of the hero as one antagonistic to history or capable of trans-
cending it, and the critical evaluation or ennobling of the Protestant
Ascendancy by the standard of a Renaissance conception of aristocracy.
The awkward and divisive hostilities latent in the Protestant Anglo-
Irishman's relation to Catholic Ireland, and in the nationalist poet's
(was he not a friend of the insurrectionary firebrand, Maud Gonne?)
relation to his Protestant class, Yeats attempted to surmount with a
sustained and — on the whole — generous effort of his creative idealising imagination. If a 'fictive race' rather than a real nation emerges, one
must be grateful for the nobility of the Yeatsian conception.

I say this as one himself a product of the 'mean roof-trees' (possibly
even a base-born product of a base bed). There is no question, however,
that Yeats's idealisation of Ireland in the semi-feudal terms he chooses
offends many readers, either on the score of its undoubted and assertive elitism — repugnant to an egalitarian age — or on the score of its
apparent lack of connection with the pressing problems, social and
political and economic, of that real Ireland enduring her great crisis
during the years of Yeats's creativity. 'A pseudo-aristocrat cultivating
a pseudo-peasant' says Brian Farrington of 'this disastrously sentimental
view'.

One may defend Yeats here by saying simply that his conception of
aristocracy owes very little to any crude urge to assert class-superiority,
and wealth and power are not valued for their own sakes. The very gap
between the average Ascendancy house in Ireland and the courts of
Urbino or Ferrara stresses the point that Yeats's aristocracy is really a
metaphor, or image.[41] In other words, it is only a dream. But a beautiful dream; the values that Yeats associates with his aristocratic society,
and which he realises in superbly eloquent and convincing poetic terms
— magnanimity, courtesy, style, permanence, tradition — are good
values, surely, values superior to those of the cult of barbarism which
has played its part in twentieth-century history and culture (and which

had its attractions for Yeats himself, as we shall see). And Yeats stresses that the encompassing of the aristocratic values demands an active and arduous discipline, a sort of soul-training; mere inheritance, and slumbering over the port, will not do, the soul's tendency being to 'natural declension':

> Life scarce can cast a fragrance on the wind,
> Scarce spread a glory to the morning beams,
> But the torn petals strew the garden plot;
> And there's but common greenness after that.

(CP, p. 229)

Thus when one calls Yeats a socially reactionary poet, referring to his feudal model, one must allow for the dignity and scope of his vision of the aristocratic life-style, his idealised enlargement of its values. Elitism need not, in literature, be a narrowing thing.[42] As regards the other charge against Yeats — the irrelevance of his archaic 'dream of the noble and the beggar-man' to the modern world — such a charge Yeats confidently ignored. He was sustained — it is what lends such authority to his poetic voice even when he is speaking in the most idealistic vein — by a life-long belief in the shaping, 'legislative' effectiveness of great images. This is derived partly from his belief in magic, partly from Shelley.[43] Yeats's own *Defence of Poetry* is the play *The King's Threshold* (1904), where the poet Seanchan chooses death rather than admit the King's argument

> ... that it was the men who ruled the world,
> And not the men who sang to it, who should sit
> Where there was the most honour.

Seanchan asserts, through the mouth of his oldest pupil, the contrary position: the poet creates, or reactivates, archetypal or ideal images which, because of their power, direct or shape human history and society:

> I said the poets hung
> Images of the life that was in Eden
> About the child-bed of the world, that it,
> Looking upon those images, might bear
> Triumphant children.

And one of these Edenic images is that of the courtly life:

> he spoke about the Court
> And called it the first comely child of the world,
> And said that all that was insulted there
> The world insulted, for the Courtly life
> Is the world's model.

(Collected Plays, pp. 109-13)

The poet's task, then, has little to do with the accurate reflection or imitation of sociological realities. Yeats's 'aristocratic' poetry he would see as serving to offer his society powerful images which simultaneously criticise the meaner values of that society and provide it with nobler goals to aspire to.[44] The poet, on this view, can never be 'irrelevant'. The same idealist view, that the creative mind, the maker of images, is the causative element in history, is the controlling idea behind the complex late poem, 'The Statues' (1938):

> . . . the men
> That with a mallet or a chisel modelled these
> Calculations that look but casual flesh, put down
> All Asiatic vague immensities,
> And not the banks of oars that swam upon
> The many-headed foam at Salamis.
> Europe put off that foam when Phidias
> Gave women dreams and dreams their looking-glass.

By this stage, Irish history as it had unfolded during Yeats's own life-time confirmed further the poet's belief in the dramatic efficacy of ideal images. The legendary Ireland of the sagas, which Yeats's own work had done so much to articulate, and which had seemed so impossibly remote from actuality, had proved not to be so. The 'filthy modern tide' may still be purged and redeemed by the powerful and subterranean workings of the imagination concerned to trace out the lineaments of ideal perfection. The last stanza of 'The Statues' runs:

> When Pearse summoned Cuchulain to his side,
> What stalked through the Post Office? What intellect,
> What calculation, number, measurement replied?
> We Irish, born into that ancient sect
> But thrown upon this filthy modern tide

And by its formless spawning fury wrecked,
Climb to our proper dark, that we may trace
The lineaments of a plummet-measured face.

(*CP*, p. 375)

To say that Yeats's concept of aristocracy is enlarging, to argue that Yeats would in a sense *define* the poet's task as being to offer his society ideal images rather than merely accurate reflections, is not, however, to explain the intense dramatic and emotional impact of his poems on ancestral houses and 'the inherited glory of the rich'. The explanation lies in Yeats's elegiac, even tragic, awareness of the transience and fragility of the aristocratic life-style he celebrated, of the frailty of his own symbol of 'traditional sanctity and loveliness'.

Robert Gregory, 'our Sidney and our perfect man', is an exemplar of aristocratic self-perfection:

Soldier, scholar, horseman, he,
As 'twere all life's epitome.

(*CP*, p. 151)

But Gregory is dead. It is not simply that the continuity of tradition is thus broken — Gregory's death, in fact, made the sale of Coole Park inevitable — but that Yeats's poetic world is rendered thereby the more vulnerable to inimical and powerful forces. Towards the end of the poem, we perceive it not just as a noble elegy, but as a Yeatsian attempt to shore fragments against the potentially ruinous forces at work in the modern world:

I had thought, seeing how bitter is that wind
That shakes the shutter, to have brought to mind
All those than manhood tried, or childhood loved
Or boyish intellect approved . . .
. . . but a thought
Of that late death took all my heart for speech.

The 'bitter wind' of 'In Memory of Major Robert Gregory' is the wind of violent destructiveness, symbolising present and future anarchy, which blows so memorably through the opening stanzas of 'A Prayer for My Daughter' (*CP*, p. 211). The storm is howling, the sleeping baby's vulnerability is beautifully suggested in the phrase 'half hid/ Under this cradle-hood and coverlid', her innocence powerfully contrasted to the 'innocence' of sheer brute force:

> I have walked and prayed for this young child an hour
> And heard the sea-wind scream upon the tower,
> And under the arches of the bridge, and scream
> In the elms above the flooded stream;
> Imagining in excited reverie
> That the future years had come,
> Dancing to a frenzied drum,
> Out of the murderous innocence of the sea.

The poem itself is framed both by 'The Second Coming', with its apocalyptic previsions of nightmarish anarchy, and by the other little prayer 'To Be Carved on a Stone at Thoor Ballylee', which less dramatically but equally bleakly anticipates the destruction of the poet's attempt to build a ceremonious place:

> I, the poet William Yeats,
> With old mill boards and sea-green slates,
> And smithy work from the Gort forge,
> Restored this tower for my wife George;
> And may these characters remain
> When all is ruin once again.
>
> > > > > > > > > > (*CP*, p. 214)

It is in this context that the virtues and values of the aristocratic life-style must be placed. The prayer for his daughter is a prayer that she be located in a tradition which may oppose the destructive anarchy of modern history:

> O may she live like some green laurel
> Rooted in one dear perpetual place . . .
> How but in custom and in ceremony
> Are innocence and beauty born?
> Ceremony's a name for the rich horn,
> And custom for the spreading laurel tree.

But the laurel tree is subject to 'Assault and battery of the wind'; the assured dignity of the conclusion nevertheless contains a buried impli-cation that ceremony and custom may be just 'names', a poet's sustain-ing fictions, without substantial reality, for 'The Second Coming' has told us that

> The blood-dimmed tide is loosed, and everywhere
> The ceremony of innocence is drowned.

The ideal image of aristocratic self-perfection, of the sanctity of its courteous innocence, is thus validated and given its powerful emotional plangency in Yeats's poetry, then, by its constant juxtaposition with the knowledge of imminent disaster. The elegiac mood excludes any possible arrogance of tone. The walls of Coole begot 'a dance-like glory'; but as the poet stands before those still-intact walls, he perceives their transience, their frailty before the indifferent desecration of history:

> Here, traveller, scholar, poet, take your stand
> When all those rooms and passages are gone,
> When nettles wave upon a shapeless mound
> And saplings root among the broken stone . . .
>
> ('Coole Park, 1929', *CP*, p. 274)

We have remarked before on Yeats's delight in committing himself, emotionally and spiritually, to lost causes, to images of heroic defeat or failure (see above, p. 90 and p. 104). But in his treatment of aristocratic values menaced by impending dissolution there is very little of the slight swagger and bravado with which he writes of the wasteful virtues of Irish patriots or individual heroes. This is probably due to his direct experience, over a long period of time, of the hospitality of Coole and the generous friendship of Lady Gregory, and to his increasing awareness as he grew older that his emotional ties were, after all, to the Anglo-Irishry. Certainly in 'Coole Park and Ballylee, 1931', the nobility of aristocratic tradition is celebrated most lyrically in a poem which is a passionate and beautiful lament for its passing, for the end of an era:

> We were the last romantics — chose for theme
> Traditional sanctity and loveliness;
> Whatever's written in what poets name
> The book of the people; whatever most can bless
> The mind of man or elevate a rhyme;
> But all is changed, that high horse riderless,
> Though mounted in that saddle Homer rode
> Where the swan drifts upon a darkening flood.
>
> (*CP*, p. 276)

As always when Yeats is at his best and most human, his least histrionic and shrill, ideal image and reality, vision and history, are at tragic odds; the swan confronts a 'darkening flood'; or rather — such is Yeats's emotional tact here, as in many of these poems — it 'drifts', a verb perfect in its suggestion of a mingling of helpless fragility, innocent purity, and aristocratic indifference. In nearly all of these 'aristocratic' poems that we have examined, right back to and including 'Upon a House Shaken by the Land Agitation', the perfection of that mode of life is under threat, a threat directly acknowledged and embodied in the poems themselves, and the tension humanises the aristocratic symbolism while simultaneously forbidding us to see Yeats's idealism as naive. The idealism of 'traditional sanctity and loveliness' and the reality of history (the darkening flood) are held in superb equipoise. And, as Dudley Young says,

> What gives his poetry such a wide metaphoric range was that his Irish situation was analogous to that of western Europe about to shatter its traditional culture in the Great War. When cataclysm comes, everyone takes to the road with his tent.[45]

In his aristocratic vein, then, Yeats could transmute his celebration of doomed things into images of compelling elegiac power and beauty, confronting the modern world like the swordsman he sometimes liked to imagine himself as being.

I want now to argue in what may seem at first to be an antithetical direction, by elaborating on that side of Yeats's work — powerful, impressive and even, in certain aspects, sinister — which celebrates not the ceremonies of innocence but the destructive forces ranged against them. The contradiction is only apparent, however; as I hope to show, this poetic 'ecstasy in the contemplation of ruin' (as Yeats referred to it) which originates in an aesthetic attitude to history, serves in the end, paradoxically, to aggrandise the imaginative portrayal of the ending of Anglo-Irish power.

To begin at the beginning, then: if Yeats's involvement with Anglo-Irish defeat and loss gave him the great ennobling images of the aristocratic poems we have looked at, it also contributed to, possibly even gave rise to, the somewhat frightening and sinister aesthetic of apocalypse which governs much of his work. That is, there is a side of Yeats which laments the passing of the swan. But there is also a side of Yeats which *relishes* the threat of the darkening flood, which finds in its dark potentialities aesthetic possibilities and creative occasions. It would be wrong to leave the impression that Yeats is primarily a poet of aristocratic stability and order. In many of his works he seems happy to see the world perish so that art may be — especially his own poems.

It hinges on his attitude to history, which is aesthetic in more comprehensive ways than has been illustrated by his application of theatrical metaphors to the 'players' of 1916. Yeats's interest in a theory or philosophy of history was applied for many years to the writing of *A Vision*; many critics, using this 'stylistic arrangement'[46] of experience as their touchstone, present Yeats's historical thinking as mainly concerned with the idea of cyclical recurrence — the circuits of the sun and moon, the Platonic Great Year, Vico, Yeats's belief in reincarnation, all being cited with varying degrees of emphasis. And many readers have traced what they see as unpleasant political and social meanings in his poetry to this cyclical vision. George Orwell may speak, in his plain blunt way, for these readers:

> Translated into political terms, Yeats's tendency is Fascist . . . the theory that civilization moves in recurring cycles is one way out for people who hate the concept of human equality . . . It does not matter if the lower orders are getting above themselves, for, after all, we shall soon be returning to an age of tyranny.[47]

There is, indeed, an offensive Nietzschean sort of swagger in some of Yeats's late poems (and prose), which does strike exactly the note that Orwell complains of —

> What matter though numb nightmare ride on top,
> And blood and mire the sensitive body stain?
> What matter? . . .
> Conduct and work grow coarse, and coarse the soul,
> What matter?

asks 'The Gyres' (*CP*, p. 337), confident that all things will run again 'on that unfashionable gyre' of a hierarchical society of workman, noble, saint. But ultimately this kind of performance is not unduly disturbing, because it is not very convincing. It is difficult to take seriously because the rhetoric is hollow and we sense the poet, through his repetitious, rhetorical questions and exclamatory tone, hectoring not only us, but himself into 'belief'.

What *is* truly alarming and disconcerting in Yeats's poetry, alarming and disconcerting because extremely powerfully felt and extremely convincingly expressed, is not his vision of a return to feudal hierarchies; it is his intense focus on the apocalyptic moments in the cyclical process, his paring down, as it were, of the cyclical idea to the point where it can only be called cyclical with a lot of qualification. Again and again Yeats presents history to us as violent disintegration or terrible annunciation. The senses of renewal and of rhythm inherent in the frequently seasonally-linked concept of the cyclical do not engage him. His most compelling myth of history (which clearly connects with his own history and the history of the Anglo-Irish) is that of crisis, loss, defeat and dissolution, often accompanied by monstrous eruptions of violence. Yet, paradoxically, Yeats seeks out or desires the apocalyptic and doom-charged moments, packed with violent potential; he makes love to his own sense of loss; because violence and loss have their own kind of terrible beauty. They are spurs to the poet's creativity, they yield him powerful metaphors, and thus the nightmare of history is aestheticised.

'Two Songs from a Play' (*CP*, pp. 239-40) are interesting examples of my point that the emphasis on the cyclical nature of Yeats's vision is rather misplaced. Richard Ellmann in *The Identity of Yeats*[48] is among many commentators who have charted the parallelisms between Astraea and Spica, Athene and Dionysus, and Mary and Christ which Yeats uses to organise the poem, and he speaks of Yeats being 'delighted by cyclical rounds'. But what we are really being asked to consider is not recurrence but the violent nature of historical annunciations, decline and disintegration, tonal qualities that must have been more marked before the addition of the last stanza with its more affirmatory conclusion. The opening stanza seems to place the speaker on a lofty vantage point where he can see, with some of the serenity of the Muses whom he serves as poet-singer, the aesthetic pattern of cyclical recurrence:

I saw a staring virgin stand
Where holy Dionysus died,
And tear the heart out of his side,
And lay the heart upon her hand
And bear that beating heart away;
And then did all the Muses sing
Of Magnus Annus at the spring,
As though God's death were but a play.

What is insisted upon, however, is the violent, unequivocally bloody

and physical nature of the apocalyptic moment, reinforced from outside the poem by our knowledge that Zeus then ate the heart and begot
Dionysus again by raping Semele, and from within the poem by the
powerful verb 'tear' and the hammering rhythm with its heavy use of
alliteration. The speaker does not see the moment as the initiation or
inauguration of a new cycle of history — indeed the syntax of the last
line 'As though God's death were but a play' separates the speaker off
from the Muses and conveys a powerful sense of subdued horror.

The second stanza moves further away from the confident singing
of the Muses with their assurance of the natural, seasonal ('at the
spring') and therefore regenerative quality of the cyclical process:

> Another Troy must rise and set,
> Another lineage feed the crow,
> Another Argo's painted prow
> Drive to a flashier bauble yet.

It is difficult to read these lines, with their ballad-like directness, without sensing their bleakness or registering, especially in the phrase
'flashier bauble', at least some of the poem's contemptuous sense of a
falling off in human achievement and aspiration. Many critics, from
Ellmann and Whitaker on, have noted Yeats's tonal modification of the
eager millenarianism of Virgil's fourth Eclogue;[49] but it has not been
sufficiently emphasised how very selective Yeats is in his treatment of
recurrence. All that significantly recurs in his dramatic cycle is violent
annunciation as prelude to or cause of general cultural breakdown, the
falling apart of even the most stable-seeming civilisations:[50]

> The Roman Empire stood appalled:
> It dropped the reins of peace and war
> When that fierce virgin and her Star
> Out of the fabulous darkness called.

Yeats's Mary is no humble handmaid of the Lord, but a *fierce* virgin;
he similarly rejects the traditional associations in his presentation of
Christ in the opening stanza of the second song. Though Christ feels
pity for man's 'darkening' thought (the participle conveys a particularly
effective and sinister implication of continuous and continuing decline),
he does not bring light. Yeats, like Nietzsche, rejects the idea of Christ
as *Lux Mundi*; this Christ comes out of darkness to usher in darkness
and — in what seems deliberate opposition to the sense of aesthetic

pattern experienced by the singing Muses earlier — formlessness. Christ's
coming subverts equally the shaping intellect of the Greek world and
the power of the Roman:

> In pity for man's darkening thought
> He walked that room and issued thence
> In Galilean turbulence;
> The Babylonian starlight brought
> A fabulous, formless darkness in;
> Odour of blood when Christ was slain
> Made all Platonic tolerance vain
> And vain all Doric discipline.

The Magnus Annus remains a theorem, for the poem's felt emphasis is
on the process of 'darkening' in history. There may be a pattern in the
cycles of history, but what Yeats stresses about the process of his cycles
is their destructiveness. Recurrence in the sense of regeneration,
renewal, is not an issue.

Yeats advances his idea most powerfully in the stanza he added
later,[51] locating the destructiveness of history and time in the very core
of human experience:

> Everything that man esteems
> Endures a moment or a day.
> Love's pleasure drives his love away,
> The painter's brush consumes his dreams;
> The herald's cry, the soldier's tread
> Exhaust his glory and his might . . .[52]

Two remarkable passages in Yeats's introduction, written in 1934, to
The Resurrection (the play that the 'Two Songs' embrace), illustrate
the emotional configurations in the view of history that the poems explore and prepare for an understanding of what some commentators
have felt to be the *volte-face* of the last two lines:

> Whatever flames upon the night
> Man's own resinous heart has fed.

Yeats writes:

> For years I have been preoccupied with a certain myth that was

itself a reply to a myth. I do not mean a fiction, but one of those statements our nature is compelled to make and employ as a truth though there cannot be sufficient evidence. When I was a boy everybody talked about progress, and rebellion against my elders took the form of aversion to that myth. I took satisfaction in certain public disasters, felt a sort of ecstasy at the contemplation of ruin . . .

And later he goes on, rhetorically:

Had I begun *On Baile's Strand* or not when I began to imagine, as always at my left side just out of the range of the sight, a brazen winged beast [a footnote reads: 'Afterwards described in my poem "The Second Coming"'] that I associated with laughing, ecstatic destruction?
('Wheels and Butterflies', reprinted in *Explorations*, pp. 392-3)

These remarks help to point up more clearly that what Yeats's vision is focused on in the 'Two Songs' is not 'eternal return', in Nietzsche's phrase, but precisely and specifically, 'disasters', 'ruin', 'destruction'. The startling paradox is that such contemplation produces not despair but 'ecstasy', because somehow or other in the Yeatsian alchemy ruin is symbiotic with creativity. Hence 'Whatever flames upon the night' is man's creativity, sprung from his 'resinous heart' — the image suggests the Phoenix-like creativity and re-creativity of man which actually *needs* destruction and ruin to flame forth the more brightly.

It follows, therefore, that Yeats can contemplate ruin 'with a sort of ecstasy' not just because ruin and disaster offend the liberal myth of progress which he associated with science and pragmatism: also, the brazen winged beast, the embodiment of 'laughing ecstatic destruction', frequently functions as the Pegasus of his work. Less metaphorically, Yeats embraces a dark myth of history as ruin and disaster and finds in it an exhilarating creative freedom and a powerful resonance of statement. The violence of history may then be seen itself as beautiful or at least as contributing to beauty. The apocalyptic or violent moment may be seen as more *authentic* than the sad waste time stretching before and after it, or as more *sublime* (Yeats yokes terror and beauty together in his version of the romantic sublime, as we can see in 'Easter 1916'). Such moments, when history can be seen in a defining or convulsive gesture, naturally lend themselves to the dramatic and image-hungry consciousness of the poet. And, of course, they may be shaped into 'befitting emblems of adversity' — we have seen in differing contexts how Yeats's sensibility impels him towards images of loss.

'Nineteen Hundred and Nineteen' (*CP*, pp. 232-7) is a masterly poem which enables us to see in some detail how Yeats processes the violence of history into characteristic and triumphant aesthetic terms. The feat is the more impressive since the violence manifests itself so near home, in the shape of the Black and Tans —

> . . . a drunken soldiery
> Can leave the mother, murdered at her door,
> To crawl in her own blood, and go scot-free . . .

The emphasis is again on the recurrent nature of disaster rather than on renewal. The opening stanza associates Hellenic Greece with the Ireland and the Europe of 1919, all lacerated by war. It asserts further the fragility and impermanence even of art, of master-works of intellect or hand, which are subject to brute contingency:

> Many ingenious lovely things are gone
> That seemed sheer miracle to the multitude,
> Protected from the circle of the moon
> That pitches common things about.

But in this first movement of the poem (stanzas 1-6) two counter-movements are set going which place the destructiveness of history in a more positive light. In the first place, and despite the sober accuracy of the reference to 'a drunken soldiery', there is a sense in which Yeats exults in the violence, since it has served to expose so ruthlessly that hated 'myth of progress' underlying liberal humanitarianism and democracy.[53] The second stanza is full of a ferocious and even triumphant contempt:

> We too had many pretty toys when young:
> A law indifferent to blame or praise,
> To bribe or threat; habits that made old wrong
> Melt down, as it were wax in the sun's rays;
> Public opinion ripening for so long
> We thought it would outlive all future days.
> O what fine thought we had because we thought
> That the worst rogues and rascals had died out.

Yeats sees violence as endemic, as part of the human psyche, and its suppression therefore as a form of hypocrisy, the failure to face its inevitability 'the half-deceit of some intoxicant/From shallow wits'. Even in the Athens of antiquity, 'Incendiary or bigot could be found'. Later in the poem, the speaker experiences the Dionysiac release of locating in himself the impulse to destruction,[54] the exulting yielding — even if momentarily — to nihilistic emotion with its purifying simplicity:

> That image can bring wildness, bring a rage
> To end all things, to end
> What my laborious life imagined, even
> The half-imagined, the half-written page.

Few poets have better understanding of the psychic appeal of violence.[55]

Secondly, the destructiveness of history may sweep away man's artifacts, but it promotes a higher good, in Yeats's eyes — it spurs continuous creativity. Thus, although Yeats begins by regretting that the 'ingenious lovely things' are not above change, not 'protected from the circle of the moon', we know from many of his other poems of this period, including 'Two Songs from a Play', that he can see mutability as a necessary condition of creation:

> Yet if no change appears,
> No moon; only an aching heart
> Conceives a changeless work of art.

('My Table', *CP*, p. 228)

To desire the end of change is to desire the end of creativity, to wish to be 'struck dumb in the simplicity of fire' (Vacillation', *CP*, p. 285), to be 'stricken deaf and dumb and blind' ('A Dialogue of Self and Soul', *CP*, p. 266) in the static artifice of eternity. As we have seen in discussing the ending of 'Two Songs', Yeats valued the process of creation more than the product, becoming more than being. 'Lapis Lazuli', written in 1936, stresses in terms rather similar to those of 'Nineteen Hundred and Nineteen', the heroic insouciance of the artist's relationship to the destructiveness of history:

> No handiwork of Callimachus,
> Who handled marble as if it were bronze,
> Made draperies that seemed to rise
> When sea-wind swept the corner, stands;

> His long lamp-chimney shaped like the stem
> Of a slender palm, stood but a day;
> All things fall and are built again,
> And those that build them again are gay.

> (*CP*, p. 339)

Here again, the link between ruin and creativity is dynamic and — paradoxically — positive, since the process, the making of art is valued more
than art as product, as finished or made.[56] History's violence, to put it
simply, constantly calls on the artist to put forth his powers.

It is in the great romantic image of his favourite swan in Section III
of 'Nineteen Hundred and Nineteen' that the aesthetic nature of Yeats's
view of the relation of artist to history is defined most clearly and compellingly:

> Some moralist or mythological poet
> Compares the solitary soul to a swan;
> I am satisfied with that,
> Satisfied if a troubled mirror show it,
> Before that brief gleam of its life be gone,
> An image of its state;
> The wings half spread for flight,
> The breast thrust out in pride
> Whether to play, or to ride
> Those winds that clamour of approaching night.

Beginning with deceptive casualness, this stanza moves to a superb
lyrical assertiveness. The swan's solitariness is emblematic of the proud
solitariness of the speaker, itself a product of his ability to cast a cold
eye on the inevitability of loss. This buoyant stoicism, this embracing
of heroic solitude, is characteristic of the Yeatsian romantic hero —
Cuchulain, Parnell, the Irish Airman, the embattled artist — and later in
this poem, the arrogant purity of isolation (possessed *naturally* by the
swan) is seen as an ultimate value surpassing even artistic fame:

> ... if our works could
> But vanish with our breath
> That were a lucky death,
> For triumph can but mar our solitude.

In so far as the adversities of history and of a man's life in time contribute to this willingly embraced solitude, they may be valuable. Nothing is here for tears.

Further, against the grim and futile circularity of the Platonic Year described in Section II, is set the straight clean line of flight of the solitary soul, leaping like the swan into 'the desolate heaven'. Clearly here is an image of the soul's integrity and independence which remains untainted by the nightmarish pollution of history. But as soon as one has put it like that — 'remains untained by' — one sees what is wrong with the phrase, and approaches the heart of Yeats's meaning. The crux is that the swan/soul will see an 'image of its state', realise its self-definition and the fullness of its being, only in a 'troubled mirror' — the troubled mirror of violent history. And only then is the speaker 'satisfied'. The beauty of the swan is inseparable from the brevity of its gleam of life, is even compounded of its sinister backcloth in 'those winds that clamour of approaching night'. (These are the same winds that scream out of the murderous innocence of the sea in 'A Prayer for My Daughter', symbolising the frenzied violence of anarchy and chaos.) In other words, the soul *needs* adversity, ruin and destructiveness to sharpen its vitality and self-awareness; nobility of gesture and of soul are impossible except in the context of their dark adversary, just as the swan's perfection, caught in the haughty moment ('The breast thrust out in pride/Whether to play, or to ride . . .'), has no meaning and is devalued unless we can allow full weight to the clamorous winds, and savour the implications of the inevitable victory of brute historical processes.

All this is emblematic of the artist's relation to history, because the artist sees clearly that all art, including his own, is doomed — yet he goes on creating, creating specifically this very poem. 'Nineteen Hundred and Nineteen' as a whole *enacts* the achievement of the solitary who looks in the troubled mirror of history for an image of his state; a prolonged meditation on violence, brutality and loss produces a great and eloquent poem. No longer 'half-imagined, half-written', the poem nevertheless declares its own helplessness in the face of destructiveness. Yet there is a romantic glamour in the whole situation (the swan confronts the night) and a buoyant energy about the whole performance that belies its theoretical gloominess of theme. The poet defines himself — and finds his subject — in his confrontation with the brazen winged beast associated with 'laughing, ecstatic destruction'. As Yeats put it in *The King's Threshold*, through the mouth of his doom-eager Seanchan:

> And I would have all know that when all falls
> In ruin, poetry calls out in joy,
> Being the scattering hand, the bursting pod,
> The victim's joy among the holy flame,
> God's laughter at the shattering of the world.
>
> (*Collected Plays*, p. 114)

Adversity and mutability are the very conditions of creativity for Yeats. Hence he hunts out, as it were, the ruinous or apocalyptic moments like a 'connoisseur of chaos' (Wallace Stevens's phrase), again and again in his work. It is in this sense that the nightmares of history may become aesthetic occasions.

Yeats's fierce joy in apocalyptic destruction undoubtedly derives in part from Nietzsche, as may be seen from the Nietzschean flavour of Martin's account of his dream in *The Unicorn from the Stars*:

> They [the unicorns] were breaking the world to pieces — when I saw the cracks coming I shouted for joy!
> And I heard the command, 'Destroy, destroy, destruction is the life-giver! destroy!'
>
> (*Collected Plays*, p. 346)

But there is more than an intellectual influence at work. That hatred for the rationalist world of liberal, Christianised democracy, the world of Newton, Locke, progress and science, which is apparent in 'Nineteen Hundred and Nineteen', explains more fully Yeats's valuation of violence. Violence is seen as a Dionysiac energy which explodes rationalism, and gives the lie to that 'pragmatical, preposterous pig of a world' (*CP*, p. 268). Yeats frequently links violence — as in 'The Magi', 'Leda and the Swan', and 'The Second Coming' — with the irruption of the supernatural into human history; the apocalyptic moment is thus midwife of a deeper sense of reality, of a sort of spirituality.

It is instructive to compare T. S. Eliot's 'Journey of the Magi' with Yeats's 'The Magi', written in 1913 (*CP*, p. 141):

> Now as at all times I can see in the mind's eye,
> In their stiff, painted clothes, the pale unsatisfied ones
> Appear and disappear in the blue depths of the sky
> With all their ancient faces like rain-beaten stones,
> And all their helms of silver hovering side by side,
> And all their eyes still fixed, hoping to find once more,
> Being by Calvary's turbulence unsatisfied,
> The uncontrollable mystery on the bestial floor.

While both poems work by confounding the traditional associations of the Christmas story, Yeats goes far beyond Eliot. In Yeats's poem, the Magi find at the end of their journey not the domestic interior of the stable with the babe in the mother's arms, the homely donkeys and cattle. Instead they perceive, or seek to perceive in a violent imaginative prolepsis, the end, not the beginning – not the Bethelehem stable, but 'Calvary's turbulence'. It is for this that they seek, to find in violent death the essence of mysterious life. For Elliot's Magi, the event was decisive, and once was enough. But the appetite of Yeats's Magi for apocalyptic and violent annunciation, their search for something beyond the rational, is not sated even by their superimposition of Christ's death on his birth (the poem enacts their telescoping or reversal of time in its last two lines, where 'Calvary's turbulence' precedes and prepares for what happens on the 'bestial floor' of the stable). They have come to sniff that 'odour of blood', which as 'Two Songs' tells us, 'Made all Platonic tolerance vain'. It is not enough. The key word of the poem is 'unsatisfied'. They represent that aspect of Yeats's own unsatisfied mind, which ranges through and over history, expecting and desiring the apocalyptic or mythical or irrational epiphany, which overturns 'ordinary' social reality in its demonstration of Dionysiac energy – 'The uncontrollable mystery on the bestial floor'. This 'uncontrollable mystery' is an amoral force, the force of the irrational, which partakes of the energy which Blake called 'Eternal Delight'.

It also betokens, as I have said already, a more authentic reality, besides which what we call civilisation or culture is merely a thin veneer, an illusion. Yeats admits the terror of the apocalyptic moment, but insists on its value as an avenue to truth, on its power to purge the 'film of familiarity' from our eyes. He says:

> All civilisation is held together by the suggestions of an invisible hypnotist – by artificially created illusions. The knowledge of reality is always in some measure a secret knowledge. It is a kind of death.
>
> *(Autobiographies*, p. 482)

If civilisation is illusion, this provides Yeats with another kind of justification for his valuation of destructiveness. These considerations are voiced explicitly in the late poem 'Meru' (*CP*, p. 333):

> Civilisation is hooped together, brought
> Under a rule, under the semblance of peace
> By manifold illusion; but man's life is thought,

> And he, despite his terror, cannot cease
> Ravening through century after century,
> Ravening, raging, and uprooting that he may come
> Into the desolation of reality:
> Egypt and Greece, good-bye, and good-bye, Rome!
> Hermits upon Mount Meru or Everest,
> Caverned in night under the drifted snow,
> Or where that snow and winter's dreadful blast
> Beat down upon their naked bodies, know
> That day brings round the night, that before dawn
> His glory and his monuments are gone.

Egypt, Greece and Rome fall before man's ravening destructiveness; the glory and the monuments are gone; but in the general context I am attempting to illustrate, it is hard to agree that this is 'Yeats in a mood of bleak and desperate pessimism'.[57] The reward of the ceaseless and destructive quest is 'reality' — a desolate reality, but reality. And 'Meru' presents this situation as inevitable. What transforms fate into freedom is the joyous embrace of such loss, the swan's bold playing or riding of the clamorous winds. The self may be asserted more gloriously for its admission of the world's ephemerality. As the Angel says in *The Hour-Glass* (1914), which takes for theme the reality of a world beyond the reach of empirical rationalism:

> Only when all the world has testified,
> May soul confound it, crying out in joy,
> And laughing on its lonely precipice.
> What's dearth and death and sickness to the soul
> That knows no virtue but itself? Nor could it,
> So trembling with delight and mother-naked,
> Live unabashed if the arguing world stood by.
>
> > (*Collected Plays*, p. 309)

Yeats's attraction towards violent apocalypse and the explosive intrusion of the irrational into human history is best exemplified in his two most famous poems of annunciation, 'Leda and the Swan' and 'The Second Coming'. It must be admitted, of course, that the fear and terror accompanying the visitation of the supernatural are given full poetic weight in each poem. It is easy enough to read 'Leda' (*CP*, p. 241) as a poem of protest against the brutally impersonal assault of the divine on the human, to put the shock and terror of the girl at the centre of the poem:

> A sudden blow: the great wings beating still
> Above the staggering girl, her thighs caressed
> By the dark webs, her nape caught in his bill,
> He holds her helpless breast upon his breast.
> How can those terrified vague fingers push
> The feathered glory from her loosening thighs?

And yet, by the end of the sonnet, the emphasis has changed. Leda has acquired 'power' through her union with the divine; she may also have acquired something of divine vision or 'knowledge', visionary insight. It is on the change in her, rather than on the historical results of the union, that the poem focuses, and the language of the conclusion suggests that Leda may have moved from terror to rapture:[58]

> Being so caught up,
> So mastered by the brute blood of the air,
> Did she put on his knowledge with his power
> Before the indifferent beak could let her drop?

The possibility of that knowledge[59] justifies the terror and the brutality. It is the Yeatsian note; in violent irrationality, in the Dionysiac frenzy, may be found truth. Writing in 1934, Yeats quotes lines from his own play *The Resurrection*:

> What if there is always something that lies outside knowledge, out-side order? . . . What if the irrational return?

— and he concludes:

> It has seemed to me of late that the sense of spiritual reality comes whether to the individual or to crowds from some violent shock, and that idea has the support of tradition.
>
> (*Explorations*, pp. 398-9)[60]

'Leda' is not only a poem which memorably embodies a moment of 'violent shock'; characteristically, that moment breeds not new life, but further destructiveness and loss:

> A shudder in the loins engenders there
> The broken wall, the burning roof and tower
> And Agamemnon dead.

Again here 'creativity' is linked to ruin; the idea is deeply rooted in Yeats's 'sense of spiritual reality'. Yet the process, as always in Yeats, is dialectical. The broken wall, the burning roof and tower in their turn beget creativity − they are 'images that yet/Fresh images beget' (*CP*, p. 281); not just the images of Yeats's own poem, but the works of Homer and the Greek dramatists.[61] In this sense, history enacts its tragic violence to provide or to issue in, the work of art. 'Leda', in one guise, is a complex and powerful restatement of the theme embodied in the closing lines of *The Green Helmet*:

> . . . till a day come that I know,
> When heart and mind shall darken that the weak may end the strong,
> And the long-remembering harpers have matter for their song.

'The Second Coming' (*CP*, pp. 210-11) is an even more ambiguous poem. In a letter to Ethel Mannin written in 1936, Yeats claimed that the poem 'written some sixteen or seventeen years ago . . . foretold what is happening' in the Europe increasingly falling under the shadow of totalitarian terror. 'I am not callous, every nerve trembles with horror at what is happening in Europe, "the ceremony of innocence is drowned".'[62] The phrase 'ceremony of innocence' recalls another Yeats with his reverence for 'traditional sanctity and loveliness', and most commentators follow the tone of Yeats's letter in seeing 'The Second Coming' as a grave prophetic denunciation of 'mob rule, unchecked violence, the impotence of the ethical will, the destruction of legitimate authority and inherited values . . . a glimpse into the nature of modern political and cultural reality':[63]

> Turning and turning in the widening gyre
> The falcon cannot hear the falconer;
> Things fall apart; the centre cannot hold;
> Mere anarchy is loosed upon the world,
> The blood-dimmed tide is loosed, and everywhere
> The ceremony of innocence is drowned;
> The best lack all conviction, while the worst
> Are full of passionate intensity.

But the poem does not end there. In his essay 'If I Were Four-and-Twenty', written in 1919, in the same year as the poem, Yeats writes:

As all realisation is through opposites, men coming to believe the subjective opposite of what they do and think, we may be about to accept the most implacable authority the world has known. Do I desire or dread it, loving as I do the gaming-table of Nature where many are ruined but none is judged, and where all is fortuitous, unseen?

(*Explorations*, p. 280)

The question is genuinely open-ended — 'Do I desire or dread it?' And if the tone of the poem's opening lines is filled with 'dread', the following lines are full of an intense prophetic excitement, the poet's exultation as a sage or seer of apocalypse shining everywhere through:

Surely some revelation is at hand;
Surely the Second Coming is at hand.
The Second Coming! Hardly are those words out
When a vast image out of *Spiritus Mundi*
Troubles my sight: somewhere in sands of the desert
A shape with lion body and the head of a man,
A gaze blank and pitiless as the sun,
Is moving its slow thighs, while all about it
Reel shadows of the indignant desert birds.
The darkness drops again; but now I know
That twenty centuries of stony sleep
Were vexed to nightmare by a rocking cradle,
And what rough beast, its hour come round at last,
Slouches towards Bethlehem to be born?

We have seen, already, in a different context, how Yeats opposes the great man and the great moment, dramatic theatricality, to the mere linear process of history, his dislike — shared with Nietzsche — for Hegelian teleology. So, in both 'Leda and the Swan' and 'The Second Coming', history as process is denied and confounded by the violent intrusion into time of the supernatural or quasi-supernatural. 'Twenty centuries' are dismissed as mere 'stony sleep'; they are only a backdrop for the truly *authentic* moments, the moments of apocalyse. In rejecting Sean O'Casey's play *The Silver Tassie*, Yeats wrote to him:

Dramatic action is a fire that must burn up everything but itself; there should be no room in a play for anything that does not belong to it; the whole history of the world must be reduced to wallpaper in front of which the characters must pose and speak.[64]

The rough beast of 'The Second Coming', the child in the cradle at Bethlehem, do not 'speak', but their intense, burning *incarnations* reduce the 'whole history of the world' to 'wallpaper'. The theatrical metaphor is appropriate, for at one level the rough beast's manifestation is a literary phenomenon.[65] It is a 'vast *image*', which appears on the speaker's quasi-incantatory repetition of 'the Second Coming!'; it disappears after its blazing appearance as behind the curtains of a theatre — 'the darkness drops again'. The brevity of the moment of intense vision is a guarantee of its poetic truth, for the poet a triumphant validation of the authenticity of his prophetic sanctity in a secular age. It is in such moments that the poet understands and embodies the creative impulse which is uniquely his because he is a poet, hence their supremely *literary* value. Yeats would argue, as he does in *Per Amica Silentia Lunae*, written in 1917 two years before 'The Second Coming', that it is for these moments that the poet lives:

> I think that we who are poets and artists, not being permitted to shoot beyond the tangible, must go from desire to weariness and so to desire again, and live but for the moment when the vision comes to our weariness like terrible lightning, in the humility of the brutes.
>
> (*Mythologies*, p. 34)

In the same essay, Yeats applies the image of the lightning flash to the visitation of the Daimon, and echoing Blake's description of the 'poet's work',[66] makes even clearer the link between the characteristic Yeatsian apocalyptic moment and creative inspiration:

> His [the Daimon's] descending power is neither the winding nor the straight line but zigzag . . . it is the sudden lightning, for all his acts of power are instantaneous. We perceive in a pulsation of the artery, and after slowly decline . . . So always it is an impulse from some Daimon that gives to our vague, unsatisfied desire, beauty, a meaning, and a form all can accept.
>
> (*Mythologies*, pp. 361-2)

The rough beast, like the 'feathered glory' of 'Leda and the Swan', is a visitation of the Daimon; Yeats's visionary moment is the basis of his claim to have 'put on knowledge' (in 'Leda' the putting on of knowledge, as we have seen, is left as rhetorical question but with an implied — in my view — affirmative answer). He has also put on 'power', in the sense that the image of apocalypse gives the poem an authoritative resonance and metaphysical grandeur from which no reader is immune. Harold Bloom says of the swan in 'Leda', 'the brute is a poet of history, writing in humans rather than words'.[67] In 'The Second Coming' we have the same thing – it is the culminating vision of the 'brazen winged beast . . . associated with laughing, ecstatic destruction', the beast as Muse. Despite the subsequent letter to Ethel Mannin, the tone of 'The Second Coming' is frighteningly exultant.[68] In the essay of 1932 on *Prometheus Unbound*, Yeats explicitly chides Shelley, as Bloom points out, 'for not sharing the attitude of the speaker of "The Second Coming" ':[69]

> Why, then, does Demogorgon . . . bear so terrible a shape? . . . Why is Shelley terrified of the Last Day like a Victorian child?
>
> (*Essays and Introductions*, p. 420)

Marx said that violence was the midwife of history; for Yeats, as many of his great creative occasions testify, it is also the midwife of poetry.

This aesthetic of apocalypse in Yeats's work may be related in the first instance to something in the general European mind of the time, expressed in many writers. Yeats himself had spoken of the advent in his time of 'the Savage God'.[70] Like all good poetic phrases, this catches our attention even as it resists our desire for closer and more analytic definition. But at least we may say that the phrase directs us to that element in the modern sensibility and in modern literature which rejects civilisation and the values traditionally associated with it – reason, order, liberal humanism, progress – and prefers unreason, violence, nihilism, chaos, the apocalyse. This represents a particularly virulent form of primitivism, which Lovejoy has defined as 'the discontent of the civilized with civilization'[71] – particularly virulent, in so far as many cultural malcontents see in modern civilisation the triumph of the especially despised bourgeois liberalism, responsible for materialism and 'Manchesterism', mass society, the commerce of cities, the vulgarities of newspapers, rulers who are ineffectual mediocrities, the loss of heroic idealism, and a pervasive effeteness. This kind of civilisation is, in Ezra Pound's words, 'an old bitch gone in the teeth'. The attitude was widespread in France and Italy in the late nineteenth century, as Julien Benda has shown, and also of course in Germany.[72] German writers (especially those influenced – as Yeats was – by Nietzsche) – Rilke, George, even Thomas Mann – tended to welcome the First World War when it came as a cleansing end to the pretence of civilisation with which they considered they had been living. Mann could write in 1915:

> Germany's whole virtue and beauty . . . is unfolded only in war . . .
> The German soul is too deep for civilization to be for her a high
> value, let alone the highest value.[73]

Spengler's *Decline of the West* of which the first instalment appeared in
1918, and which received Yeats's seal of approval for the congruence of
its ideas with those of *A Vision*, is written to demonstrate the inevitability of coming doom. It struck a resonant chord — in the literature
of the period there is 'a widespread determination to welcome such a
downfall as Spengler predicted'.[74]

A sadder and a wiser Mann than the essayist of 1915 wrote his great
novel *Dr Faustus* just at the end of the Second World War. He describes
the career of the composer Leverkühn who sells himself in the interests
of powerful artistic achievement to the power of barbarism. This story
is counterpointed by an account, given us through the horrified eyes of
the humanist Zeitblom, of Germany's slide into the barbarities of the
Nazi regime. Mass gives a brilliant analysis of the appeal of prophetic
visions of cultural disintegration, and of the propinquity of prophecy and
emotional complicity. Zeitblom, referring to the powerful and compelling apocalyptic visions of his composer friend, tells us that he has
experienced 'in his very soul how near aestheticism and barbarism are
to each other: aestheticism as the herald of barbarism.' He also medi-
tates on the effect of listening to a circle of poets, intellectuals and men
of business who meet in a Munich drawing room in the '20s to discuss
the political developments of the day, to mount an 'all-embracing
critique of the bourgeois tradition', and to anticipate the coming of
'absolute power':

> In the end it all came down to dictatorship, to force, for with the
> demolition of the traditional national and social forms through the
> French Revolution an epoch had dawned which, consciously or not,
> confessedly or not, steered its course toward despotic tyranny over
> the masses; and they, reduced to one uniform level, atomized, out of
> touch, were as powerless as the single individual.
> 'Quite right, quite right. Oh indeed yes, one may say so!' zur
> Höhe assured us, and pounded with his feet. Of course one may say
> so; only one might, for my taste, dealing with this description of a
> mounting barbarism, have said so with rather more fear and trembling
> and rather less blithe satisfaction . . . I did not for a moment conceal

from myself that with an acuity worthy of note they had laid their
fingers on the pulse of the time and were prognosticating accord-
ingly. But I must repeat that I should have been so endlessly grateful . . . if they themselves had been more alarmed over their findings
or had opposed to them a little ethical criticism. They might have
said: Unhappily it looks as though things would follow this and this
course. Consequently one must take steps to warn people of what is
coming and do one's best to prevent it. But what in a way they were
saying was: it is coming, it is coming, and when it is here it will find
us on the crest of the moment. It is interesting, it is even good,
simply by virtue of being what is inevitably going to be, and to
recognize it is sufficient of an achievement and satisfaction. It is not
our affair to go on to do anything against it. − Thus these learned
gentlemen, in private. But that about the satisfaction of recognizing
it was a fraud. They sympathized with what they recognized; without this sympathy they could not have recognized it. That was the
whole point . . .[75]

This is not the whole point about Yeats, even in his prophetic-
apocalyptic vein, of course. Nevertheless, much of his work provides
evidence for Frank Kermode's view that what he calls 'the sense of an
ending' is 'as endemic to . . . modernism as apocalytic utopianism is to
political revolution',[76] and buttresses Lionel Trilling's argument, in an
impressive essay that ranges over writers like Lawrence, Gide, Conrad,
Sir James Frazer, Nietzsche and Dostoevski, that

> . . . the characteristic element of modern literature, or at least of the
> most highly developed modern literature, is the bitter line of hos-
> tility to civilization which runs through it.[77]

Mann's insight usefully indicates, while evaluating, the aesthetic and
psychological appeal and power of an art which asserts the flimsiness of
liberal democracy and which contemplates its collapse with a sort of
perverse excitement.[78]

Once again, however, Yeats's 'sense of an ending' can be traced, like
all other aspects of his work, to his Irish cultural situation. Born into
the Protestant Ascendancy, he experienced its loss of power with the
rise of the Catholic middle class and the establishment of a Catholic
bourgeois Free State. This shaped him as a conservative revolutionary −
he longed to destroy the despised present in order to recapture an
idealised past in an imaginary future. Hence the excoriation of the

'filthy modern tide' as it manifested itself in Ireland; hence his arch-
aising art which offered Ireland ideal images of a legendary heroic past
and of a vanished courtliness, which he hoped might model and shape a
nobler future. But he could not, in the end, escape the predicament of
his Anglo-Irish roots; and the history of the Anglo-Irish in his time was
one of decline and fall. Despite an early and determined attempt to
assimilate with Gaelic, Catholic and nationalist Ireland, Yeats gradually,
and with increasing power and pride, came to realise his identity with
Anglo-Ireland. And from this identification comes the transvaluation of
defeat, defeat and loss made beautiful. We have already examined, in
'Nineteen Hundred and Nineteen', how very much the beauty of the
symbolic swan depends on its courageous facing of the clamorous and
irresistible winds that will bring the night. Precisely the same image
turns up in Yeats's most powerful expression of his Anglo-Irish identity
and inheritance, in the testament of 'The Tower' (*CP*, pp. 222-3):

> It is time that I wrote my will;
> I choose upstanding men
> That climb the streams until
> The fountain leap, and at dawn
> Drop their cast at the side
> Of dripping stone; I declare
> They shall inherit my pride,
> The pride of people that were
> Bound neither to Cause nor to State,
> Neither to slaves that were spat on,
> Nor to the tyrants that spat,
> The people of Burke and of Grattan
> That gave, though free to refuse —
> Pride like that of the morn,
> When the headlong light is loose,
> Or that of the fabulous horn,
> Or that of the sudden shower
> When all streams are dry,
> Or that of the hour
> When the swan must fix his eye
> Upon a fading gleam,
> Float out upon a long
> Last reach of glittering stream
> And there sing his last song.

That intensely beautiful image of the swan is not just emblematic of the poet Yeats singing in the teeth of adversity, but emblematic of the whole Anglo-Irish class, whose passing instructed Yeats, more than anything else, in the aesthetics of endings.

This breaking of a culture he revered certainly contributed to his projection outwards on world history a myth of defeat and disintegration felt in his bones. He came to find authenticity and — with the help of Nietzsche — 'tragic joy' in ruin. But there is also a sense in which Yeats's violent myth of world history is called in to serve an imaginative aggrandisement of Anglo-Irish loss. That is, Yeats's repeated patterns of metaphor and symbol tend to link the destruction of a local culture, the fall of the Great House, with the operations of the Savage God who embodies the meaning of history in so much of Yeats. To do this, to see the 'ceremonies' of that local culture as drowned in the 'blood-dimmed tide' of world anarchy, is to imbue Anglo-Irish history in its last phase with a glamorous grandeur. For to see Ascendancy collapse as part of a world collapse is enormously to dignify its passing; the disappearance of the Ascendancy may then be seen not as some irrelevant sideshow, but as paradigmatic of a major historical watershed.[79] The eloquence and sonority of Yeats's symbolism makes us feel that in witnessing the end of Coole House, for example, we are experiencing a universal catastrophe:

> Where fashion or mere fantasy decrees
> We shift about — all that great glory spent —
> Like some poor Arab tribesman and his tent.

It is instructive to contrast with the tragic and apocalyptic grandeur of Yeats's treatment of Anglo-Irish downfall the caustic words of Standish O'Grady, an acquaintance and one of Yeats's 'beautiful lofty things':

> Aristocracies come and go like the waves of the sea; and some fall nobly and others ignobly. As I write, this Protestant Anglo-Irish aristocracy, which once owned all Ireland from the centre to the sea, is rotting from the land in the most dismal farce-tragedy of all time, without one brave deed, without one brave word . . .

And again, addressing the landlords of Ireland, O'Grady employs theatrical metaphors, of a kind to which Yeats's imagination lent itself but in a very different tone:

> Your career is like some uncouth epic begun by a true poet, con-
> titnued by a newspaper man, and ended by a buffoon; heroic verse,
> followed by prose, and closed in a disgusting farce. Then *plaudite*,
> and *exeunt omnes*. The curtain falls on two centuries of Irish history,
> and such centuries . . .[80]

Though Yeats was aware of the shortcomings of the Anglo-Irishry in reality, the Anglo-Irishry as an *ideal* class of cultured, benevolent yet proud, even arrogant, natural rulers appealed enormously to him. And how many of Yeats's ideals are inseparable from a framework of heroic defeat and loss! He could not accept O'Grady's 'play', especially such a fall of the curtain, and hating comedy and farce, rewrote the ending in sombre dignity. In Yeats's version, the rough beast of destructiveness slouches not just through world history but through Irish Ascendancy landscapes, incorporating them also inside its own aura of lurid grandeur. And the poet finds for himself a most congenial role as elegist of a culture, a role where his sense of caste can be satisfactorily married with his apocalyptic romanticism to produce befitting emblems of adversity:

> . . . this hand alone,
> Like some last courtier at a gypsy camping-place
> Babbling of fallen majesty, records what's gone.

> (*CP*, p. 138)

4 JAMES JOYCE: FROM INSIDE TO OUTSIDE AND BACK AGAIN

Yeats and Synge, though of the Ascendancy ethos, attempt to embody and define in their work, across that cultural divide, a personal sense of innerness with Ireland and its culture. Joyce seems to provide an almost too neat contrast, at first sight; the native who wants to get out of the stifling constrictions of his culture, who chooses the path of rejection and exile, and who, far from wishing to be accounted one of that distinguished company 'who sang to sweeten Ireland's wrong', insists on the wide division between the solitary and detached artist and his paralysed society. This insistent emphasis in Joyce's work (especially the earlier work) may be misleading; first, the reader may neglect or simplify the real nature of Joyce's relationship with Ireland, taking Stephen Dedalus's Luciferian rejection of fatherland as unqualified triumph; second, it may lead, especially when put alongside Joyce's technical virtuosity, to a facile endorsement of the view that for Joyce supreme value lies in Art and that his hero is the Artist. In fact, though Joyce offers an unsparingly critical view of Ireland, he was unable to commit himself wholly to the simple romantic model of the artist as victim of his society. Byronically shaking its dust from his feet. The romantic-heroic view of the artist, held so firmly by Yeats, certainly appealed to him, but was in the nature of a psychological compensation rather than a dogma, and from the beginning of his career, with the publication of *Dubliners*, he was aware of its limitations. Joyce moves consistently and steadily from the mountain-top, where 'unfellowed, friendless and alone', the artist disdainfully — and somewhat ridiculously — flashes his antlers,[1] to the intimacy of Eccles Street. He shows that the artist must learn to shake hands with the citizen, or at least have a cup of cocoa with him; and the affirmation of the values of the social man, the member of a community, is the more convincing because of the posture of extreme rejection from which Joyce began — and needed to begin.

A history and a tradition are of enormous value to a writer in offering a consolidation of a sense of identity, of continuity and of community. But only, it would seem, if the writer can take some pride in that tradition. So Yeats, sustained from the start by a sense of the nobility of the Anglo-Irish tradition in Ireland encapsulated in the

151

impressive roll he inclined to call more and more in his later years —
Swift, Grattan, Burke, Goldsmith, Congreve, Berkeley, Lord Edward
Fitzgerald, Robert Emmet, Parnell, Wilde — and simultaneously feeling
free of the great English literary tradition, could assert, in turning to
the sagas and legends of heroic Ireland and to the folk-lore of the
peasantry, the nobility of his own chosen version of the native Irish
tradition, and simply ignore what he did not wish to see. The Anglo-
Irishman may pick and choose among the shattered fragments of Irish
culture; he may seek identity, but with the freedom of his own inborn
detachment. The native Irishman has no such option and lacks the
splendour of the kind of heritage Yeats was able to invoke as consolation for a history frequently perceived, to use Stephen Dedalus's word,
as nightmare. He is obsessed with the sense of a gapped or fractured
culture, arising from the dispossession of a language, a sense memorably
conveyed in the thought of Stephen Dedalus in his discussion with the
English dean of studies:

> He felt with a smart of dejection that the man to whom he was
> speaking was a countryman of Ben Jonson. He thought: — The
> language in which we are speaking is his before it is mine. How
> different are the words *home, Christ, ale, master*, on his lips and on
> mine! I cannot speak or write these words without unrest of spirit.
> His language, so familiar and so foreign, will always be for me an
> acquired speech. I have not made or accepted its words. My voice
> holds them at bay. My soul frets in the shadow of his language.
>
> (*A Portrait*, p. 194)

He is obsessed with a sense of failure, gripped by a 'politics fatally construed as a theology', in Denis Donoghue's phrase,[2] oppressed — in
Joyce's case — by a theology construed as a denial of individuality. For
Joyce, whose own family's slide into poverty and squalor functioned as
a kind of domestic analogue of the sorry history of his country, the
sense of constriction in Ireland was overwhelming. As he said, in a lecture in Trieste in 1907, of the Irishman's plight:

> The economic and intellectual conditions that prevail in his own
> country do not permit the development of individuality. The soul of
> the country is weakened by centuries of useless struggle and broken
> treaties, and individual initiative is paralysed by the influence and
> admonitions of the church, while its body is manacled by the police,
> the tax-office, and the garrison. No one who has any self-respect stays

in Ireland, but flees afar as though from a country that has under-gone the visitation of an angered Jove.[3]

For Joyce, then, the sense of freedom and even liberation which both Yeats and Synge found in aspects of Irish life and culture was simply not available; such freedom had to be fought for and won by silence, exile and cunning, by a series of willed, even histrionic detachments. Only when he had fought clear of the chrysalis of constriction could he begin to see his cultural background with a more benign, if always ironic, eye.

I would argue that the origins of Joyce's art, which is frequently seen as proud and arrogant in its highly individual techniques and apparently encyclopaedic claims, lie in a deep sense of cultural inferiority which Joyce feels is the Irishman's heritage, and of which the thoughts of Stephen and the words of Joyce himself quoted above give only some indication. Such a feeling, significantly, is not to be found in Yeats and Synge, who do not have the mentality of the defeated and colonised. Joyce saw Irish history as ignoble from the very start; Ireland had sold herself into English hands because the first English adventurers 'came to Ireland at the repeated requests of a native king'; and she sold herself again in the Act of Union of 1800, because although bribery and corruption were rife it was nevertheless an Irish Parliament at Dublin which legislated itself out of existence. Joyce comments sourly: 'From my point of view, these two facts must be thoroughly explained before the country in which they occurred has the most rudimentary right to persuade one of her sons to change his position from that of an un-prejudiced observer to that of a convinced nationalist.'[4]

Further, having sold herself cheaply to the English, through her history Ireland has repeatedly sold, in betrayal, her great men. The fall of Parnell was, of course, Joyce's most potent image of Irish treachery; occurring in his childhood, it left an indelible mark on him, as is shown most clearly, perhaps, in the magnificent Christmas dinner episode in *A Portrait*. The single instance became the basis of a general theory; in a Triestine newspaper article on John O'Leary, written in 1907, Joyce succinctly explains the failure of Fenianism in the nineteenth century:

And why this disintegration of a movement so well organised? Simply because in Ireland, just at the right moment, an informer always appears.[5]

And again, in 1910, Joyce offers the same generalisation to his Triestine readers: Ireland 'has betrayed her heroes, always in the hour of need and always without gaining recompense'.[6] These comments make it possible to accept some of Stephen Dedalus's diatribes as Joyce's own. Images of betrayal and of the ignoble servility of his country lurk near the surface of Stephen's mind, and may be triggered by the slightest of occasions, as in the brief encounter with the flower-girl:

— Buy them lovely ones, will you, sir? Only a penny.
— Did you hear what I said? asked Stephen, bending towards her. I told you I had no money. I tell you again now.
— Well, sure, you will some day, sir, please God, the girl answered after an instant.
— Possibly, said Stephen, but I don't think it likely.

He left her quickly, fearing that her intimacy might turn to gibing and wishing to be out of the way before she offered her ware to another, a tourist from England or a student of Trinity. Grafton Street, along which he walked, prolonged that moment of discouraged poverty. In the roadway at the head of the street a slab was set to the memory of Wolfe Tone and he remembered having been present with his father at its laying. He remembered with bitterness that scene of tawdry tribute. There were four French delegates in a brake, and one, a plump smiling young man, held, wedged on a stick, a card on which were printed the words: *Vive l'Irlande!*

(*A Portrait*, p. 187)

Stephen's sense of poverty here clearly goes beyond the financial. The girl becomes an image of willing servility, and the semi-ridiculous twinges of shame before the imagined English tourist[7] and the remembered Frenchmen show Joyce's insight into the touchy consciousness of those who feel dispossessed of any history to be proud of.

In this general connection it is important to see that Joyce attacks the Roman Catholic Church in his writings less on theological grounds or from a purely personal standpoint than for what he designates as its social and historical role in Ireland. He consistently presents it as another imperial power, another mighty source for the inculcation of servility. Ireland's loyalty to Rome is the worse since Rome sold Ireland to the English in the time of Henry II. But 'Ireland's compliance is so complete that it would hardly murmur if tomorrow the pope, having already turned it over to an Englishman and an Italian, were to turn their island over to some *hidalgo* of the court of Alphonso [the King of Spain] who found himself momentarily unemployed'.[8]

In the opening episode of *Ulysses*, Stephen is aware that he is the servant of two masters, the British Empire and the holy Roman Catholic
and apostolic Church. For him, as for Joyce, there is little doubt as to
which is the more formidable oppressor, since the Church can exert
moral and spiritual, as well as social, financial and political, control.
'The Roman, not the Sassenach, was . . . the tyrant of the islanders',
thinks Stephen in *Stephen Hero*, a point Joyce expresses directly in his
own voice in one of his newspaper articles:

> I confess that I do not see what good it does to fulminate against the
> English tyranny while the Roman tyranny occupies the palace of the
> soul.[9]

In fact, Joyce is most vitriolic about the Church precisely at those
moments where he senses its identity and common cause with that
other imperial tyranny; behind much of the Parnellite anti-clericalism
he inherited from his father can be glimpsed a sense of thwarted
nationalism raging before an unshakeable combination of forces. In
Stephen Hero having described Stephen passing 'the great cow-like
trunks of police constables' (representing the secular empire), Joyce
goes on:

> These wanderings filled him with deep-seated anger and whenever
> he encountered a burly black-vested priest taking a stroll of plea-
> sant inspection through these warrens full of swarming and cring-
> ing believers he cursed the farce of Irish Catholicism: an island . . .
> the inhabitants of which entrust their wills and minds to others
> that they may ensure for themselves a life of spiritual paralysis,
> an island in which all the power and riches are in the keeping of
> those whose kingdom is not of this world, an island in which Caesar
> . . . confesses Christ and Christ confesses Caesar that together they
> may wax fat upon a starveling rabblement which is bidden ironically
> to take to itself this consolation in hardship 'The Kingdom of God is
> within you'.
>
> (pp. 150-1)

Joyce liked the central image here well enough to use it in his own
voice years later in his satirical broadside, 'Gas from a Burner', which
combines a number of the attitudes we have been examining:

This lovely land that always sent
Her writers and artists to banishment
And in a spirit of Irish fun
Betrayed her own leaders, one by one.
'Twas Irish humour, wet and dry,
Flung quicklime into Parnell's eye;
'Tis Irish brains that save from doom
The leaky barge of the Bishop of Rome
For everyone knows that Pope can't belch
Without the consent of Billy Walsh.
O Ireland my first and only love
Where Christ and Caesar are hand and glove![10]

In Joyce's history, then, Ireland has sold herself twice over, to different masters who make common cause in enforcing servility on the nation. Servility, like the foot and mouth disease of which Mr Deasy is so afraid, has become endemic. Thus the students Joyce presents, in both *Stephen Hero* and *A Portrait*, are indeed a sorry lot, cravenly adjusting their moral and aesthetic standards to the dictates of their Church, anxiously committed to Mr Dedalus's belief that the way to an employers' heart is to possess a priestly seal of approval (itself ironic, given Mr Dedalus's Parnellite views). Another aspect of this inescapable servility, in Joyce's view, is evidenced in the qualities of wit and eloquence for which the Irish are allegedly famed, which the Joycean sense of cultural inferiority transmutes into only another form of ingratiation with the English master. Hence he writes of Oscar Wilde:

In the tradition of Irish writers of comedy that runs from the days of Sheridan and Goldsmith to Bernard Shaw, Wilde became, like them, court jester to the English.[11]

It is a situation presented vividly in his fiction as at the beginning of *Ulysses*, where the jester Mulligan puts on a series of pantomime sketches for the stolid Englishman, Haines, and attempts to persuade Stephen, too, to perform, so that money may be forthcoming from 'the oxy chap'. Ireland is 'destined by God to be the everlasting caricature of the serious world'.[12]

In such a context Irish art can only be 'the cracked looking-glass of a servant'. The vividness of Joyce's sense of his country's social and political failure rather than the arrogance of a youthful aesthete, sure of the one true road to Parnassus, is what underlies his depiction of

Ireland's cultural and artistic inferiority. There is no consolation in
thoughts of a golden past. As he says in his 1901 pamphlet 'The Day
of the Rabblement': 'A nation which never advanced so far as a miracle-
play affords no literary model to the artist, and he must look abroad'.[13]
The tone is very close to what we find in *A Portrait*, where Stephen
thinks on the nationalist Davin:

> His nurse had taught him Irish and shaped his rude imagination by
> the broken lights of Irish myth. He stood towards this myth upon
> which no individual mind had ever drawn out a line of beauty and to
> its unwieldy tales that divided against themselves as they moved down
> the cycles in the same attitude as towards the Roman catholic relig-
> ion, the attitude of a dullwitted loyal serf.
>
> (p. 184)

The present, despite − or indeed, because of − the Irish revival offers
just as little as the past. It is a long way from the noble ideals of Coole
Park to the squalid pettiness and futility of the *Eire Abu* Society's
concerts, which Joyce presents in the *Dubliners* story 'A Mother'. As
for the Gaelic League, and the Gaelic Athletic Association (founded by
Michael Cusack, the 'Citizen' of *Ulysses*), having created a few vivid
pictures of the embarrassing parochiality and self-admiration of typical
evening meetings in *Stephen Hero*, Joyce writes of this aspect of the
cultural revival:

> The liberty they desired for themselves was mainly a liberty of cos-
> tume and vocabulary: and Stephen could hardly understand how
> such a poor scarecrow of liberty could bring . . . serious human
> beings to their knees in worship. As in the Daniels' household he had
> seen people playing at being important so here he saw people playing
> at being free . . . A glowing example was to be found for Ireland in
> the case of Hungary, an example, as these patriots imagined, of a
> long-suffering minority, entitled by every right of race and justice to
> a separate freedom, finally emancipating itself. In emulation of that
> achievement bodies of young Gaels conflicted murderously in the
> Phoenix Park with whacking hurley-sticks . . .
>
> (pp. 66-7)

Joyce's sense of being trapped inside a servile and inferior culture was
therefore very real and not in the least a pose invented to justify an
elitist artistic credo. One may detect in many of the passages cited a

desire to redeem this culture in some way. But here Joyce had few
roads to go. The constitutional path to some measure of freedom
seemed utterly discredited and moribund in the aftermath of the
Parnell debacle. As for the spirit of republican nationalism, what Joyce
called 'the irreconcilable temper', he had little taste for extremism,
believed devoutly in his betrayal theory of Irish history, and always
hated physical force, as Frank Budgen among others testifies.[14] The
portrait of the Citizen in *Ulysses*, though a comic *tour-de-force*, shows
Joyce's distaste for even the rhetoric of the 'irreconcilables'. Turning
from political to more purely cultural considerations, he could find, as
we have seen, no sense of a sustaining artistic tradition; in Joyce's eyes,
the Irish heroic age had produced only 'unwieldy tales', and as for the
folk-lore of the Gaelic-speaking Ireland, he would see nothing in it but
'senility'.[15] It was not just that Joyce did not know the Irish language;
he knew that the majority of his Anglicised countrymen did not know
it either, and dramatises the point crushingly in the opening episode of
Ulysses, where his Cathleen ni Houlihan has become a bemused old
milkwoman who fails completely to understand when addressed in Irish
— by an Englishman.

Though Yeats was as ignorant of Irish as Joyce, he was free of the
native's disabling and self-lacerating sense of Irish cultural inferiority
which possessed the young Joyce. Hence the literary movement which
he and his own work did so much to inspire could celebrate, without
embarrassment or a sense of incongruity, an Anglo-Irish version of the
heroic past, and of the 'spirituality' of the Irish peasantry. Joyce could
never have been a member of the Yeatsian school. He felt there was a
basic falsity in Yeats's view of the Irish past as dynamic, denied that
great legends were the mother of great nations:

> If an appeal to the past in this manner were valid, the fellahin of
> Cairo would have all the right in the world to disdain to act as
> porters for English tourists. Ancient Ireland is dead just as ancient
> Egypt is dead. Its death chant has been sung, and on its gravestone
> has been placed the seal.[16]

Secondly, Joyce was a totally urban man who had a contempt for the
idiocy of rural life, in part natural, in part no doubt a product of Irish
sensitiveness to the *Punch*-like view of Paddy-with-the-Pig-in-his-Kitchen.
His conversations with Arthur Power in Paris, and in particular his dismissal of Synge's portrait of peasant Ireland,[17] confirm in maturity the
attitudes expressed with youthful vigour in *Stephen Hero*, not only in

the depressing picture of Mullingar as representative of country life, but in Stephen's argument with Madden on the peasant:

— But you despite him — he's not clever enough for you.
— Now, you know, Madden, that's nonsense. To begin with he's cute as a fox — try to pass a false coin on him and you'll see. But his cleverness is all of a low order. I really don't think that the Irish peasant represents a very admirable type of culture.
— That's you all out! Of course you sneer at him because he's not up-to-date and lives a simple life.
— Yes, a life of dull routine — the calculation of coppers, the weekly debauch and the weekly piety — a life lived in cunning and fear between the shadows of the parish chapel and the asylum.

(p. 59)

Third, apart from being uninterested in Ireland outside Dublin, Joyce was temperamentally opposed to the idealising tendency built into the Yeatsian vision of rural Ireland and the past — something which also troubled Synge. As early as the paper he delivered to his college's Literary and Historical Society in 1900, titled 'Drama and Life', Joyce had committed himself to a view of the matter of art not only of great importance for his own future development but one which might have been constructed deliberately as an antithesis to Yeats's epic, heroic and romantic view:

Life indeed nowadays is often a sad bore . . . Epic savagery is rendered impossible by vigilant policing, chivalry has been killed by the fashion oracles of the boulevards. There is no clank of mail, no halo about gallantry, no hat-sweeping, no roystering! The traditions of romance are upheld only in Bohemia. Still I think out of the dreary sameness of existence, a measure of dramatic life may be drawn. Even the most commonplace, the deadest among the living, may play a part in a great drama. It is a sinful foolishness to sigh back for the good old times, to feed the hunger of us with the cold stones they afford. Life we must accept as we see it before our eyes, men and women as we meet them in the real world, not as we apprehend them in the world of faery. The great human comedy in which each has share, gives limitless scope to the true artist, today as yesterday and as in years gone.[18]

Joyce values 'the classical temper' above 'the romantic temper', defining it as 'a constant state of the artistic mind' which, 'ever mindful of limitations, chooses rather to bend upon these present things';[19] and, also in *Stephen Hero*, writes that the truly modern spirit is 'vivisective':

> Vivisection itself is the most modern process one can conceive. The ancient spirit accepted phenomena with a bad grace. The ancient method investigated law with the lantern of justice, morality with the lantern of revelation, art with the lantern of tradition. But all these lanterns have magical properties: they transform and disfigure. The modern method examines its territory by the light of day.
>
> (p. 190)

Though Joyce had the highest admiration for Yeats as a poet, his holding views like this clearly put him outside the fringes of the revival, the only aspect of contemporary Irish culture which even Joyce had to admit had achieved work of distinction; and thus increased, inevitably, his sense of artistic isolation. The vision of himself as an isolated critical realist surrounded by romantics, mystics and seers achieves rumbustious definition and satirical brio in the verses of 'The Holy Office' of 1904:

> But all these men of whom I speak
> Make me the sewer of their clique.
> That they may dream their dreamy dreams
> I carry off their filthy streams
> For I can do those things for them
> Through which I lost my diadem,
> Those things for which Grandmother Church
> Left me severely in the lurch.
> Thus I relieve their timid arses,
> Perform my office of Katharsis.[20]

Hence the promulgation of isolation as the radical principle of artistic economy first made in 'The Day of the Rabblement' in 1901 and reiterated in *Stephen Hero* is not made simply in deference to a Byronic view of the artist as romantic outcast and rebel. No doubt Joyce derived some personal comfort from a sense of being supported by a literary stereotype, of course; but, as I have tried to show, isolation was not so much chosen as forced on him, chiefly by a characteristically Irish sense of cultural inferiority, and by the nature of his literary aims (which had nothing to do with the creation of stereotypical postures). Though Joyce proceeded to make a virtue of a necessary isolation, it is difficult to see his work as a glorification of the autonomous world of the godlike artist, contemplating its own perfection. At the age of nineteen, after all, as we have seen, he had proclaimed the programme he was to follow: 'Life we must accept as we see it before our eyes, men and women as we meet them in the real world, not as we apprehend them in the world of faery.' His special difficulty was that the culture of which he was a product seemed to offer such peculiarly unpromising material to the artist, and his greatest temptation was that of simple rejection and negation. Joyce certainly wanted to be an artist; equally certainly he wanted somehow or other to express the culture which had produced him, not simply to forget it, as Shaw and Wilde had done.

It is often said that Joyce, having had to reject Irish models, found his artistic sustenance in Europe. And this is true, but I think it might be more accurate to say that at the crucial point in his development he found, not Europe *tout court*, but Scandinavia, and especially two writers who had made great art, in Joyce's view, from countries just as insignificant as Ireland, Norway and Denmark. In the context I have tried to illustrate, it was inevitable that the Danish novelist Jakobsen, and the Norwegian dramatist Ibsen, should mean more to Joyce than any native tradition or cultural group. They each had the fundamental credentials – unglamorous, provincial, even stifling backgrounds, yet a resolute desire to treat these backgrounds realistically – to depict, in Joyce's own words, 'men and women as we meet them in the real world, not as we apprehend them in the world of faery'. Jakobsen's influence on Joyce is less well-known than Ibsen's, but should not be underestimated. Joyce himself was not afraid of mentioning Flaubert and Jakobsen in the same breath; perhaps this may be better understood if his life, and the subject matter of Jakobsen's novel *Niels Lyhne*, begun in 1875 and finished in 1880, is briefly described. Jakobsen, the son of a prosperous merchant of Thisted, a remote town in north-west Jutland, was sent to Copenhagen University in 1868 when he was twenty-one years old. He became a botanist, and affronted the pieties of his background by translating *The Origin of Species* and *The Descent of Man* into Danish. From this came his novelist's interest in the position of, and the pressures on, a freethinker in a conservative and hostile society.

In conversation with Georg Brandes, in 1875, just before beginning work on *Niels Lyhne*, Jakobsen looked back at the development of free thought in the immediately preceding generation:

> . . . this free thought proved to be not very easy to pass through the
> world with, and in fact impaired one's career, talent, position and
> relation to one's friends, and one found that one had not merely
> shut oneself out of the granaries of Egypt, but that one missed the
> remaining traditions that fed one's spiritual growth; in short that one
> was made to rely on one's self to a frightful degree; one found, on
> the whole, that the liberty one had gained was a heavy burden to
> bear. The consequence was that some people could not endure it any
> longer, and deserted.

He went on to describe the subject of *Niels Lyhne* in these words:

> It will be a chronicle of youth. It is youth, which in the novel I am
> writing, grows, loves, chatters, fails, fights, is disillusioned and swept
> away. By its virtues and its vices, by its cowardice and its ruin, I
> will show how difficult it is for a man to be a freethinker in a coun-
> try like Denmark, with the siren-voices of tradition and the memories
> of childhood on one side and the censoriousness of society on the
> other.[21]

These siren-voices are obviously pre-figurative of the 'nets' flung at the
free soul to hold it from flight in Joyce's novel of youth; as indeed,
more generally, Jakobsen's own scientific and sceptical posture in relation to life foreshadows Joyce's praise of what we have seen him refer
to as the 'vivisective' modern spirit. And both writers clearly share an
admiration for the heroism of the independent soul, and an apprecia-
tion of the power of society's 'censoriousness'. But the parallels are
more specific, too. The young Joyce must have found Jakobsen's
account of Niels Lyhne's relation to the culturally nationalist 'Danish'
movement especially interesting and sustaining, in the light of his own
view of the, in many ways similar, Irish revival outlined above:

> With unquestioning faith [Niels] had shut his eyes to much that
> attracted him, in order to see more plainly in the great night of the
> Eddas and Sagas; he had been deaf to many things that called him,
> in order to listen to the mystic, natural sounds of the songs of the
> people. Now he had at length perceived that he was under no physi-
> cal necessity to be either Old-Norse or Romantic; that it was simpler
> to proclaim his doubts himself than to put them in the mouth of

Gorm Lokedyrker, and more rational to find expression for the
mystery of his own being than to call to the cloister walls of the
Middle Ages and hear his words returned to him with the faintness
of an echo. He had, indeed, always been alive to the new ideas of the
time, but he had been too busy listening to the manner in which
these ideas were dimly foreshadowed in the past, to hear the clear
and distinct message that the present had to give . . .[22]

The Dane reminded the young Irishman that he was not quite alone in
his attitudes; and the affinities between Jakobsen and Joyce help us to
see that Joyce's interest in European culture was not a means of escaping from Ireland, but a way of learning how he should treat Ireland in
his art. *Niels Lyhne* at once criticises its own culture and yet, in existing,
gives proof that that culture is not entirely moribund.

But though Joyce admired Jakobsen, he worshipped Ibsen. Under-
standably, for the young Dubliner conscious of the poverty of his culture and the squalor of his family context, the obscure provincial from
insignificant Norway who had achieved a European reputation became
a compellingly powerful hero-figure. This Joycean identification of the
situations of the two artists' struggles is obvious, and is the major explanation of Joyce's continuing admiration for the work of an artist which
is, in the end, so different from his own – not least in the almost total
absence of humour and the comic spirit in Ibsen. Though Joyce wrote
to Ibsen, in the letter thanking Ibsen for his notice of Joyce's review of
When We Dead Awaken 'Do not think me a hero-worshipper', the rest
of the letter belies this, revealing the almost painful intensity of Joyce's
identification:

I am sure if you go back along your own life to the time when you
were an undergraduate at the University as I am, and if you think
what it would have meant to you to have earned a word from one
who held as high a place in your esteem as you hold in mine, you
will understand my feeling . . . I have sounded your name defiantly
through a college where it was either unknown or known faintly
and darkly . . . But we always keep the dearest things to ourselves.
I did not tell *them* what bound me closest to you. I did not say how
what I could discern dimly of your life was my pride to see, how
your battles inspired me – not the obvious material battles but those
that were fought and won behind your forehead – how your wilful
resolution to wrest the secret from life gave me heart, and how in
your absolute indifference to public canons of art, friends and

shibboleths you walked in the light of your inward heroism.[23]

Ibsen then was for Joyce an important symbolic figure, the artist as hero, rising in Daedalean fashion above the mean and petty circumstances of his environment.

In his essay on 'Ibsen's New Drama', Joyce wrote of Ibsen's handling of the character of Irene:

> . . . [he] treats it, as indeed he treats all things, with large insight, artistic restraint, and sympathy. He sees it steadily and sees it whole, as from a great height, with perfect vision and an angelic dispassionateness, with the sight of one who may look on the sun with open eyes.

Richard Ellmann and Ellsworth Mason comment that this

> . . . image of artistic detachment was to grow, with some assistance from Flaubert, into Stephen Dedalus' picture of the artist 'like the God of creation . . . within or behind or beyond or above his handiwork, invisible, refined out of existence, indifferent, paring his fingernails.'[24]

And in *Stephen Hero*, there are more approving words for 'the impersonal manner of the artist' (Ibsen).[25] Now, it seems to me that we should be careful not to put too much emphasis on these aspects of Joyce's admiration of Ibsen, on, that is, Joyce's view of Ibsen as the Daedalean artist-hero and on his praise for Ibsen's dispassionate impersonality, if this emphasis leads us, as it tends to do, to interpret Joyce's early work as indicative or expressive of his own need to reject utterly his Irish context, in escaping to the lofty vantage-point of the god-like artist from which that context can be viewed with the purest and coldest irony. That, though it has its truth, is not the whole truth. The most profound significance of Ibsen for Joyce is not that his work offered the young Irishman a model of how to reject one's culture; on the contrary, what Joyce stresses in writing directly or indirectly of this time is that from Ibsen (and, to a lesser extent, from Jakobsen) he learned to come to terms with his culture, flying by the nets of the romantic idealisations of Yeats, the political chauvinism of the nationalists, and the sterility of pure aestheticism. Thus, in *Stephen Hero* Ibsen is first introduced as one who is able to mediate between two different worlds, the real and the imaginative:

The spectacle of the world which [Stephen's] intelligence presented to him with every sordid and deceptive detail set side by side with the spectacle of the world which the monster in him, now grown to a reasonably heroic stage, presented also had often filled him with such sudden despair as could be assuaged only by melancholy versing. He had all but decided to consider the two worlds as aliens one to another — however disguised or expressed the most utter of pessimisms — when he encountered through the medium of hardly procured translations the spirit of Henrik Ibsen. He understood that spirit instantaneously.

(p. 45)

And, in more high-flown vein, the young Joyce himself in his paper 'Drama and Life' praised Ibsen with the same significant emphasis: he 'stands a mediator in awful truth before the veiled face of God'.[26] The example of Ibsen as 'mediator' underlies the important and more extended statements of *Stephen Hero*, where Joyce draws a famous distinction between the romantic and classical tempers:

The artist, he imagined, standing in the position of mediator between the world of his experience and the world of his dreams — a mediator, consequently gifted with twin faculties, a selective faculty and a reproductive faculty. To equate these faculties was the secret of artistic success: the artist who could disentangle the subtle soul of the image from its mesh of defining circumstances most exactly, and re-embody it in artistic circumstances chosen as the most exact for it in its new office, he was the supreme artist.

(p. 82)

'The world of experience' is given its due importance here, and the lesson Joyce learned in Ibsen is stated even more profoundly a little later:

The romantic temper, so often and so grievously misinterpreted, and not more by others than by its own, is an insecure, unsatisfied, impatient temper which sees no fit abode here for its ideals and chooses therefore to behold them under insensible figures. As a result of this choice it comes to disregard certain limitations. Its figures are blown to wild adventures, lacking the gravity of solid bodies, and the mind that has conceived them ends by disowning them. The classical temper on the other hand, ever mindful of limitations, chooses rather to bend upon these present things and so to work upon them and fashion them that the quick intelligence may go beyond them to their meaning which is still unuttered. In this method the sane and joyful spirit issues forth and achieves imperishable perfection, nature assisting with her goodwill and thanks.

(p. 83)

The example of Ibsen, then, in whom Joyce saw pre-eminently the 'classical temper' showed him a way out of what I have called his 'special difficulty' — that the culture of which he was a product seemed to offer such unpromising, even inimical, material to what the young man saw as the artistic function — and enabled him to overcome the temptation of simple rejection and negation. Joyce had been tempted, as he tells us in *Stephen Hero*, 'to consider the two worlds [of "reality" and of "art"] as aliens one to another'; Ibsen's lesson was that of Mr Stein, in Conrad's *Lord Jim*, that one must 'in the destructive element immerse'. All this helps to explain the excitement with which Joyce responded to Ibsen's last play in his own first published work. Joyce clearly understands the central issue of *When We Dead Awaken*, commenting on Rubek that 'it strikes him yet more forcibly that there are great gulfs between his art and his life', that he comes to see 'in their true light his own feelings towards his art', and going on to quote:

> *Rubek*. . . . all the talk about the artist's vocation and the artist's mission, and so forth, began to strike me as being very empty and hollow and meaningless at bottom.
> *Maja*. Then what would you put in its place?
> *Rubek*. Life, Maja.[27]

Joyce had to find his own way of treating 'life', of course; but what needs to be emphasised strongly is that even before he had written any creative prose, he had realised that he must commit himself to the reality of Irish subject-matter, however inglorious that matter was. Joyce's only 'escape' from Dublin was not to be through rejecting it, but through a deeper understanding of it, achieved through his art. He 'chooses rather to bend upon these present things'. In that crucial artistic sense, Joyce is committed to Ireland, whatever her imperfections, from the very start. One has had to labour the point to a certain extent, because failure to appreciate it has led to an insistent emphasis on the tone and significance of *Dubliners*, Joyce's first major work, which seems to me to be frequently wrong-headed. Thus Gerald Gould in the *New Statesman* of 27 June 1914, in one of the earliest reviews, though praising Joyce's 'genius', goes on to say of *Dubliners*:

> Mr Joyce seems to regard this objective and dirty and crawling world with the cold detachment of an unamiable god.[28]

And John Gross, in his recent study says that —

> *Dubliners* is above all a work of rejection. Sullen or sluggish, ignoble or despondent, the citizens circulate to no purpose; the very rounds which they stand one another in the pubs come to sound like so many turns of the treadmill. If nothing which exactly deserves to be called tragic happens, neither does anything hopeful or exhilarating — and on every side there is evidence of petty degradation. As the indictment of an entire city, it ranks with Stendhal's unyielding verdict on Grenoble in *La Vie de Henri Brulard*: 'that town which I still hate, for it is there that I learned to know man'.[29]

These fairly representative comments on the 'cold detachment' of *Dubliners* imply that Joyce's attitude to his subject-matter was purely purgative, as it were; he had to 'get Ireland out of his system', indicting and rejecting it. Far from seeing the book as evidence of Joyce's 'classical' commitment to 'these present things', such a reading, undoubtedly influenced by the young Joyce's actual choice of exile, sees it as a necessary act of hatred, a ruthless severing of umbilical ties. Lost in that confusing border country between Joyce's life and his art, many critics respond to *Dubliners* as if the stories are the work of the jaundiced Stephen Dedalus.[30] It is certainly true that Joyce's statements of intent, or description of his aim, have an undoubtedly critical flavour. At an early stage in the composition, he wrote to a friend, C. P. Curran:

> I am writing a series of epicleti — ten — for a paper. I have written one. I call the series *Dubliners* to betray the soul of that hemiplegia or paralysis which many consider a city.[31]

And to his dilatory and dithering publishers, Joyce wrote in terms which confirm the critical, dissective, Flaubertian import of this:

My intention was to write a chapter of the moral history of my country and I chose Dublin for the scene because that city seemed to me the centre of paralysis. I have tried to present it to the indifferent public under four of its aspects: childhood, adolescence, maturity and public life. The stories are arranged in this order. I have written it for the most part in a style of scrupulous meanness . . .[32]

These remarks, and others on the general 'atmosphere' of his stories,[33] might be taken as sufficient proof, especially when buttressed by the appropriate bit of biographical reference, that *Dubliners* is 'above all a work of rejection'.

As if this was not enough, however, we have to take into account here the nature of critical reactions to the elaborateness of Joyce's art. Joyce's own reference to the arranged order of the stories, in the letter cited above, clearly indicates that he wants us to see *Dubliners* as something unified, not a loose bundle of stories held together merely by geographical or topographical setting. And the critics, fortified by their knowledge of the teasing intricacies of the later Joyce, have gladly taken the hint. The thematic unity given by Joyce's conception of Dublin as 'the centre of paralysis' has been explored very fully by the critics. And this is clearly appropriate, given the actual paralysis of the old priest in the opening story 'The Sisters', and the boy-narrator's musing on the word: 'it sounded to me like the name of some maleficent and sinful being. It filled me with fear, and yet I longed to be nearer to it and to look upon its deadly work.' (p. 7). Most critical discussion then goes on to illustrate how the successive stories play variations on this major theme, showing the 'deadly work' of a force almost palpable, threatening, thwarting, and constantly defeating any potentialities for moral or spiritual or emotional development in the self or selves of the various Dubliners depicted. Other suggestively linked or repeated thematic ideas or situations may then be related back to this central matrix, as Peter K. Garrett illustrates in discussing the recurrent fantasies of escape entertained by the Dubliners:

The most frequent form of paralysis is captivity, both imposed by the deadening environment and produced by the characters' own moral weaknesses. Joyce, the artist who achieved self-realization by leaving Ireland, repeatedly writes of characters who can only dream of escape. For the boys of 'An Encounter' and 'Araby' the dream dwells on the Wild West or the exotically named bazaar, but the quests for 'adventures' end in frustration or disappointment. Eveline cannot bring herself to escape to Argentina; in 'The Boarding House' Bob Doran longs 'to ascend through the roof and fly away to another country' ... but is instead trapped into marriage. Already married, Little Chandler in 'A Little Cloud' dreams of becoming a poet and escaping to London, 'to live bravely like Gallaher' ... and in 'The Dead' Gabriel Conroy thinks of going to the Continent to escape Irish provincialism. Repeatedly the impulse toward escape is frustrated; paralysis is reasserted. The characteristic motion of Joyce's Dubliners is not linear flight away from their stifling city but a circular motion, like the obsessive speech of the pervert in 'An Encounter', 'slowly circling round and round in the same orbit' ... The same circle of captivity is described by Lenehan's wanderings in 'Two Gallants' and is acted out by Gabriel Conroy as he tells the story of the old horse that went round and round the monument ... It is the pattern of lives caught in the deadly, paralyzing round of obsession or habit.[34]

I have quoted this at length because it is a clear and intelligent example of 'main-stream' criticism of *Dubliners*, arising from the perception of thematic unity, and indicating towards its conclusion how individual motifs from the separate stories may be seen as serving the informing moral vision of the whole collection. That such a critical approach may also suggest that the experience of reading *Dubliners* becomes a rather automatic 'checking off' of devices intended to denote or connote paralysis, and that the book itself is a somewhat flat, monotonous and monocular application of a restrictive thesis, is an unfortunate side-effect to which we will return.

The critics who stress the thematic unity of the collection are closely related to a school of critics who take the hunt for unity to much greater, and in my view, highly unproductive extremes. Thus, Richard Levin and Charles Shattuck in 'First Flight to Ithaca: A New Reading of Joyce's *Dubliners*' argued in 1944[35] that, like *Ulysses*, these short stories are integrated by a pattern of correspondence to the *Odyssey* of Homer. For example, the 'fine decent tart' of a slavey in 'Two Gallants' is seen as a debased Nausicaa, apparently mainly on the grounds that she wears a blue serge skirt, white blouse and a sailor hat, clothing suggestive of the sea — we must remember that Nausicaa was princess of a seagoing people, and first met Ulysses on the beach. Similarly, and on equally unconvincing grounds, Levin and Shattuck argue that Polly Mooney, the 'little perverse madonna' of 'The Boarding House' is a debased Aphrodite, the foam-born goddess (we must note that Polly's

eyes were 'grey with a shade of green throught them', and the sea is —
sometimes — grey green). And in discussing Gabriel Conroy's carving
of the goose at supper, his speech of tribute to his aunt's hospitality,
and the subsequent events at the Gresham Hotel, they see close parallels to Ulysses's slaughter of the suitors and reunion with Penelope.
'So faithfully does Joyce follow these main lines of Homeric action
that he twice sets asterisks to mark Homeric book-divisions.'[36]

This particular criticism need not detain us long, since the crudity of
the 'retrospective intentionalism', in the attempt to discover patterns of
symbols in *Dubliners* simply *because* Joyce used such patterns in
Ulysses, is obvious.[37] However, the Levin-Shattuck article is of some
historical importance in that it encouraged critics in a feeling that there
must be an unsuspected elaborateness in the art of the stories. Thus
Brewster Ghiselin states:

> To this first demonstration of a latent structural unity in *Dubliners*
> must be added the evidence of its even more full integration by
> means of a symbolic structure so highly organized as to suggest the
> most subtle elaborations of Joyce's methods in his maturity.[38]

Thematic unity ('paralysis'), and even structural unity (the enactment
of the Homeric story) are not enough for Ghiselin; for him it is 'a novel,
the separate histories of its protagonists composing one essential history', 'a movement of the human soul . . . through various conditions of
Christian virtue and stages of deadly sin, toward or away from the font
and the altar and all the gifts of the two chief sacraments provided for
its salvation'.[39] In arguing for this Hibernian version of *The Pilgrim's
Progress*, Ghiselin lays heavy stress on religious images and ideas, especially the 'symbols, sacraments and doctrines of the Catholic Church',
and few foods mentioned by Joyce get away unscathed from the
Ghiselin exegetical net; the wine and crackers of the first story are
obviously sacramental, and Ghiselin goes on: 'Again and again throughout *Dubliners* such substitutes for the sacred elements of the altar
recur, always in a secular guise: "musty buiscuits" and "raspberry
lemonade", porter and "a caraway seed" '[40] (And Lenehan's plate of
peas and ginger beer?)

While comparatively few critics endorse this kind of elaborate analogical exegesis of Joyce's book, it has played a part in encouraging a
pervasive feeling that *Dubliners* is a work of cold dissection, in which
fairly hapless butterflies are pinned to a board by a young artist who
measures the distance between himself and his victims by means of a

virtuosic technique. Frank O'Connor, himself a short story writer, may serve to illustrate my point. O'Connor is by no means an 'analogical exegete', but is clearly aware of the Levin-Shattuck-Ghiselin school, and up to a point goes some of the road with them. O'Connor focuses less on the 'symbolic' details of the individual stories and their integration, however, than on the precision and almost fanatical perfectionism which he sees in Joyce's style. He analyses paragraphs from 'Araby' and 'Two Gallants', and damns Joyce with the praise that he uses words as they had never before been used in English, except by Pater — 'not to describe an experience, but so far as possible to duplicate it. Not even perhaps to duplicate it so much as to replace it by a combination of images — a rhetorician's dream'. This style, according to O'Connor, is intended firstly to exclude the reader from the action, making him merely gaze on beautifully finished images — 'Understanding, indignation, or compassion, which involve us in the action and make us see it in terms of our own character and experience, are not called for'. Secondly, the perfection of style is an oblique but powerful assertion of authorial tyranny; O'Connor says that Joyce 'has deprived his submerged population of autonomy', that it is submerged not so much 'by circumstances but by Joyce's own irony'.[41] Irony here is made up of the remote classical perfection of the style, the clinical placing of significant details, the resolute repression — save on the odd occasion — of any overt statement of authorial attitude.

Thus it is easy to see how critical attention to the qualities of Joyce's art in *Dubliners* feeds into critical emphasis on the hostility of the artist to his subject-matter, and leads to the conclusion of John Gross that *Dubliners* 'is above all a work of rejection'. It is true that only a particularly wrong-headed sentimentalist could see in Joyce's stories a warm and loving book, a sort of Dublin *Cranford*. However, one must surely challenge the implication that concern with style necessarily involves an assertion of the primacy of style. One must reject the more extreme analogical criticism as simply wrong and distorting. In general, the qualities of Joyce's art in the stories — the elements of structural and thematic unity, the care with details, the mastery of juxtaposition, and so on — should not blind us to the possibility that, *pace* O'Connor, 'understanding, indignation and compassion' play an important part in the overall vision of the stories, qualifying the overt and much discussed critical irony.

'Eveline', for example, has generally been seen — when it is noticed at all — as indicating Joyce's unequivocal attitude of ironic contempt for the 'paralysis' afflicting the Dublin denizens who have not the courage to do what Joyce himself did — escape by exile from a stifling environment. The vivid picture of defeated helplessness at the end of the story, when Eveline finds herself unable to get on the ship for Buenos Ayres with her Frank, might be seen as a dramatic snap-shot of paralysed Dublin itself:

> No! No! No! It was impossible. Her hands clutched the iron in frenzy. Amid the seas she sent a cry of anguish! 'Eveline! Evvy!' He rushed beyond the barrier and called to her to follow. He was shouted at to go on, but he still called to her. She set her white face to him, passive, like a helpless animal. Her eyes gave him no sign of love or farewell or recognition.
>
> (pp. 42-3)

One cannot, however, simply separate this conclusion from what has gone before it. Joyce gives us a very full and sympathetic portrait of the psychological pressures of Eveline's situation. The life she has known may not have been particularly pleasant, but it is the only life she has known, and to go to Buenos Ayres is to lose it forever. She is only nineteen, she has her responsibility to her younger brothers and sisters to whom she stands as a mother (and, by implication, a shield against their father's irresponsibility and potential violence), and being a muddled human rather than a clear-headed and decisive critic, she even has some warmth of feeling towards her father:

> Her father was becoming old lately, she noticed; he would miss her. Sometimes he could be very nice. Not long before, when she had been laid up for a day, he had read her out a ghost story and made toast for her at the fire. Another day, when their mother was alive, they had all gone for a picnic to the Hill of Howth. She remembered her father putting on her mother's bonnet to make the children laugh.
>
> (p. 41)

Indeed, Joyce's structuring of his brief story is designed not so much to show that Eveline fails a crucial moral test at the North Wall quay, but to show that the choice, the chance of freedom, was never really there for her. Her nature is subdued to what it works in, like the dyer's hand — the monotonous harshness of her work at the Stores and at home, the wearying squabbles over money to do the shopping, the attempt to keep the house and the residual family together. The very littleness of Eveline's life render her incapable of the momentous step of emigration and exile; but to understand this, as Joyce makes us understand, leads to compassion rather than condemnation. The critical view that would simply classify 'Eveline' as a kind of *quod erat demonstrandum* of the 'paralysis' thesis of *Dubliners* – which is how the story is made to sound, especially by those wishing to stress the artistic unity of the collection – is probably the result, in part, of a sort of buried biographical approach. The closeness of Joyce's works to his life has always caused critical problems. In the case of 'Eveline', critics who fail to register the sympathy in the story are probably in the grip of what Warren Beck has called a 'persistent false stereotype' of Joyce himself; Joyce seen as 'the wholly defiant rebel, whose self-assurance was absolute, whose uprooting produced no wilting, and whose personal severance from everything native to him was as simple as boarding ship'.[42] By the light of this stereotype, Eveline's failure to board ship is to be taken as proof of the author's condemnation of her.

I begin with 'Eveline' because the character is so helpless, the story so economical as to suggest a clinical vivisection, that if one perceives a humane tolerance and sympathy even here, then *a fortiori* one may be more receptive to it in more complex stories. (Joyce must not be sentimentalised, of course; in 'Eveline' the sharpness of eye for the ironic detail – 'the coloured print of the promises made to Blessed Margaret Mary Alacoque' – in a sense helps to validate the paramount note of compassion.) Joyce shows in 'Eveline', also, his wonderful ability to modulate from the impersonal narrator's voice into a voice which is not quite the character's, in any direct sense, but which impersonates, as it were, the character's voice. This 'ventriloqual' shading into the character's mode of speech or thought ('Her father used often to hunt them in out of the field with his blackthorn stick; but usually little Keogh used to keep *nix* and call out when he saw her father coming') goes beyond the routine technique of letting us see things from an individual point of view. In capturing the flavour of the individual's personal idiom, it brings us very close to him or her, and hence is another device by which Joyce may invoke our sympathies.

Thus even Lenehan in 'Two Gallants' is presented to us not entirely unsympathetically, though his aim and the general context of the story make 'the special odour of corruption' which Joyce intended to 'float over' *Dubliners* particularly noticeable. In part it is Joyce's visual details which allow us to see something of Lenehan's desperation:

His breeches, his white rubber shoes, and his jauntily slung waterproof expressed youth. But his figure fell into rotundity at the waist, his hair was scant and grey, and his face, when the waves of expression had passed over it, had a ravaged look.

(p. 52)

But more than this, the stylistic flexibility mentioned above steers us imperceptibly between the narrator's 'neutrality' and Lenehan's perception of the stunted nature of his lonely life:

When he had eaten all the peas he sipped his ginger beer and sat for some time thinking of Corley's adventure. In his imagination he beheld the pair of lovers walking along some dark road; he heard Corley's voice in deep energetic gallantries, and saw again the leer of the young woman's mouth. This vision made him feel keenly his own poverty of purse and spirit. He was tired of knocking about, of pulling the devil by the tail, of shifts and intrigues. He would be thirty-one in November. Would he never get a good job? Would he never have a home of his own? He thought how pleasant it would be to have a warm fire to sit by and a good dinner to sit down to. He had walked the streets long enough with friends and with girls. He knew what those friends were worth: he knew the girls too. Experience had embittered his heart against the world. But all hope had not left him. He felt better after having eaten than he had felt before, less weary of his life, less vanquished in spirit. He might yet be able to settle down in some snug corner and live happily if he could only come across some good simple-minded girl with a little of the ready.

(p. 62)

The passage marks Lenehan's moral and emotional bankruptcy (the colloquial glibness of the last phrase, especially) but marks it from the inside; and while one cannot say *comprendre, c'est tout pardonner*, the effect is much more sympathetic than it would be were the authorial criticism to be overt, *de haut en bas*, as in Joyce's depiction of Mrs Mooney in the next story, 'The Boarding House': 'She dealt with moral problems as a cleaver deals with meat' (p. 68).

Such inner presentation, with its potential for arousing some kind of sympathetic understanding in the reader, is to be found not just in 'Eveline' and 'Two Gallants', but in 'The Sisters', 'An Encounter' and 'Araby', with their boy-narrators, and in 'A Little Cloud' and 'Clay' (where Joyce brilliantly captures the naive sadness of little Maria), to say nothing of 'The Dead'. It is therefore difficult to agree with the implications of S. L. Goldberg's verb when he says that each story 'vivisects its material'.[43] Critical rigidity tends to set in unless the individuality of each story is allowed to emerge from the thematic overview. Thus even a sensitive critic like Peter Garrett, in discussing the motif of fantasies of escape from Dublin in the passage quoted earlier, may produce a distortion. He draws on that dangerous and simplifying biographical contrast that has already been commented on: 'Joyce, the artist who achieved self-realisation by leaving Ireland, repeatedly writes of characters who can only dream of escape'.[44] It follows that 'escape' is a good, and that Eveline should have gone to Argentina; and that the limitations of the escape fantasies themselves — the dream of the Wild West in 'An Encounter', of the exotically titled bazaar in 'Araby', of the spurious European glamour in 'After the Race'— are simply a means by which the artist measures more fully the inept delusions that are cause as well as symptom of the prevailing paralysis. As Garrett puts it — 'Repeatedly the impulse towards escape is frustrated; paralysis is reasserted.'[45]

A brief discussion of 'A Little Cloud' may help to show how this tracing of 'repeated' thematic and moral ideas in *Dubliners* can distort the integrity of the individual story. Little Chandler, the timid clerk, is presented as a second-rate sensitive soul, with buried artistic longings fanned somewhat by the Celtic Twilight spirit of the time. All this Joyce amusingly and incisively delineates:

> He tried to weigh his soul to see if it was a poet's soul. Melancholy was the dominant note of his temperament, he thought, but it was a melancholy tempered by recurrences of faith and resignation and simple joy. If he could give expression to it in a book of poems perhaps men would listen. He would never be popular: he saw that. He could not sway the crowd, but he might appeal to a little circle of kindred minds. The English critics, perhaps, would recognise him as one of the Celtic school by reason of the melancholy tone of his poems; besides that, he would put in allusions . . . It was a pity his name was not more Irish-looking. Perhaps it would be better to insert his mother's name before the surname: Thomas Malone Chandler; or better still: T. Malone Chandler.
>
> (p. 80)

The prospect of meeting, after a long period, his colourful friend Ignatius Gallaher, whom he 'had known under a shabby and necessitous guise', but who is now 'a brilliant figure on the London Press', evokes

in Chandler that distaste for his immediate environment which runs
through many of the Dubliners:

> For the first time his soul revolted against the dull inelegance of
> Capel St. There was no doubt about it: if you wanted to succeed
> you had to go away.
>
> (p. 79)

It quickly turns out that the dream of escape embodied in or symbolised for Chandler by Gallaher is a delusion. Gallaher is a vulgarian,
whose experience of the wider world presents itself merely as salacious
tabloid gossip, whose confident manner is the outward expression of a
mean little egotism. The important point is that Little Chandler sees
through him too − it is not left simply to the reader to measure the
ironic disparity between *his* valuation of the patronising loud-mouth
and Little Chandler's. For Chandler begins to 'feel somewhat disillu-
sioned', is not pleased by Gallaher's 'accent and way of expressing himself', senses 'something vulgar in his friend which he had not observed
before'. And he quickly picks up the tone suggestive of the return of
the conquering hero to a provincial backwater, everywhere in Gallaher's
remarks, as well as the significance of Gallaher's 'little card-party' that
will preclude a visit to Chandler's home:

> He was sure that he could do something better than his friend had
> ever done, or could ever do, something higher than mere tawdry
> journalism if he only got the chance. What was it that stood in his
> way? His unfortunate timidity! He wished to vindicate himself in
> some way, to assert his manhood. He saw behind Gallaher's refusal
> of his invitation. Gallaher was only patronizing him by his friend-
> liness just as he was patronizing Ireland by his visit.
>
> (p. 88)

Thus, though still attracted by the idea of escape, Chandler has sufficient insight to perceive the hollowness of what Gallaher stands for.
The coda of the story describes with great economy how Chandler faces
and treats another temptation − an introspective plunging into Byronic
posturing, a caressing of his own 'melancholy' as another kind of escape-
route from 'the thin tight lips' and the 'unconscious and ladylike' face
of his wife. Torn between a voluptuous melancholic fantasising and the
insistent reality of his baby boy's wailing crying, his tension and self-
control snaps in a shouted imprecation which terrifies the baby. (In all
his work, Joyce is a brilliant portrayer of the frayed nerve-ends and
petty tragedies of humdrum domesticity.) The shock of reality cauter-

ises his Byronic fantasising ('It was useless, useless! He was a prisoner for life'), and the story ends:

> Little Chandler felt his cheeks suffused with shame and he stood back out of the lamp light. He listened while the paroxysm of the child's sobbing grew less and less; and tears of remorse started to his eyes.
>
> (p. 94)

Again the important point is that Little Chandler himself has reached a perception quite close to the reader's own. (He is, in this respect, quite deliberately contrasted with Farrington, another 'child-abuser', in the next story 'Counterparts'.) Such a perception, and such a version of the alternatives to Dublin life, make it hard to fit 'A Little Cloud' into that pre-set critical mould: 'Repeatedly the impulse towards escape is frustrated; paralysis is reasserted', in Garrett's words. One could just as legitimately say that Joyce is criticising, in stories like 'A Little Cloud' which involve dreams of escape, that 'romantic temper' which will not 'bend to these present things'. Life, even in Dublin, is not something to be simply rejected; the characters are not necessarily to find their self-realisation by taking the extreme step of their creator. And in so far as even the naive and timid clerk Chandler comes himself to see in his own way that a proper perception and insight into his own situation is the beginning of wisdom, to that extent is his situation not quite hopeless. The irony with which Joyce treats him is not corrosive, and is balanced by sympathetic understanding, itself a product of Little Chandler's own ability to understand.

Many critics of *Dubliners* have, quite rightly, explained Joyce's fictional method in terms of the notion of epiphany, defined in *Stephen Hero*:

> By an epiphany he [Stephen] meant a sudden spiritual manifestation, whether in the vulgarity of speech or of gesture or in a memorable phase of the mind itself. He believed it was for the man of letters to record these epiphanies with extreme care, seeing that they themselves are the most delicate and evanescent of moments.
>
> (p. 216)

Joyce himself collected such 'showings forth', usually of spiritual or emotional hollowness revealed in tiny or trivial incidents or fragments of dialogue.[46] But in *Dubliners* he extends the principle to make the whole story, often flat and trivial in itself, resonant with larger meanings which the 'open-ended' form of the stories (ending often, as in 'The

Sisters', 'Counterparts' and 'Grace' abruptly in the midst of dialogue) leaves to crystallise in the reader's mind. We must take note, however, that the *Stephen Hero* formulation distinguishes two kinds of epiphany, one where the extended insight depends chiefly upon the reader, and one where the character in the story, 'in a memorable phase of the mind itself' perceives as much, or almost as much, as the reader and the author. The 'naturalistic-objective' epiphany, and the 'subjective-psychological' (to borrow Warren Beck's terminoloy) produce quite different effects and tones. Where we have stories of the first kind, in which the 'vulgarity' or hopelessness of the characters is made quite clear to us, but is veiled from the characters by their crassness, moral sloth or ignorance, the effect is that of Flaubertian ironic dissection. Such stories would be 'After the Race', 'The Boarding House', 'Counterparts', 'Ivy Day in the Committee Room', 'A Mother' and 'Grace'. Eveline and Maria may hardly be said to understand themselves and their situations, but the evident sympathy of the author with them must make one hesitant about placing 'Eveline' and 'Clay' with this more satiric group of stories. And it might be remarked in passing that Joyce's evident relish of the conversational eccentricities of his father's seedy-genteel Dublin world, captured so perfectly in the dialogue of 'Ivy Day' and 'Grace' and to bear such magnificent humorous fruit in *Ulysses*, qualifies the hostility of the satiric intent of those stories.

In the second kind of story, 'The Sisters', 'An Encounter', 'Araby', 'A Little Cloud', 'A Painful Case' and — pre-eminently — 'The Dead', the 'subjective-psychological' nature of the epiphanies is indicated by the characters' coming to an increased awareness. This may be melancholy, as in 'A Little Cloud', or bitter, as in 'Araby', or even a kind of death, as in 'A Painful Case'.[47] But what one wishes to stress is that such stories — a not inconsiderable proportion of the whole — are evidence of Joyce's refusal to throw the blanket of 'paralysis' over all his Dubliners. *Pace* O'Connor, he does not deprive all of his submerged population of 'autonomy' — they have capacities for insight, even growth. They are human, after all, and we are allowed to feel their humanity, perhaps the more touchingly because their lives are minor and obscure. *Dubliners*, in fact, far from being the product of an aloof and sardonic artificer, may be seen as the first clear evidence of the 'democratic spirit' — for want of a better phrase — which informs Joyce's writing. Or, as Warren Beck puts it, more polemically:

. . . in *Dubliners* he avoided modern literature's two offences against the spirit — the first a pseudo-aristocratic or coterie presumption

that acute awareness is the prerogative of an elite, however consti-
tuted; or secondly, a fictitious repeopling of the world with jerky
automata to enact the artist's delusion that his own absurdity is
universal but a comprehension of it is his unique gift.[48]

Indeed, the very concept of the epiphany marks Joyce's openness to
experience, his reverence for the real. The ordinary phenomena of an
objective, 'real' world may be instinct with meanings for the attentive
observer, not, as in the *chosisme* of the French new novel, or in the
artfully contrived bafflement of absurdist literature, merely proof of
the random contingency of the world. The artistic method of *Dubliners*,
based on the epiphany notion, implies a relationship of respect between
the artist and the subject-matter he chooses for his material. As Joyce
had said in 1900, in words with a strong bearing on my argument for
seeing *Dubliners* as less restricted to the ironic demonstration of a mor-
dant thesis than most critics allow:

> Still I think out of the dreary sameness of existence, a measure of
> dramatic life may be drawn. Even the most commonplace, the
> deadest among the living, may play a part in a great drama ... Life
> we must accept as we see it before our eyes, men and women as we
> meet them in the real world, not as we apprehend them in the world
> of faery. The great human comedy in which each has share, gives
> limitless scope to the true artist ...[49]

These words from 'Drama and Life' read almost like a prospectus for
Dubliners.

For all the book's complexity, the principles behind the thematic
organisation of *A Portrait of the Artist as a Young Man* are indicated to
us in an almost schematic way in Stephen's excited words to his friend
Cranly during their last long conversation together, which develops
from Stephen's 'unpleasant quarrel' with his mother about his lapse
from religious observances. Stephen says:

> I will not serve that in which I no longer believe, whether it call itself
> my home, my fatherland, or my church: and I will try to express
> myself in some mode of life or art as freely as I can and as wholly as
> I can, using for my defence the only arms I allow myself to use —
> silence, exile, and cunning.

(p. 251)

This summarises the action of the book which we have been reading – the story of Stephen's rebellion against the three forces which have in different ways threatened his freedom; his family, Ireland, with its curious mixture of moral torpor and political fanaticism, and the Church, that 'grey spouse of Satan'. And there is the complementary story of Stephen finding his sense of identity as an artist.

A quick reading of *A Portrait of the Artist as a Young Man* might well cause the reader to hesitate before assenting to the view of *Dubliners* which I have tried to argue, because *A Portrait* seems to assert the principles of the absolute heroism of the artist and the nullity of the *canaille* who surround him. To read it thus, however, is to read the book too quickly. While Joyce allows Stephen due credit for his idealistic commitment to art, the major thrust of the novel is directed towards emphasising the necessary – and indeed inescapable – ties between 'life', however unglamorous, and 'art'. Thus the artistic vision behind *Dubliners* is being re-stated and re-worked in a more complex and more ironic mode.

No reader has any difficulty in assenting to the power of the forces Stephen faces. The two great bravura exhibitions of Joyce's art in the novel, the argument over Parnell at the Christmas dinner-table, justly celebrated as one of the great episodes of modern European fiction, and the massive sermons on death and hell in the third chapter, are absolutely convincing. In the first, Stephen is 'terror-stricken', in the second, he ends up vomiting 'profusely in agony'. Almost as good is the novel's precise notation of the Dedalus family squalor, rendered with a scrupulous meanness of description carried over, as it were, from *Dubliners*: the watery tea, the crusts of fried bread, the yellow dripping, the box of pawn tickets, its lid 'speckled with louse-marks', and all the furniture (including the grotesquely inaccurate and battered alarm-clock) of the breakfast-table described at the beginning of the fifth chapter enforce a sense of violent disjunction between Stephen's imaginative world and the sordid reality which surrounds him.

The power of these forces ranged against Stephen, and the convincingness with which they are realised in Joyce's art, give Stephen's rebellion and his commitment to personal freedom a markedly heroic flavour, embodied in the rhetoric of his Luciferian *non serviam* quoted above. From one point of view, Stephen is the artist as hero, and many aspects of Joyce's presentation of him support such a reading. He recognises, for instance, and is ready to face, the isolation attendant on the artistic vocation. He goes on to say to Cranly in the episode already cited:

I do not fear to be alone or to be spurned for another or to leave whatever I have to leave. And I am not afraid to make a mistake, even a great mistake, a lifelong mistake, and perhaps as long as eternity too.

(p. 251)

This is not a remark made on the spur of the moment. Earlier, after his interview with the priest who tries to persuade him to enter a Jesuit novitiate, Stephen reflects that 'his destiny was to be elusive of social or religious orders', that he 'was destined to learn his own wisdom apart from others or to learn the wisdom of others himself wandering among the snares of the world' (p. 165). So this is a chosen isolation — the artist stands apart from the common herd. The heroic implications of this posture are a commonplace in the literature of romanticism; further, the reader of Joyce will compare Stephen's stance with the words of Joyce himself, first in the polemic broadside 'The Day of the Rabblement' (1901):

No man, said the Nolan, can be a lover of the true or the good unless he abhors the multitude; and the artist, though he may employ the crowd, is very careful to isolate himself.[50]

And in the satirical squib of 1904, 'The Holy Office' Joyce again makes of isolation a cardinal virtue:

Where they have crouched and crawled and prayed
I stand the self-doomed, unafraid,
Unfellowed, friendless and alone,
Indifferent as the herring-bone,
Firm as the mountain-ridges where
I flash my antlers on the air.[51]

The romantic rhetoric of this is as extreme as anything to be found in Stephen's often over-heated musings on the artist's destiny in *A Portrait*.

Further, in Stephen's allusions to 'wandering among the snares of the world' and to his willingness to risk 'a lifelong mistake', another attribute of the heroically isolated artist is implied. That is his omnivorous appetite for experience, his readiness to encounter and suffer the moral abysses, the craters of the spirit, to fall and sin in his existential quest, to be willing to enter 'the gates of all the ways of error and glory', as Stephen puts it to himself at the moment of his ecstatic apprehension of his true vocation. Indeed, it may even be said that the courage 'to err, to fall' is the *sine qua non* of the artist's separate and special powers, marking him off most firmly from the timid common souls. Thus Stephen remarks to Davin, in a famous passage, in defence of the more lurid aspects of his private life which he has revealed to the shocked young nationalist:

> The soul is born . . . first in those moments I told you of. It has a slow and dark birth, more mysterious than the birth of the body. When the soul of a man is born in this country there are nets flung at it to hold it back from flight. You talk to me of nationality, language, religion. I shall try to fly by those nets.
>
> (p. 207)

This idea is rephrased by the Stephen of *Ulysses*, who remarks of Shakespeare: 'A man of genius makes no mistakes. His errors are volitional and are the portals of discovery.'[52]

The reader's sense of Stephen's heroic apartness is based not only on what he says or thinks explicitly about it, but on a vivid and dramatic contrast, set up especially in the last chapter, between himself and the dull and muddy-mettled fellows who are his university acquaintances. They are concerned almost solely with worldly success — with the passing of examinations, with getting jobs, with earnest measurings of the relative merits of posts in Liverpool as against Irish country practices. A persistent, if relatively unobtrusive, imagery marks the appearance of these acquaintances. Moynihan's face is 'snoutish', Temple's expression is 'equine', his mouth 'flecked by a thin foam' and his voice 'bleating', Lynch's head 'brought before Stephen's mind the image of a hooded reptile'; Donovan is pig-like, his small fat-encircled eyes 'vanishing in his pallid bloated face'; and Cranly's favourite term of abuse is 'bloody ape'. Stephen's attempt to forge courageously his aesthetic theory in this unpromising context enables us to see him almost literally as one condemned to cast pearls before swine.

The heroic implications in Stephen's view of art and the artist reach their logical, if most extreme, point at the end of his discourse to Lynch on aesthetics, when he proclaims that the artist is like the 'God of creation', that there is an analogy between 'the mystery of aesthetic' and 'that of material creation' (p. 219). The assumption of godlike powers here is obviously connected with Stephen's half-serious, half-whimsical casting of Cranly in the role of confessorial John the Baptist to Stephen as Messiah ('Then he is the precursor. Item: he eats chiefly belly bacon and dried figs' (p. 252.)) and with the tone of such rhapsodic musings as 'O! in the virgin womb of the imagination the word was made flesh' (p. 221). Even if he does not consistently attribute to himself godlike or messianic powers, Stephen's view of the artist's role is consistently sacramental. As Cranly says to him, 'Your mind is super-saturated with the religion in which you say you disbelieve.' (p. 244). So it is perhaps inevitable that he sees himself as 'a priest of the eternal imagination, transmuting the daily bread of experience into the radiant body of ever-living life' (p. 225), and that his aesthetic theory is mainly a transvaluation of religion concepts. The point here is that such a self-conception increases the flavour of the heroic surrounding Stephen, not only in its own claim, but since it calls to our mind the numerous un-flattering portraits of literal priests in the novel. One need only com-pare Father Arnall's method of working on the conscience to Stephen's heroic aspiration, based on a conception of the artist as priest, 'to forge in the smithy of my soul the uncreated conscience of my race' (p. 257).

Joyce seems to underpin this view of Stephen as isolated, daring, courageous artist-hero in a striking way, by departing from naturalistic probabilities in the imposition of the unlikely name of Dedalus on this Irish family. Though critics have argued that there is an ironic emphasis in this bold use of mythic symbolism, that Stephen is more probably to be identified with the hubristic son of Daedalus, the Icarus whose 'waxen wings did mount above his reach', as Marlowe put it, the posi-tive implications of the name are more evident in the novel. This is especially marked at the crucial moment of Stephen's perception of his vocation in Chapter 4:

> Now, as never before, his strange name seemed to him a prophecy
> . . . Now, at the name of the fabulous artificer, he seemed to hear
> the noise of dim waves and to see a winged form flying above the
> waves and slowly climbing the air. What did it mean? Was it a quaint
> device opening a page of some medieval book of prophecies and
> symbols, a hawk-like man flying sunward above the sea, a prophecy
> of the end he had been born to serve and had been following through
> the mists of childhood and boyhood, a symbol of the artist forging
> anew in his workshop out of the sluggish matter of the earth a new
> soaring impalpable imperishable being?
>
>   (p. 173)

That Stephen is not shown realising the artistic potential in him in any concrete way (or, at least, convincing way, since the villanelle is a watery performance) in the novel does not mean that the reader must take passages like this ironically. In the context of oppressive banality which surrounds him, and which is so finely captured with Joyce's

laconic mastery, Stephen's search for himself, and his high-minded
aspirations, do show up in a very favourable light. Joyce believed that
the artist must 'disentangle the subtle soul of the image from its mesh
of defining circumstances' and re-embody it in art — another statement
of the concept of epiphany. To do this, he must disentangle himself
first from his own mesh of defining circumstances, 'fly by those nets',
as Stephen puts it to Davin. This is a brave, even noble, undertaking,
and *A Portrait* presents it as such. Rejecting the fashionable ironic
reading of the book[53] which turns the portrait of the artist into 'the
dissection of a second-rate aesthete', John Gross says — rightly, in my
view — that

> . . . the tone and over-all momentum of the book . . . are not prim-
> arily those of a cautionary tale. If they were, and if Stephen's condi-
> tion was really hopeless, Joyce could legitimately be taxed with a
> certain gratuitous cruelty: why dispatch so small a victim at such
> length, in such intimate detail, when he might have been decently
> disposed of in a short story?[54]

What Joyce does in *A Portrait* is to measure, with great psychological
penetration and even with compassion (qualities for which the word
'irony' is a poor and misleading substitute), the cost of Stephen's 'brave
undertaking', the cost in human terms and also in terms of art.

First, it is clear that the isolation which the young man proudly
displays as proof of his credentials as an artist is not just or simply a
freely chosen stance, a commitment of the will, but deeply rooted in
Stephen's psychology, something into which he is from an early age
conditioned. To the young boy at school, feeble of body and weak of
sight, hanging around the edge of the football game, 'all the boys
seemed to him very strange'. He does not understand their language,
bemused by Athy's sexual references in the infirmary, baffled by the
meaning of 'smugging'. He must go alone to confront the rector, aware
that 'all the fellows were looking after him as they went filing by'.
Home, which might have proved a rock of security in counterpoise to
the disagreeable life of school, becomes merely another focus of his isolation, as his terrified ignorance tries to comprehend the furious passions
of the adults at the Christmas dinner-table. The boy's detachment, a
concomitant of his sense of isolation, is clearly in origin a purely defensive reaction to ugly realities pressing in on him:

He was angry with himself for being young and the prey of restless

foolish impulses, angry also with the change of fortune which was
reshaping the world about him into a vision of squalor and insin-
cereity. Yet his anger lent nothing to the vision. He chronicled with
patience what he saw, detaching himself from it and tasting its
mortifying flavour in secret.

(p. 69)

His academic abilities, and the achievements attained despite his consciousness of the 'squalor of his own mind and home' only serve to isolate him further — rebuked by a teacher at Belvedere for 'heresy' in an
essay, he is aware of 'a vague general malignant joy' among his class-
mates, though 'nobody spoke to him of the affair'. In the brilliantly
depicted episode of the visit to Cork with his father, Stephen's loneliness reaches new levels of intensity because of the virulence of his sense
of sin; the real world becomes insubstantial to him, his past has 'faded
out like a film in the sun', and he needs to repeat his name and the
name of his father and their hotel to hold on to a sense of identity. His
father's maudlin but real gregariousness aggravates the problem:

Stephen watched the three glasses being raised from the counter as
his father and his two cronies drank to the memory of their past.
An abyss of fortune or of temperament sundered him from them.
His mind seemed older than theirs: it shone coldly on their strifes
and happiness and regrets like a moon upon a younger earth. No life
or youth stirred in him as it had stirred in them.

(p. 98)

The fears and terrors of childhood, the family's slide into squalor,
and his overpowering sense of sin and guilt, are just as important in
shaping Stephen's sense of isolation as anything we may be inclined to
attribute to the 'artistic temperament'. In fact, Joyce's penetrating
study of the psychology of this isolated individual could be interpreted
along familiar Freudian lines; Stephen embraces art as a compensation
for his loneliness or psychological deformation, and his proclamation of
the value of isolation to the artist is simply making a virtue of necessity.
As he develops, he sees his problem clearly:

He saw clearly too his own futile isolation. He had not gone one step
nearer the lives he had sought to approach nor bridged the restless
shame and rancour that had divided him from mother and brother
and sister. He felt that he was hardly of the one blood with them but

stood to them rather in the mystical kinship of fosterage, fosterchild and fosterbrother. (p. 101)

But to see the problem is not to solve it. Much later, after his repentance, he still finds it easier to try to love God than to try to love his neighbour, knowing that 'to merge his life in the common tide of other lives was harder for him than any fasting or prayer'; and there is a certain inevitability in his answer to Cranly's question — 'Do you love your mother?':

> Stephen shook his head slowly.
> — I don't know what your words mean, he said simply.
>
> (p. 244)

This retreat from reality, the fear or timidity in response to the otherness of other people, the refusal to commit himself in an outgoing way to the world, is a marked pattern in Stephen's psychological make-up, and there is a considerable irony in his final rhapsodic entry in his diary: 'Welcome, O life! I go to encounter for the millionth time the reality of experience'. But the irony is not cold or hostile; Stephen has been rendered so intimately, and the psychological pressures on him so concretely, that the reader does not feel disposed to condemn. Besides, we should not lose sight of the simple but important point that at the close of the novel Stephen is still very young.

It is only when we have some understanding of Stephen as an 'ordinary' human being that we can begin to understand the significance of art to him, the peculiar direction his theory of art takes him in, and the large theme of Joyce's novel which is the relationship of art and life. In a sense we may say that Stephen's isolation, stemming from fear (in various shapes and guises) connects with a desire for the safety of a substitute world of words. This process, too, begins early in his life.

Words are intensely, almost tactilely, real for Stephen, their associations unpredictable but vivid, as we see when the schoolboy phrase 'McGlade's suck' leads his mind to the washbasin of the Wicklow Hotel. They may be beautiful, like 'wine', or sinister and baffling, like 'smugging'. Significantly, they offer from the first an escape from painful reality. Stephen calls up, in the misery of the cold football field, the little spelling jingle 'Wolsey died in Leicester Abbey' and reflects:

> It would be nice to lie on the hearthrug before the fire, leaning his head upon his hands, and think of those sentences.
>
> (p. 10)

And in the infirmary, he remembers the doleful dirge that his nurse Brigid has taught him ('Farewell, my mother!/Bury me in the old churchyard/Beside my eldest brother . . .'):

> How beautiful and sad that was! How beautiful the words were where they said *Bury me in the old churchyard*! A tremor passed over his body. How sad and how beautiful! He wanted to cry quietly but not for himself: for the words, so beautiful and sad, like music.
>
> (p. 24-5)

More interestingly, we see him shape and alter reality to fit his verbal world, in the passage where he interprets the young Eileen's sexual flirtatiousness in terms of phrases from the liturgy. Eileen's hands are 'like ivory; only soft':

> She had put her hand into his pocket where his hand was and he had felt how cool and thin and soft her hand was. She had said that pockets were funny things to have: and then all of a sudden she had broken away and had run laughing down the sloping curve of the path. Her fair hair had streamed out behind her like gold in the sun. *Tower of Ivory. House of Gold.* By thinking of things you could understand them.
>
> (p. 44)

The irony of this last sentence is clear.

But again, Joyce is not asking us to judge the boy Stephen harshly. It would clearly be ridiculous to put that kind of weight on these examples of Stephen's early obsession with words, to condemn him as someone for whom words replace people, objects and sensations. He is a boy. What is important about Joyce's depiction of Stephen's early life is that it renders the shape of his mind, makes psychologically justified and even inevitable his flight to words as substitute or compensation for chill realities. Thus, for example, we are prepared for this typical reaction of the older Stephen, sunk in sin but prefect of the sodality of the Blessed Virgin Mary.

> The imagery of the psalms of prophecy soothed his barren pride . . . When it fell to him to read the lesson towards the close of the office he read it in a veiled voice, lulling his conscience to its music.
>
> (p. 108)

This pattern reasserts itself constantly; Stephen's instinct of remorse at the poverty and neglected state of his brothers and sisters, his 'pain of spirit' at the weariness behind their innocent voices singing glees in the sordid family kitchen, glides easily into and is quelled by a literary allusion, full of the comforting music of generalisation:

> And he remembered that Newman had heard this note also in the broken lines of Virgil, *giving utterance, like the voice of Nature herself, to that pain and weariness yet hope of better things which has been the experience of her children in every time*.
>
> (p. 168)

A harmless and wholly understandable configuration of the boy's psychology has clearly hardened into an habitual pattern of mind in the young man; language, especially literary language, has become his narcotic.

Books, naturally, exert a potent influence on the young Stephen, and again the tendency is for him to prefer their insubstantial images to the reality around him, and indeed to interpret reality in the terms of those images. Besotted with the image of Mercedes from *The Count of Monte Cristo*, he abandons his boyish games — 'he wanted to meet in the real world the unsubstantial image which his soul so constantly beheld'. His initial reaction to Dublin, after the sudden flight 'from the comfort and revery of Blackrock', is coloured by his reading. He wanders through the docks and quays, noting the corks 'bobbing on the surface of the water in a thick yellow scum', the bales of merchandise and the crowds of porters, but this new and busy world produces within him a feeling of dissatisfaction:

> . . . amid this new bustling life he might have fancied himself in another Marseille but that he missed the bright sky and the sun-warmed trellises of the wineshops. A vague dissatisfaction grew up within him as he looked on the quays and on the river and on the lowering skies and yet he continued to wander up and down day after day as if he really sought someone that eluded him.
>
> (p. 68)

All this, again, is a commonplace of romantic adolescence; but in the case of Stephen, with this strongly introverted and introspective nature, it bites deeper than usual. So that we find him near the end of the novel conveying to his diary his still-powerful desire to seek out 'unsubstantial images':

> Michael Robartes remembers forgotten beauty and, when his arms
> wrap her round, he presses in his arms the loveliness which has long
> faded from the world. Not this. Not at all. I desire to press in my
> arms the loveliness which has not yet come into the world.
>
> (p. 255)

Even a Dublin prostitute, with her patter and her 'huge doll . . . with
her legs apart in the copious easy-chair beside the bed', cannot escape
the shadow of Mercedes. In Stephen's fantasy, he meets Mercedes in a
quiet trysting place, and in a moment of 'supreme tenderness', as he
imagines it, 'weakness and timidity and inexperience would fall from
him'. In the middle of the narrow dirty streets and 'foul laneways' of
Dublin's night-town, Mercedes manifests herself: 'Goodnight, Willie
dear!'. And the literary fantasy, obscene doll notwithstanding, takes its
shape:

> In her arms he felt that he had suddenly become strong and fearless
> and sure of himself.
>
> (p. 104)

The verbal counterpoint between this and the weakness, timidity, and
inexperience of the earlier reference is too deliberate to be accidental.

Stephen's two attempts at creative writing – both poems to 'E–C–',
as he Byronically calls her – reveal again the extent of the gap between
Stephen's world of words, and reality. Joyce describes brilliantly the
vivacious, flirtatious girl, 'sprays of her fresh warm breath' hanging
gaily in the frosty air, the stirred but timid boy, the 'lank brown horses'
of the last tram rubbing their noses together, and the frustration of the
boy alone on the deserted tram: 'he tore his ticket into shreds and
stared gloomily at the corrugated footboard'. It is precisely these
details, bringing the scene so vividly to life, which Stephen filters out in
his poem on the event:

> . . . all those elements which he deemed common and insignificant
> fell out of the scene. There remained no trace of the tram itself nor
> of the tram-men nor of the horses: nor did he and she appear vividly.
> The verses told only of the night and the balmy breeze and the
> maiden lustre of the moon . . . [When he had finished] he went into
> his mother's bedroom and gazed at his face for a long time in the
> mirror of her dressing-table.
>
> (pp. 72-3)

The distaste for 'corrugated footboards' in the sanctified realm of early love poems, and the soulful narcissism of adolescence, we are all familiar with and have experienced, no doubt, for ourselves. But this is, if not damningly conclusive, one more stroke in a cumulative portrait of how the boy and adolescent may be father to the young man.

For the famous villanelle, on which so much critical ink has been spilt, is surely simply a more complex version of the same process of aesthetic filtering which the younger Stephen employed on his tryst at the last tram. In each case, the poem is ludicrously at odds with the world of real experience out of which it comes. The composition of the villanelle is described in terms which suggest a masturbatory fantasy — 'Towards dawn he awoke . . . His soul was all dewy wet . . . Her nakedness yielded to him . . . and like a cloud of vapour or like waters circumfluent in space the liquid letters of speech, symbols of the element of mystery, flowed forth over his brain' (p. 221). It is made 'from cloud on cloud of vague circumstance', and is, in its way, a rather good specimen of the 'yellow book' poetry of the decadent nineties, the 'lure of the fallen seraphim' a poetic analogue to one of Beardsley's drawings. The critical point is partly the disparity between the languorous *femme fatale* of Stephen's poem and the real girl who flirts with Father Moran, or who might read out his poem over the tapping of egg-shells at breakfast (memories and previsions which accompany the composition of the poem). The poet, of course, has always the right to cast over his subject 'the light that never was, on sea or land'. We may feel here, however, that Stephen's 'light' is unusually lurid. What the whole episode stresses also is the fragility of Stephen's creative impulse, and — again — the way in which it represents a desire to escape from realities. The merest touch of the 'sordid' paralyses Stephen's inspiration:

> Smoke went up from the whole earth, from the vapoury oceans, smoke of her praise. The earth was like a swinging swaying censer, a ball of incense, an ellipsoidal fall. The rhythm died out at once; the cry of his heart was broken.

(p. 222)

A fine example of the subtlety of Joyce's indirect presentation, this passage is meant to recall to us the context which the word 'ellipsoidal' has in Stephen's subconscious mind, a context inimical to his fragile verses. At the physics lecture, the professor's attempt to distinguish between 'elliptical' and 'ellipsoidal' had prompted Moynihan's lewd jeer — 'What price ellipsoidal balls! chase me, ladies, I'm in the cavalry!'

Stephen's imaginative world is a world of 'beauty', in the most Paterian sense of the word, and it cannot survive the merest brush of the wing of an alternative world. (Joyce insists on the point by his very refusal to underline, in any explicit way, the significance of the word 'ellipsoidal'. The cry of Stephen's imagination is broken on a tenuous association.

Many details in Joyce's presentation of the process of Stephen's making the poem indicate how, for the young man at this stage, 'art' is an escape, a separate world. Again, there is no point in being severely moralistic about this. Joyce is ready to make us see the admirable side of Stephen's struggle to create in spite of depressing surroundings – we register the lumpy pillow, the candlestick with the paper socket, the dirty plate from last night's supper, the substitution for proper paper of the cigarette packet with – a fine touch – its one cigarette, and we register these with full force. But there is such a violent contrast between that world and the lavish-limbed erotic paradise of the villanelle, that we are alerted to the obviously compensatory nature of Stephen's imaginative excursion:

> He spoke the verses aloud from the first lines till the music and rhythm suffused his mind, turning it to quiet indulgence . . . The full morning light had come. No sound was to be heard; but he knew that all around him life was about to awaken in common noises, hoarse voices, sleepy prayers. Shrinking from that life he turned towards the wall, making a cowl of the blanket and staring at the great overblown scarlet flowers of the tattered wallpaper. He tried to warm his perishing joy in their scarlet glow.
>
> (p. 226)

The 'rose and ardent light' of his initial inspiration declines into the tattered wallpaper flowers, as 'overblown' as Stephen's own style. 'The priest of the eternal imagination', as Stephen has seen himself only a few lines before, becomes the comic 'shrinking' monk, cowled in his blanket, his face to the wall.[55]

In other words, this Stephen, like the earlier creation in *Stephen Hero*, has 'all but decided to consider the two worlds [the real and the imaginative] as aliens one to another', and in many ways Joyce presents the Stephen of the later book as being at greater hazard. Stephen in *A Portrait* does not find a saving mediator in Ibsen, and seems more fully committed to his substitute world of words. What we have seen so far would certainly bear out Harry Levin's point:

> Emotion is integrated, from first to last, by words. Feelings, as they

filter through Stephen's sensory apparatus, become associated with phrases. His conditioned reflexes are literary.[56]

And he goes on to make the point that Stephen 'exalts the habit of verbal association into a principle for the arrangement of experience'. Stephen may thus make a neat, self-enclosed — and hence safe — world for himself, and his love for, and power over, words may even lend his verbal universe an appealing intensity or beauty. But the price paid is a high one. 'Words alone are certain good?' Stephen's mind drives a wedge between itself and what Charles Tomlinson calls 'the proper plenitude of fact',[57] and in doing so, shuts him off damagingly from the fertile realities of experience. People, places and objects dwindle into mere items of furniture in Stephen's mind. The characteristic emphasis on the word over the thing signified by the word, and the equally characteristic subjectivity of his associative processes are neatly illustrated by his musing on 'ivory', a word in his head itself because of its link with another word, 'ivy':

The word now shone in his brain, clearer and brighter than any ivory sawn from the mottled tusks of elephants. *Ivory, ivoire, avorio, ebur*. One of the first examples that he had learnt in Latin had run: *India mittit ebur*; and he recalled the shrewd northern face of the rector who had taught him to construe the Metamorphoses of Ovid in a courtly English, made whimsical by the mention of porkers and potsherds and chines of bacon.

(pp. 182-3)

Dublin itself becomes merely a trigger for Stephen's literary reflexes —

The rainladen trees of the avenue evoked in him, as always, memories of the girls and women in the plays of Gerhart Hauptmann . . . His morning walk across the city had begun, and he fore-knew that as he passed the sloblands of Fairview he would think of the cloistral silver-veined prose of Newman; that as he walked along the North Strand Road, glancing idly at the windows of the provision shops, he would recall the dark humour of Guido Cavalcanti and smile; that as he went by Baird's stonecutting works in Talbot Place the spirit of Ibsen would blow through him like a keen wind, a spirit of wayward boyish beauty; and that passing a grimy marine dealer's shop beyond the Liffey he would repeat the song by Ben Jonson which begins:

I was not wearier where I lay.

(pp. 179-80)

The measure of Stephen's trapped subjectivity of response here, his heavily literary approach to reality is given by Leopold Bloom's alert and unceasing interest in the details — sights, sounds, and smells — of the physical life of his Dublin (and for that matter, by the Stephen of *Ulysses* attempting himself to move towards Bloom's attitude, to 'hold to the now, the here' of experience).

It is, of course, Stephen's tendency to substitute words, literary allusions, and associative patterns of verbal symbolism for people, for the realities of human relationships, that marks most damagingly how violent a grip the disease of the 'romantic temper' has on him — as James Maddox glosses it, 'the disease of seeing the world as subservient to one's own imperial self'.[58] We have already seen how his mind evades the human pain implicit in the sight of his neglected brothers and sisters by transmuting the experience into some phrases from the cloistral silver-veined prose of Newman. Emma Clery is the chief focus for Stephen's evasive literary strategies. Unable, as even the first mention of their meeting in the novel (at the last tram after the party) makes clear, to approach Emma directly, Stephen images her in a series of symbolic or iconographic displacements which gratify his literary imagination while shifting her out of the area of possible positive action. Yeats found balm for his frustrations in transmuting the living Maud Gonne into the archetypal — and mythically unapproachable — Helen of Troy. In a naturally more adolescent mode, Stephen prefers to see Emma as either the temptress of his villanelle, or the 'bat-like soul' symbolising 'the secret of her race'. And, further, as Charles Peake well says, discussing Stephen's views of Emma as manifested in the last chapter:

> Emma is for Stephen a female body in which his imagination can locate the sexual appeal of the prostitute, the spiritual uplift of the Virgin and the rhapsodic inspiration of the Muse-girl on the shore.[59]

The metamorphoses of Emma are necessary for Stephen because 'she is also the chief threat to his assumed detachment'. Towards the end of the novel, Stephen himself momentarily sees that he has buried Emma (who may well *be* a simple, boring Irish *bourgeoisie*) under the weight of his own literary fantasising. He describes in his diary how he has met her in Grafton Street, and how she enquired in a friendly way about his plans.

> She shook hands a moment after and, in going away, said she hoped

I would do what I said.

Now I call that friendly, don't you?

Yes, I like her today. A little or too much? Don't know. I liked her and it seems a new feeling to me. Then, in that case, all the rest, all that I thought I thought and all that I felt I felt, all the rest before now, in fact . . . O, give it up, old chap! Sleep it off!

(p. 256)

Stephen needs more 'sleep', more rest, that is, from his own labyrinthine introspection, so that he can experience more of these 'new feelings', and in doing so come to appreciate the multifaceted otherness of reality. The hermetic nature of his verbal universe is, more than anything else, what separates him off from Bloom with his 'depersonalized form of consciousness',[60] from the Bloom awareness of the reality of 'the ordinary universe', as Denis Donoghue has termed it,[61] which enables Bloom to 'encounter the reality of experience' in a way that the young Stephen can — characteristically — talk about rather than achieve. Significantly, it is in the 'Aeolus' chapter of *Ulysses*, with Bloom's presence for the first time hovering near, that Stephen thinks to himself: 'Dublin. I have much, much to learn'.

Inevitably, Stephen's immersion in his own verbal universe is reflected in his theory of art, which he expounds at length to Lynch in the last chapter of *A Portrait*. With S. L. Goldberg — who has written what I find the most convincing account of this much discussed episode[62] — I would argue that Stephen's theory of art is certainly not Joyce's (though clearly there are many points of contact) and that its chief significance is dramatic; that is, it serves to round out the portrait of a young artist which we have been given by demonstrating — very accurately in psychological and philosophical terms — what sort of theory such a character as we have got to know would come up with. We see, for example, why Stephen's theory verges towards formalism, as it does in its denial that proper art should produce any 'kinetic' effects. 'Desire' and 'loathing' are the kinetic emotions specified, but the theory is so sweeping that it is easy to see that Stephen leaves no place for art to engage in any way with its essential task, the valuation of and discrimination between human sympathies, antagonisms, emotions, ideas and choices. 'The esthetic emotion is therefore static', he says, and this is only possible because Stephen has managed to divorce the 'esthetic emotion' from what we may call the moral emotion. Stephen's position is philosophically untenable, but psychologically totally comprehensible and convincing; he wants to assert the autonomy of art with such passion precisely because of the intolerably heavy pressures of moralising didacticism that he has encountered in his own background – in his father's clichéd gentleman's code ('never peach on a fellow', 'mix with gentlemen'), in his country's nationalist pieties ('be true to your country'), and, of course, in the Church ('The priest had answered that Victor Hugo had never written half so well when he had turned against the church as he had written when he was a catholic'). These pressures lead him to insist on the totally separate nature of art, to drive the dissociative wedge between life (as he knows it) and art, too far in. He makes of art a self-enclosed formal phenomenon, as can be seen especially clearly in his definition of *consonantia*, which, with *integritas* and *claritas* is one of the essential constituents of beauty, and a stage in the apprehension of beauty. 'You feel the rhythm of its structure' [the structure of the object of perception]', says Stephen, but 'structure' here could be any sort of formal arrangement, the question of the human significance or importance of any such formal arrangement being completely evaded. As Goldberg says of the cumulative weight of Stephen's argument:

> Subtly but inevitably, he suggests that as the artist is isolated from his society so art is isolated from life. His rejection of *kinesis* seems all too like a rejection of emotion rather than a demand for its purification, for a true impersonality; it hints at a fear of reality rather than a welcoming acceptance of it in order to transform it and express it in another mode. In the long run, Stephen extends the exile of the artist to the exile of art.[63]

What is most impressive about Joyce's art in the closing chapters of *A Portrait* (which students often find less immediately effective than the childhood and boyhood chapters) is that we cannot doubt the authenticity of Stephen's committment to his artistic vocation, and the moral courage involved in making such a choice in such a context; but likewise, we are made to feel the psychological inevitability of the damagingly limited aesthete's position that Stephen adopts. It is implicit in the very first of the sequence of thoughts and events relating to Stephen's crucial choice (the last term of which is the hammering out of the aesthetic theory), when Stephen had wondered whether –

> ... being as weak of sight as he was shy of mind, he drew less pleasure from the reflection of the glowing sensible world through the prism of a language many-coloured and richly storied than from the contemplation of an inner world of individual emotions mirrored

perfectly in a lucid supple periodic prose. (p. 171)

Stephen's 'mirror' remains turned inwards, and this affects not just his attitude to experience but, inevitably, his aesthetic theory. The point is highlighted, as critics have pointed out, by Joyce's deliberate omission from his portrait of the artist as a young theorist of any mention of the crucial idea of ephiphany, discussed at length in *Stephen Hero*. The notion of epiphany involves an opening of the self to the fullest possible perceptual impact of the detail, or details, of the objective world in all its unique particularity. There is thus a *fusion* of objective fact and subjective consciousness, in which neither bludgeons the other out of sight. It is not just an aesthetic or an epistemological concept, but the major moral idea in Joyce's art. As Maddox says, citing Mr Duffy and Gabriel Conroy,

> . . . the vocabulary of 'subject' and 'object' takes on a new meaning at those moments when a character can transcend his own ego to understand what is beyond himself.[64]

The Stephen of *A Portrait* is frequently too afraid of what is beyond himself. This may seem at first sight a surprising statement to make of this Luciferian rebel, and indeed Stephen is not afraid of making his heroic rejections. His fear is that of the thorough-going romantic spirit, the fear of the ordinary, the hum-drum, of what the young Joyce in his 'Drama and Life' essay had called 'the dreary sameness of existence' (and to which the young Joyce had committed his own art). And so, again and again in *A Portrait*, we find Stephen retreating from that reality into his alluring world of words, from the sloblands of Fairview to Newman's silver-veined prose.

To sum up, Stephen's theory may seem comprehensive in its approach to the potentially beautiful, and, despite the significant omission of the epiphany idea with which the Stephen of the earlier draft had been credited, we may even agree that the merit of the theory as expounded to Lynch is that Stephen argues that 'beauty is manifested in a *relationship* between observer and observed, governed by the fundamental character of human apprehension'.[65] But what Goldberg calls 'barren formalism' is still there; Stephen's theory does not leave room for discrimination between humanly significant patterns in the beautiful object, and mere patterns. The theory as it stands cannot explain why *King Lear* is more 'beautiful' than a chamber-pot, or the butcher boy's basket to which Stephen directs Lynch's attention, since

Stephen takes the work of art, or the beautiful object, purely on its own terms, and makes no attempt to place it in a wider frame of reference. Further, while theoretically Stephen is prepared to admit that anything may be beautiful provided that the perceiving mind registers its wholeness, harmony and radiance, in practice Stephen has a very limited, ninetyish or Paterian sense of the beautiful. As we have seen, he constantly filters out the sordid, disagreeable or humanly painful elements in experience; for him, these are 'so many voices offending and threatening to humble the pride of his youth'. Though he sees himself as 'a priest of the eternal imagination', it is precisely the 'daily bread of experience' which Stephen finds it most difficult to deal with in art. The Stephen of *A Portrait* is not capable of creating 'The Pisgah Sight of Palestine' (with all its 'scrupulous meanness') which the Stephen of *Ulysses* offers in the 'Aeolus' episode. His conception of beauty and art is too anaemic, and the young Joyce's words may be turned against him:

> . . . beauty is as often anaemic spirituality as hardy animalism. Then, chiefly because beauty is to men an arbitrary quality and often lies no deeper than form, to pin drama to dealing with it, would be hazardous. Beauty is the swerga [the heaven of Gods in Hindu literature] of the aesthete; but truth has a more ascertainable and more real dominion.[66]

A Portrait of the Artist as a Young Man, then, asserts the necessity for the artist to stick close to life. Stephen must encounter, and learn to enter, the empirical world of Bloom. However, as John Gross says, it is certainly not simply a cautionary tale. Apart from the narrative technique which, though in the third person, sees everything from Stephen's point of view and hence brings us sympathetically close to him, Joyce's understanding of the pressures on Stephen, and the forces which make him what he is, creates in the reader an attitude towards him compounded of admiration and compassion in at least equal measure to any tincture of contemptuous amusement at his pretensions. The imaginative balance between satiric irony and compassion which, as I have argued, is a marked feature even in *Dubliners*, is held even more skilfully in *A Portrait*. In a sense, this means that social reality, the city, Dublin, is affirmed even more strongly, for all its obvious and glaring imperfections. For Joyce organises *A Portrait* around Stephen's sense that there is a fundamental opposition between the imperial imagination of the artist and the mundanities of his society, and then allows Stephen's imagination, which seems to control the selection of incident and to dictate the rhythm of the action, to play out the conflict with all the cards stacked in its favour, as it were. And yet, the ultimate effect of *A Portrait* is to show the nature of the dead-end into which Stephen manoeuvres himself by cutting himself off, imaginatively, so totally from what surrounds him. Joyce's affirmation of the importance of the 'daily bread of experience' is all the more convincing in *A Portrait* because he has taken the long way round to making it, through the sympathetic investigation of an artistic sensibility that wishes either to dominate reality possessively, or to retreat from it to contemplate 'an inner world of individual emotions mirrored perfectly in a lucid supple periodic prose'. Joyce's great strength, and his saving sanity, is that for all his belief in the value of art, his 'classical temper' forbids him to make of art an end in itself; and that the greatest wordsmith in the history of the novel shows himself to be aware of the limitations of words and of the danger of making them one's holy grail.

In discussing *Ulysses* during its composition, Joyce remarked to his friend Frank Budgen: 'Stephen no longer interests me to the same extent. He has a shape that can't be changed'.[67] While one sees Joyce's point and the implied comparison with that 'all-round man', Bloom, it would be a mistake to see Stephen's function in the novel as simply that of foil to Bloom (neurotic, intellectual bachelor *v.* sane, common-sensical married man). In fact Stephen does 'change' from the character we have seen in *A Portrait of the Artist*, and his struggles to come to a more mature sense of his own identity and a more inclusive view of the nature of art provide an engrossing and indispensable strand of the novel's rich tapestry.

Stephen is recognisably basically the same young man of *A Portrait*, but in *Ulysses* comes across as a much more sympathetic character, an effect in keeping with the general atmosphere of humorous tolerance which pervades Joyce's masterpiece. Obviously his mother's recent death and his reaction to it play a large part in projecting this more human Stephen. Some critics take a very harsh line on Stephen's grief and remorse (which seems to me utterly convincing and moving), finding in his emotional recollections too much Gothic horror and 'self-pity'.[68] But perhaps it is an occasion or situation where a young man might be allowed such emotions. Bloom, after all, has had ten years to assimilate the death of Rudy. My main point, however, is that this deep distress has humanised Stephen in a fertile and hopeful way.

He is more aware of the mysterious and irreducible otherness of experience, for example. The reality of his mother's separate existence
comes before his mind, in a way we never saw in the earlier book, in
this brief, intense passage, where a poem (Yeats's) points him towards
experience rather than, as hitherto, away from it:

> Fergus' song: I sang it alone in the house, holding down the long
> dark chords. Her door was open: she wanted to hear my music.
> Silent with awe and pity I went to her bedside. She was crying in her
> wretched bed. For those words, Stephen: love's bitter mystery.
> Where now?
> Her secrets: old feather fans, tasselled dancecards, powdered with
> musk, a gaud of amber beads in her locked drawer. A birdcage hung
> in the sunny window of her house when she was a girl. She heard
> old Royce sing in the pantomime of Turko the terrible and laughed
> with others when he sang:
>
> > I am the boy
> > That can enjoy
> > Invisibility.
>
> (pp. 7-8)

And his later reflections, in Mr Deasy's schoolroom, on Cyril Sargent
and his mother mark a long step forward from the Stephen who cannot
understand even the meaning of Cranly's question 'Do you love your
mother?' For Sargent, dull-witted and graceless, on his cheek 'a soft
stain of ink . . . date-shaped, recent and damp as a snail's bed' (what a
master of accurate observation Joyce is) — Sargent too is loved from
the womb. Stephen raises Cranly's points about mother-love again for
himself, and directs some contemptuous irony at his own earlier arrogance:

> Was that then real? The only true thing in life? His mother's pros-
> trate body the fiery Columbanus in holy zeal bestrode. (p. 25)

His mother's memory, his mother's ghost, returns to haunt Stephen
frequently during the day. He cannot free himself of it. Many readers
interpret things differently, seeing Stephen's defiant shout of Siegfried's
heroic 'Nothung!', at the climax of the 'Circe' episode, when he confronts his mother for the last time, and smashes her ghostly image as he
smashes the chandelier, as a kind of exorcism of his death-fixated
neuroses. Joyce is clearly aware of the morbid and inhibiting aspects of
Stephen's Hamlet-like persistence in mourning; but a central meaning in

the book, which Stephen must learn, is that one cannot fly by the nets of one's past. The past is part of the baggage on the flight. Hence our last view of Stephen in the 'Circe' episode asserts the continuing power of his mother's memory over him; he lies curled in the foetal position, murmuring 'thickly with prolonged vowels' the Yeats song forever associated with her death. The implications are clear; the past cannot be exorcised, only come to terms with. The crushing limitation of Stephen's imperious and imperial imagination involved here is at the same time an assertion of the reality principle which underlies the novel. Like Ibsen's Brand (whose slogan is 'All or Nothing'), Stephen (who cries out 'With me all or not at all' (p. 549)) discovers that the world cannot be made in his own image. It is the pain involved in the discovery that makes the Stephen of *Ulysses* so much more sympathetic.

The impact of the 'mercurial Malachi', Buck Mulligan, on the reader's sense of the book's energy (an energy denied by a school of critics who see *Ulysses* as anticipatory of Robbe-Grillet's dreary *chosiste* novels) is equalled only by his importance in qualifying our views of Stephen. Mulligan's desire to 'Hellenise' Ireland and his contempt for the provinciality of Irish culture ('A new colour for our Irish poets: snot-green' (p. 3)) pre-empts one of the positions that had set Stephen proudly apart from his peers in *A Portrait*; and is expressed with a joyous zest which Stephen's bitter asperities never rise to, as in his parody of Synge in the library episode, where even Stephen has to laugh:

> It's what I'm telling you, mister honey, it's queer and sick we were, Haines and myself, the time himself brought it in . . . 'Twas murmur we did for a gallus potion would rouse a friar, I'm thinking, and he limp with leching . . . And we to be there, mavrone, and you to be unbeknownst sending us your conglomerations the way we to have our tongues out a yard long like the drouthy clerics do be fainting for a pussful.
>
> (p. 188)

Further, Mulligan's persistent and cheerful blasphemy, evidenced in the parody of the Mass with which he opens the novel and in his 'Ballad of Joking Jesus' throws a crude but nevertheless humorously balanced light over the dark intensities of Stephen's heroic *'non serviam'*. As he says to Stephen, 'you have the cursed jesuit strain in you, only it's injected the wrong way' (p. 6). Again, Stephen's theory of art, expressed in his argument for the closeness of the relation between

Shakespeare's life and his works, especially *Hamlet*, is immediately
deflated and parodied by Mulligan's 'play for the mummers', called
Everyman His Own Wife or A Honeymoon in the Hand, which implies
a view that art is masturbatory.[69]

Mulligan's pre-empting or parodying of Stephen's positions makes
him in every way a much more powerful antagonist than anyone
Stephen has encountered in *A Portrait*. He represents a threat to
Stephen in a deeper and more pervasive way, also, in his 'mercurial'
(Buck's own word) ability to be all things to all men, to be indifferent
to contradictions in himself ('Do I contradict myself? Very well then, I
contradict myself' (p. 15)), in his protean slipperiness of identity. In
all these ways, he is like Mosca, the parasite of Volpone, in one of
Joyce's favourite authors, Jonson:

> But your fine, elegant rascal, that can rise
> And stoop, almost together, like an arrow;
> Shoot through the air as nimbly as a star;
> Turn short as doth a swallow; and be here,
> And there, and here, and yonder, all at once;
> Present to any humour, all occasion;
> And change a visor swifter than a thought,
> This is the creature had the art born with him . . .

This type threatens Stephen who is throughout the novel in the toils of
a deep crisis about the nature and reality of his own identity, and
struggles to come to a sense of his own enduring self. The presence of
Mulligan in *Ulysses*, then, shapes our attitude to Stephen in a complex
way; on the one hand, his 'hyperborean' stance, his cheerful blasphemy,
his wit and verbal dexterity lessens our sense of Stephen's special
apartness, undercutting his 'heroic' status; on the other, his 'spirit of
denial',[70] the absence in him of anything approaching integrity, shows
Stephen up in a more favourable and more sympathetic light.

It is not, however, just that the reader sees Stephen differently in
the wider perspectives offered by *Ulysses*. Stephen himself has advanced in several ways. He is, for example, capable now of directing an
ironic gaze at his more arrogant youthful poses. In the 'Proteus' episode,
he mocks his own narcissism and the precious nature of his literary
aspirations:

> Reading two pages apiece of seven books every night, eh? I was
> young. You bowed to yourself in the mirror, stepping forward to

applause earnestly, striking face. Hurray for the Goddamned idiot!
Hray! No-one saw: tell no-one. Books you were going to write with
letters for titles. Have you read his F? O yes, but I prefer Q. Yes,
but W is wonderful. O yes, W. Remember your epiphanies on green
oval leaves, deeply deep, copies to be sent if you died to all the great
libraries of the world, including Alexandria? Someone was to read
them there after a few thousand years . . . When one reads these
strange pages of one long gone one feels that one is at one with one
who once . . .

(p. 37)

And in 'Scylla and Charybdis', he measures with disgust the gap between
his pretensions and the actuality of achievement:

Fabulous artificer, the hawklike man. You flew. Whereto? Newhaven-
Dieppe, steerage passenger. Paris and back. Lapwing. Icarus. *Pater,
ait*. Seabedabbed, fallen, weltering, Lapwing you are.

(p. 199)

In one sense, there is as little balance here as in those earlier extensive
musings which 'flattered his mild proud sovereignty' (*A Portrait* p. 169);
Stephen's self-disgust is as emotionally extremist as his egotism. But,
though the tone clearly measures Stephen's painful instability, he has
progressed towards a sense of his own limitations which is at least the
beginnings of wisdom. In conversation with Arthur Power, Joyce
remarked in words that have a clear application to Stephen (and to
Bloom):

What makes most people's lives unhappy is some disappointed
romanticism, some unrealizable or misconceived ideal. In fact you
may say that idealism is the ruin of men, and if we lived down to
fact, as primitive man had to do, we would be better off.[71]

This is a kind of Joycean paraphrase of Dr Johnson's words on 'that
hunger of imagination which preys incessantly upon life',[72] a tragic
hunger from which we all inevitably and by our nature suffer, and to
which Stephen's character and circumstances have rendered him peculiarly prone. But there is a visible and sustained effort on his part to
move towards the 'classical temper' as Stephen struggles through the
day in *Ulysses*.

Apart from the ironic self-scrutiny to which he now more regularly
subjects himself, Stephen can be seen trying to temper the rampant
Platonism of his mode of thought as we have come to know it in *A*

Portrait, where, impatient of accidents and externals, his mind seeks to intuit the essences of things. In 'Nestor', for example, whose 'art' according to Joyce's scheme is history, Stephen toys with the Blakean notion that history is inferior to 'Vision or Imagination' which 'is a Representation of what Eternally Exists, Really and Unchangeably'.[73] By contrast, history may only be

> Fabled by the daughters of memory. And yet it was in some way, if not as memory fabled it. A phrase, then, of impatience, thud of Blake's wings of excess. I hear the ruin of all space, shattered glass and toppling masonry, and time one livid final flame. What's left us then?
>
> (p. 21)

'And yet it *was* in some way' — history cannot be simply dismissed as irrelevant. Stephen is partly attracted to Blake's position because it seems, in denying the reality of history, to offer a way out of seeing history as a nightmarish and weary succession of meaningless violence ('Time shocked rebounds, shock by shock. Jousts, slush and uproar of battles, the frozen death-spew of the slain, a shout of spear spikes baited with men's bloodied guts' (p. 30); or, alternatively, to offer an escape route from Mr Deasy's teleological view: 'All history moves towards one great goal, the manifestation of God' (p. 31). This view tends, from a different angle, to strip the particularities of history of any self-sustaining significance, as well as implying, of course, a theological imperative which Stephen is reluctant to accept. Tentatively in this chapter Stephen is moving towards a position which is outlined more fully in 'Proteus' and 'Scylla and Charybdis' which affirms the significant particularity of *quidditas* of the events and personalities of history (and hence of personal experience inside the historical continuum):

> Had Pyrrhus not fallen by a beldam's hand in Argos or Julius Caesar not been knifed to death? They are not to be thought away. Time has branded them and fettered they are lodged in the room of the infinite possibilities they have ousted. But can those have been possible seeing that they never were? Or was that only possible which came to pass? . . . It must be a movement then, an actuality of the possible as possible.
>
> (p. 22-3)

That is, history may be conceived of as a record of potentialities which managed to realise themselves in actuality. The hopeful bearing of this on Stephen's desire to realise his own personal potential inside the nets of history is obvious. And further, in a clipped and abbreviated way, Stephen in this 'Nestor' chapter offers a version of Joyce's crucial epiphany idea, when he rejects Mr Deasy's 'one great goal': 'That is God . . . A shout in the street' (pp. 31-2). This need not be taken (as Mr Deasy takes it) as youthful blasphemy; rather, it is a cryptic mode of asserting that the meaning of existence may be located in multitudinous manifestations; indeed, that we can only penetrate to essence through accident, through, that is, the outward signs of the inner reality. We can only know the world through our senses, not through direct (angelic) intuition of its essence. We find Stephen at the beginning of the next chapter stressing to himself the 'ineluctable modalities' of the visible and the audible, the inevitability and primacy of our sensory mode of perception of reality, or (putting it the other way round) the inevitably phenomenal or accidental way in which reality offers itself to us. Hence, as Stephen muses:

> Signatures of all things I am here to read, seaspawn and seawrack, the nearing tide, that rusty boot. Snot-green, bluesilver, rust: Coloured signs.
>
> (p. 33)

In fact, throughout 'Proteus', Stephen strives after an awareness of the world as a world of process and change, hence infinitely variable yet possessing an underlying reality behind its often ephemeral phenomena. It is independent of his mind. 'See now. There all the time,without you: and ever shall be, world without end' (p. 34).

All this is evidence of growth in Stephen, of his attempt to limit the sway of his imperious, even Luciferian ('The mind is its own place') intellect and imagination by admitting and forcing himself to face the world of process and ever-varying phenomena – the world in which Bloom swims naturally. This is hard for Stephen, since his ordering and controlling mind fears swamping and the loss of identity. As Maddox says in a good account of 'Proteus': 'philosophically, [Stephen] is a Platonist reluctantly forcing himself to become an Aristotelian'.[74] In the larger terms of the book this overall distinction is clear, and provides a kind of pattern: Stephen's abstract, highly verbal and somewhat hermetic mind needs to be brought into contact with Bloom's concrete world of ever-changing innumerable sensations; likewise Bloom, ever in danger of being overwhelmed by the sheer flux of experience, could possibly use some of Stephen's conceptualising powers.

Against the booming Platonism of AE and the others in 'Scylla and

Charybdis' (the 'yogibogeybox' voices that maintain 'Art has to reveal to us ideas, formless spiritual essences' (p. 173))), Stephen comes to a full realisation and (inner) assertion of the significance of some of these thoughts and words from earlier in the day. In doing so, he defines his relationship to reality in terms which indicate a new respect for 'the now, the here':

> John Eglinton, frowning, said, waxing wroth:
> — Upon my word it makes my blood boil to hear anyone compare Aristotle with Plato.
> — Which of the two, Stephen asked, would have banished me from his commonwealth?
>
> Unsheathe your dagger definitions. Horseness is the whatness of allhorse. Streams of tendency and eons they worship. God: noise in the street: very peripatetic. Space: what you damn well have to see. Through spaces smaller than red globules of man's blood they creepy-crawl after Blake's buttocks into eternity of which this vegetable world is but a shadow. Hold to the now, the here, through which all future plunges to the past.

(pp. 174-5)

And it is out of such an attitude that Stephen creates his 'Pisgah Sight of Palestine or the Parable of the Plums', related first on the Dublin streets of 'Aeolus', and later to Bloom in the security of Eccles Street. (Bloom is actually on the fringes during Stephen's first account, but misses it because of Myles Crawford's 'K.M.R.I.A.'.)

The context of Stephen's parable is provided by the windy rhetoric of the newspaper office, the scene opening with the highfalutin bombast of Doughy Dan Dawson's reported speech on the beauties of 'Erin, Green Gem of the Silver Sea' (p. 115) — stuff so powerful as to give Simon Dedalus 'a heartburn on the arse', and drive him forth to drink. At a higher level, J. J. O'Molloy quotes 'a polished period' from a speech of Seymour Bushe, KC. The allusion to the Moses of Michelangelo in this speech leads 'Professor' MacHugh to quote extensively from the famous speech of John F. Taylor on the analogy between the Irish and the Jews, both oppressed by mighty empires, both ready to defend and uphold their own cultural values, even as Moses bore in his arms 'the tables of the law, graven in the language of the outlaw' (p. 133). Stephen, a 'chip of the old block' (p. 134), reacts to all this by suggesting an adjournment for drinks. He is more polite than his father, merely reflecting inwardly on MacHugh's 'That is oratory': 'Gone with the wind . . . Dead noise' (p. 133). He is also more creative than his father, and it is on the way to the pub that he offers his parable.

The most obvious point to be made about it is that it is Stephen's 'dagger definition', achieved by contrast, of the fustian rhetoric he has just been subjected to. In subject matter, Moses on Pisgah is replaced by Anne Kearns and Florence MacCabe, two elderly spinsters, on Nelson's Pillar. At least one implication of this is that they are just as interesting in what the young Joyce called 'the dreary sameness of [their] exist-ence' as the prophet-heroes of the world. It is the relentless detail of the short episode, what the young Joyce called the 'scrupulous meanness' of the style that he employed in *Dubliners*, that more than anything else hammers home the thoughts of Stephen on the implications of the grandiloquent rhetoric he has been listening to:

> — They buy one and fourpenceworth of brawn and four slices of panloaf at the north city dining rooms in Marlborough street from Miss Kate Collins, proprietress . . . They purchase four and twenty ripe plums from a girl at the foot of Nelson's pillar to take off the thirst of the brawn. They give two threepenny bits to the gentleman at the turnstile and begin to waddle slowly up the winding staircase, grunting, encouraging each other, afraid of the dark, panting . . .

(p. 135)

Stephen has plunged into the details of Dublin life just as boldly as Mulligan dived into the Forty Foot pool, and has urged himself on with three significant asides to himself, which focus on his subject and on the desire to follow it through: 'Dublin. I have much, much to learn' (p. 134); 'Dubliners' (just before he begins the story); and 'On now. Dare it. Let there be life.' (p. 135).

But there is, of course, a thematic implication in Stephen's parable. It suggests that the Irish, however strongly the parallels between them and the Israelites may be drawn, are not really capable of the same heroic and prophetic and compelling vision. The two old women sit under the statue of Nelson, itself a symbol of Ireland's colonial status (and obviously felt to be a potent symbol — the IRA finally blew it up in the 1960s). They look down and see nothing but churches, about the identities of which they remain uncertain. They make no sense of anything — for them Nelson is merely a 'onehandled adulterer'.[75] Thus Stephen indicates their rigid — because unconscious — bondage to Caesar and to God, giving a sombre local application and a name to the words he had spoken of himself to the Englishman Haines in the opening episode:

— I am the servant of two masters . . . the imperial British state . . . and the holy Roman Catholic and apostolic church. (p. 18)

The Irish are not Mosaic visionaries, and as Richard Ellmann sums it up, Stephen tells his own 'Parable of the Plums'

> . . . as foil to Taylor's parallel, as the blade of truth amid the airbags of oratory. There is no Moses on Pisgah, there is no promised land, only two old women spitting out plum-stones from the top of Nelson's pillar.[76]

Yet — and this is what the non-Irish reader may find most difficult to see — the parable is not a Dantesque vision of hell, or a dry run for *The Waste Land*. Stephen gives 'a sudden loud young laugh as a close'. There is no need to interpret this as a kind of nervous hysteria; rather, although Stephen clearly means to puncture the high-flown quasi-heroical rhetoric of the whole discussion, he is also — like any good, and sane, satirist — partly in love with his mean subject. The sort of comic gusto that Joyce himself unleashes on the stunted men, gnomes, crones, drunken navvy, scrofulous children and the 'famished snaggle-tusks of an elderly bawd' (p. 412) in 'Circe' — a heaping up of grotes-queries that pushes things over the edge into comedy — is also observable in Stephen's loving detail, in all its absurdity, in this parable:

> Anne Kearns has the lumbago for which she rubs on Lourdes water given her by a lady who got a bottleful from a passionist father. Florence MacCabe takes a crubeen and a bottle of double X [i.e. strong Guinness] for supper every Saturday.
>
> (p. 135)

Swift is also a master of the unnecessary, detail — it is this, above all, that sweetens satire, in giving us the sense of the author's delighted zest. Joyce has it in abundance; but even Stephen, here, shows he has it. Clearly this is a very different young man from the composer of the villanelle of the temptress. Short though it is, the 'Pisgah Sight of Palestine' suggests the new and more profitable direction of Stephen's aesthetic aspirations. We are convinced that the young man who relates this sardonic vignette has it in him to write *Dubliners*, where the stories are equally laconic and open-ended. Indeed, certain aspects of *Ulysses* are also in this miniature — again, the open-ended quality, but also that zest in the unrelenting piling up of realistic detail which in the end produces a comic effect.

Perhaps it is through his theory about Shakespeare, revealed to a sceptical group in the National Library of the 'Scylla and Charybdis' episode, that Stephen adds most to our sense of the change in him and also to our understanding of some basic premisses of the novel itself. The theory has been very ably commented on, notably by Goldberg and Maddox, and my account will concentrate on only a few salient points. Stephen argues that the older and sexually aggressive Ann Hathaway seduced the young Shakespeare, dealing a heavy blow to his self-confidence, and imposed marriage on him. Unable to cope with this or with her, Shakespeare left Stratford for London (as far away 'as corrupt Paris lies from virgin Dublin', Stephen pointedly remarks), to begin his career. The wound rankled, however, and its pain intensified when Shakespeare discovered that Ann had committed adultery with his brothers Edmund and Richard. The birth of a granddaughter to some extent reconciled him with his Stratford life, but he never really forgave Ann. These facts of his life, and his obsession with lust and adultery, are written into all of his works (for example, two of the really evil characters of his work are called Edmund and Richard, and the birth of his granddaughter is echoed in the solace brought by the young girls of the last plays — Marina, Miranda, Perdita — to older suffering men).

Hamlet is the key play, because it is in this work that Shakespeare expresses in art his understanding of himself and his life. He is driven to creation by the compulsive neuroses of his personality, but to some extent frees himself of those emotional and psychological fetters by being able to give them artistic shape. Stephen argues for the significance of Shakespeare acting the part of King Hamlet's ghost, denying that Shakespeare — as is most commonly believed — identified with Prince Hamlet. He ties it neatly together:

> Is it possible that the player Shakespeare, a ghost by absence, and in the vesture of buried Denmark, a ghost by death, speaking his own words to his own son's name (had Hamnet Shakespeare lived he would have been Prince Hamlet's twin) is it possible, I want to know, or probable that he did not draw or foresee the logical conclusion of those premises: you are the dispossessed son: I am the murdered father: your mother is the guilty queen. Ann Shakespeare, born Hathaway?

(p. 177)

One does not have to accept Stephen's argument as literally true — in fact he himself denies that he believes in it. But on the higher level he is asserting an important truth. The central general meaning of his theory, in which he links most ingeniously and appositely scraps of whatever biographical information (or speculation) on Shakespeare that we have to lines and phrases from the works, is that the artist's life and the artist's work have a symbiotic relationship; the art grows directly out of the life, and reflects back directly on that life, since it is only through his art that the artist can come to understand himself as a man, and hence to understand his relationship with the world around him. The Stephen of *A Portrait* had driven a large wedge between art and life; his theory here shows a considerable advance in wisdom in giving such weight to what he simply ignored in the earlier novel, the dynamic relationship between the artist's life and his work. Stephen steers with brilliant intellectual energy between the Charybdis of 'yogibogeybox' Russell's Platonism ('Art has to reveal to us ideas, formless spiritual essences') and the Scylla of Mulligan's mocking nihilism (Mulligan attempts, with his grotesque parodic style, to reduce Stephen's theory to the proposition that art is masturbation: 'Every Man His Own Wife').

The Shakespeare theory offers us much more than simply an insight into Stephen's changed views on art and its human reference, though this is of crucial importance because, as Goldberg says of the theory, 'here, if anywhere, is something like a mature aesthetic of his [Joyce's] own'.[77] The organisation and meaning of *Ulysses* are implicated at many points and in many ways in this scene in the library. For instance, the chapter enables us to see more clearly than at any previous point the nature of the link that the novel is to forge between Stephen and Bloom (who, as in 'Aeolus', is again present on the fringe of the stage dominated by Stephen). Stephen as artist naturally identifies with Shakespeare as the type of all artists, but Bloom is, in fact, in experiential terms much closer to Shakespeare than Stephen is. He is impotent before his dominant wife Molly, 'belief in himself' — in relation to Molly, at any rate — 'has been untimely killed' (p. 185). Like Shakespeare, he has to bear with the knowledge of his wife's adultery. As Shakespeare lost his son Hamnet, so Bloom has lost his son Rudy. And — a point emphasised strongly by Stephen in his discourse — Shakespeare had a strong sense of property, was a substantial citizen. Bloom, too, is canny in his financial dealings ('the prudent member') and is much more comfortably off (as is revealed in 'Ithaca') than most of those he meets during the day, whose exemplar is the shabby-genteel hand-to-mouth Simon Dedalus. So, Shakespeare is not just a great artist, but a cuckold-citizen, failed husband, bereaved father, and indeed finds all the material of his art in his ordinary painful man's life. The artist needs the man. Hence the significance of the moment in 'Circe':

> *Stephen and Bloom gaze in the mirror. The face of William*
> *Shakespeare, beardless, appears there, rigid in facial paralysis,*
> *crowned by the reflection of the reindeer antlered hatrack in the*
> *hall.*
>
> (p. 536)

('Facially paralysed', because Shakespeare, like Stephen and Bloom, or
any man, will always remain to some extent a victim of his own psychological and emotional problems.) Shakespeare, then, is both Stephen
and Bloom. And so, of course, is James Joyce.

Closely bound up with his views on *Hamlet* is Stephen's conception
of the nature of paternity. The idea of fatherhood dominates the symbolic action of *Ulysses*, from Mulligan's sneer in the opening chapter,
which arises in the context of a mention of *Hamlet* — 'O, shade of
Kinch the elder! Japhet in search of a father!' (p. 16). Stephen says in
the library:

> Fatherhood, in the sense of conscious begetting, is unknown to man.
> It is a mystical estate, an apostolic succession . . .
>
> (p. 195)

At a fairly obvious level, if paternity is a thing of the spirit, a 'mystical
estate', Stephen's words justify the sense in which we may see Bloom,
in his experience, maturity, and yearning for the lost son,'as Stephen's
'father'. More complicatedly, there is the sense in which Stephen may
become Bloom's father and even father of himself: that is, if he succeeds
in becoming a mature and self-understanding artist:

> When Rutlandbaconsouthamptonshakespeare or another poet of the
> same name in the comedy of errors wrote *Hamlet* he was not the
> father of his own son merely but, being no more a son, he was and
> felt himself the father of all his race, the father of his own grand-
> father, the father of his unborn grandson.
>
> (p. 196)

Art is the means by which a man may achieve the spiritual paternity
(the wisdom, maturity and self-knowledge) of his own self, thus trans-
cending — temporarily at least — the conditions of his own psychological entrapment. Thus, Stephen's theory of Shakespeare is also a mirror
reflecting on the conception and creation of *Ulysses* itself. Stephen
tells himself, in the course of his argument: 'See this. Remember'
(p. 180), and a little later says: 'So in the future, the sister of the past, I

may see myself as I sit here now but by reflection from that which then I shall be' (p. 183). Very clearly here the artist that Stephen hopes to become is telling himself to write the novel we are reading: Stephen and Joyce fuse for a moment, like Stephen and Bloom in the Shakespearean reflection of Bella Cohen's mirror, as Stephen hopes to be able to look back in the future on his own past with understanding.

Throughout *Ulysses*, for all his sympathetic qualities, his growing insights, and his intellectual brilliance, Stephen remains a character suggesting potentiality rather than realisation. Bloom, by contrast, is the 'all-round man', realised fully — in all his imperfections — both by himself and by his creator. His self is actualised in his experience. Without too much exaggeration, we could say that he is the most fully rounded character in literature. Joyce himself remarked to Frank Budgen:

> I see him from all sides, and therefore he is all-round . . . But he is a complete man as well — a good man. At any rate, that is what I intend he shall be.[78]

Bloom's consciousness, though much less intellectually penetrating than Stephen's, is extremely inclusive. It swings between the poles of roseate — and sometimes sentimental — optimism and a hopeless pessimism, between shrewd and humorous self-reliance and disabling masochism, between delusive fantasising and common-sensical empiricism. In a way these contradictions, inside which Bloom lives quite at ease, define his personality, but they make it difficult for the critic to 'put a pin in that chap' (p. 44). This is, of course, a major contribution to our sense of the overwhelming reality of Bloom; his elusiveness is that of life itself. Nevertheless, in his moral bearing, as it were, his actions, his decisions, and in the overall response of his consciousness to what befalls him (since in this novel consciousness is very much a form of action), it is easy to agree with Joyce that he is a good man.

Much of his day is taken up by little practical acts of kindness, whose very lack of ostentation reveal them as stemming from a habitual trait of personality in him. Thus, he helps Dignam's widow financially (even paying her a visit), helps the blind stripling to cross the street, and of course he helps Stephen to recover some equilibrium after the *Walpurgisnacht* of 'Circe'. Particularly striking in the crude, boozy male-oriented atmosphere of Dublin is his compassion for the pains of Mrs Purefoy in her protracted labour. He visits the lying-in hospital to enquire after her, and in the varying textures of Joyce's style in this chapter ('Oxen of the Sun'), often dismissed as the extravagance of a technical virtuoso, we can suddenly see Bloom as genuinely being a 'verray parfit gentil knight':

> Some man that wayfaring was stood by housedoor at night's on-coming. Of Israel's folk was that man that on earth wandering far had fared. Stark ruth of man his errand that him lone led till that house.
>
> (p. 367)
>
> . . . And sir Leopold that was the goodliest guest that ever sat in scholars' hall and that was the meekest man and the kindest that ever laid husbandly hand under hen[79] and that was the very truest knight of the world one that ever did minion service to lady gentle pledged him courtly in the cup. Woman's woe with wonder pondering.
>
> (pp. 370-1)

In this chapter Bloom comes off very well by comparison with the young students and their hangers-on. Indeed, throughout the day — and into Molly's night-thoughts, even — Bloom is seen as superior to the Dublin males, for whom he is, at best, an outsider (because of his Jewishness) and, more commonly, a butt. Dublin males, like Joyce's own father, can be extremely amusing in their ready and vituperative wit; but, as they are seen in *Ulysses*, they have little of the rationalism, moderation or tolerance of Bloom, and for his compassion, charity and genuine love of his family they tend to substitute, as in the 'Sirens' episode, a flatulent sentimentality based on not much more than a liquorish sense of pub-fellowship. Intermittently, and somewhat grudgingly, some of his peers acknowledge something of his quality:[80]

> Davy Byrne, sated after his yawn, said with tearwashed eyes: — And is that a fact? Decent quiet man he is. I often saw him in here and I never once saw him, you know, over the line.
> — God almight couldn't make him drunk, Nosey Flynn said firmly . . . — He's not too bad, Nosey Flynn said, snuffling it up. He has been known to put his hand down too to help a fellow. Give the devil his due.
>
> (p. 166)

Moderation and tolerance are not normally 'heroic' virtues, but in the context of 'Cyclops' Bloom's standing up for them against the virulent rhetoric of the nationalist Citizen ('All wind and piss like a tanyard cat', as the Nameless One caustically characterises that hero), against the hostility and suspicion of the whole group of drinkers, who think — mistakenly — that Bloom has made a killing on the Gold Cup but won't buy his round,[81] and against the nihilistic reductiveness of the Nameless One, as the narrator is called in 'Circe' — in this context Bloom's stand is heroic:

> — And I belong to a race too, says Bloom, that is hated and persecu-
> ted. Also now. This very moment. This very instant . . .
> — Right, says John Wyse. Stand up to it then with force like men.
>   That's an almanac picture for you. Mark for a softnosed bullet.
> Old lardyface standing up to the business end of a gun. Gob, he'd
> adorn a sweepingbrush, so he would, if he only had a nurse's apron
> on him. And then he collapses all of a sudden, twisting around all
> the opposite, as limp as a wet rag.
> — But it's no use, says he. Force, hatred, history, all that. That's not
> life for men and women, insult and hatred. And everybody knows
> that it's the very opposite of that that is really life.
> — What? says Alf.
> — Love, says Bloom. I mean the opposite of hatred.
>
> (p. 317)

Our sense of the heroism of the Bloom voice of sanity in this great, and extremely funny, chapter is increased by its being the only episode, with the exception of 'Penelope', where he is seen entirely through other eyes. This, and the pack mentality rampant among the other drinkers in Barney Kiernan's, highlights him as not just solitary (the scapegoat, the outsider) but as exceptional.

This is not just a side of himself that Bloom puts on show only in public. We know from his most private thoughts that he is as firmly 'on the side of life' as any Lawrentian hero, without the Lawrentian hero's apocalyptic and sometimes awkward rhetoric or his tendency to proselytise. In the chapter where we first meet him, Bloom suffers a sudden and horrific vision of the East and the Jewish race as exhausted:

> Sodom, Gomorrah, Edom. All dead names. A dead sea in a dead
> land, grey and old . . . Dead: an old woman's: the grey sunken cunt
> of the world.
> Desolation.
> Grey horror seared his flesh.

But in a very characteristic manner he shakes this off, via a combination of evasion, interest in the world around him, and assertion of the simple pleasures of life:

> Well, I am here now. Morning mouth bad images . . . Blotchy brown
> brick houses. Number eighty still unlet. Why is that? . . . To smell
> the gentle smoke of tea, fume of the pan, sizzling butter. Be near
> her ample bedwarmed flesh. Yes, yes.
>
> (p. 54)

And later, in the Glasnevin cemetery after Dignam's funeral, with its
melancholy associations for Bloom of the deaths of his father and his
son, he once again asserts his sense of life's value:

> Enough of this place. Brings you bit nearer every time. Last time I
> was here was Mrs. Sinico's funeral. Poor papa too. The love that
> kills. And even scraping up the earth at night with a lantern like that
> case I read of to get at fresh buried females or even putrefied with
> running gravesores. Give you the creeps after a bit. I will appear to
> you after death. . . . There is another world after death named hell. I
> do not like that other world she wrote. No more do I. Plenty to see
> and hear and feel yet. Feel live warm beings near you. Let them
> sleep in their maggoty beds. They are not going to get me this
> innings. Warm beds: warm full blooded life.
>
> (p. 107)

This is the more convincing because of the way in which we have just
seen Bloom encounter the idea of death, and the memory of loved ones'
death, with great fullness, with compassion, curiosity, and even an alert
good humour. He can see death without the horrified and disabling
agony of Stephen, but also without any of the callousness that is exemplified in Buck Mulligan.

It is one thing to praise Bloom for the mature stoicism of his attitude to mortality; none of us can do anything about death. What about
his attitude to the far from inevitable adultery of his wife with Blazes
Boylan? I am sure that it is Bloom's action – or lack of action – in
this respect that more than anything else lies behind the 'ironic' reading
of *Ulysses*, the critical view, that is, which sees the characters as futile
and the whole as a Joycean vision of a Dublin Waste Land. From the
morning moment when Bloom picks up Boylan's letter to Molly with
its 'bold hand', he has a shrewd idea that the rehearsal of 'Love's Old
Sweet Song' is not the only item on the afternoon's agenda. He specu-
lates frequently on the act to come, usually in a frame of mind which
already accepts it as unalterable. He sees Boylan at several points, and
though he sometimes seems to be nearing a point of acting, as when he

sees Boylan's jaunting car ('Follow. Risk it. Go quick. At four. Near now. Out' (p. 250)), more frequently he experiences panic (pp. 171-2) or deliberately and very obviously tries to shut the whole thing out of his mind. Further, there is evidence in Bloom's thoughts, and in the workings of his subconscious as revealed in the 'Circe' episode, that he participates voyeuristically in his own cuckolding. Bloom is here at his lowest ebb, his most degraded:

BOYLAN

(*To Bloom, over his shoulder.*) You can apply your
eye to the keyhole and play with yourself while I just go
through her a few times.

BLOOM

Thank you, sir, I will, sir. May I bring two men chums to
witness the deed and take a snapshot? (*He holds an oint-
ment jar*). Vaseline, sir? Orangeflower? . . . Lukewarm water?
. . .

(p. 535)

The masochist tendencies in his nature, marked throughout, seem to run rampant in his attempt to come to terms with the relationship of Boylan and Molly. Frank Budgen suggests that Bloom really wants it to happen, first because Bloom's Jewishness seeks to express itself in suffering and, denied its traditional outlet in religious observances, since Bloom is secular, chooses this sexual humiliation. This is not very convincing, since Bloom's Jewishness does not run very deep and has as its main functional role in the novel the setting apart of Bloom as, like Stephen, an outsider. Budgen's next point is, however, suggestive and interesting, meshing in with many details and aspects of the novel:

Linked to the fatalism of the Oriental and organically connected with his Jewish and personal masochism is the homosexual wish to share his wife with other men. He is surrounded with acquaintances, yet he is a lonely man, condemned never to experience the warmth of male fellowship — incapable, perhaps, of accepting it were it offered him. That his wife is possessed by other males gives him a physical contact with them at second hand. It is an underground substitute for noisy back-slapping, arm-gripping comradeship.[82]

But whatever reasons we find, the contrast between Bloom the cuckold and Ulysses the ferocious slayer of his wife's suitors seems to buttress the view that Joyce is commenting on Bloom's inadequacy and taking an ironic view of the conditions of modern 'heroism'.

In fact, Joyce told Budgen that in Homer 'the slaughter of the suitors always seemed to me un-Ulyssean',[83] and his aversion to blood and violence is attested by many witnesses apart from Budgen. If we begin by accepting that Joyce does not necessarily consider Bloom's failure to call out Boylan to a duel, or to slap a divorce petition on Molly, to be moral weaknesses or ridiculous timid abasements, we can perhaps come to see how even Bloom's behaviour over the Boylan business may have positive aspects. He is, for a start, ready to accept some of the blame for the situation. As he muses during the 'Sirens' episode (which takes place very near the time of the adulterous encounter):

> I too, last my race. Milly young student. Well, my fault perhaps. No son. Rudy. Too late now. Or if not? If not? If still? He bore no hate. Hate. Love. These are names. Rudy. Soon I am old.
>
> (p. 27)

The breakdown of his marital relationship is a fact of a more intractable order of reality than the entry of Boylan into his bed; and it is Bloom's hardest task to try to come to terms with that in the course of the day. His attitude *does* change — he moves from a position of eager escapism, in which he does not wish to confront the fact materialised, as it were, in Boylan, to equanimity. As Goldberg well says:

> His attitude can be easily mistaken for a completely passive resignation. In fact, it is something rather different, an *active* resignation, so to speak.[84]

That is, he comes to see his situation in a wider perspective, as an aspect of a universal human fate, as part of the pain of living, and in seeing it thus can accept it more easily without ever generalising the particular case out of existence; Molly always, in his mind, 'can knock spots off them' (p. 356) and his love for her, as hers for him, subsists through their mutual infidelities, a source of inextricable strength and pain.

The movement towards equanimity does not take place because of a sudden blinding flash of insight. Like everything else in *Ulysses*, it is based on a series of fragmented little events or moments of reflection. For example, in the carriage on the way to Paddy Dignam's interment, Bloom thinks about the marriages of his companions. Simon Dedalus is a widower; Mr Power keeps a woman ('Not pleasant for the wife. Yet they say, who was it told me, there is no carnal' (p. 86)); and the sympathetic Martin Cunningham has an even worse time:

> And that awful drunkard of a wife of his. Setting up house for her time after time and then pawning the furniture on him every Saturday almost. Leading him the life of the damned. Wear the heart out of a stone that. Monday morning start afresh. Shoulder to the wheel.
>
> (p. 89)

Bloom draws no conclusions, but we certainly, and he possibly, may think that comparatively speaking Bloom could be in a worse marital mess.

As we have seen, he becomes ready to accept some of the blame for the mess, which leads not to despair but to a sense of some hope: 'Too late now. Or if not?' And nearly simultaneously in this 'Sirens' episode, he moves towards a forgiveness of Molly and a tolerance of himself based on a sense of the general lot, arising, significantly, from a sentimental song — Joyce never forces a philosophical abstractness on Bloom:

> Thou lost one. All songs on that theme. Yet more Bloom stretched his string. Cruel it seems. Let people get fond of each other: lure them on. Then tear asunder. Death . . . Human life . . . Gone. They sing. Forgotten. I too.
> And one day she with. Leave her: get tired. Suffer then. Snivel. Big Spanishy eyes goggling at nothing . . . Yet too much happy bores.
>
> (p. 263)

(The slight touch of self-pity in the vision of Molly suffering after his departure helps to validate the 'equanimity' of tone here.) Later in the day he is able to relate Molly's behaviour to a natural law of attraction:

> Back of everything magnetism. Earth for instance pulling this and being pulled. That causes movement . . . Because it's arranged. Magnetic needle tells you what's going on in the sun, the stars. Little piece of steel iron. When you hold out the fork. Come. Come. Tip. Woman and man that is. Fork and steel. Molly, he. Dress up and look and suggest and let you see and see more and defy you if you're a man to see that and, like a sneeze coming, legs, look, look and if you have any guts in you. Tip. Have to let fly.
>
> (p. 357)

And still later, history comes to the aid of natural laws to widen still
further his perspective on his own position. In the 'Eumaeus' chapter,
the subject of discussion is a more famous adultery, that of Parnell and
Kitty O'Shea. Bloom reflects:

> Whereas the simple fact of the case was it was simply a case of the
> husband not being up to the scratch with nothing in common
> between them beyond the name and then a real man arriving on the
> scene, strong to the verge of weakness, falling a victim to her siren
> charms and forgetting home ties . . . North or south however, it was
> just the wellknown case of hot passion, pure and simple, upsetting
> the applecart with a vengeance and just bore out the very thing he
> was saying, as she also was Spanish or half so, types that wouldn't
> do things by halves, passionate abandon of the south, casting every
> shred of decency to the winds.

(pp. 612-13)

Here, too, blame for himself combines with a willingness to allow for
the natural 'hot-bloodedness' of Molly.

At the end of the day, then, Bloom is able to think of Molly's adultery with more 'abnegation and equanimity' than envy (of Boylan) or
jealousy (of Molly). It is partly his fault; Molly's nature is as it is;
Boylan is young and 'subject to impulses'; and what has happened is
'not as calamitous as a cataclysmic annihilation of the planet in conse-
quence of collision with a dark sun', less reprehensible than many
another crime; and finally he sees the act 'as more than inevitable,
irreparable' (pp. 693-4). Bloom's victory is a victory over the destructive feelings in himself — feelings of self-loathing as well as the more
obvious feelings of fear, envy and jealousy. By deploying the full range
of his emotional resources — in short, his maturity — he has managed
to come to terms with his marital problems without denying their
reality, or the reality of Molly as a person, and without lapsing into a
hopeless apathy. There is no total rapprochement with Molly — such
neat, cut-and-dried solutions occur only in what Joyce scornfully called
'literature';[85] but, nevertheless, Bloom has successfully met and mastered
a painful personal crisis in a way which does not necessarily make him
seem inferior to the blood-boltered Ulysses of Homer.

Yet for all his good qualities, Bloom remains a human character, not
a paragon. The account given above of Bloom's acts of kindness, of his
tolerance and moderation, of the fundamental sanity of his belief in
'life', of his humour and common-sense, and of his ability to employ his
experience and some of those qualities in coming to terms with a pro-

foundly disturbing threat, might tend to suggest that Joyce sentimental-
ises him. Part of the power of Joyce's 'all-round' vision of Bloom is
that we are never in danger of confusing him with that modern stereotype, the 'little man' with the heart of gold, as presented in the films of
Chaplin or in the novels of H. G. Wells. Joyce shows us that, despite his
good qualities, Bloom is severely limited, and not only in his marital
relations. He is, on the whole, less honest than Stephen in his response
to the painful aspects of experience, more prone to flee to anodynes,
as is seen most clearly in his coy epistolary flirtation with Martha and
in his masturbatory encounter with Gerty on the beach. He is more of
a natural survivor than is Stephen, but there are moments when one
cannot help feeling that his resignation, his acceptance of the brute
forces of process and change, is a mode of denying his own individuality and of shifting off his shoulders any sense of personal moral responsibility; as he lapses into the grateful bath at the end of the 'Lotus-
Eaters' chapter, so does he lapse − occasionally − into a comforting
sense of helplessness which makes him a mere pawn of the nightmare
of history:

> Things go on same; day after day: squads of police marching out,
> back: trams in, out . . . Dignam carted off. Mina Purefoy swollen
> belly on a bed groaning to have a child tugged out of her. One born
> every second somewhere. Other dying every second. Since I fed the
> birds five minutes. Three hundred kicked the bucket. Other three
> hundred born . . . Cityful passing away, other cityful coming,
> passing away too: other coming on, passing on. Houses, lines of
> houses, streets, miles of pavement, piledup bricks, stones. Changing
> hands . . . No one is anything.

(p. 153)

And there is no getting away from his responsibility for the bad state of
affairs between Molly and himself. This produces some of the novel's
most deeply ironic moments, 'ironic' in a sense that the more sardonic
Flaubert, for all Joyce's admiration of him, rarely reaches. For example,
in the 'Oxen of the Sun' episode, Bloom, as we have already seen, is
the compassionate spokesman for woman in her trauma of child-bearing
and childbirth. In a very obvious way he stands for 'life' against the
crude and callow jests of his younger companions. But, as the Junian
rebuker, who has temporarily assumed the narrator's role, puts it, in
defence of Molly:

> Unhappy woman she has been too long and too persistently denied

her legitimate prerogative to listen to his objurgations with any other feeling than the derision of the desperate . . . It ill becomes him to preach that gospel [the gospel of 'life']. Has he not nearer home a seedfield that lies fallow for the want of a ploughshare? A habit reprehensible at puberty is second nature and an opprobrium in middlelife. If he must dispense his balm of Gilead in nostrums and apothegms of dubious taste to restore to health a generation of unfledged profligates let his practice consist better with the doctrines that now engross him.

(p. 391)

Thus, though this is one of the chapters in which Bloom emerges as most sympathetic, simultaneously we see him in his impotent fatuity, preaching what he does not or cannot practise. And it is significant that the ironic consciousness here is not Bloom's. It is not that Bloom has not a capacity for self-irony. On the contrary. But he is much less able to see the larger patterns of his life than Stephen is able to see his. His inability to extrapolate, to conceptualise, to see the wood behind the trees, which is his great strength, is also his great weakness. Or perhaps a different way of putting it would be to say that while Bloom is aware of the rhythm of his life, he is much less capable than the younger Stephen of being able to do anything to change that life. Thus he is rather like the Shakespeare of Stephen's theory — a man of much experience but trapped inside the confines of that experience. Stephen says of Shakespeare, and *mutatis mutandis*, his words have application to Bloom:

> He goes back, weary of the creation he has piled up to hide him from himself, an old dog licking an old sore. But, because loss is his gain, he passes on towards eternity in undiminished personality, untaught by the wisdom he has written or by the laws he has revealed.

(p. 185)

The novel gives full weight to Bloom's fallibility and failings, then, and yet despite this (or because of this), we are led to see and feel him as a man of 'undiminished personality', as a complete man and a good man, in Joyce's own words. His choice of Bloom as hero may be related to his own etymology of the name Odysseus, which he believed to be *outis* (nobody) and Zeus — hence 'the divine nobody, at once unique and nondescript'.[86]

The significance of making such a choice, in the context of Irish literature, and much modernist literature, lies in the humane democracy of vision it implies. Ireland is very much a victim of its hero-fixations, of a compensatory or aggressive myth of heroism and the Heroic Individual. Yeats's art is wholly imbued with the heroic ideal, with towering presences whose mere shadow renders the casual comedy of ordinary daily life meaningless:

> Had Cosgrave eaten Parnell's heart, the land's
> Imagination had been satisfied . . .

Synge's work is more sceptical of the myths of heroism, yet he too has the urge to make his own Irish hero and creates the noble peasant of the West. Even O'Casey offers us a heroic class — his suffering women of the slums clad in the robes of their apolitical sanctity. Literature may be harmless enough, but not — as Yeats himself came to see — when it imposes its simplified images on an all-too-receptive national imagination:

> We had fed the heart on fantasies,
> The heart's grown brutal from the fare.

(CP, p. 230)

Parnell, Pearse, Cuchulain, the masked Provisional, his heart enchanted to a stone — how refreshingly different from all these is cuckold Bloom! Joyce wrote in a letter to Stanislaus in 1905:

> I am sure that the whole structure of heroism is, and always was, a damned lie . . .[87]

The creation of Bloom provides a very full gloss on the meaning of the letter, indicating Joyce's humanistic view of the importance of the individual, his belief in unspectacular virtues, and his own 'classical temper' which 'bends upon these present things'.

In the wider context of modern literature, Joyce is also set apart. Unlike the other literary liberators of his time, who are high bourgeois, he is distinct because he is, as V. S. Pritchett puts it, 'the cad, the lower-middle-class man'.[88] This enables him to treat Bloom without condescension or a shuddering aversion — compare Eliot in *The Waste Land* holding 'the young man carbuncular' at arm's length with his fastidious tongs. Joyce's hero is the enemy for nearly all of the high priests of modern culture — one of the low, 'the traipsing city man whose habits and language have been debased',[89] and whose very job — advertisement canvasser — marks him down as lost in that ephemeral,

superficial 'filthy modern tide' (Yeats's phrase) which Pound, Eliot,
Yeats himself and — from his different angle — Lawrence spill so much
ink in excoriating. Joyce looks on Bloom and the 'world' of which
Bloom is the representative calmly and unhistrionically. Nothing is
sentimentalised, but nor does Joyce see Bloom and his world as part
of that 'immense panorama of futility and anarchy which is contemporary history', to use Eliot's phrase from his review of *Ulysses*.[90]
Rather, Joyce might say in the words of Augustine which he puts into
the mind of Stephen in the 'Aeolus' chapter:

> It was revealed to me that those things are good which yet are cor-
> rupted which neither if they were supremely good nor unless they
> were good could be corrupted.

(p. 180)

In its valuation of Bloom *Ulysses* strikes an extremely effective blow
for the much-despised 'modern civilisation', then. Arising from that
valuation comes the sanity of Joyce's mockery of the apocalyptic
stance, so often adopted by the great literary reactionaries as a response
to their.vision of the modern age as a waste land. One of the funniest
moments in what is a very funny book comes when Bloom overhears a
snatch of conversation between George Russell (AE), the eminent
visionary, and a young friend:

> — Of the twoheaded octopus, one of whose heads is the head upon
> which the ends of the world have forgotten to come while the other
> speaks with a Scotch accent. The tentacles . . .
> They passed from behind Mr Bloom along the curbstone. Beard and
> bicycle. Young woman.

(p. 154)

This turns up again in burlesque form in 'Circe', where Florry Talbot's
comment 'They say the last day is coming this summer', made with
'obese stupidity', triggers one of Joyce's most exuberant mocking
flights in which the second coming vanishes in a welter of ridiculous
detail:

> (*A rocket rushes up the sky and bursts. A white star falls from it,
> proclaiming the consummation of all things and second coming of
> Elijah. Along an infinite invisible tightrope taut from zenith to
> nadir the End of the World, a twoheaded octopus in gillie's kilts,
> busby and tartan filibegs, whirls through the murk, head over heels,
> in the form of the Three Legs of Man*)

THE END OF THE WORLD
(*With a Scotch accent*.) Wha'll dance the keel row, the keel row, the keel row?

(p. 481)

After such knowledge, what possibility of solemnity? Yeats's rough beast here suffers its most ludicrous sea change.

But Bloom, though the most important character of the novel, is not its all. It would be wrong to give the impression that Joyce intended *Ulysses* to be a portrait of the advertisement canvasser as hero. What are we to make of the juxtaposition of Stephen and Bloom, of the significance (if any) of their 'relationship'? Arnold Kettle is in no doubt:

> The relationship between Bloom and Stephen, on which the whole pattern of the book depends, is a fraud, whose only significance is imposed from above by a vast apparatus of what can often only be described as verbal trickery. The tragedy of *Ulysses* is that Joyce's extraordinary powers, his prodigious sense of the possibilities of language, should be so deeply vitiated by the sterility of his vision of life.[91]

The book does indeed suggest at many points a fundamental link between the two men. It is not just that Bloom is seeking for a son and that Stephen — less consciously — is looking for a father, though this is the weightiest aspect of their relationship. The sense that Joyce is hinting at some deep kinship between the two is mediated in hundreds of other ways. So both are threatened by coarse 'usurpers' in Boylan and Mulligan, both are 'exiles' in different ways in Dublin, both are grieved during the day by the memory of bereavement, both share a distaste for violence and believe in achieving inner moral victories over their enemies, both have lapsed from the beliefs of their fathers, and so forth. And even at a lower level there are parallels; both are dressed in black during the day, both are keyless, both think of *Hamlet* (at very different levels of complexity, to be sure). So we are clearly meant to think of the two of them as a pair.

And yet throughout the novel we are also aware of the great differences between them. More than 'name, age, race, creed' (p. 638), as the impersonal catechism of 'Ithaca' puts it, are the separating forces between them. As we come to know them intimately, we see that the very shape of their minds, the rhythm of their thoughts, make it unlikely that they could ever achieve any real or enduring contact in their

daily lives. Stephen is involved in trying to impose a meaningful shape
on his life, to abstract patterns from the flux around him. He is capable
of shutting out, or greatly reducing, the bombardment of discrete
details from the world of process apprehended by the senses. In 'his'
chapters, we are for quite long periods in a mental world generated by
Stephen's intelligence. While he knows he must open himself more to
the sensorily grasped empirical world of phenomena, he fears to do so
to the point where he might lose a sense of his own identity. Bloom, on
the other hand, is wholly immersed in the phenomenal and empirical
world, an involvement symbolised by his love for water, emblem of
that world, 'fresh cold neverchanging everchanging water'. Stephen,
significantly, is 'hydrophobe, hating partial contact by immersion or
total by submission'. Maddox sums up and extends the point, to cover
Bloom's frequent plunges away from emotional crises into the safety of
consideration of trivial details of the physical world (the unlet state of
'number eighty' to recover from his vision of desolation referred to
above, a study of his fingernails in the 'Hades' episode to recover from
the sight of Boylan):

> Bloom . . . is not simply attracted to the phenomenal world. At his
> most painful moments, he is psychologically addicted to it, since it
> serves as his chief refuge from revolutionizing thought. He is in this
> respect the precise opposite of Stephen, who suffers a kind of
> spiritual anemia from being so removed from Bloom's world.
> Stephen is incomplete because he has only mental solutions to his
> problems; he can only *imagine* his desired commitment to the
> world. Bloom is incomplete because his nature is so completely
> subdued to what it works in. Immersed in the physical world, he is
> incapable of a depersonalized distance from himself, and so he
> cannot grasp even the nature of his own dilemma.[92]

They are very different, then, in the very structures of their minds and
emotional responses to experience, and the 'Ithaca' chapter sets its
impersonal seal on what we already know; that even when they do get
together, the real contact between them is inevitably limited:

> Were their views on some points divergent? Stephen dissented
> openly from Bloom's views on the importance of dietary and civic
> self-help while Bloom dissented tacitly from Stephen's views on the
> eternal affirmation of the spirit of man in literature.
>
>   (p. 627)

Bloom's proposal of asylum 'promptly, inexplicably, with amicability, gratefully' declined (p. 656), and aware of the 'irreparability of the past' and the 'imprevidibility of the future' (p. 657), he is also aware that his various plans for bringing about future meetings between the two of them are unlikely to be realised. Stephen's feelings are more opaque to us, but as Clive Hart has argued,[93] we can easily imagine that Stephen has not freed himself, or tried to free himself, from his bondage to Church, state, family, only to enter another kind of bondage to Bloom. They part, and in one of the novel's great passages, Joyce emphasises the solitude of the human lot:

> Alone, what did Bloom feel?
> The cold of interstellar space, thousands of degrees below freezing point or the absolute zero of Fahrenheit, Centigrade or Réaumur.
> (p. 665)

What are we to make of all this, in view of the novel's apparently heavy insistence on the theme of the quest for paternity and sonship? Clearly the shadowy and insubstantial coming together of Stephen and Bloom could be seen as evidence that Joyce is stressing the futile and ironic aspects of human relationships, that the whole elaborate network of literal and symbolic ties drawn between Bloom and Stephen is there simply to be exploded, that Joyce's vision of life is, in Kettle's word, sterile. Kettle would argue that the paternity metaphor exists only at the symbolic level, *is* only a metaphor, and, not buttressed by the *action* or 'plot' of the novel, reveals a 'fraud', a hollow piece of 'verbal trickery' at the heart of *Ulysses*. Behind this sort of view is the Jamesian criterion that the novelist must not 'tell' us, much less imply, but *show* us; mixed with more than a dash of the Lawrence-Leavis emphasis on 'felt life' as vital to the health of any work of art − on this view, the reality of a novel must come mainly from its representational qualities, for which mere symbolic structures are no substitute. Hence, the encounter of Bloom and Stephen can have no real positive moral significance. For these reasons, a critic who finds Joyce's linking of Stephen and Bloom either merely 'literary' or an ironic demonstration of the futility of life will be unconvinced by A. Walton Litz's argument about the meeting of the two as being a complex statement about psychological potentialities:

> On the literal level, bounded by the twenty hours of the novel's action, Stephen and Bloom are mock-heroic figures; but on the figurative level they take on heroic and creative possibilities. Having

confined himself to a realistic time-scheme which made impossible the actual dramatization of that growth of personality so characteristic of the conventional novel, Joyce vested this element in his symbolic structures. To paraphrase Santayana, *Ulysses* is mock-heroic in immediacy, but heroic in perspective.[94]

Before considering more fully the precise significance of this 'figurative level', it is possible to confront the Kettle argument more directly. There is, that is, a more comprehensive realism in the 'resonant unfulfilment' of the Bloom-Stephen relationship. It is not just that it would have been intolerably sentimental to have an ecstatic *rencontre* between the two, in which Bloom finds his lost son and Stephen perceives a personified manifestation of the Maturity for which he is seeking. Such a conclusion would have smacked over-much of the conventional literary plot, in which life is artificially arranged or abridged in accordance with the dictates of the plot-pattern. Even more than Virginia Woolf in her famous statement on modern fiction,[95] Joyce objected to the falsification of life by the imposed requirement of 'telling a story'. In conversation with Arthur Power, who questioned him 'is literature to be fact or is it to be an art?' Joyce replied:

> It should be life . . . and one of the things I could never get accustomed to in my youth was the difference I found between life and literature.[96]

— and he also in Power's presence mounted a spirited attack on what he saw as the creaking conventionalities of plot in Hardy's *Tess of the D'Urbervilles*. He told Stanislaus that 'literature' was 'a parody of life', and Stanislaus records:

> More than he objected to the succession of thrilling incidents carefully worked out so as to keep the interest alive, my brother objected to the literary psychology which he found everywhere in fiction. He said that literature provided men and women with false consciences, literary consciences.[97]

Although *Ulysses* does 'tell a story' (after a fashion), it is one of the book's great achievements to free 'conversation, anecdote, thought, desultory impression, image and happening' from their 'long subordination to plot'.[98] No book can be 'life' of course, but *Ulysses* comes as close as any book to capturing the feel of the texture of life in all its random contingency, shot through with moments of illumination and significance. All of us live the sense of Eliot's line: 'We had the experience but missed the meaning'. Just as the very exhaustiveness of the techniques employed to define Bloom paradoxically serves to demonstrate that there is an indefinable essence at his core, and hence asserts the mysterious freedom of the individual personality, so the thematic inconclusiveness of Joyce's handling of the Bloom-Stephen relationship is, in part, a way of suggesting the protean slipperiness of life, whose patterns are more subtle and complex than the plot patterns of literature would have us believe. Some people would find this a depressing thought; I find the idea that life cannot be pinned down a most cheering thought. There is a humility, as well as a vivifying comic sense, in *Ulysses*; this enormously 'written' book, one of the most 'literary' of novels, demonstrates in its handling of character and 'plot' the limitations of literature as a representational art. The whole novel is full of 'metaphors of incompleteness', through which, as Maddox says, 'the book describes itself',[99] and of which the glancing contact and rebound of Stephen and Bloom is only the most obvious.

So one may counter Kettle's assertion that a fraud has been perpetrated on us firstly by arguing thus, that Joyce is attempting to push the novel form towards a greater degree of inclusive realism, that life rarely has its neat ends. Again to quote Eliot:

> There is no end, but addition: the trailing
> consequences of further days and hours . . .

Alternatively, one may assent to the notion that the book's essential meaning is vested in symbolic structures, in 'significances imposed from above', but argue for a deeper and rounder understanding of these significances. The paternity motif is only a symbol for Joyce himself, and we are not to attempt to interpret the Bloom-Stephen relationship literally. At the level of simple character comparison and contrast, Joyce's art of the unspoken implication makes clear the gifts that each character has the potentiality to offer the other; Stephen would benefit from acquiring something of Bloom's resilience and unself-conscious engagement in the 'everchanging neverchanging' empirical processes of life, Bloom from acquiring something of Stephen's refusal to allow himself to be totally submerged in the flux of phenomena, his strenuousness of effort to perceive significant form in experience and make it operative in his own life. But even this, important though it is, is not the fundamental implication of the juxtaposition of Stephen and Bloom. Together they represent vital aspects of Joyce's own mind, polarities which the novel brings to a finely achieved stasis. Joyce combines in himself at last, and comprehensively, the citizen, the ordinary suffering and surviving man, and the artist. Stephen and Bloom are divided counterparts of his own self, and his capacity to enter fully, imaginatively and morally, into each of them, represents a triumphant act of self-understanding and self-integration. As Goldberg puts it:

> All discussion about whether or not their relationship is 'consummated' in 'Ithaca' is . . . beside the point. Clearly it is not, nor could it be . . . The controlling irony of *Ulysses* is that neither Stephen nor Bloom is capable of fully understanding himself or the other − Stephen needs Bloom's relative freedom, Bloom needs Stephen's knowledge and imagination. The only person who can understand and express them is Joyce. Their union is therefore impossible *within* the action of *Ulysses*. It takes place far beyond it − the end to which the life represented in the action moves as its 'one great goal' − in that 'intense instant of imagination' when 'that which I was is that which I am and that which in possibility I may come to be'. The 'consummation' is the act whereby the artist, like God, by understanding himself, the Son, and all creatures, conceives and utters his Word, yet 'remains within, or behind or beyond or above his handiwork'. The consummation of the action of *Ulysses* is *Ulysses* itself.[100]

The relevance of Stephen's theory about Shakespeare's life and art as a key to understanding this aspect of *Ulysses* is clear. Stephen and Bloom are entirely credible, that is, as individual characters; but through them and the tenuous link he creates between them, Joyce is able to explore and define the nature of his own personality and experience. Stephen says it memorably, in summing up the autobiogrpahical basis of Shakespeare's art:

> He found in the world without as actual what was in his world within as possible. Maeterlinck says: *If Socrates leave his house today he will find the sage seated on his doorstep. If Judas go forth tonight it is to Judas his steps will tend.* Every life is many days, day after day. We walk through ourselves, meeting robbers, ghosts, giants, old men, young men, wives, widows, brothers-in-love. But always meeting ourselves.
>
> (p. 201)

The stress on the necessary impersonality of art, much underlined in modern aesthetics since Eliot's famous utterance in 'Tradition and the Individual Talent',[101] combined with Stephen's words in *A Portrait* (usually quoted out of context), has directed attention away from the consistently autobiographical nature of Joyce's work. *Ulysses* is the triumphant culmination of a development begun as early as 1904, when Joyce wrote the brief story 'A Portrait of the Artist' in one day. It was rejected by the editors of the journal *Dana*, but nevertheless Joyce had begun his life's work. As Ellmann says:

> At the age of twenty-one Joyce found he could become an artist by writing about the process of becoming an artist, his life legitimizing his portrait by supplying the sitter, while the portrait vindicated the sitter by its evident admiration for him.[102]

By the time of *Ulysses*, the 'evident admiration' has been qualified by an inclusive maturity of vision and sceptical tolerance; but the book is still, in its complex way, a portrait of James Joyce.

Hostile critics may find this an even more 'sterile' way of looking at *Ulysses* than seeing it as a projection of ideas about paternity and sonship which founders under the weight of its own symbolic superstructures. One can only reply that Joyce has a wonderful capacity for objectifying his inner world and his emotional selves, so that one is never conscious in the reading of any claustrophobic narrowness; on the contrary, here is a book which seems to offer God's plenty. Joyce himself affirmed the inevitability of his kind of autobiographical art — at the time of the earliest imaginative stirrings of *Ulysses*, in 1908, he lashed out at the psychologist Paul Bourget:

> 'Psychologist! What can a man know but what passes inside his own head?' Stanislaus replied, 'Then the psychological novel is an absurdity, you think? and the only novel is the egomaniacs? D'Annunzio's?' Joyce replied 'I said as much in my pamphlet' ['The Day of the Rabblement'].[103]

The 'egomania' takes an extremely satisfying creative form in *Ulysses* where it is projected on and diverted through a great gallery of vividly realised characters. Yet, in the end, Joyce would have agreed with his great contemporary on the provenance of his brilliant and variegated 'circus animals'; for Joyce, as for Yeats,

> . . . all the ladders start
> In the foul rag and boneshop of the heart.

(CP, p. 392)

Ulysses is not, of course, an ordinary novel, and my omission so far of
any detailed discussion of the technical virtuosities of the book — the
Homeric parallel, the numerous parodies and pastiches of differing
literary styles, the encylopaedic lists and catalogues, the elaborate use
of motif and leitmotif — may have given a misleading impression.
Certainly the 'story' becomes increasingly submerged roughly after the
mid-point of the book under a welter of intrusive authorial devices of
style; form and content seem to go increasingly in different directions
in chapters like 'Sirens', 'Cyclops', 'Oxen of the Sun', 'Circe' and
'Ithaca'. And certainly the stylistic pyrotechnics alienate many readers;
even Ezra Pound commented somewhat sourly on the receipt of the
'Sirens' episode: 'New style per chapter not required.'[104] By concen-
trating as I have done on Stephen and Bloom I have tried to suggest
that Joyce believes, as much as any other more conventional novelist,
in the reality of individual character, and that *Ulysses* need not necessarily be regarded as a freak or sport. But clearly no reading of the
novel can omit an attempt to assess the meaning and significance of its
elaborate battery of literary artifices.[105]

At one level, the technical complexity of *Ulysses* is simply a direct
product of that sense of cultural inferiority which was Joyce's inheritance as a Catholic Irishman, and which we began this essay by discussing. Joyce had, in fact, a far more thorough and elaborate formal education than Yeats, yet, unlike Yeats, felt himself 'a shy guest at the
feast of the world's learning', and knew that the language which he used
so masterfully was nevertheless not his by ethnic inheritance. *Ulysses*,
with its many styles, is one Irishman's attempt to take on the might of
the dominant and noble English literary tradition, and 'outdo' it. To
put it in the form of the newspaper headlines that Joyce employed in
the 'Aeolus' chapter, one might say: BOGTROTTER MAKES GOOD.
Joyce would show in *Ulysses* that what his own Little Chandler called
'the Celtic note' was not all that there was to the Irish literary imagination. The aggressive modernism of the techniques is itself a side-swipe
at the 'Cuchulanoid' (Synge's epithet) writers of the Irish revival.[106]

Less combatively, Joyce's cultural inheritance contributes to the
complexity of *Ulysses*. His Catholic background gave him a taste not
only for the coherence but also for the baroque ramifications of Catholic theology.[107] Just as he transposed his temporary desire to become a
priest into a commitment to the priesthood of art, so did he transpose
his love of out-of-the-way information, abstruse learning and 'encyclo-
paedism' — all imbibed from his Jesuit masters — into the labyrinth of
Ulysses, 'this chaffering allincluding most farraginous chronicle' (p. 405).

The baroque ornamentation in *Ulysses* — the forced correspondences, the disproportion between information required by the reader and the excess of ingenuity which goes into supplying it (as when Bloom's turning on of a tap produces a description of the Dublin waterworks system (pp. 631-2)) — is also present in *Tristram Shandy*, and both novels owe their common mode to imaginations profoundly influenced by scholasticism.[108] Joyce, who could spend days happily poring over outdated compendia of useless knowledge, remarked approvingly to Arthur Power in Paris that he thought that the imagination of contemporary Europe was becoming medieval again, in its consciousness and values. He went on, in words which capture well, if metaphorically, that pedantic obsessiveness which is strongly marked in *Ulysses* as in writers like the late lamented Flann O'Brien:

> There is an old church I know of down near Les Halles, a black foliated building with flying buttresses spread out like the legs of a spider, and as you walk past it you see the huge cobwebs hanging in its crevices, and more than anything else it reminds me of my own writings . . . And in my opinion one of the most interesting things about Ireland is that we are still fundamentally a medieval people, and that Dublin is still a medieval city . . . Take Yeats, for example, he is a true medievalist with his love of magic, his incantations and his belief in signs and symbols, and his later bawdiness. *Ulysses* is also medieval but in a more realistic way.[109]

Pedantry, medievalism, scholasticism — whether taken seriously or as a source of comic enjoyment — do not touch much of a chord in the Anglo-Saxon imagination, but are deeply rooted in the Irish.[110] In this sense, Joyce is as much 'home-grown' as cosmopolitan or avant-garde in his stylistic audacities.

From another angle, it is the very absence of a trammelling — or sustaining — literary tradition in Ireland, at least in the English language, which might be seen as conducing most powerfully to the imaginative exhaustiveness of *Ulysses*, to that attempt to 'get everything in', of which the multiplicity of stylistic modes is as much evidence as the sheer density of information about what Dublin looked like, smelt like, sounded like, on a particular day in 1904 when Throwaway won the Gold Cup at distant Ascot. Stanislaus speaks of his brother's attempt to create a world as being related to the Irish cultural problem:

> In Ireland, a country which has seen revolutions in every generation,

> there is properly speaking no national tradition. Nothing is stable in
> the country; nothing is stable in the minds of the people. When the
> Irish artist begins to write, he has to create his moral world from
> chaos by himself, for himself. Yet, though this is an enormous dis-
> advantage for a host of writers of good average talent, it proves to be
> an enormous advantage for men of original genius, such as Shaw,
> Yeats or my brother.[111]

Hence, finally, the stylistic and technical developments of *Ulysses* may
be ascribed to various factors in his Irish background, and are not
necessarily to be put down to European literary viruses that Joyce
picked up during his long exile. In fact, Joyce did not know all that
much about contemporary developments in European literature, and as
time went on spent even less time trying to find out about them.[112]

At a more strictly literary level, Joyce's rejection of the conventions
of the traditional novel, especially — as we have seen — in regard to the
structuring of 'events' into a literary 'plot' — forced him to seek or to
impose other unifying devices on his novel, lest it should seem to par-
take itself of the random contingency of the world it describes.[113] The
Homeric parallel is clearly the most important structuring device of this
kind, and will be discussed more fully in a moment. The patterning of
the paternity or quest theme, with the extended references to
Shakespeare and *Hamlet*, and the moral-aesthetic key to the entire
action contained in 'Scylla and Charybdis', we have already examined.
And although the stream of consciousness technique may seem to have
its own tendencies to fragmentation, in fact Joyce distinguishes the
modes of consciousness of Stephen and Bloom so precisely by that
ventriloqual style first seen in embryo in some of the *Dubliners* stories
that the form of each consciousness as we come to know it provides a
strong sense of organisation throughout the first half of the novel at
least, and is latent in the rest of the book.

For similar unifying reasons, Joyce works many of the realistic
phenomena of this Dublin day up into motifs. The weight of realistic
detail is one of the chief factors making for our sense of *Ulysses* as an
overwhelmingly naturalistic novel; the patterned re-appearance in fact
or thought of many of these details — the throwaway, Plumtree's
Potted Meat, H.E.L.Y'S, M'Intosh, Bloom's cake of soap, and many
others — betoken the Daedalean artificer side of Joyce. Many readers
of Joyce feel irritated by his heavy use of motifs, seeing in it proof of
an essentially mechanistic turn of mind, by which a merely superficial
unity is imposed from above by an author drawing attention to nothing

much more than his own efficient card-index system, as it were. One could defend Joyce from this kind of criticism by a simple appeal to experience; real life itself throws up motifs and coincidences all the time, is a blend of the random and the patterned, contains the casual and the causal in equal proportions. A sense of life like that embodied in *Ulysses*, at least in regard to this particular topic, is to be found in that other great artist of the city, Dickens:

> On the coincidences, resemblances, and surprises of life Dickens liked especially to dwell, and few things moved his fancy so pleasantly. The world, he would say, was so much smaller than we thought it; we were all so connected by fate without knowing it and people supposed to be far apart were so constantly elbowing each other; and tomorrow bore so close a resemblance to nothing half so much as yesterday.[114]

Besides, it would be wrong to leave the impression that Joyce's use of motifs represents nothing more than an ingenious ordering device. They often contribute a lot to the comedy and the pathos of the novel. For example, Bloom's eye idly catches, early in the day, the advertisement in the newspaper:

> *What is home without*
> *Plumtree's Potted Meat?*
> *Incomplete.*
> *With it an abode of bliss.*

(p. 67)

A random detail, it nevertheless has its ironic reference to the state of affairs in Eccles Street. After his visit to the cemetery, and nearer lunchtime, it enters his head again in the context of reflections on the art of his own profession, advertising. Bloom reflects scornfully on the ineptitude of Wisdom Hely's ideas on advertising as compared to his own grandiose schemes:

> His ideas for ads like Plumtree's potted under the obituaries, cold meat department.

(p. 143)

At lunch, thinking about cannibalism and the unfortunate end of the reverend Mr MacTrigger, he laughs again at the stupid siting of the ad — 'Dignam's potted meat' (p. 160). And then late at night in the Eccles Street kitchen, Bloom sees the remains of Molly's and Blaze's love-feast:

. . . four conglomerated black olives in oleaginous paper, an empty
pot of Plumtree's potted meat, an oval wicker basket bedded with
fibre and containing one Jersey pear . . .

(p. 635)

Most poignantly, and in one of our last sights of Bloom, this insignificant grocery item 'achieves', as Joyce said in a different place, 'its
own epiphany':

What did his limbs, when gradually extended, encounter? New clean
bedlinen, additional odours, the presence of a human form, female,
hers, the imprint of a human form, male, not his, some crumbs,
some flakes of potted meat, recooked, which he removed.

(p. 691)

Again and again in *Ulysses*, the things and objects that make up 'the
land of Phenomenon' (p. 378) are given this sort of human resonance;
the objective universe is suffused with the personalities of its per-
ceivers.[115]

Such notable critics as Ezra Pound and A. Walton Litz have seen the
Homeric parallel as mainly a structural device, a necessary scaffolding
inside which to contain the enormously heterogeneous material of the
book, and of more use to the author than of significance to the reader.
Litz says that Pound was right in his early judgement of the Homeric
framework:

These correspondences are part of Joyce's medievalism and are
chiefly his own affair, a scaffold, a means of construction, justified
by the result, and justified by it only.[116]

Most critics, however, feel that the relationship between Homer and
Ulysses goes beyond the merely structural to involve questions of sub-
stantive and informing values. And here is where the argument rages.
On the one hand, one may say that the gap between the heroic values
of Homer and modern values creates a critical irony directed by Joyce
at the squalid futility of modern life, in the mode perfected by Eliot:

Where are the eagles and the trumpets?
Buried beneath some snow-deep Alps.
Over buttered scones and crumpets
Weeping, weeping multitudes
Droop in a hundred A.B.C.'s.

On the other hand, it can be — and has been — argued that the Homeric parallel is a means whereby Joyce can give expression to his archetypal vision of humanity, the view (worked out even more fully in *Finnegans Wake* with its Viconian structure) that human types and human situations repeat one another through history.[117] Richard Ellmann, who gives one of the best accounts of Joyce's use of his 'sources' in Homer and Shakespeare for *Ulysses*, says:

> Joyce felt more than most writers how interconnected literature is, how to press one button is to press them all . . . In his library was Georges Polti's *Les Trente-six situations dramatiques*, in which hundreds of works, and some incidents of history and modern life, were conflated to show that all made do with three dozen basic plots. This was a literal working out of Joyce's contention in his undergraduate paper, 'Drama and Life', that the laws of human society are changeless. That one hero should gall the kibe of another seemed therefore second nature.[118]

On this view, the *Odyssey* offers an archetype for modern man, which Bloom fills out quite genuinely, for all that his heroic weapon is transmuted into a cigar, 'one of your prime stinkers' (p. 288).

My own view is a modified version of the 'archetypal' reading. That is, I believe that there are fundamental correspondences between the moral and even some of the physical situations of both Ulysses and Bloom (and, to a lesser extent, of Stephen and Telemachus); both have to confront temptations, dangers, enemies. This sounds rather vague and inclusive, but then archetypal patterns do tend to be rather vague and inclusive. At certain points in the novel the correspondences are particularly obvious. For example, in Homer Ulysses makes sure with the beeswax in his crew's ears that they will not be able to hear the dangerously beautiful music of the siren's songs, but ties himself to the mast so that he will be able to hear the songs but not give way to them. Bloom listens, out of sight, to the sentimental songs of Simon Dedalus and his cronies in the Ormond bar, but his only, slightly later, contribution to the music is a fart done under the protective rumble of a passing tram (the prudent member at it again). Thus, like Ulysses, Bloom half-yields to temptation — the temptation, in his case, of immersing himself in the maudlin self-pity generated by the cloying emotionality of the songs, but saves himself by his good sense; his Ulyssean ability to see through the merely illusory charms of the siren-songs. Similarly, when he stands with upraised ashplant over Bella

Cohen in the brothel (p. 551), there is a strong visual reminder of Ulysses, his sword upraised over Circe; Bloom achieves victory over his own masochistic urges and the lures of the brothel, and 'rescues' Stephen, thanks to the moly of his own prudence, common-sense and practicality.

In these general situations, in their both being 'men of many devices', in many moral qualities, in being husbands, fathers, sons, 'lovers', and exiles, it is possible to argue for a genuine affinity between Homer's hero and Joyce's. But it is difficult to push the argument too far without toppling into absurdity.[119] That is, while we may feel the force of the *overall* parallel between the two wandering heroes, the elaborate working out of correspondences between incidental details in Homer's story and Joyce's Dublin day, the desperate attempts to find modern equivalents for a whole range of events, persons, and things in the heroic world – this is surely risible. Calypso regaled herself with ambrosia and nectar; Joyce gives Molly her breakfast-time cream, ordinarily reserved solely for her. When Ulysses met Ajax in Hades, Ajax treated him coldly, being still angry about Ulysses' victory over him in the contest for the arms of Archilles. Joyce has John Henry Menton snub Bloom in the cemetery –

> Got his rag out that evening on the bowling green because I sailed inside him. Pure fluke of mine: the bias.
>
> (p. 107)

The island of Aeolus was surrounded by a wall of bronze; so Joyce begins his 'Aeolus' chapter with a picture of the trams and tram-lines, the 'rows of cast steel', which encircle the heart of the hibernian metropolis. The Lestrygonians swooped down on Ulysses' friends at Lamos, and drowned or ate them. So Joyce has Bloom feed, at the Liffey, the gulls, who 'swooped silently two, then all, from their heights, pouncing on prey. Gone. Every morsel' (p. 142); in the same 'Lestrygonians' chapter, Bloom half remembers a limerick:

> *There was a right royal old nigger. Who ate or something the some-things of the reverend Mr MacTrigger.*
>
> (p. 160)

Because Joyce believed, with Bérard, that the small islands of the Sirens were flowery, the dining tables in the Ormond Hotel have flowers set on them, and Miss Douce preens for Boylan 'a bosom and a rose' (p. 251). Ulysses blinded the one-eyed Cyclops with a sharpened club heated in the fire. So Joyce practically swamps the reader in the

'Cyclops' chapter with references to blindness — Stuart Gilbert mentions some of them:

> . . . the boxer 'whose right eye was nearly closed', the narrator's desire, happily suppressed, to kick Garryowen 'where it wouldn't blind him', and we hear of that occult sewer, the 'blind intestine'. The first remark, indeed, of the narrator — an imprecation of the sweep who 'near drove his gear into my eye' — is an obvious recall of the blinding of the giant, and the huge club of . . . Odysseus . . . has its pigmy caricature in Mr Bloom's 'knockmedown cigar'.[20]

Finally — to end a catalogue that could go on and on — we might just note that, following up the Circean analogies, Zoe the whore replies to Bloom's question 'Where are you from?' — airily or labouredly, depending on taste — 'Hog's Norton where the pigs play the organs' (p. 475) (Stephen is playing the piano in Bella Cohen's establishment — naturally).

Now, how is the reader to respond to this kind of ingenuity which marks Joyce's treatment throughout *Ulysses*? Surely not with the reverential solemnity of Stuart Gilbert, who gives the impression that Joyce's reworking of the details and motifs of the *Odyssey* is an entirely successful transplantation of heroic epic to modern. Nor does the comic disproportion in the examples I've cited (ambrosia to cream, contest for the armour of Achilles to a bowls match, etc.) necessarily imply that Joyce is scornfully belittling the triviality of modern life. Whether one prefers the 'archetypal' reading of *Ulysses* or the ironic, surely what the exhaustive ingenuity of Joyce's relentless hunting out of correspondences chiefly does is to draw attention to itself. I have referred to the comprehensiveness of Joyce's attempt to link the Homeric story with his own as desperate and risible; but I mean deliberately desperate, deliberately risible. The book constantly and overtly makes us aware of its own procedures; part of our experience of reading it is our sense of the grossly *imposed* quality of the mythic structure. And, further, this sense, this awareness, is a large factor in our enjoyment of *Ulysses*.

There are two different ways in which this works. Firstly, there is the enormous gusto in the way Joyce goes about solving the almost impossible tasks he sets himself. In the second half of the novel especially, no reader can fail to feel that the author with his prodigious inventiveness and variety of style has himself moved to the forefront of the book, and become in a sense the hero. Joyce himself is revealed as being, like Ulysses, a man of many devices. The almost crazy zest with

which Joyce transmutes the Odyssean incident in which the companions of Ulysses killed some of the oxen of Helios on Thrinacia into his
own 'Oxen of the Sun' is a particularly fine example of what I mean.
There *is* a link between what happens in the Joyce chapter and what
happens in Homer, but the reader is far more aware of the exuberant,
free-wheeling, baroque *form* of the chapter than of any compelling
similarity between *events* on Thrinacia and in 'Horne's house'
(p. 368).[121] The same is true even in the less extravagant 'Cyclops',
where Joyce portrays Homer's physical giant partly through what he
called gigantism of style. The citizen's handkerchief is hauled out after
he has 'spat a Red Bank oyster out of him right in the corner':

> The much treasured and intricately embroidered ancient Irish face-
> cloth attributed to Solomon of Droma and Manus Tomaltach og
> MacDonogh, authors of the Book of Ballymote, was then carefully
> produced and called forth prolonged admiration.

(p. 316)

'Prolonged' is the word – Joyce goes on in this vein for another page.

It is not only in connection with the underlying Homeric myth that
we are led to feel in the second half of *Ulysses* the flagrant yoking together by violence of matter and manner. Each chapter treats the story
with its Homeric overtones in such wildly differing stylistic ways – we
have a fugue ('Sirens'), a mock-epic ('Cyclops'), a sentimental trashy
novelette ('Nausicaa'), a comic survey of prose-styles ('Oxen of the
Sun'), an expressionist drama ('Circe'), and an allegedly scientific catechism ('Ithaca'). Each of these styles contributes something dramatically and morally to the novel, as we saw, for example, in discussing
how the parodies in 'Oxen of the Sun' help to fill out the characterisation of Bloom. But taken all together, what these varied stylistic extravagances do is to make us aware of the comic author enjoying himself,
gambolling happily in the exercise of his power. This is a major feature
of comedy in general (and *Ulysses* is a great comic book); whereas the
writer of tragedy or the naturalistic writer always try to give the impression that they have no selective control over their material, but must
simply follow the iron inevitabilities laid down by life, the comic writer
is unabashedly present, pulling the strings as overtly as he likes (one
thinks of Shakespeare's cheerful unconcern for psychological probabilities at the end of *Twelfth Night*, for example, or Sterne's leaving
characters frozen on stairways or at keyholes through his lengthy discussions with the reader on how to write the book in front of him, or
Fielding's authorial intrusions in *Tom Jones*, or Ben Jonson's joyous

heaping of intrigue upon intrigue in *Volpone* and *The Alchemist*).

Thus the very ingenuity of *Ulysses* provides much of its comic appeal — the sheer zest and gusto that has gone into the *doing* of it, which Budgen's record captures so admirably. Notoriously, of course, when speaking of what is funny, *de gustibus non est disputandum*. Leaving the subject, then, we may turn to the charge that the extraordinary heterogeneity of Joyce's exercises in style in the latter part of the book, however funny in individual execution, fragments whatever unity the novel might be said to have. I do not think this is true, not so much because I would argue that the Homeric parallel *is* organically binding — its self-defeating, deliberately mechanical over-elaboration has already been commented on — but because of the solidly specified reality of Bloom and Stephen and Molly[122] and the connections between them; in other words, because of the human character and events of the book. So firmly established is our sense of the reality of character and environment in the first half of *Ulysses* that Joyce can afford, in a sense, to play his technical virtuosities around that reality later on. W. J. Harvey, writing of Dickens's *Bleak House*, makes a point of great relevance to the total effect of Joyce's work:

> I would say that one of the reasons for its greatness is the extreme tension set up between the centrifugal vigour of its parts and the centripetal demands of the whole. It is a tension between the impulse to intensify each local detail or particular episode and the impulse to subordinate, arrange and discipline. The final impression is one of immense and potentially anarchic energy being brought — but only just — under control. The fact that the equipoise between part and whole is so precariously maintained is in itself a tribute to the energy being harnessed.[123]

Energetic gusto, manifested in the extraordinary complexity of the book's techniques, played off against scrupulous fidelity to the naturalistic details of life — this tension in *Ulysses*, as in *Bleak House*, does indeed characterise the reader's experience of Joyce's novel. But in Joyce, 'the fascination of what's difficult' points in a comic direction. There is irony in the use of the Homeric myth, but an irony directed not at the pettiness of the modern world. As Joyce deploys his mythic correspondences, especially as the stylistic patterning becomes ever more elaborate, and *style* itself comes to embody or represent Homeric *incident*, we can sense — and share — his own laughter at the workings of the literary imagination itself. 'How's that for high?' he asks us, and we smile in reply. Pretty high.

Joyce's use of myth in *Ulysses* is usually seen as aligning his work with a major trend in some of the greatest of modern artists — Eliot, Yeats, Mann in certain moods, Picasso, Stravinsky — namely, the employment of myth to universalise, to provide coherence, to link the frightening present to the stable past. Eliot went so far as to say of Joyce that his use of myth had 'made the modern world possible in art'.[124] Hence Yeats, believing that great myths are the mother of great nations, can ask with all the compelling seriousness of his rhetorical *gravitas*:

When Pearse summoned Cuchulain to his side,
What stalked through the Post Office?

Hence Eliot, feeling with Yeats the 'formless spawning fury' of 'this filthy modern tide', also attempts to control modern experience by filtering it through the archetypes of his shaping myths in *The Waste Land*, and expects us to feel that the insights provided by the mythic procedure are impersonal, universal, 'true'.

Joyce is, in fact, quite different in his use of myth.[125] The point again is in the outrageously imposed quality of the mythic structure in *Ulysses*. I have argued, firstly, that this makes for comedy (and 'comic' is not a word one would readily apply to the art of Yeats and Eliot). Perhaps an even more important result of the reader's sense of the blatant gratuitousness of the link made between myth and reality in *Ulysses* could be expressed like this. The comically elaborate attempt to force the Dublin characters and their day into the mythic straitjacket is designed deliberately to fail. That is, the employment of myth becomes a way of affirming the dense specificity of Dublin, the autonomy of this naturalistic world of Plumtree's Potted Meat and Epp's cocoa, of pubs and trams and newspapers, of songs and theatres and advertising placards. Even more, of course, the irreducible individuality of the human characters of the place, whether major figures like Bloom or briefly glimpsed loungers like Nosey Flynn ('Look at his mouth. Could whistle in his own ear. Flap ears to match' (p. 161)), is affirmed, as much by their stubborn refusal to put on the Homeric clothes that the author exaggeratedly foists on them as by the vividness of observation that goes into creating them. The real irony of *Ulysses* is that Joyce's use of a whole arsenal of literary devices and techniques directs our attention to the fact that life can never really be 'captured' by literature. This amounts to a humane — even humble — acknowledgement of the mysterious otherness and, above all, reality of what lies outside the artist's own imagination. Joyce, despite his great verbal genius, does not see the word as fully capable even of representing reality, let alone replacing it. The imperious shaping imagination of the artist is a reality, too, of course, a reality fully demonstrated in the technical complexity of *Ulysses*; but Joyce shows it deadlocked in comic *stasis* with the intransigent and irreducible otherness of reality. The artist is not God. In the delightful interplay between technical extravagance and what Henry James called 'solidity of specification' in *Ulysses*, Joyce imparts a benevolent and humorous benediction on the reconciliation of the pattern-making Stephen and the realistic, empirical Bloom sides of himself. It is a great achievement of an imagination that can only be called, again, thoroughly democratic. The humanity of Bloom is affirmed the more in that, despite the intense scrutiny he is subjected to, the ordeal, as it were, of dissection by various literary techniques, in the end he triumphantly eludes total definition, is not to be fixed 'in a formulated phrase . . . pinned and wriggling on the wall'. Or, as John Gross puts it:

> Characters are deliberately played off against techniques, and not merely for comic effect, either. Bloom is exposed to surrealist ridicule in 'Circe', ruthlessly parodied in 'Eumaeus', put through the mangle in 'Ithaca', and in every case he survives the ordeal . . . Bloom's humanity remains proof against lurid mutations, dismissive judgments, even against the more dessicated sections of 'Ithaca'. First and last he is the same man: an identity crisis is not part of his 'modern' luggage.[126]

Finally, the novel's affirmation of individual identity and of 'the ordinary universe' is the more convincing precisely because Joyce takes such a convoluted road to his conclusion. The complex and brilliant intellectuality of the book's techniques validate its overall 'message' of tolerant acceptance of reality by inoculating that sense of the engaging, continuing, unpredictable variety of life and of people against the easy sentimentality of the middlebrow cliché.

This is the great gift of Joyce's art to Irish life and culture; a tolerant, democratic humorous acceptance which is everywhere informed with intelligence. His work is resolutely anti-heroic (though Bloom is 'a good man') in a country obsessed with heroes and hero-worship. He consistently ridicules violence and apocalyptic thinking in an Ireland sodden with both. Yet he is equally scathing on the sentimentalised view of

Ireland, and could hardly be said to stand for the pieties of the De Valera view of a cosy, Catholic nation of home-lovers — in the 'Circe' episode, Bloom's defence of himself against various charges constitutes a devastatingly comic parody of domestic Ireland, of 'loveful households in Dublin city and urban district . . . model young ladies playing on the pianoforte or anon all with fervour reciting the family rosary round the crackling Yulelog' (p. 440).

From *Dubliners* right through to *Ulysses*, his critique of Irish chauvinism, blather and sentimentality is unsparing. But he does not look away from the real world, from 'the dreary sameness of existence', the commonplace, in disgust. Unlike Yeats, he does not look into the past for the compensatory glories of Irish heroic myths, or for the dignity of Ascendancy tradition (unavailable to him, in any case). 'The daily spite of this unmannerly town' does not drive him into isolation and the pursuit of 'beautiful lofty things'. Rather, believing that 'the great human comedy in which each has share gives limitless scope to the true artist today as yesterday', he strives in his works first to understand, and then to reconcile himself — and us — to the human comedy in its Irish manifestation.

Joyce's rejection in his art of the rural, peasant Ireland so important to Yeats, and even more to Synge, is neither a virtue nor a vice, but a simple reflection of his unredeemably urban nature. Joyce simply accepts the city as a major fact of modern living, especially in *Ulysses*. As Frank Budgen says:

> . . . it is not by way of description that Dublin is created in *Ulysses*. There is a wealth of delicate pictorial evocation in *Dubliners*, but there is little or none in *Ulysses* . . . It is not a decor to be modified at will but something as native to [the characters] as water to a fish.[127]

There are moral implications, however, in precisely this unhistrionic and unostentatious mode of treating the city. Joyce, more than most artists, humanises the city since, as Budgen has seen, we only know it through the perceptions of characters to whom it is a phenomenon every bit as natural as 'cold Clare rock and Galway thorn'. It is not the Dantesque hell of Eliot's *Waste Land*, nor the Great Bad Place it seems to be to the essentially archaicising imaginations of Yeats and Synge. For Joyce it simply *is*. Once again, we see Joyce 'bending upon these present things'. But in the fullness of his realisation of the city in *Ulysses*, it is impossible not to feel his affectionate tolerance of the place he left physically but never stopped writing about.

Joyce's attitudes of acceptance and tolerance may be attacked on the grounds that they betoken a political quietism verging towards indifference. Phillip Herring, for example, argues that Joyce's art is essentially static and that therefore he wanted Ireland to stay as his frozen image of her, a 'gallery of paralytic portraits'.[128] Conor Cruise O'Brien had taken the point further in his introduction to *The Shaping of Modern Ireland* by suggesting that there is a connection between 'the comic' and 'the static' in Joyce, as there is in the stories of the Ascendancy writers Somerville and Ross:

> Indeed one could argue that the most characteristically Irish thing about the old landlord class was its inability to take Irish affairs wholly seriously: just as the caricatures of Somerville and Ross resemble the brilliant frozen social scenes of *Ulysses* through their intimations of a world both futile and changeless. Somerville and Joyce . . . saw through the Gaelic League, the Gaelic Athletic Association, the world of the Citizen and the new crooked County Councillors, but they did not see through them to anything in particular or at least not to anything Irish or anything moving and growing.[129]

Several beginnings of an answer could be advanced to this charge, at least on behalf of Joyce. Firstly, at a fairly simple level, there is the point made by Frank Budgen that the writing of *Ulysses* took Joyce about eight years. 'For half of that time all Europe was at war: and peace, when it came, was as disturbing as, though less destructive than, war. Several revolutions shook the world . . . No permanence was in the air'.[130] And of course, Joyce's own country was convulsed with revolution, war and civil war during this time. Perhaps, then, there was a psychological factor at work behind the quietism of *Ulysses*. This is, in a way, to cede part of O'Brien's point, but at least to free Joyce from the charge of blindness, for during the composition of the novel Joyce *knew* that Ireland and Europe had undergone dramatic changes. But, perhaps, and more fundamentally, the quietism of *Ulysses* makes its own valid political point, and even a courageous point, to a nation obsessed with the theology of its own politics, and ever-prone — as recent history all too painfully reminds us — to retreat from the complexities of living into the simplicities of violence. As Bloom says, with most un-Joycean directness:

Force, hatred, history, all that. That's not life for men and women,
insult and hatred. And everybody knows that it's the very opposite
of that that is really life. (p. 317)

Just as Joyce refused to drive a wedge between art and life, so he
refused to drive a wedge between politics and life. His whole art is
designed to stress the wrongness and futility of trying to ignore the
bewildering but enriching context of ordinary life. This is, of course,
what the 'hearts with one purpose alone' *must* do as they drive on to
their next knee-capping. Recently the Ulster poet, James Simmons,
when asked why he was not writing now (in 1978) about the continuing Northern Irish troubles, replied that when all this is over, there will
still be difficult marriages and the perennial problems of human relationships. Perhaps Joyce too felt about an earlier period of Irish convul-
sions that politics is a part rather than the whole of life. At any rate,
'quietism' may not, in Joyce's case, be equated simply with 'indifferen-
tism'. For an Irish writer of any time, but perhaps especially of Joyce's
time, there is an inescapable political context. Who would say that the
tolerant geniality of *Ulysses* is a less attractive stance than the heroic
bitterness which has fuelled Irish history, and which expresses itself still
on the streets of Belfast and Derry?
Yeats wrote:

Out of Ireland have we come.
Great hatred, little room,
Maimed us at the start.
I carry from my mother's womb
A fanatic heart.

(*CP*, p. 288)

The art of James Joyce in its honesty, inclusiveness, intelligence and
humour is at least part of the antidote for this sad condition.

5   SEAN O'CASEY: HEARTS O' FLESH, HEARTS O' STONE, AND CHASSIS

Sean O'Casey was born in 1880 in the Dublin slums, one of thirteen children, eight of whom died in childhood.[1] His father and mother, especially his father, who worked for the proselytising Irish Church Mission, were fervent Protestants; hence the young O'Casey knew not only squalor, poverty and malnutrition – the common lot of the slum-dwellers – but also his isolation in the midst of warrens of tenements that were overwhelmingly Catholic. Perhaps this isolation, aggravated by the ill-health and partial blindness of his boyhood days, played a formative part in shaping the fiercely independent spirit of the man, whose long life was one long struggle, a series of variations on contro-versial issues. O'Casey was active in the Gaelic League, in the Republi-can movement and – above all – in the Labour movement. And far more than any of the other writers with which this study is concerned, he lived in an often terrifyingly immediate way through the travails accompanying the making of modern Ireland – the great Dublin Lock-Out in 1913 which led to the formation first of the Irish Citizen Army (of which O'Casey was secretary), then of the Irish Volunteers; the Easter Rising of 1916; the guerrilla war of independence; the civil war between Free-Staters and Republicans, which followed on the signing of the Treaty with Britain, and which ended only in 1923. O'Casey knew these ten years of violence and bloodshed intimately – as a tene-ment dweller in a cycle of carnage that was peculiarly urban, he could hardly help doing so. And from the political and social mayhem of Ireland between 1913 and 1923, O'Casey made the plays for which he is still best-known, all of which were performed at the Abbey theatre: *The Shadow of a Gunman* (1923), which deals with the guerrilla war; *Juno and the Paycock* (1924), which is set during the civil war; and *The Plough and the Stars* (1926), last of the three but dealing with the chronologically earliest period, that of the Rising itself. Though O'Casey did not tackle directly the Dublin Lock-Out, which in many ways was for him the crucial experience of his life, until the rather bad propagand-ist drama called (with heart-sinking militancy) *The Star Turns Red* (1940), its shadow informs the perspective that he brought to bear in writing his Abbey plays.

Thus, we have here a man of independent intelligence, with a natur-

ally lively observation, untrammelled by literary preconceptions and
unbowed by the distortions of dramatic theory. Not only that, but a man
passionately interested and involved in politics and political ideas. His
experience, at first hand, of so many of the conflicting organisations and
ideas in that strife-torn Ireland, taken along with those other qualities,
might be seen as confirming that O'Casey is the artist who offers most
to those who would understand the boiling Irish stew of patriotism,
violence, colonial subjugation, and war. Like Joyce, O'Casey is urban,
where Yeats and Synge are not; but unlike Joyce, O'Casey confronts
the immediate history of his own time with a characteristic head-on
directness, and with an accessibility which has always made his drama
seem more realistic than anything in Joyce, whose 'realism' is severely
qualified for many readers by the mandarin complexities of his style.

However, O'Casey's work, for all its popularity and apparent 'obvious-
ness', needs in my view to be approached with caution. He can be
uproariously funny ('Joxer's song, Joxer's song - give us wan of your
shut-eyed wans' is one of the finest lines in Irish literature, a small
masterpiece of observation and characterisation), he can be enormously
moving, his skill in manipulating the tragi-comic rhythm of his actions
is superb, and he has, as Lady Gregory was the first to tell him,[2] a
great gift for the creation of character on the stage; but overall, his
achievement is flawed.

Reviewing the critics of O'Casey, Ronald Ayling says in the introduction to his useful anthology of essays:

> Another substantial body of polemic writing . . . masquerades as
> literary or dramatic criticism when it is, in reality, motivated by
> political, nationalist, and/or religious beliefs. For this reason the
> majority of Irish writings on O'Casey is invalidated as *literary*
> criticism.[3]

These are words that the Irish critic does well to pay heed to, especially
perhaps, as in the present case, the Northern Irish critic with the current
Northern tragedy sitting on his pen, who finds something inadequate in
O'Casey's treatment of a previous tragic decade. But perhaps to be Irish
does not necessarily handicap the critic of O'Casey? It is true that we
must be careful not to go outside his plays and write the social or political tracts for the times that O'Casey did not; we must be on our guard
against the danger that Ayling points to of importing illegitimate extra-
literary factors into our consideration of O'Casey. Yet one can surely
go too far in the other direction. O'Casey's plays themselves are superbly

polemical; they are soaked in Irish history, politics and social life. In a sense it is a greater insult to these impressive plays *not* to engage with the issues and opinions that O'Casey felt so passionately about. He would be the last man in the world to wish that his plays be removed from the arena to the safe *cordon sanitaire*, as it were, of purely 'literary' discussion (even if such a thing were possible).

Besides, admirers of O'Casey — and I would count myself one, though well this side of idolatry — have their own 'polemical' ploys. On the one hand, we are told to be literary, academic critics and to filter out our own personal political and social bias. When, however, having tried to do this, we still find ourselves with some 'critical' objection to O'Casey, his defenders can pull the rug from under our feet by invoking the (extra-literary?) hardship of O'Casey's life, which serves both as excuse for O'Casey and as something to make us feel uncomfortable in our smugly academic security. The procedure can be observed neatly at work even in such a good critic as John Jordan, who writes:

> There are occasions, in reading O'Casey, when one loses patience with his lads and lasses, so ardent, so selfconsciously gay, so ostentatious in their pursuit of culture. And then I think of the first three volumes of his great autobiography, and am humbled by that record of mind and imagination and above all enthusiasm, surviving the bitter and bloody arena of the slums in Victorian and Edwardian Dublin.[4]

O'Casey's life is genuinely heroic, a tremendous battle against almost unbearable hardship, and something which predisposes all of us enormously in his favour. But, of course, the hard life does not inevitably and of itself guarantee a flawless art which is beyond criticism. It is to a consideration of that art as manifested in the three Dublin plays that I now wish to turn, hoping to avoid the sterilities both of 'polemics' and of a merely polite academicism. O'Casey is too important for that, especially at a time when his 'world in chassis' would seem to have a tragic relevance to Ireland's north-east corner.

The critical consensus on O'Casey's Dublin plays is that they present an anti-heroic vision of the Irish struggle, in which the rarefied and theoretical ideals of sacrifice and heroic commitment are measured against the ordinary lives of the people, and are found wanting; indeed, in which the politics of nationalism are seen as being fundamentally inimical to what David Krause calls 'the essential human situation — bread on the table and love in the heart'.[5] 'Ordinary life' then becomes *the* standard of value in O'Casey's dramatic world — 'human nature and its necessity – the flux of petty, unheroic life that creeps beneath the surface of great historical moments – provide the dramatic centre of these plays', says Michael Kaufman,[6] and the 'great historical moments' impinge on this life in a destructive and negative way. Krause, Kaufman and other critics agree that Seumas Shields in *The Shadow of a Gunman* makes the point that governs the entire 'trilogy':[7]

> It's the civilians that suffer; when there's an ambush they don't know where to run. Shot in the back to save the British Empire, an' shot in the breast to save the soul of Ireland.
>
> (p. 132)

The people are the victims of a situation that lies outside them and which initially they do not comprehend, until it forces itself damagingly into their tenements. They – especially the women – and not the patriots and political activists, become the heroes of the plays, their heroism consisting partly in their rejection of the stony-hearted politics that surround them, partly in simply *being* and *surviving*. As Krause says of O'Casey's characteristic stress:

> If O'Casey says nothing else, in most of his plays, he certainly insists that his people are *more important* than 'the larger political tragedy' which threatens to destroy them.[8]

This is certainly an accurate description of O'Casey's model of the relationship of 'ordinary life' to 'politics' in the plays. The critical questions are how *convincingly* the plays dramatise this situation, how compellingly O'Casey embodies his valuations both of human 'ordinary' life and of 'inhuman' idealisms, and whether his work has internal conherence, whether in depicting a 'world in chassis' it manages to avoid partaking of that chassis.

The Shadow of a Gunman is a powerful and bitter play which, partly because it is O'Casey's first successfully produced play, has not received the attention given to *Juno* and *The Plough*. Set in a tenement at the height of the guerrilla war of independence, the play describes – in a more clipped and sardonic mode than Synge's *Playboy* – the nature of false heroism and heroic posturings. Donal Davoren, a self-indulgent and insipidly romantic poet, who shares a room with the more earthy and 'primitive' Seumas Shields, a pedlar, is thought because of the gossip and surmise of his fellow tenement-dwellers to be one of the IRA gunmen who are fighting the Black and Tans. Davoren is flattered by the attention he is given by them as a result of this quite untrue image of him, and plays along with it, especially for the sake of the impression he makes on young Minnie Powell —

> Minnie is attracted to the idea, and I am attracted to Minnie. And what danger can there be in being the shadow of a gunman?
>
> (p. 124)

The posturing and sham rhetoric which so liberally besprinkles the first act is exposed in all its hollowness by the terrifying reality of a Black and Tan midnight raid on the tenement, in which Minnie is killed, having been found hiding bombs which she believes are Davoren's. He and Shields have only been concerned to save their skins, and as the curtain falls, Davoren is brought up against his hollowness:

> Ah me, alas! Pain, pain, pain ever, for ever! It's terrible to think that little Minnie is dead, but it's still more terrible to think that Davoren and Shields are alive!
>
> (p. 156)

Even here, it may be noted, the confrontation with his own evasion is itself expressed in the evasive clichés which constitute the kind of poetry Davoren writes.

The play's action then, as critics have often noted, is an urban version of the basic idea of *The Playboy of the Western World*, in which the imaginative fantasies of those around him create a new personality for the central young man. But there is here none of Synge's sense of the creative possibilities of fantasy, of the idea that it can function purpose-fully and positively. Christy Mahon is genuinely transformed by the end of his play, but Davoren is and remains deeply contemptible. This is partly dramatised through the obvious thinness of his 'poetic' personality, which expresses no genuine sense of experience, but in petulant reaction from the sordid circumstances in which he finds himself and in childish irritation at the frequent interruptions he has to put up with in the crowded tenement, can only find consolation in a debased literariness. The self-indulgence is clear at the beginning of Act II, where what we see is the 'sensitivity' of a second-rate soul, pointed up by the references to the genuinely revolutionary Shelley:

> *Davoren*. The cold chaste moon, the Queen of Heaven's bright isles,
> Who makes all beautiful on which she smiles;
> That wandering shrine of soft yet icy flame,
> Which ever is transformed yet still the same.
> Ah, Shelley, Shelley, you yourself were a lovely human orb shining

through clouds of whirling human dust. 'She makes all beautiful
on which she smiles.' Ah, Shelley, she couldn't make this thrice
accursed room beautiful. Her beams of beauty only make its
horrors more full of horrors still. There is an ugliness that can only
be destroyed, and this is part of that ugliness. Donal, Donal, I fear
your last state is worse than your first.

> [He lilts a verse, which he writes on the pad before him]
> When night advances through the sky with slow
> And solemn tread.
> The queenly moon looks down on life below,
> As if she read
> Man's soul, and in her scornful silence said:
> All beautiful and happiest things are dead.

(p. 125)

The irony of Davoren's supposed role as patriot and protector of the
people in the real war, which is one of the things his queenly moon looks
down upon, is specially pointed by his *fin-de-siècle* conception of his
poet's role. When Shields criticises Davoren's kind of poetry, a little later
in this Act, Davoren expresses his contempt for 'the people':

Shields. . . . I don't know much about the pearly glint of the morning
   dew, or the damask sweetness of the rare wild rose, or the subtle
   greenness of the serpent's eye — but I think a poet's claim to
   greatness depends upon his power to put passion in the common
   people.
Davoren. Ay, passion to howl for his destruction. The People! Damn
   the people! They live in the abyss, the poet lives on the mountain-
   top . . . To the people the end of life is the life created for them;
   to the poet the end of life is the life that he creates for himself;
   life has a stifling grip upon the people's throat — it is the poet's
   musician.

(p. 127)

Even in his contempt, Davoren can only talk in stale formulas. Christy
Mahon is a more genuine poet in every way, not least because Christy
does not see himself (except occasionally, and then always with a diminu-
tion of his eloquence) as a poet at all.

In his relationship with Minnie, Davoren begins by firmly dissociating
himself from what he sees as the sham-heroics of republican nationalism:

A man should always be drunk, Minnie, when he talks politics — it's
the only way in which to make them important . . . Oh, we've had

enough of poems, Minnie, about '98, and of Ireland, too.
(pp. 106-7)

Even Robert Emmet, in Davoren's view, 'would have lived on if he could; he died not to deliver Ireland. The British Government killed him to save the British nation.' O'Casey stresses this realistic, even cynical side to Davoren's political — or apolitical — attitudes to dramatise more strikingly the egoism and self-indulgence in Davoren's willing acceptance of the glamorous mantle of the gunman in which Minnie clothes him. This follows immediately:

Minnie. . . . I know what you are.

Davoren. What am I?

Minnie [in a whisper]. A gunman on the run!

Davoren. [too pleased to deny it]. Maybe I am, and maybe I'm not.

Minnie. Oh, I know, I know, I know. Do you never be afraid?

Davoren. Afraid! Afraid of what?

Minnie. Why, the ambushes of course; *I'm* all of a tremble when I hear a shot go off, an' what must it be in the middle of the firin'?

Davoren. [delighted at *Minnie*'s obvious admiration; leaning back in his chair, and lighting a cigarette with placid affectation]. I'll admit one does be a little nervous at first, but a fellow gets used to it after a bit, till, at last, a gunman throws a bomb as carelessly as a schoolboy throws a snowball.
(pp. 109-10)

The stage direction, as well as the words, show the complacency of Davoren's acquiescence in the lie; unlike Christy, who strives in *The Playboy* energetically and continuously to make a reality of the heroic image which is projected on him, Davoren is completely and 'placidly' passive. Christy is spurred on by a real love for Pegeen, but Davoren is not in love with Minnie. He loves only himself, and is merely flattered by Minnie's hero-worship — as Shields says to him later 'You think a lot about her simply because she thinks a lot about you, an' she thinks a lot about you because she looks upon you as a hero'. The action bears this out. When the compromising bombs are found in the room as the Tans begin their raid, Minnie alone is able to act, and her action, even her presence, is hardly noticed by Davoren, who 'reclines almost fainting on the bed' and who, paralysed by fear, is 'only semi-conscious' (Shields 'sits up in an attitude of agonised prayerfulness'). Her death is the price of Davoren's pretensions. There is nothing subtle about O'Casey's portrait of this posturing poetaster, but this does not detract from its power. It is a comprehensive indictment of the Irish tendency to romanticise

violence, and to respond to that romanticism of violence. The ineptitude
of Davoren, his incapacity to act in *any* way, serves to highlight O'Casey's
satirical point. People are killed for and by even the shadow of a gunman.

Seumas Shields seems, at first sight and as the other major character
of the play, to be intended as a realistic and down-to-earth foil to the
insipidly romantic Davoren. We have already noted his wariness of the
kind of mind that gives itself to rhapsodies on 'the pearly glint of the
morning dew, or the damask sweetness of the rare wild rose', and his
awareness of the indulgent fantasies that cling around the idea of the
gunman's glamour inseparable from the Davoren-Minnie relationship.
He serves further to deflate the heroicising that accumulates around the
idea of Ireland's legendary past, remarking comically of a pair of braces
— among the wares that he peddles — that 'they'd do Cuchullian, they're
so strong' (promptly the pair that he is wearing himself snap as he bends
down), and sneering at his landlord, 'oul' Mulligan would call himself a
descendant of the true Gaels of Banba . . . Oh, Kathleen ni Houlihan,
your way's a thorny way!' And above all, Shields is given the words that
many critics feel lie at the heart of O'Casey's anti-heroic vision of the
Irish troubles. They have been much quoted, but need to be quoted
again, for in a way they do encapsulate that intended vision. As Davoren
and Shields lie in bed just before the Black and Tan raid, Davoren refers
to Shields's republican past, and he replies with disarming honesty:

Davoren: I remember the time when you yourself believed in nothing
         but the gun.
Seumas: Ay, when there wasn't a gun in the country; I've a different
         opinion now when there's nothin' but guns in the country . . . An'
         you daren't open your mouth, for Kathleen ni Houlihan is very
         different now to the woman who used to play the harp an' sing
         'Weep on, weep on, your hour is past', for she's a ragin' divil now,
         an' if you only look crooked at her you're sure of a punch in th'
         eye. But this is the way I look at it — I look at it this way: You're
         not goin' — you're not goin' to beat the British Empire — the
         British Empire, by shooting' an occasional Tommy at the corner of
         an occasional street. Besides, when the Tommies have the wind up
         . . . they let bang at everything they see — they don't give a God's
         curse who they plug . . . It's the civilians that suffer; when there's
         an ambush they don't know where to run. Shot in the back to
         save the British Empire, an' shot in the breast to save the soul of
         Ireland. I'm a Nationalist meself, right enough, — a Nationalist
         right enough, but all the same — I'm a Nationalist right enough; I

believe in the freedom of Ireland, an' that England has no right to
be here, but I draw the line when I hear the gunmen blowin' about
dyin' for the people, when it's the people that are dyin' for the
gunmen! With all due respect to the gunmen, I don't want them
to die for me.

(pp. 131-2)

This unheroic moral realism, often compared to Falstaff's pragmatic
views on the field of battle at Shrewsbury ('What is honour? A word . . .
Who hath it? He that died a-Wednesday.'), lies behind the action of *The
Shadow of a Gunman* and also structures the plots of *Juno* and *The
Plough*. Thus, Shields's words not only offer a powerful critique of
Davoren's 'placid affectation' of the gunman's role and all that ensues
from it, but have an authorial weight to them.

Yet the strength of *The Shadow of a Gunman* is partly in the fact
that Shields is no mere author's mouthpiece. In his own way, he is as
contemptible as Davoren, though less predictable, and hence a genuinely
dramatic character. Davoren seems to be in the right in characterising
Shields as somebody whose religion, like his life, is based on fear. Shields,
with 'a snarling laugh of pleasure' exults in the idea of Shelley 'doing a
jazz-dance' in hell, because, he says, he rejoices 'in the vindication of
the Church and Truth'. Davoren's reply is amply borne out in the play:

You know as little about truth as anybody else, and you care as little
about the Church as the least of those that profess her faith; your
religion is simply the state of being afraid that God will torture your
soul in the next world as you are afraid the Black and Tans will
torture your body in this.

(p. 97)

Shields has a great contempt for Irish laziness and incompetence, dramatised near the beginning of the play ('And still we're looking for freedom
— ye gods, it's a glorious country!'); the point is that he embodies laziness
and incompetence in himself. O'Casey's opening description of him in
the stage-direction tells us that 'in him is frequently manifested the
superstition, the fear, and the malignity of primitive man'. The 'primitive'
quality in Shields gives him a dramatic advantage over the ethereally
watery Davoren, and he has his telling moments; but his behaviour
during and after the Tans' raid is servile, cowardly in the extreme, and
totally self-interested. Even Davoren shows some sense of shame —
Shields's refrain, repeated at least eight times, is a variation on the theme
'I hope to God Minnie'll say nothin''. When Minnie's death is reported,
Shields merely says 'She did it off her own bat — we didn't ask her to

do it' (a callousness anticipated in his reaction to the death of his gunman friend Maguire — 'How am I goin' to get back the things he has
belongin' to me . . .?'). Worst of all, he shows himself just as susceptible
as the other characters in the play to the endemic vice of false posturing,
falsifying, in as gross a manner as the impostor and braggart Dolphie
Grigson, the nature of his behaviour during the raid:

> *Grigson.* . . . says I 'a man can only die once, an' you'll find Grigson
> won't squeal.' 'God, you're a cool one,' says the other, 'there's no
> blottin' it out.'
> *Shields.* That's the best way to take them; it only makes things worse
> to show that you've got the wind up. 'Any ammunition here?'
> says the fellow that come in here. 'I don't think so,' says I, 'but
> you better have a look.' 'No back talk,' says he, 'or you might get
> plugged.' 'I don't know of any clause', says I, 'in the British Con-
> stitution that makes it a crime for a man to speak in his own
> room,' — with that, he just had a look round, an' off he went.
> (pp. 154-5)

This is particularly unpleasant since Shields knows that Minnie, the only
character to show any 'coolness' in the face of the raid, has just been
arrested; in what he says there is a repellent mixture of braggadocio,
callousness, and relief that the seizure of Minnie has drawn off the Tans.

So, for all his deflationary realism, and his grasp of the essential
nature of urban guerrilla warfare as O'Casey presents it ('It's the civilians
that suffer'), Shields is himself deeply flawed. We can begin to perceive
that the pattern of oppositions in the play is not a simple and sentimental
one, not, that is, an opposition between stony-hearted gunmen (whether
republicans or Tans) and warm and life-loving civilians. Shields's words
in his long speech quoted above are often cited in relation to all three
Dublin plays, and cited out of context, in such a way as to imply that
O'Casey is offering us the simple, sentimental model. Whether or not
this is true of *Juno* and *The Plough*, it is not true of *The Shadow of a
Gunman*. For Davoren and Shields are 'civilians' — but, as we have seen,
they are contemptible, and are in large measure responsible for Minnie's
death. In fact, despite Shields's set-speech, the real gunman of the piece,
the cheery Maguire (whom admittedly we see for only a brief moment)
seems rather more attractive than the two central figures.

This is where it becomes important to keep O'Casey's plays separate
from each other in our minds, and to resist the understandable temptation to see them as a trilogy, informed by the same vision in every case.

The crucial distinction of Shields's key speech is that between gunmen, on the one hand, and 'civilians' or 'the people' on the other, with a strong implication that the civilians are merely passive spectators at, or victims of, the gunmen's activities. But this is not what we actually see in the play. What we actually see is the complicity of the people with the gunmen, a rather different thing.

Davoren, for instance, despite his belief that 'we've had enough of poems about '98', quickly allows himself a spurious share in the glamour that hangs round the IRA. Tommy Owens is a simpler and even more contemptuously drawn type of the blathering republican windbag:

> Two firm hands clasped together will all the power outbrave of the heartless English tyrant, the Saxon coward and knave. That's Tommy Owen's hand, Mr Davoren, the hand of a man, a man — Mr Shields knows me well.
>
> [He breaks into song]
> High upon the gallows tree stood the noble-hearted three,
> By the vengeful tyrant stricken in their bloom;
> But they met him face to face with the spirit of their race,
> And they went with souls undaunted to their doom! . . .
> God save Ireland ses the hayros, God save Ireland ses we all,
> Whether on the scaffold high or the battle-field we die,
> Oh, what matter when for Ayryinn dear we fall! . . .
> I'm bloody well tired o' waitin' — we're all tired o' waitin'. Why isn't every man in Ireland out with the IRA? Up with the barricades, up with the barricades; it's now or never, now an' for ever, as Sarsfield said at the battle o' Vinegar Hill. Up with the barricades — that's Tommy Owens . . .
>
> (pp. 112-13)

Tommy is a typical tenement-dweller, but, as this shows, the republican infection (as O'Casey tends to see it) has permeated the tenements. This sort of stuff, of course, effectively devalues the rhetoric, and by extension, the ideals of the republican movement, by turning all into a longwinded mouthing of platitudes and slogans. ('All wind and piss like a tanyard cat', as Joyce's nameless Dubliner remarks of similar effusions of the egregious Citizen.) And of course, as in similar instances throughout the play, the sense of ridicule is heightened by our knowledge that the focus of all this inflated bombast, Davoren, is himself a sham.

O'Casey's treatment of Mrs Henderson and Mr Gallogher, in the extended scene where they bring Mr Gallogher's letter of complaint about domestic harassment to the attention of the 'Gentlemen of the

Irish Republican Army' (in the person of Davoren), is not really different from his presentation of Owens. They, too, have a simple — or simple-minded — belief in the efficacy of the movement Davoren supposedly represents. Mrs Henderson ingratiates herself, as she thinks, with Davoren by praise of Mr Gallogher's children:

> It ud make your heart thrill like an alarm clock to hear them singin' 'Faith of Our Fathers' an' 'Wrap the Green Flag Roun me'.
>
> (p. 123)

and Mr Gallogher, 'half apologetically and half-proudly' chimes in 'Faith an' Fatherland, Mrs Henderson, Faith an' Fatherland.' And on hearing the news of the ambush out near Knocksedan, Mrs Henderson says 'That's the stuff to give them'.

Clearly it would be wrong to overemphasise the bloodthirstiness or the nationalist commitment of Mrs Henderson and Mr Gallogher in this scene: it is there less as evidence of a real political outlook, than as evidence of an inability to grasp political issues in any but the most superficial terms. But that then becomes part of O'Casey's criticism of this crowded tenement life, its unthinking and garrulous endorsement of the mythology of 'the men that are fightin' for Ireland's freedom'. Most critics would disagree, seeing in scenes like this proof of O'Casey's warm interest in the rich comedy of ordinary life, which he sets up as an opposing value to the destructive values of theoretical and abstract idealism, the false and inhuman pieties of nationalist politics. Here, these critics would argue, we have the classic O'Casey confrontation between 'hearts of flesh' and 'hearts of stone', and the humour and comedy in the letter scene of *The Gunman* underwrites the dramatist's belief in the ordinary people. David Krause, for instance, speaking in general of this aspect of O'Casey's work, says:

> ... the humour in his plays reveals a native vigour and shrewdness in his characters which ironically becomes a means of survival in a shattered world ... His humour saves him and his characters from despair. In the midst of anti-heroic laughter there can be no total catastrophe.[9]

Humour and comedy may well function in this way in O'Casey's other plays, but it is hard to accept such a valuation in the case of *The Gunman*.

For surely the comedy of the Henderson-Gallogher episode is bitter comedy, compounded of a mixture of contempt for the delusions of the 'ordinary people' and of laughter *at* their folly. Where is their 'native

vigour and shrewdness'? Apart from their uncritical parroting of the
nationalist catch-cries, which O'Casey has already savaged in the presentation of Tommy Owens, the whole scene turns on the ludicrous
disproportion of the request that the IRA 'bring their guns' to sort out
a tenement squabble. O'Casey presents them as a gallery of Dickensian
imbeciles, Smikes and Sloppys (lacking the saving 'holy fool' touch):

> *Mrs Henderson*. . . . I'll ask you to read the letter, which I'll say, not
> because you're there, or that you're a friend o' mine, is as good a
> letter as was decomposed by a scholar. Now, Mr Gallicker, an'
> don't forget the top sayin'.
> [*Mr Gallogher* prepares to read; *Minnie* leans forward to listen;
> *Tommy* takes out a well-worn note-book and a pencil stump, and
> assumes a very important attitude.]

(pp. 116-17)

The tableau freezes them in attitudes of respectful awe before the
mystery of the written word, which turns out to be ridiculous rhodo-
montade, but is only the more appreciated for its farcical quasi-legal
orotundity ('To All to Whom these Presents come . . . ventures to say
that he thinks he has made out a Primmy Fashy Case . . . in the above
written schedule.'). And as Mrs Henderson's introductory remarks
indicate, much of the laughter in the scene depends upon the solemn mis-
use of language in malapropisms ('decomposed') and general ignorance
— 'there's two k's in shockin'', 'my unvarnished respectability', 'that's a
parrotox' — 'It may be what a parrot talks, or a blackbird, or for the
matter of that, a lark', 'the matter specified, particularated, an' expanded
upon in the letter, mandamus or schedule,' 'you will be supernally positive of a hundred thousand welcomes'. Raymond Williams is surely right
about this kind of scene when he says 'It is done from the inside, this
tenement life, but with an eye on the audience, on external and
"educated" reactions.'[10] Except that this is not a fault in *The Shadow
of a Gunman*, save to those who would wish to argue the sentimental
case for the humour and warmth of O'Casey's tenement dwellers; the
mocking, bitter comedy is totally consistent with the play's overall
sardonic sense that 'gunmen' *and* 'people' (*pace* Shields) are locked
inside a corporate and pervasive fantasy.

The death of Minnie Powell might be interpreted as a near-perfect
illustration of Shields's thesis about the separation of gunmen from
people and how the people die for the gunmen rather than, as Fluther
Good would say, vice-versa. She is young and innocent, and many would
argue that her love for Davoren, with its tragic consequences, illustrates

the way in which the private and 'domestic' world of personal emotion is tragically at the mercy of the outer world of politics and violence. Such a reading is based largely on the unassailable fact that O'Casey's other women, Juno, Nora Clitheroe and Bessie Burgess for example, are the main victims of war and also the real heroines of the plays, in their endurance and suffering, and their realistic hostility to the fantasies and dreaming of their men-folk.

Minnie, however, should not be linked too readily to those other women. It is true that she has much more genuine courage than Davoren, Shields, Tommy Owens or Dolphie Grigson. But she is the means whereby O'Casey gives the most bitter turn of the screw to his dramatic action. That is, Minnie's love for Davoren, who is after all revealed consistently as an insipid nonentity, is based almost entirely on the glamour of the gunman's mystique.

> *Minnie.* . . . Poetry is a grand thing, Mr Davoren, I'd love to be able to write a poem – a lovely poem on Ireland an' the men o' '98.
> *Davoren.* Oh, we've had enough of poems, Minnie, about '98, and of Ireland, too.
> *Minnie.* Oh, there's a thing for a Republican to say! But I know what you mean: it's time to give up the writing an' to take to the gun.
> (p. 107)

She believes that a man should die willingly for his country, and is shocked and thinks Davoren is 'only jokin'' when he denies this. Thus, even more than the other characters in the play, Minnie is a victim of illusion and self-delusion, like them in imaginative complicity with the romantic mystique of 'the fellas in th' trench-coats'. She sacrifices herself to a hollow effigy, and though her end has therefore an ironic pathos, her ignorance and illusion prevent her achieving tragic dignity.

The portrait of Minnie then is not designed to make us feel the saving sanity of a woman's love in the destructive world of nationalist politics, but is the culminating touch in O'Casey's portrayal of a whole society given over to illusion. Shields is wrong about Minnie being 'an ignorant little bitch that thinks of nothin' but jazz dances', and wrong about her courage; but much of what he says is penetrating:

> A Helen of Troy come to live in a tenement! You think a lot about her simply because she thinks a lot about you, an' she thinks a lot about you because she looks upon you as a hero – a kind o' Paris . . . she'd give the world an' all to be gaddin' about with a gunman.

An' what ecstasy it ud give her if after a bit you were shot or hanged; she'd be able to go about then – like a good many more – singin', 'I do not mourn me darlin' lost, for he fell in his Jacket Green'. An' then, for a year an' a day, all round her hat she'd wear the Tricoloured Ribbon O, till she'd pick up and marry someone else – possibly a British Tommy with a Mons Star.

(p. 130)

It is true that Minnie looks upon Davoren as a hero, and there is nothing in the play to suggest that there is more substance than this to her love. (This contributes, ironically, to the play's strength as a play, since O'Casey is always uneasy and hollowly rhetorical in his attempts to delineate genuine romantic or sexual love.) Further, there is nothing in the play to suggest that her devotion to the republican cause is anything more than superficial, since it finds expression only in tags and slogans. In this respect she is like Tommy Owens, only less long-winded. Her decisive – and courageous – act in hiding the bombs is based solely on her feelings for Davoren, which are in their turn, as we have seen, compromised by her bedazzled vision of the gunman's mystique.

Shields's bitterness in his characterisation of Minnie is not quite O'Casey's bitterness, for he sees and communicates the pathos of her situation and allows her virtues, especially her courage which so exposes the masculine posturing, their full weight. Yet, in the end, *The Shadow of a Gunman* is a peculiarly bitter play. Everyone in it is trapped inside a collective fantasy, with the possible exception of Shields, and he is devalued by his craven cowardice. The play is thus wholly consistent in tone, however negative – a memorable indictment of not just a few gunmen but of a whole 'country gone mad'. Though O'Casey's earliest play, it has an inner coherence, and is unmarred by the indulgence and sentimentality which weaken, in crucial ways, the more famous *Juno and the Paycock* and *The Plough and the Stars*.

It is a critical commonplace that the hostility of O'Casey's attitude to the politics of Ireland between 1916 and 1923 was due to the fact that he believed that the 'revolution' was a revolution about and for the wrong things, a nationalist rebellion rather than a social and economic revolution. Jack Lindsay in his essay 'Sean O'Casey as a Socialist Artist', for example, says that the great Dublin Lock-Out of 1913 was the high-water mark of O'Casey's experience and provided him with the criteria that never left him:

Essentially he went on judging all the phases of the political struggle that followed, in terms of that experience; and to the extent that

they distracted the Irish people from the goals that Larkin had set
before them, he found them wanting. The aim that controls all the
Abbey plays is the passionately felt need to force people up against
the ways in which they have been cheated, lured away from the true
struggle, and made to serve alien causes.[11]

And O'Casey himself, admittedly from the perspective of 1949, offers
substantiating evidence for Lindsay's assertion, when he writes in the
fourth volume of his autobiography, *Inisfallen Fare Thee Well*:

Two fierce fights were going on for liberty: one on the little green
dot in the world's waters, called Ireland; and the other over a wide
brown, grey, blue, and scarlet expanse of land, later to overflow into
the many-coloured, gigantic bloom of the Soviet Union. The first for
a liberty of the soul that was to leave the body and mind still in
prison; the other for the liberty of the body that was to send the soul
and mind as well out into the seething waters of a troubled world on
a new and noble adventure.[12]

The implications are clear; economic exploitation and poverty are the
real enemies of O'Casey's slum dwellers, and nationalist politics and
republican activism are obfuscating diversions from the 'true struggle'.

In *The Shadow of a Gunman*, as we have seen, O'Casey concentrates
on satirising the delusive fantasising to which the republican mythology
gives rise. In that play, the poverty is more a setting than a thematic
issue – at least in any explicit way. In his next work, *Juno and the
Paycock*, poverty and the facts of poverty move more to centre stage,
as it were, becoming a felt issue in the play. When it opens, Mary the
daughter is on strike. Juno's weary pessimism about the efficacy of trade
union activity elicits Mary's defiant 'It doesn't matther what you say,
ma – a principle's a principle' – a phrase which becomes an ironic
leitmotif in the play. Juno's response to this shows the immediate
repercussions of the loss of Mary's – presumably small – contribution
to the family's finances:

Yis; an' when I go into oul' Murphy's tomorrow, an' he gets to know
that, instead o' payin' all, I'm goin' to borry more, what'll he say
when I tell him a principle's a principle? What'll we do if he refuses
to give us any more on tick?

(pp. 6-7)

Juno, in fact, bears the full weight of the harassed economic anxiety which is endemic to the family's situation. She has to rush off to her own menial job to keep the house going, and almost all of her appearances in the first act, up to the arrival of Bentham with the news of the legacy, reflect her awareness of the burdens imposed on her by her maimed son, and, above all, her feckless husband:

> You'd think he was bringin' twenty poun's a week into the house the way he's going on. He wore out the Health Insurance long ago, he's afther wearin' out the unemployment dole, an' now, he's thryin' to wear out me! An' constantly singin', no less, when he ought always to be on his knees offerin' up a Novena for a job!
>
> (pp. 5-6)

The few jobs that do come along are presented as being in the gift of clerical patrons. Ironically, it is the aspiring secretary of the trade union whom O'Casey employs to dramatise the point:

> Father Farrell is just afther stoppin' to tell me to run up an' get him ['Captain' Boyle] to go to the new job that's goin' on in Rathmines; his cousin is foreman o' the job, an' Father Farrell was speakin' to him about poor Johnny an' his father bein' idle so long, an' the foreman told Father Farrell to send the Captain up an' he'd give him a start . . .
>
> (pp. 8-9)

The world of *Juno and the Paycock* is, then, a world of desperate make-shifts against destitution, a world of pawn-tickets, borrowing, scrounging, and – in the case of the Paycock – endless bibulous fantasising and drunken escapism designed to shield him from the uncomfortable aware-ness of economic realities, which his wife must face without illusions.

In this context, the major plot device of the false legacy serves to expose, in a tragi-comic way, the incapacities of the Boyle family – the Captain's prate of Consols being down half per cent, Mary's bedazzle-ment by the smoothly fatuous Bentham, Johnny's hope that they will be able to buy themselves out of the context of war – even Juno, despite her knowledge of her husband's character, is thankful that he 'won't have to trouble about a job for awhile', and carries a gramophone, unlikeliest of immediate necessities, back from Henry Street, on credit. The great festive celebration in the second act, with the family and Mrs Madigan and the ubiquitous Joxer, is brilliantly and successfully comic;[13] but it also dramatises, under the boozy and sentimental camaraderie, the stunted and thwarted nature of the tenement's aspira-tions, the pathos of its ignorance of the real exploitative world of money and business, and the childishness of the belief that the illusory money can of itself make an impregnable bulwark of security. The first law of poverty in O'Casey's dramatic world is that people are not in control of their lives. They cannot, even when the money seems a real possibility, escape the trap to which they are habituated — the Captain's blather remains substantially the same whether he is poor or 'rich', drunk or 'sober'. The last act — a prolonged and powerful portrait of disintegration — systematically strips bare the ugly realities which the false expectations raised by the legacy could only momentarily disguise. Bentham has fled, leaving Mary pregnant, Mr Nugent and Mrs Madigan reclaim their property, Joxer pockets the last bottle of stout, like a true 'butty', and — most memorably — the very furniture is removed from under the distraught mother's eyes.[14]

Thus the realities of economic deprivation are hammered home in *Juno* more directly than in *The Shadow of a Gunman*. And in so far as Bentham, the middle-class man, is responsible to a large extent, with his 'banjaxed' will, and desertion of Mary, for the particular shape that the Boyles' disaster takes, O'Casey may be seen as pointing up the economic argument of the play; Bentham, patronising, cheating, irresponsible, is exploitation in action. As Seamus Deane says 'Bentham . . . can be seen as the representative of those ills which afflict the Boyles, and Tancreds and all others in the tenement.' It is true that he is a wooden figure, a melodramatic stereotype and is, in dramatic terms, thoroughly unconvincing. As Deane goes on to say of Bentham as a symbol of exploitation and indifference: 'He is seen to represent these forces but there is no way in which one could argue that he persuasively embodies them'.[15] Certainly I would not wish to attempt such an argument; what I wish to stress here is O'Casey's emphasis on the grim economic realities which confront his characters. Bentham is, dramatically speaking, a bungle, but the bungle does not destroy the play; his presence, however imperfectly achieved, shows the nature of O'Casey's overall conception.

Thus far *Juno* is a coherent and unified play. Where does the civil war between Republicans and Free Staters fit in with this portrait of tenement poverty? It would not be quite accurate to say that the play breaks in two here, that there is no organic connection made by O'Casey between poverty and nationalist politics, along the lines suggested by Jack Lindsay's comment quoted above. When Juno introduces Johnny to Bentham in the first act, she says:

My son, Mr Bentham; he's afther goin' through the mill. He was only a chiselur of a Boy Scout in Easter Week, when he got hit in the hip; and his arm was blew off in the fight in O'Connell Street. [*Johnny* comes in] Here he is Mr Bentham; Mr Bentham, Johnny. None can deny he done his bit for Irelan', if that's goin' to do him any good.

Johnny [boastfully] . I'd do it agen, ma, I'd do it agen; for a principle's a principle.

Mrs Boyle. Ah, you lost your best principle, me boy, when you lost your arm; them's the only sort o' principles that's any good to a workin' man.

Johnny. Ireland only half free'll never be at peace while she has a son left to pull a trigger.

Mrs Boyle. To be sure, to be sure — no bread's a lot better than half a loaf.

(pp. 30-1)

Johnny is clearly from the same stable as Tommy Owens in *The Shadow of a Gunman*, the emptiness of his sloganising pointed up not just by Juno's weary realism here, but by his cowering timidity throughout the play — the exchange serves to dramatise the opposition between what O'Casey sees as 'alien causes' and the true facts of tenement life. And later in the play another mother makes the same kind of point about her son. As Mrs Tancred goes out with some neighbours, past the party in the Boyles' room, to the funeral of her murdered son, Juno sympathetically invites her in for a 'cup o' tay':

Mrs Tancred. Ah, I can take nothin' now, Mrs Boyle — I won't be long afther him.

First Neighbour. Still an' all, he died a noble death, an' we'll bury him like a king.

Mrs Tancred. An' I'll go on livin' like a pauper.

(p. 54)

This is O'Casey's most explicit effort to show that the Irish struggle was about the wrong things. The satiric direction and overall thrust of the play's ideas would seem to be clear.

In fact, this is precisely what is not the case. Any prose summary of the play will always make it seem more coherent than the actual theatrical or literary experience of the play itself. Something is awry in O'Casey's vision and his art.

Mrs Tancred's words suggest, as do many of Juno's remarks about Johnny, the essential *irrelevance* of Irish politics to the fundamental issues of living. Yet her entry, her prayer that 'hearts o' stone' be replaced by 'hearts o' flesh' (which Juno is to repeat at the play's climax), and the sombre off-stage funeral procession which closes the second act, while Johnny faces his nemesis in the shape of the Mobilizer — all this is intended to introduce into the play the tragic note, in a way that what we may call the 'poverty theme' never does. So what is seen as irrelevant is simultaneously presented to us as the source of the play's deepest emotional moments. Johnny's fate is ostentatiously adumbrated for us throughout the play, in his fear and in his vision of the blood-boltered Robbie Tancred kneeling before the statue in his room, itself preceded by Bentham's melodramatically apposite theory of the relationship between sensational murders and the seeing of ghosts. And his death provides the play's emotional and dramatic climax, since it is on Juno's reactions that O'Casey bases his claim for the special heroism of her great-souled humanity:

> Maybe I didn't feel sorry enough for Mrs Tancred when her poor son was found as Johnny's been found now — because he was a Diehard! Ah, why didn't I remember that then he wasn't a Diehard or a Stater, but only a poor dead son! It's well I remember all that she said — an' it's my turn to say it now: What was the pain I suffered, Johnny, bringin' you into the world to carry you to your cradle, to the pains I'll suffer carryin' you out o' the world to bring you to your grave! Mother o' God, Mother o' God, have pity on us all! Blessed Virgin, where were you when me darlin' son was riddled with bullets, when me darlin' son was riddled with bullets? Sacred Heart o' Jesus, take away our hearts o' stone, and give us hearts o' flesh! Take away this murdherin' hate, an' give us Thine own eternal love!
>
> (p. 87)

'An' it's my turn to say it now' — Juno takes her supreme place in the line of O'Casey's innocent and suffering women, victims not so much of poverty as of an illusory and hate-filled politics.

It is Irish politics, then, which is the essential and dynamic opponent of the maternal humanism of Juno (the same is true, of course, in the case of characters like Nora Clitheroe and Bessie Burgess in *The Plough and the Stars*). But that humanism, the belief in what Krause calls 'bread on the table and love in the heart', is presented as being a product of a refusal, or an inability, to attempt to grapple with the political issues. O'Casey consistently tries to suggest that the hearts of stone and the hearts of flesh live in two different and totally separated worlds, and that true morality for his hearts of flesh consists in maintaining the separation, in a complete and healthy scepticism about what Juno refers to as 'principles' — 'principles' which the play suggests have nothing to

them but sloganising bombast, anyway. Juno's heroic humanity, in
short, like her husband's unreconstructed humanity, is possible only
because she is apolitical, or even anti-political.

And yet the war is the stressed fact, *the* situation which dominates
the lives of the people. After Mrs Tancred's exit in the second act, Boyle
remarks (in patent untruth, given the presence of the maimed Johnny
and Mrs Tancred's own words):

> We've nothin' to do with these things, one way or t'other.

Juno's reply is instructive, if instructively confusing:

> I'd like to know how a body's not to mind these things; look at the
> way they're afther leavin' the people in this very house. Hasn't the
> whole house, nearly, been massacreed? There's young Dougherty's
> husband with his leg off; Mrs Travers that had her son blew up be a
> mine in Inchegeela, in Co. Cork; Mrs Mannin that lost wan of her
> sons in an ambush a few weeks ago, an' now, poor Mrs Tancred's
> only child gone west with his body made a collandher of. Sure, if it's
> not our business, I don't know whose business it is.

(p. 56)

While Juno admits the impact of the war, and expresses a human horror
at it in generalised terms, the claim that it is her 'business' is never explored in any meaningful way in the play. Our sense of the 'ordinary
humanity' of the people is, as we have seen, dependent on our sense of
their freedom from any kind of political outlook, from the dehumanising
effect of 'principles', because O'Casey, here as elsewhere, sees (nationalist) politics as taking place in a separate world from that of the human.
The politics are a deformation of, and a threat to, the human, and
O'Casey's suffering women are the authorially endorsed mouthpieces of
this view. There is something simple-minded and sentimental about this.
For, as Juno's own words show, 'politics' are central to life in the
tenement — 'Hasn't the whole house, nearly, been massacreed?' Since
'principles' and 'politics' do demonstrably have such a major impact, it
is simple-minded to ignore them, and sentimental to pretend that
humanity consists in ignoring them. The simplemindedness and sentimentality are not Juno's so much as O'Casey's. The dramatist lapses
from the 'picture' to the crude 'diagram', to employ George Eliot's
distinction, mainly because his presentation of the inimical world of
politics is dramatically so tenuous and muddled. Note that the objection
here is not a political one — O'Casey has a perfect right to see the Irish

struggle in as hostile a way as he wishes, and while *The Shadow of a Gunman* may make uncomfortable viewing for an Irish nationalist, it is, as we have seen, a valid and consistent work of art. In *Juno*, however, we are asked to feel the irrelevance of nationalist politics *and* their centrality, at the same moment. These politics focus and embody the tragedy, yet O'Casey does not begin to try to explore the forces behind the tragedy, so that we feel a hollowness at the play's core. The powerful rhetoric of the speeches of Mrs Tancred and Juno insists on the weight of the dynamic and inimical 'principles' of political activism, which can and do erupt into people's lives, wrecking them; they *are* everybody's 'business'. But, in the drama, the characters are only 'human' to the extent that they do not concern themselves with politics, and so we have the Captain and Joxer, and above all Juno. The play urges contradictory and incoherent claims on us, which severely limit the dramatic effectiveness of Juno herself as the 'great' character; she is O'Casey's reality principle, confronting the differing fantasy worlds of the Captain and Johnny — for it is as a fantasy world that O'Casey presents Johnny's world — with her stoic and rational endurance which is intended to expose those worlds. But in the latter case it is a sham confrontation, Juno only being permitted by her creator to engage with the political world in any meaningful sense when the author wishes to use that world to direct our attention further to her 'humanity'. The result is curiously lopsided; Juno is human because she isn't interested in politics, and when politics force themselves on her in tragic terms, it is only so that she can proclaim the more loudly her humanity by rejecting the more emotively those very politics. It is the classic case of O'Casey's 'two worlds' principle — one world full of political male braggarts and cowards, the other world full of apolitical female realists seeking bread on the table and love in the heart. And the two worlds simply spin past each other, never really meeting, giving only the illusion of contact or conflict. Juno is really saying 'Why don't politics just go away?' Why indeed, we may sigh with her, if we can believe that true humanity is freedom from political taint. But even if we can swallow that, we are apt to become uneasy when we find the despised politics, bombastic, cowering and empty by turns in the case of Johnny, caricatured in the Captain ('If th' worst comes . . . to th' worse . . . I can join a flyin' . . . column . . . I done . . . me bit . . . in Easther Week . . .'), becoming the chief means towards, the major focus of, Juno's achievement of 'tragic' status. O'Casey is having it both ways; Johnny is a fool in his politics, his death a logical and inevitable result of his folly — yet we are asked, through and because of Juno, to see it as tragedy. Hence, and for all the apparent earthiness of her character, Juno remains ultimately and stubbornly insubstantial. She is one of 'the saved women of O'Casey', as Seamus Deane puts it in a striking phrase that captures the essence of O'Casey's unconvincingness, 'that protestant elite stricken with the grace of humanity in the damned male realm of nationalist politics'.[16]

The really striking success of *Juno and the Paycock* is the relationship between Captain Boyle and the parasitical Joxer. Lady Gregory was right to tell O'Casey that his strong point was characterisation – she might have been more precise with *comic* characterisation. Even O'Casey's stage-directions, in his introduction of these two magnificent clowns, are irresistibly rich. Of the Captain:

> His neck is short, and his head looks like a stone ball that one some-times sees on top of a gate-post . . . His walk is a slow consequential strut.

Of Joxer:

> He may be younger than the *Captain* but he looks a lot older. His face is like a bundle of crinkled paper . . .
>
>   (pp. 9-10)

The Captain's glorious lying, and Joxer's constant provocation of it, shows their mutual irrepressibility, their almost aristocratic disdain for mere truth:

> *Joxer*. God be with the young days when you were steppin' the deck of a manly ship, with the win' blowin' a hurricane through the masts, an' the only sound you'd hear was, 'Port your helm!' an' the only answer 'Port it is, sir!'
>
> *Boyle*. Them was days, Joxer, them was days. Nothin' was too hot or too heavy for me then. Sailin' from the Gulf o' Mexico to the Antanartic Ocean. I seen things, I seen things, Joxer, that no mortal man should speak about that knows his Catechism. Ofen, an' ofen, when I was fixed to the wheel with a marlin-spike, an' the win's blowin' fierce an' the waves lashin' an' lashin', till you'd think every minute was goin' to be your last, an' it blowed, an' blowed – blew is the right word, Joxer, but blowed is what the sailors use . . .
>
> *Joxer*. Aw, it's a darlin' word, a daarlin' word.
>
> *Boyle*. An', as it blowed an' blowed, I ofen looked up at the sky an' assed meself the question – what is the stars, what is the stars?
>
>   (pp. 25-6)

And throughout, Joxer's very funny and relentless quoting of stale tags
— 'Oh, that's shockin''; ah, man's inhumanity to man makes countless
thousands mourn!' he laments of the stolen stout-bottle, allegedly lifted
by Nugent, actually reposing in Joxer's own pocket — is matched by
the Captain's ability to rise to a genuine poetry, even if it is usually the
poetry of disintegration:

> [Taking a sixpence from his pocket and looking at it] Wan single,
> solitary tanner left out of all I borreyed . . . [He lets it fall] The last
> o' the Mohicans . . . The blinds is down, Joxer, the blinds is down!
> (p. 88)

The very success of the Captain and Joxer as dramatic characters,
however, poses its own kind of threat to the unity of vision, the coherence of standpoint, towards which *Juno and the Paycock* strives.
O'Casey's gift is characterisation — we may say that these two characters
run away with the play. This happens in differing ways, but there is an
overall connection between these ways and between them and the
uneasily contrived exploitation of politics, in the manner examined
above, to stretch Juno out on the rack of tragedy or pathos. The parts
of the play are *seriatim* more convincing than the whole.

For example, we have seen how O'Casey stresses — again mainly
through Juno, in her tones of weary realism or of desperate nagging —
the facts of poverty, and the nearness of the wolf to the Boyle door.
Presumably the feckless irresponsibility of her husband (and her husband's 'butty') is intended to highlight once again the deluded fantasising
of O'Casey's male world by contrast with the clear-sighted and con-
structive ability of the women to face facts. A highly laudable and moral
— and sane — approach, in life. But on O'Casey's stage things do not
quite work out like that. The huge comedy of Boyle and Joxer, in their
inventive escapism, in their posturing, in their superb bombast, is, quite
simply, too enjoyable for us to feel like condemning them. This is not a
matter of individual sentimentality, a weak-kneed reflex of generous
tolerance to a pair of 'lovable rogues'. As many critics have rightly
pointed out, the sources of O'Casey's conception of the Captain and
Joxer, and the sources of their appeal to us, lie deep in comic conventions
and archetypes hallowed by time. The Captain is essentially the *miles
gloriosus* of classical comedy, Joxer the parasite as Plautus and Terence
— and Ben Jonson — might have seen him. There is nothing in the least
academic about O'Casey, but he had served his dramatic apprenticeship
at the feet of Shakespeare and Boucicault,[17] and had an admirable

practical knowledge of the age-old stuff of comedy. The *miles gloriosus*, his parasite, and their deflation are brilliantly handled in this episode from Act I:

> *Boyle*. Let her hop in; we may as well have it out first as at last. I've made up me mind — I'm not goin' to do only what she damn well likes.
>
> *Joxer*. Them sentiments does you credit, Captain; I don't like to say anything as between man an' wife, but I say as a butty, as a butty, Captain, that you've stuck it too long, an' that it's about time you showed a little spunk.
>
> How can a man die betther than facin' fearful odds,
> For th' ashes of his fathers an' the temples of his gods?
>
> *Boyle*. She has her rights — there's no denying it, but haven't I me rights too?
>
> *Joxer*. Of course you have — the sacred rights o' man!
>
> *Boyle*. Today, Joxer, there's goin' to be issued a proclamation be me, establishin' an independent Republic, an' Juno'll have to take an oath of allegiance.
>
> *Joxer*. Be firm, be firm, Captain; the first few minutes'll be the worst: if you gently touch a nettle it'll sting you for your pains; grasp it like a lad of mettle, an' as soft as silk remains!
>
> [Voice of Juno outside] Can't stop, Mrs Madigan — I haven't a minute!
>
> *Joxer* [flying out of the window]. Holy God, here she is!
>
> *Boyle* [packing the things away with a rush in the press]. I knew that fella ud stop till she was in on top of us!
>
> (pp. 27-8)

This is O'Casey at his very best. The problem is that our enjoyment of and delight in the Captain and Joxer — and every audience groans with pleasure when they appear, strutting or sidling — draws off our sympathy from Juno, and hence weakens O'Casey's stress on the poverty and its seriousness in the lives of the tenement dwellers. Juno is in no sense a Malvolio of the tenements, since she has no over-weening self-regard, but in the context of comic archetypes activated by the Captain and Joxer, she functions as an obstructive figure, blocking our sense of comic release and catharsis with the reminders of necessity; and we feel like adapting Sir Toby Belch's question, putting it in the mouth of the Captain, and addressing Juno: 'Dost thou think, because thou art virtuous, there shall be no more half-uns in Foley's snug?' Enid Welsford in her scholarly study of the fool in literary history, makes this general point in her conclusion:

> Under the dissolvent influence of his [the fool's] personality the iron
> network of physical, social and moral law, which enmeshes us from
> the cradle to the grave, seems — for the moment — negligible as a web
> of gossamer. The Fool does not lead a revolt against the Law, he lures
> us into a region of the spirit where, as Lamb would put it, the writ
> does not run.[18]

This is true of Falstaff, to whom Captain Boyle is frequently compared.
And when Miss Welsford goes on to make the point of Falstaff and those
like him that they offer 'a safety valve for unruliness, a wholesome
nourishment to the sense of secret spiritual independence of that which
would otherwise be the intolerable tyranny of circumstances', her words
seem particularly apposite to a play like *Juno and the Paycock* where
the 'intolerable tyranny of circumstances' is given such specific economic
and political embodiment. These circumstances are focused in Juno, or
focused by Juno, with her worries about getting credit from oul' Murphy,
about getting jobs for her husband, about looking after her maimed son;
and — however reprehensible such an attitude may be, or however differently we would respond in real life — we turn with relief from her
nagging ("'Tisn't Juno should be her pet name at all, but Deirdre of the
Sorras, for she's always grousin'") to the comic, irresponsible and feckless
world of the Captain and his butty.

That feeling, that delight, is the strongest and least compromised
emotion, dramatically speaking, in the play. But thematically, O'Casey
wants us to condemn this irresponsibility and fecklessness, partly
because it damages the family unity and integrity, the idea of the family
and domestic harmony being for Juno, as it is for Nora Clitheroe in *The
Plough and the Stars*, and for O'Casey himself, the major and controlling
value. We are also to condemn the Captain's irresponsible fantasising
because O'Casey — and many of his commentators — connects it, in
some not very clear way, with the more inhuman fantasising that fills
the minds of the Republicans with their chimera of a 'free Ireland'.
Hence Johnny: 'Ireland only half free'll never be at peace while she has
a son left to pull the trigger'. Hence the Captain, and Joxer's introduction to Bentham:

> This is Joxer Daly, Past Chief Ranger of the Dear Little Shamrock
> Branch of the Irish National Foresters, an' oul' front-top neighbour,
> that never despaired, even in the darkest days of Ireland's sorra.

Joxer. Nil desperandum, Captain, nil desperandum.

(p. 49)

And hence, most memorably, the drunken words that reverberate in our minds from the play's final scene:

Boyle. If th' worst comes . . . to th' worse . . . I can join a . . . flyin' . . . column . . . I done . . . me bit . . . in Easther Week . . . had no business . . . to . . . be . . . there . . . but Captain Boyle's Captain Boyle!

Joxer. Breathes there a man with soul . . . so . . . de . . . ad . . . this . . . me . . . o . . . wn, me nat . . . ive l . . . an'!

Boyle [subsiding into a sitting posture on the floor]. Commandant Kelly died . . . in them . . . arms . . . Joxer . . . Tell me Volunteer Butties . . . says he . . . that . . . I died for . . . Irelan'!

(p. 88)

Thus drunken irresponsibility is seen as simply a more overt version of the disease of the heroic dream that affects the nationalists, and opposed to it, again, is the suffering, realistic woman.

But there is another way (apart from our enjoyment of the brave comedy of the two loafers, and which indeed underwrites, in terms of the play's specific message, our ease of conscience in that enjoyment) in which O'Casey confuses the pattern. The Captain and Joxer are resolutely uninterested in politics, save as the spur to drunken or vain-glorious rhetoric. Since, apart from the unintegrated moment when she argues that the politics is everybody's business, it is the burden of Juno's appeal and of her total significance in the play that involvement in politics is a deformation of the truly human, there is a sense in which the Captain's irresponsible fecklessness means that he is automatically on the side of the 'hearts o' flesh': 'We've nothin' to do with these things, one way or t'other.' The point is that in the terms the play sets up, Boyle's drinking and lying and boasting are bound to seem more attractive — they are 'human failings', with the emphasis on 'human' — than the inhuman abstract fanaticism of those who urge, like the Mobilizer, the sacrifice of everything to Ireland.

So, these great layabouts who dominate the play successfully trample its coherence to pieces. It is not a matter of objecting, on theoretical grounds, to O'Casey's habitual formula of tragi-comedy, which has been ably defended, as a form, by David Krause and J. L. Styan[19] among others. Rather, it is a matter of O'Casey's uncertain manipulation of the Captain and Joxer in terms of the play's overall intention. Their comedy is thoroughly exploited by O'Casey, and enormously enjoyed by the audience who respond to their archetypal dimension. This, however, makes it harder to respond sympathetically to Juno, who carries the burdens of reality on her back. Nevertheless, we should condemn Boyle and Joxer because of their anarchism in regard of the endorsed family values, the affront that they give to the spirit of maternal humanism which is extolled through Juno. And then, in a further twist, their ordinary make-shift ne'er-do-well pettiness becomes a positive, is made to focus a derogatory light (to use a Flutherian epithet) on the activities of the 'hearts o' stone': the Captain's end (drunk) is preferable to Johnny's (dead), yet Johnny's death provides Juno, and the play, with an emotional climax which seems somewhat contrived. O'Casey's art in this play does not merely describe a world 'in chassis': it partakes of that chassis.

The Plough and the Stars, produced at the Abbey theatre two years after *Juno*, in 1926, is more integrated than that earlier play. O'Casey's sense of the effectiveness of dramatic juxtapositions, which works rather factitiously at the end of *Juno*, is brilliantly demonstrated in the second and fourth acts of *The Plough*. They are superbly theatrical, and operate to convey, in a cause and effect, a 'before' and 'after' manner, the central O'Casey thesis, which is once again the dehumanising effect of abstract idealism of the nationalist variety. In the second act, the chief technical device for the manipulation of dramatic juxtaposition and contrast is the projection into the pub of the silhouette and words of the nationalist orator; colloquial bar-chat and bar-rhetoric can then be brought up against a very different kind of rhetoric:

> It is a glorious thing to see arms in the hands of Irishmen. We must accustom ourselves to the thought of arms, we must accustom ourselves to the sight of arms, we must accustom ourselves to the use of arms . . . Bloodshed is a cleansing and sanctifying thing, and the nation that regards it as the final horror has lost its manhood . . . There are many things more horrible than bloodshed, and slavery is one of them!
>
> (pp. 193-4)

This, and the other three speeches by the orator which occur through the act, O'Casey took almost *verbatim* from various addresses Padraic Pearse gave in 1914 and 1915, only altering them to reinforce our sense of the dogmatism and the blood-lust.[20] P. S. O'Hegarty remarks of these rhetorical calls to action, and particularly of the last one ('they have left us our Fenian dead, and, while Ireland holds these graves, Ireland, unfree, shall never be at peace!'):

[It] is one of the great Irish national orations. It cuts like a trumpet call, like the sword of the Lord, like a gleam of beauty, right across the squalidity, the maudlinism, the spinelessness, which was Ireland at the time; just as the Rising itself came, suddenly and like a sign from Heaven.[21]

O'Hegarty was, interestingly enough, a member of the Supreme Council of the Irish Republican Brotherhood. Hence it is not surprising that he gets O'Casey's emphasis in this act almost exactly wrong. Rather as in *The Shadow of a Gunman*, O'Casey stresses firstly the *link* between the orator's fanatical rhetoric and the collective excitement and virulence of rhetoric of the people in the bar, the frenzied collusion in delusion. Peter and Fluther come rushing in:

> *Peter* [splutteringly to *Barman*]. Two halves ... [To *Fluther*] A meetin' like this always makes me feel as if I could dhrink Loch Erinn dhry! ...
> *Fluther*. Jammed as I was in th' crowd, I listened to th' speeches patherin' on th' people's head, like rain fallin' on th' corn; every derogatory thought went out o' me mind, an' I said to meself, 'You can die now, Fluther, for you've seen th' shadow-dhreams of th' past leppin' to life in th' bodies of livin' men that show, if we were without a titther o' courage for centuries, we've vice versa now!' Looka here. [He stretches out his arm under *Peter*'s face and rolls up his sleeve] The blood was BOILIN' in me veins!
>
> (pp. 194-5)

Of course, this serves not only to indicate the collusion, imaginatively, between the excited drinkers and the nationalist orator, but also to parody and deflate his rhetoric. His stern call to dedication becomes an aspiration to drink Loch Erinn dry, and the comic reductivism of Fluther's image of 'th' shadow-dhreams of th' past leppin' to life', supplemented as it is by his established verbal tics ('derogatory', 'vice versa'), is obvious. The pattern is repeated — minus the comedy, but with equal clarity — in the entry, near the end of the act, of Clitheroe and Brennan of the Citizen Army and Langon of the Volunteers. O'Casey's stage-direction reads in part: 'Their faces are flushed and their eyes sparkle; they speak rapidly as if unaware of the meaning of what they said. They have been mesmerized by the fervency of the speeches.' In other words they too are drunk in their own way.

Capt. Brennan [catching up The Plough and the Stars] . Imprisonment
for th' Independence of Ireland!
Lieut. Langon [catching up the Tri-colour] . Wounds for th' In-
dependence of Ireland!
Clitheroe. Death for th' Independence of Ireland!
The Three [together] . So help us God!

(pp. 213-14)

The chant-like, formal nature of this antiphon is O'Casey's way of conveying the ritualised hollowness of what is being said; the full effect is
delivered, pat, in the last act when each of the three has his prayer come
true. It is not a case of the orator's words 'cutting across' anything here
(*pace* O'Hegarty), but of them finding an all-too-ready echo in a
'mesmerised' populace.

In the same way, further, the orator's references to national and
international wars simultaneously unleash the verbal Donnybrook
between Mrs Gogan and Bessie Burgess (who are also caught up in the
pervasive bubbling excitement of the night), and are then mocked in
their sweeping assumption of Irish aspiration and high-mindedness by
the pettiness and complete self-absorption of the women in their 'war'.
And of course the females' furious fight is paralleled by the bawling-
match between Fluther and the Covey. The general effect of all this is
quite clear: the ideals and rhetoric of nationalism are, in the Covey's
words, 'all dope', but in their lofty bloodthirstiness heady dope. The
emotional excitement of the meeting triggers a responsive violence of
speech and deed in the people, but this takes grotesque and absurd
forms, and serves to throw back on the 'high' nationalist rhetoric an
ironic, parodic and deflationary light. The grouping of characters, the
increasing tempo of the action, the dramatic effectiveness of the
speaker's silhouette looming over the bar and itself reinforcing the sense
of the disembodied spectral fanaticism of what he preaches, the juxtaposition of the prostitute and all the boozing with the swirl and colour
of the flags and the uniforms (a juxtaposition which so enraged the first
Abbey audiences)[22] – through all this turbulent act O'Casey really does
manage to convey his sense of a whole city giving itself up to a kind of
madness. The consumptive Mollser's words at the end of the first act –
'Is there anybody goin', Mrs Clitheroe, with a titther o' sense?' – take
on ever greater appositeness as the second act unrolls.

The purpose of the final act is to show how the chickens have come
home to roost. Outside, Dublin burns, and the melancholy lilting chant
from the streets which punctuates the act, 'Red Cr . . . oss, Red Cr . . . oss!
Ambu ... lance, Ambu ... lance!', shows O'Casey using one of his favourite

'poetic' devices with great power and economy. Inside, Bessie's attic serves to ram home visually the terrible poverty of the tenements (by contrast, the Clitheroes' room, below Bessie's, which we have seen in the first act, has seemed spacious and almost elegant). The brass standard-lamp with its fancy shade, the crimson silk dress, both looted, only show up the more the torn and dirty wallpaper, the tin kettle and the other signs of near destitution. (At this point we may remember that Bessie's son — presumably her only financial prop — is involved in another, greater war in Flanders.)

But the two worlds, the outer world of flame and destruction and the inner world of poverty, are dynamically connected. A pane in one of Bessie's small windows has been shattered by a bullet. Beside the card-playing men — a touch which brilliantly and horribly naturalises and familiarises sudden death — rests the coffin which contains the victims of both the poverty and the war; the bodies of the consumptive Mollser, and of Nora's baby, still-born as a result of Nora's fright and shock when her husband rejected her pleas to stay with her, and turned back to his fighting — and dying. The realities, with which O'Casey in all his plays opposes the 'blather' of evasion and the high-flown abstractions of idealistic rhetoric, have not before in his work been so powerfully presented. This is largely due to the fact that here the principles of those realities are articulated by the whole setting and situation, and are not, as in the cases of Juno, or even, in his different way, of Shields, the property of one heroic or clear-sighted character. It is true that O'Casey rubs his point in in local details of the act, as when Fluther ironically jeers at Peter:

> If they make any attack here, we'll send you out in your green an' glory uniform, shakin' your sword over your head, an' they'll fly before you as th' Danes flew before Brian Boru!
>
> (p. 240)

The fatuity of the dream of martyrdom for Ireland is further expressed in a simple but effective juxtaposition a little later, when Brennan gives his account of Clitheroe's death:

> He took it like a man. His last whisper was to 'Tell Nora to be brave; that I'm ready to meet my God, an' that I'm proud to die for Ireland.' An' when our General heard it he said that 'Commandant Clitheroe's end was a gleam of glory'. Mrs Clitheroe's grief will be a joy when she realizes that she has had a hero for a husband.
> *Bessie.* If you only seen her, you'd know to th' differ.

[*Nora* appears at door . . . She is clad only in her nightdress; her hair, uncared for for some days, is hanging in disorder over her shoulders. Her pale face looks paler still because of a vivid red spot on the tip of each cheek. Her eyes are glimmering with the light of incipient insanity . . .

(p. 244)

But the major force of the act comes from the dramatisation of the whole situation, from O'Casey's at last and successfully bringing together in a convincing and meaningful way the outer world of politics and war and the inner world of the domestic life of the tenements. In the created situation, 'humanity' cannot be kept insulated from a 'politics' brought vividly before us. Clitheroe is dead, his baby is dead, his wife is insane, Langon has been horribly wounded, even the death of one of the soldiers comes bloodily 'on stage' in the words of Sergeant Tinley:

> Private Taylor; got 'it roight through the chest, 'e did; an 'ole in front of 'im as 'ow you could put your fist through, and 'arf 'is back blown awoy! Dum-dum bullets they're using.
>
> (pp. 254-5)

The great stroke is the death of Bessie (a death full of irony since Bessie is vehemently anti-Republican), who is shot by members of the army in which her own son serves, and dies because of her care and concern for Nora, who in her incipient insanity has exposed herself to danger for a husband who is already dead:

> *Bessie* [with an arrested scream of fear and pain] . Merciful God, I'm shot, I'm shot, I'm shot! . . . Th' life's pourin' out o' me! [To *Nora*] I've got this through . . . through you, you bitch, you! . . . O God, have mercy on me! . . . [To *Nora*] You wouldn't stop quiet, no, you wouldn't, you wouldn't, blast you! Look at what I'm afther gettin' . . .
>
> (p. 258)

That 'you bitch' is masterly, counteracting the obvious dangers of sentimentality and adding yet another level of irony.

The high-flown theories of the glory of war, and the inhuman false-ness of the bombastic attitudes and rhetoric which ran rampant in the second act, are thus in this last act, thoroughly exposed. O'Casey has one final turn of the screw left in his fine climax. This is dramatised through the two British soldiers, Corporal Stoddart and Sergeant Tinley. Earlier in the act Corporal Stoddart, especially, seemed to stand for the professional soldier's indifference to death:

'ello. [Indicating the coffin] This the stiff? . . . Was she plugged?
The Covey. Ah, no; died o' consumption.
Corporal Stoddart. Ow, is that all? Thought she moight 'ave been
plugged.

(pp. 248-9)

But in the great last moments of the play, we see something else. The
irony of the chorus in which they join, 'Keep the 'owme fires burning',
as the 'glare in the sky seen through the window flares into a fuller and
deeper red', is sufficiently obvious. What we also realise — it is O'Casey's
final comprehensive routing of the false values of militarism in any shape
or form — is that, as the two 'professionals' sit drinking their cups of
tea in Bessie's attic, while her corpse stiffens on the floor in front of
them, they too are essentially and fundamentally domestic — they
'dream of 'owme'.

The last act of *The Plough and the Stars* is perhaps O'Casey's finest
and most sustained piece of writing, with hardly a flaw. Despite this,
however, the play as a whole has its weaknesses. The relationship between Nora and Clitheroe which is destroyed comprehensively by the
politics and the fighting is clearly intended to highlight the tragedy of
those politics by providing the contrasting what-might-have-been idyll-
image of domestic affection and security and love. The problem is that
the false poeticism in O'Casey's handling of the language of love never
begins to convince us that there is any real or moving substance to the
love relationship. 'Little, little, red-lipped Nora', exclaims Clitheroe,
and Nora dutifully takes up the banal phrase — 'Send him away, an' stay
with your own little red-lipped Nora'. This is hollow, and O'Casey seems
to feel the hollowness, for he attempts to eke out or step up the 'feeling'
with a song. But the song is itself trite, though one critic says of it,
amazingly enough:

> Filled as it is with images of youth, romance, spring, and the restora-
> tive powers of nature the ballad is an effective metaphor for that
> period before the Rising, a time of peace, potential and tranquil
> love.[23]

Effective metaphor? Most of all, what this ballad does is to remind us
that O'Casey at one time, and for the honourable cause of making a
bob or two, wrote verses for Christmas cards:

Th' violets were scenting th' woods, Nora,
Displaying their charm to th' bee,

> When I first said I lov'd only you, Nora,
> An' you said you lov'd only me! ...
> The trees, birds, an' bees sang a song, Nora,
> Of happier transports to be,
> When I first said I lov'd only you Nora,
> An' you said you lov'd only me!
>
> (pp. 186-7)

When O'Casey has Nora repeat this song in the last act with Clitheroe dead and her own sanity going, he takes a risk in the cause of pathos which simply does not come off. Strained and far-fetched rhetoric persists throughout the relationship and always weakens the dramatic impact of moments that are meant to be intense, as when Nora begs Clitheroe, in the third act, to stay with her rather than seek succour for his wounded comrade:

> No, no, no, I'll not let you go! Come on, come up to our home, Jack, my sweetheart, my lover, my husband, an' we'll forget th' last few terrible days! ... I look tired now, but a few hours of happy rest in your arms will bring back th' bloom of freshness again, an' you will be glad, glad ... glad!
>
> (pp. 233-4)

It is not an isolated failure in O'Casey — as Thomas Kilroy points out,[24] a similar contrived diction and overworked rhythm informs the language of Harry and Jessie in *The Silver Tassie*, of Ayamonn and Sheila in *Red Roses For Me*, and of Manus and Foorawn in *The Bishop's Bonfire*. Kilroy does not mention, but he could have mentioned, Jerry and Mary in *Juno and the Paycock*; even when the relationship isn't central to the play, O'Casey betrays his habitual unease and 'poeticism':

> *Jerry* [appealingly]. Mary, what's come over you with me for the last few weeks? You hardly speak to me, an' then only a word with a face o' bittherness on it. Have you forgotten, Mary, all the happy evenin's that were as sweet as the scented hawthorn that sheltered the sides o' the road as we saunthered through the country?
>
> (p. 18)

But it is not just the overblown and sentimental language in which it is dramatised that prevents us acceding to O'Casey's urge that we should see in the Clitheroes a tragic image of human relations usurped by political fanaticism. Jack Clitheroe is vain, shallow, egotistical and foolish. He gave up the Citizen Army in a fit of sulks because he was not made a Captain, and his main reason for wishing to be a Captain, apparently, is the desire to swank it in a new uniform and a Sam Browne belt. He muses enviously, just after his entry in the first act, on the luck of Captain Brennan 'showing himself off' in the big meeting, in his uniform, carrying the flag of the Plough and the Stars. And we have already seen how in the second act, he is presented as a mesmerised dupe of the high-flown rhetoric of the orator. In other words, his devotion to the nationalist cause is entirely superficial. In fact, though he is younger, and does not look like 'the illegitimate son of an illegitimate child of a corporal in th' Mexican army', the character whom he most resembles is the wholly ridiculous Peter, also a sucker for uniforms — the 'green coat, gold braided, white breeches, top boots, frilled shirt, slouch hat with white ostrich plume and ceremonial sword' of the Foresters — and for windy rhetoric. Now, the critical point at issue is that while it is perfectly fair for O'Casey to ask us to view Clitheroe as yet another in his long line of foolish and bemused nationalists, it is not permissible that he then asks us, through the heavily sentimentalised mouth of Nora, to take Clitheroe's death as in some way tragic. O'Casey cannot have his cake and eat it too; we simply don't care much, one way or the other, about Clitheroe. As before in O'Casey, the weight of the pathos comes to rest on the shoulders of his suffering — and apolitical — women, a pattern, by now predictable, with its own tendencies to sentimental over-simplification. Once again braggart and posturing males are shown up by the womenfolk — Nora, Rosie Redmond, Bessie. Rosie functions most effectively of the three, because least sentimentally, neither wife nor mother (apart from Bessie's off-stage son, we see her maternal solicitude for Mollser), but prostitute:

Barman [wiping counter]. Nothin' much doin' in your line tonight, Rosie?

Rosie. Curse o' God on th' haporth, hardly, Tom. There isn't much notice taken of a pretty petticoat of a night like this . . . They're all in a holy mood. Th' solemn-looking dials on th' whole o' them an' they marchin' to th' meetin'. You'd think they were th' glorious company of th' saints, an' th' noble army of martyrs thrampin' through th' streets of paradise. They're all thinkin' of higher things than a girl's garthers.

(pp. 192-3)

Her down-to-earth pragmatism serves throughout that second act to mock the idealistic claims being made outside and inside the bar; though, even here, there is a faint touch of the stereotype in the warm-hearted tart with common-sense. Again, it is perfectly in order — though historically inaccurate to the Ireland of those years — for O'Casey to suggest that his womenfolk somehow (miraculously?) contrive to escape the political and nationalist virus rampant and endemic in his men. But, given the basically naturalistic thrust and design of his plays, the implicit claim that he is 'telling it like it is, or was', we cannot but be aware of the strain, of the factitiousness, in O'Casey's created world where this kind of politico-sexual apartheid seems so firmly established.

The pattern is too simple, then. And apart from this strange division between male hearts of stone and female hearts of flesh, over-simplification is the main charge to be brought against O'Casey's whole treatment of nationalists and nationalism, not just in *The Plough and the Stars* but in the other work also. Raymond Williams is surely right in saying:

> . . . this people's dramatist writing for what was said to be a people's theatre at the crisis of this people's history, is in a deep sense mocking it at the very moment when it moves him. The feelings of the fighters, in that real history, are not dramatically engaged at all; all we see and hear is the flag, the gesture, the rhetoric. The need and the oppression are silent, or at best oblique in some consequent action.[25]

One is not asking here that O'Casey should have betrayed his own feelings and presented Republican nationalism in a heroic light, but rather that he should not have betrayed the complexities of his chosen subject in so facile a fashion. Yeats, for example, had many reservations about nationalist idealism and aspiration, but succeeded in embodying in his work, along with those reservations and despite his aversion from the naturalistic mode which O'Casey employs, a fuller and more genuine understanding of the power and the appeal of nationalist ideology to a deprived and oppressed population. O'Casey never sees — or at least never presents in his plays with any understanding — the important role played by nationalist ideology in offering to and creating in his deprived slum dwellers a necessary sense of dignity and pride. For him it is always, and too neatly, a wholly spurious ideology; its defining characteristics mere vainglory, the love of empty show and bombast. So we get his hollow men — Tommy Owens and Davoren, Johnny and the Mobilizer, Clitheroe, Langon, Brennan, and more. 'A principle's a principle', says Johnny, but O'Casey sees no principle at all in nationalism. It is an unnecessary diversion from the true struggle, which should be the social and economic one. This may have been so, and one may even agree with O'Casey's 'Would that it had been otherwise!' O'Casey's plays offer no explanation of how nationalism operated so powerfully as a 'diversion', however, of how even a man like the labour leader James Connolly threw in his lot with nationalism. F. S. L. Lyons, speaking of Connolly's choice in his magisterial history, *Ireland since the Famine*, writes:

> In choosing to place political action first and the reshaping of society second in his order of priorities, he was surely obeying a sound instinct. In the circumstances of his time, indeed, he could hardly have done otherwise.[26]

Nationalism was, fortunately or unfortunately, the most dynamic force in Irish politics. But O'Casey will not allow this, with the resulting simplification of the dramatic pattern. And the simplification is never far away from contradiction. His desire to show up the nationalist ideology as wholly spurious makes his slum dwellers ridiculous, even sometimes contemptible, since they fall so easily for what are seen as totally empty postures. And this, even while O'Casey is simultaneously trying to assert his people's fundamental humanity, warmth, humour, etc. A phrase of Raymond Williams is again apt — 'surface warmth over a deeply resigned contempt'.[27]

The point is of importance, not solely as a way of trying to pin down the sense of confusion which permeates O'Casey's dramatic vision. Much of the misunderstanding and misreading of the Northern Ireland situation of today is due to a similar failure to appreciate the power of nationalist ideology, especially in what are in a sense Northern versions of O'Casey's tenements, the ghettos of Derry and Belfast. These places too are full of economic deprivation, high unemployment, and appalling social conditions. And yet there too, as in O'Casey's Dublin, the tricolour means more than the Red Flag. Eamonn McCann, himself a committed and articulate socialist, would, like O'Casey, wish it were otherwise. But in his recent book *War in an Irish Town*, dealing mainly with events since 1969 in Derry, he does not allow his socialist interpretation to override his sense of realities; he refuses to write off the nationalist ideology as the straw man, the empty shadow, of O'Casey's plays:

> The main reason why Republican rhetoric about the past continues to evoke a gut response from many people in Ireland is that most of it is true. That it is encrusted with myth alters nothing essential. Some people need myths, need them to glorify their history in order to push away the grim reality of the way they have to live now. If the traditional Republican account of Irish history has been most fervently believed in the Catholic ghettos of the North . . . it is because

the people who live there, ground down by oppression and with no apparent possibility of escape, have needed an ennobled history, have needed to postulate a line of continuity between the glorious struggles of the past and a liberation yet to come. When a man lives in a world of bookies' slips, varnished counters and Guinness spits he will readily accept an account of the past which invests his living with dignity.[28]

What McCann sees, and what O'Casey does not see, despite their similar general orientation, is that to desire that Irish politics should be concerned with economic change, with 'bread on the table', rather than with 'myth', does not permit one to take the wish for the deed and turn the 'myth' into empty caricature. It is possible to dislike the nationalist myth yet to recognise its power, to admit that − as Yeats saw so clearly − myth may be not so much a swerve away from reality, as another mode of reality. O'Casey's opposition of politics to 'genuine humanity', which results in the hollow and superficial portrayal of nationalism in his work, prevents him getting to grips with his subject in any serious way. Plays which, on the surface, tell us so much about Ireland's political upheavals earlier in the century, in reality tell us very little; and, with their damaging and sentimental oversimplifications of (nationalist) political realities, offer even less insight into the complexities of the present situation in the North.

On February 1, 1913, a columnist who wrote under the pseudonym of 'Euchan' wrote an article in *The Irish Worker* called 'The Labour Movement: Labour and its Relation to Home Rule'. The argument was that Labour should realise that its true fight was not for Home Rule, but against capitalism, and it made the following point:

In its present position Ireland is comically pathetic. Its subconscious mind is away back in glories of the past, while its conscious mind is occupied in up-to-date political manoeuvring, with a sort of pious hope that the glories of the past will be revived when the political intriguing will be successful. The past, however, is for ever past. Ireland can never again be the glorious nation it was. The present age is a commercial one, and all that the British political bosses desire is that Ireland will become a cohesive, active and willing part of the British commercial empire, and Ireland will undoubtedly become so after Home Rule is established.[29]

This position is very close to what O'Casey himself was to come to feel, and it is part of the implied or explicit criticism of nationalist thought and rhetoric in the three Dublin plays, especially *The Plough and the Stars*. But in 1913, O'Casey felt very differently, and engaged in controversy with 'Euchan' in *The Irish Worker*, adopting an intemperately 'Irish Ireland' position and rhetoric. On 22 February, for example, O'Casey ends an article titled '"Euchan" and Ireland, a Challenge to a Verbal Combat', with these words:

> The delivery of Ireland is not in the Labour Manifesto, good and salutary as it may be, but in the strength, beauty, nobility and imagination of the Gaelic ideal. I am one of those who has entered into the labour of our fathers; one of those who declare — by the fame of our forefathers; by the murder of Red Hugh; by the anguished sighs of the Geraldine; by the blood-dripping wounds of Wolfe Tone; by the noble blood of Emmet; by the death-wasted bodies of the famine — that we will enter into our inheritance or we will fall one by one. Amen.[30]

Here lies a good part of the explanation of O'Casey's contemptuous and even vituperative portrait of nationalists and nationalism in his plays; in the special degree of recoil and revulsion from an attitude and a rhetoric he had once himself so ardently espoused. O'Casey's attitude in the plays to nationalist politics is that of the reformed alcoholic to drink. From one extreme to the other, for O'Casey is — and this is partly what distinguishes him from Joyce, whose work seems to share something of what has come to be known as O'Casey's 'anti-heroic vision', but which is in fact much more in control of its emotional attitudes — an extremist, a man of imbalance. Parenthetically one may remark that O'Casey's sympathetic presentation of the apolitical women of his plays probably stems from personal experience; he is offering tribute to his long-suffering mother, whose life was concerned not with politics but with rent and food and the struggle against the dirt and disease of the tenements.[31] An admirable personal attitude and devotion, but when it fuses with his personal recoil from nationalist politics we get a lop-sided art.

Finally, a point often made in O'Casey's defence or commendation is that the richness and vigour of his dramatic language excuses or covers a multitude of flaws. The dynamism and energy that O'Casey so signally filters out of Irish· politics may then be found in the extravagantly humorous or abusive speech of his characters, and the plays themselves found resplendent with a kind of 'poetry', itself an expression of O'Casey's reverence for 'life', or the life force. Such a view is sometimes, in fact, a way of switching off the critical faculties, for the much easier substitution of some cliché behind which lurks the myth of 'the Irish gift for language'. Sometimes O'Casey's language has indeed a pithily forceful energy and sinew, as in Juno's 'you can skip like a goat into a snug' and 'don't be actin' as if you couldn't pull a wing out of a dead bee'; or in these examples from *The Plough and the Stars*:

(a) Y'oul' hypocrite, if everyone was blind you'd steal a cross of an ass's back! (p.230).

(b) Th' whole city can topple home to hell, for Fluther! (p.237).

(c) Fight fair! A few hundhred scrawls o' chaps with a couple o' guns an' Rosary beads, again' a hundhred thousand thrained men with horse, fut, an' artillery . . . an' he wants us to fight fair! D'ye want us to come out in our skins an' throw stones? (p. 255)

And, of course, there are many more examples of genuinely vigorous dramatic speech in O'Casey, a number of which have already been cited in the course of this essay. But there is another, weaker kind of language in O'Casey, apart from the false poeticism in his rhetoric of love which has already been commented on. It emerges partly in the increasing reliance on verbal tics and mannerisms and malapropisms, generally designed for comic effect, which can be observed steadily on the flow from *The Shadow of a Gunman* up to *The Plough and the Stars*, where they seriously intrude. Thus, Fluther uses the word 'derogatory' with wearying frequency — at least seven times before the (relatively early) entry of Nora in the first act; and Mrs Gogan has her own tricks: 'Ah, she is and she isn't. There's prettiness an' prettiness in it . . . there's politeness and politeness in it . . . Ah, they do an' they don't . . . It is an' it isn't'. Since this also occurs in the opening exchanges, and since we have also old Peter's stock cry 'God Almighty, give me patience' (at least three times in the opening episode, with only slight variations), and his frequent references to being 'twarted an' tormented', we sense O'Casey's somewhat mechanical reliance on a simple audience response.

More seriously, where the language is meant to be more colourful and to move beyond the verbal tic, there is frequently a damaging self-consciousness about it, as if it is designed to make the audience sit up and take notice of its extravagance. Fluther says:

Is a man fermentin' with fear to stick th' showin' off to him of a thing that looks like a shinin' shroud?

(pp. 168-9)

Mrs Gogan shares this fondness for alliteration and for the redundant epithet which has the preservation of alliterative effects as its main purpose:

> . . . he might come staggerin' in covered with bandages, splashed all over with th' red of his own blood, an' givin' us barely time to bring th' priest to hear th' last whisper of his final confession, as his soul was passin' through th' dark doorway o' death into th' way o' th' wondherin' dead.
>
> (p. 216)

The Covey, too, has caught the infection:

> . . . it's not long since th' fathers o' some o' them crawled out o' th' shelterin' slime o' the sea.
>
> (p. 171)

And when it is not alliteration, it is a quasi-Biblical orotundity, or a combination of both, as in Peter's —

> . . . to have to listen to that Covey's twartin' animosities, shovin' poor, patient people into a lashin' out of curses that darken his soul, with th' shadow of th' wrath of th' last day!
>
> (p. 174)

(The quasi-Biblical note that informs many of the evangelical Bessie's speeches is, dramatically speaking, more justified — but of course it loses some of its point because O'Casey spills his rhetorical 'colours' so unrestrainedly over the other characters' speech.) The flaccidity of the syntax — we may compare Synge's much greater control and artistry in this respect — is also a marked feature of the passages quoted. It is as if O'Casey confused amplitude with energy, and is particularly noticeable as an inert device in the flytings of Bessie and Mrs Gcgan:

> . . . an' steppin' from th' threshold of good manners, let me tell you, Mrs Burgess, that it's a fat wondher to Jennie Gogan that a lady-like singer o' hymns like yourself would lower her thoughts from sky-thinkin' to stretch out her arm in a sly-seekin' way to pinch anything dhriven asthray in th' confusion of th' battle our boys is makin' for th' freedom of their counthry!
>
> (p. 228)

The Irish reputation for linguistic extravagance is itself a product of the historical development of the country alongside its powerful and imperial neighbour. It is dangerous, as Seamus Deane says of this kind of reputation, 'especially when given to small nations by a bigger one which dominates them. By means of it, Celts can stay quaint and stay put; extravagance is their essence and fact not their forte.'[32] Unfortunately, 'quaintness' is exactly the quality of much of O'Casey's rhetoric in *The Plough and the Stars*: one feels that either O'Casey is too aware of the English audiences who had greeted his earlier plays with enthusiasm, or that – as frequently happens in the Irish psyche – he has actually come to believe in the myth of the 'Elizabethan' richness of Irish speech. Either way, the language of *The Plough and the Stars* trades too easily on the indulgence of the audience for an expected 'comic' blather. Its colour and 'energy' are too frequently factitious – ironically, too 'literary', not earned by observation but created by a few devices such as alliteration, heaped-up epithets, and heaped-up clauses.

For this reason, one must disagree with Jack Lindsay's point in his influential essay, where he gamely argues the political worth of O'Casey, and relates this to his language:

> But, beyond any such particular cases [i.e. O'Casey's 'heroic' women], what conveys an effect of rich energies which have not yet found their occasion, is something deeper, more diffused, embedded in the whole method of characterization and above all in the speech of the people – a conviction of great human potentialities and powers of enjoyment and action. And so, paradoxically, it is through the babblers and fantasists ... that we feel the possibilities of great positive liberations.[33]

We have only to ask ourselves – what 'possibility of great positive liberation' is suggested in the figures of Captain Boyle and Joxer, O'Casey's most successful babblers and fantasists? There is a genuine energy and imaginative power in the Paycock, and his language rarely if ever rings false; but surely not even O'Casey asks us to see in him Ireland's hope. His 'powers of enjoyment' are convincingly mediated through a successful and enormously funny rhetoric, but the whole conception is of a man locked inside his own world, and quite happy with it, and anxious to keep the world of positive action at bay. And then, finally, as regards the 'energy' of much of the language of O'Casey's other men and women, it simply is not there; it is either self-deceiving blather that we are to criticise for its evasions, or merely a product of O'Casey's collusion with a received view of Irish eloquence.

Much of this may seem very hard on a dramatist who has given us one highly coherent and consistent play, a few superbly funny and memorable characters, and at least two or three intensely and magnificently theatrical scenes;[34] whose subject-matter seems more than ever relevant to an Ireland still convulsed by violent politics; and who achieved all that he did despite the most arduous conditions of existence. But, as Thomas Kilroy says of O'Casey, 'it is not his feeling or his honesty that is in question . . . but the capacity to occupy the chosen subject with discrimination'.[35] And for all O'Casey's incidental felicities and local successes, one would have to reply to the question by saying that in the Dublin plays the chosen subject is not handled with such discrimination.

NOTES

Notes to Chapter 1

1. See, for example, H. Howarth, *The Irish Writers, 1880-1940: Literature under Parnell's Star* (Rockliff, London, 1958); U. M. Ellis-Fermor, *The Irish Dramatic Movement* (Methuen, London, 1939); James W. Flannery, *W. B. Yeats and the Idea of a Theatre: The Early Abbey Theatre in Theory and Practice* (Yale University Press, New Haven and London, 1976); W. I. Thompson, *The Imagination of an Insurrection: Dublin, Easter 1916* (Oxford University Press, New York, 1967); R. Loftus, *Nationalism in Modern Anglo-Irish Poetry* (Wisconsin University Press, Madison, 1964); Malcolm Brown, *The Politics of Irish Literature: From Thomas Davis to W. B. Yeats* (Allen and Unwin, London, 1972); Peter Costello, *The Heart Grown Brutal: The Irish Revolution in Literature, from Parnell to the Death of Yeats, 1891-1939* (Gill and Macmillan, Dublin, 1977).

2. The most comprehensive and consistently illuminating history of Ireland in the period in question is by F. S. L. Lyons, *Ireland since the Famine* (Fontana, London, revised edn 1973). Other good histories are J. C. Beckett's *The Making of Modern Ireland, 1603-1923* (Faber and Faber, London, 1966), and R. Dudley Edwards's *A New History of Ireland* (Gill and Macmillan, Dublin, 1972). Each, especially Lyons, includes an extensive bibliography.

3. Patrick O'Farrell, *England and Ireland since 1800* (Oxford University Press, London, 1975), p. 2.

4. Cited in L. P. Curtis, Jr, *Anglo-Saxons and Celts: A Study of Anti-Irish Prejudice in Victorian England* (Bridgeport, Conn., 1968), p.50.

5. Cited O'Farrell, p.69.

6. Cited Curtis, *Anglo-Saxons and Celts*, p.84.

7. Cited D. G. Boyce, *Englishmen and Irish Troubles* (Cape, London, 1972), p.29. In the same speech Lord Salisbury made clear the political implications of the colonialist attitude when cross-fertilised by racial prejudice: 'You would not confide free representative institutions to the Hottentots for instance.'

8. An anonymous article in *Punch*, in October 1862, shows neatly how the unflattering English view of the Irish was widely diffused through the 'popular' culture:

> A gulf, certainly, does appear to yawn between the Gorilla and the Negro. The woods and wilds of Africa do not exhibit an example of any intermediate animal. But . . . a creature manifestly between the gorilla and the negro is to be met with in some of the lowest districts of London and Liverpool . . . It comes from Ireland, whence it has contrived to migrate; it belongs in fact to a tribe of Irish savages: the lowest species of the Irish Yahoo. When conversing with its kind it talks a sort of gibberish. It is, moreover, a climbing animal, and may sometimes be seen ascending a ladder laden with a hod of bricks . . . The somewhat superior ability of the Irish Yahoo to utter articulate sounds, may suffice to prove that it is a development, and not, as some imagine, a degeneration of the gorilla.

L. P. Curtis, Jr, in *Apes and Angels: The Irishman in Victorian Caricature* (David and Charles, Newton Abbot, 1971), has shown how the rise of ethnological and anthropological studies in Victorian England, plus the impact of Darwinism, gave a new 'scientific' impulse to the simianisation of Paddy.

9. Curtis, *Anglo-Saxons and Celts*, p.51.

10. Conor Cruise O'Brien's *States of Ireland* (Hutchinson, London 1972),p.51, is largely an attempt to come to terms with the Northern Irish problem; but putting that problem as he does in terms of historical attitudes and prejudices, he says many things, especially in two chapters entitled respectively 'Songs of the Irish Race' and 'Colonists and Colonized', that I wish I had said first.

11. Cited in Nicholas Mansergh, *The Irish Question, 1840-1921* (George Allen and Unwin, London, 1965), pp.88-9.

12. The Anglo-Irish Elizabeth Bowen makes the extremely perceptive point: 'Ireland for the Irish had been the politician's promise, yet to be made good. *Irishness* for the Irish was the Gaelic League's promise, subtler and more essential' (*Bowen's Court*, Longman's, London, 1942, p.400).

13. *The Revival of Irish Literature: Addresses by Sir Charles Gavan Duffy, Dr. George Sigerson, and Dr. Douglas Hyde* (London, 1894), p.118. Paradoxically, and bearing out the general drift of my argument about Ireland's cultural complexity, Hyde was a Protestant Anglo-Irishman. Later he was to be President of the Free State.

14. Cited in Lady Gregory, ed., *Ideals in Ireland* (At the Unicorn, London, 1901), p.36.

15. O'Brien, *States of Ireland*, p.67.

16. Joseph Lee, *The Modernisation of Irish Society, 1848-1918* (Gill and Macmillan, Dublin, 1973), p.130.

17. *Davis, Mangan, Ferguson? Tradition and the Irish Writer*. Writings by W. B. Yeats and by Thomas Kinsella (Dolmen Press, Dublin, 1970), pp.60-1. Corkery's book was published in 1931.

18. Lee, *Modernisation of Irish Society*, p.94.

19. *Ibid.*, p. 96.

20. Cited in Howard Smith, *Ireland: Some Episodes from Her Past* (BBC Publications, London, 1974), p.115.

21. Cited in Peter Costello, *The Heart Grown Brutal*, p.189. Costello does not give the date of the radio broadcast from which these words come. But that does not really matter – the present writer remembers hearing 'Dev' many times on Radio Eireann, and he always worked something like this in.

22. See Gregory, *Ideals in Ireland*, pp.16-21.

23. *Parnell and his Island* (London, 1887). There Moore speaks of 'a primitive country and barbarous people'.

24. Gregory, *Ideals in Ireland*, p.50.

25. This is discussed more fully in Lyons, *Ireland since the Famine*, in Lee, *The Modernisation of Irish Society*, and particularly well in Alexander J. Humphreys, *New Dubliners: Urbanisation and the Irish Family* (Routledge and Kegan Paul, London, 1966).

26. Raymond Williams, *Keywords: A Vocabulary of Culture and Society* (Fontana, London, 1976), p.194, shows how the word 'peasant' became a loose term of abuse, or died out, or had a purely literary usage, in England from about the late eighteenth century.

27. See Humphreys, *New Dubliners*, who shows that as late as 1949, of 116 parents of 58 spouses included in his sample, only 31 were born and raised in Dublin; 67 were children of farmers, 9 children of farm labourers. Costello, *The Heart Grown Brutal*, confirms the general point I am making; that the majority of the Abbey theatre audiences were fairly close to the soil, but wanted to think themselves as far away from it as possible.

28. Frank O'Connor, *The Backward Look: A Survey of Irish Literature* (Macmillan, London, 1967), p. 154.

29. J. C. Beckett, *The Anglo-Irish Tradition* (Faber and Faber, London, 1976),

p. 11. It is important to note that the Protestants of Northern Ireland, or Ulster as it was then more properly called, are not under discussion here. They were mainly of Scottish and strongly Presbyterian origin; and 'Anglo-Irish' usually refers to Protestants of what we now call the south of Ireland. It is hardly necessary to add at this stage in Irish history that the 'religious' labels denote wide cultural, political and even racial differences, and have little to do with disagreements over the status of the Blessed Virgin Mary or the question of transubstantiation.

30. Edmund Curtis, *A History of Ireland* (Methuen, London, 1936; sixth edn 1950), p.284.

31. Beckett, *The Anglo-Irish Tradition*, pp. 87-8.

32. The two key dates are probably 1829, when the Catholic Emancipation Act was passed, and 1869 when the Anglican Church of Ireland was disestablished. The latter Act, as Beckett says (p.110), marked an unmistakeable step towards the British Government's abandonment of the Anglo-Irish.

33. Cited in Gerald Griffin, *The Wild Geese* (Jarrolds, London, 1938), p.24.

34. Elizabeth Bowen, *Seven Winters: Memories of a Dublin Childhood* (Longmans Green, London, 1943), pp.44-5.

35. Cited in Frank Tuohy, *Yeats* (Macmillan, London, 1976), p.120.

36. Cited in Terence de Vere White, *The Anglo-Irish* (Gollancz, London, 1972), p.199.

37. Vivian Mercier, *Beckett/Beckett* (Oxford University Press, New York, 1977), p.26.

38. *Ibid.*, pp.31-2.

39. Cited in de Vere White, *The Anglo-Irish*, p. 59.

40. Yeats, *Essays and Introductions*, p.519.

41. See Allen Tate, ed., *T.S. Eliot: The Man and His Work* (Chatto and Windus, London, 1967), p.20. 'H. J.' is, of course, Henry James.

42. The allusion is to Oscar Wilde's 'The Decay of Lying' (1898): 'I can quite understand your objection to art being treated as a mirror. You think it would reduce genius to the position of a cracked looking-glass.' From *The Artist as Critic: Critical Writings of Oscar Wilde*, ed. Richard Ellmann (W.H. Allen, London, 1970), p.307.

43. Kinsella, *Tradition and the Irish Writer*, p.65.

44. *Ibid.*, pp.64-5.

Notes to Chapter 2

1. See Robin Skelton, *J.M. Synge and His World* (Thames and Hudson, London, 1971), p.12. Landlordism was deep in the Synge blood — yet another brother, Robert, managed and owned estates in Argentina.

2. T. R. Henn, ed., *The Plays and Poems of J.M. Synge* (Methuen, London, 1963), p.1.

3. 'I was painfully timid, and while still very young the idea of Hell took a fearful hold on me. One night I thought I was irretrievably damned and cried myself to sleep in vain yet terrified efforts to form a conception of eternal pain. In the morning I renewed my lamentations and my mother was sent for. She comforted me with the assurance that the Holy Ghost was convicting me of sin and thus preparing me for ultimate salvation.' (*CW*, vol.2, p.4).

4. See David H. Greene and Edward M. Stephens, *J.M. Synge, 1871-1909* (Macmillan, New York, 1959), p.23.

5. Letter to *The Irish Statesman* (vol.11, no.9), 3 Nov. 1928, p.169. One

might note that this letter was written long after Synge's death, and some years after the qualified triumph of Irish nationalism.

6. 'Synge seemed by nature unfitted to think a political thought, and with the exception of one sentence, spoken when I first met him in Paris, that implied some sort of Nationalist conviction, I cannot remember that he spoke of politics or showed any interest in men in the mass, or in any subject that is studied through abstractions and statistics.' ('J. M. Synge and the Ireland of his Time' (1910), in Yeats, *Essays and Introductions*, p.319.)

7. Nicholas Grene, *Synge: A Critical Study of the Plays* (Macmillan, London, 1975), p.8.

8. See, for example, the fragment of a scenario called 'National Drama', and also 'Deaf Mutes for Ireland', *CW*, vol.3, pp.218-26.

9. Synge had first become interested in the peasant way of life during his lonely boyhood ramblings in Wicklow. His travels in Germany and his studies in Celtic civilisation while in France further deepened his interest in folklore.

10. Cited Lee, *The Modernisation of Irish Society*, p.5. See also Humphreys, *New Dubliners*.

11. Arthur Power, *Conversations with James Joyce*, ed. Clive Hart, (Millington, London, 1974), p.33.

12. 'Give up Paris. You will never create anything by reading Racine, and Arthur Symons will always be a better critic of French literature. Go to the Aran Islands. Live there as if you were one of the people themselves; express a life that has never found expression.' (Yeats, *Essays and Introductions*, p.299).

13. See Daniel Corkery's judgement, in *Synge and Anglo-Irish Literature* (Mercier Press, Cork, 1966, originally published 1931), p.56: 'He remained long enough [on Aran] to be troubled with the thought that he could never become more to the islanders than a stranger. This trouble he openly cries out again and again. It is the "cry over the abyss", the forlorn wail of the tribeless. Because he raised it, he differed from his fellow Ascendancy men.'

14. Robin Skelton, *The Writings of J. M. Synge* (Thames and Hudson, London, 1971), p.39. We may contrast to the primitivist strain in Synge Chekhov's rejection of Tolstoy's primitivism, in a letter of 1894: 'Reason and justice tell me there's more love for humanity in electricity and steam than in chastity and vegetarianism. War's evil, litigation's evil. But that doesn't mean I have to wear clogs and sleep on a stove with a workman and his wife and that sort of thing.' (R. Hingley, *A New Life of Anton Chekhov*, (Oxford University Press, London, 1976, p.75).

15. Corkery, *Synge and Anglo-Irish Literature* p.121.

16. Frank O'Connor in *The Backward Look* (pp.167-8), describes succinctly how Yeats made of primitivism a sort of 'universal' scheme of religion, aesthetics and politics. What is more it is a scheme that can impress people so different as Russell, Moore, Synge and Lady Gregory, all of remarkable intelligence. Like all universal systems it is basically simple: to escape the vulgarity of Victorian religion one returns to mythology and magic; to escape the commonplaces of journalism one goes back to peasant speech; to break the tyranny of actor-managers one simplifies acting and stage design, and to re-energize the theatre one brings back the miracle and mystery plays . . . though the problems are different, the answer is the same – a stream is purer nearer its source.'

17. The line is from 'The Municipal Gallery Revisited' (*CP*, p.369), and is explicitly linked with Synge:

John Synge, I and Augusta Gregory, thought
All that we did, all that we said or sang
Must come from contact with the soil, from that
Contact everything Antaeus-like grew strong.

We three alone in modern times had brought
Everything down to that sole test again,
Dream of the noble and the beggar-man.

18. Skelton, *The Writings of J.M. Synge*, may be taken to exemplify the
attitude of most contemporary critics of Synge's 'documentaries': 'The narrator's
involvement in his own interpretations is such that the whole book becomes
much less the account of a series of visits to strange islands than an account of an
introspective myth-making which feeds upon any evidence that supports it' (p.35).

19. Corkery, *Synge and Anglo-Irish Literature* p.79.

20. An analogous sensibility — in some respects at least — may be found in the
autobiography and some of the poetry of Edwin Muir, whose Orkney is almost a
literal as well as an imaginative Eden and whose move to Glasgow and 'the big
world' — to use the Irish phrase — is presented as a kind of fall from natural grace.
(See Muir's autobiography.)

21. See Alan J. Bliss, 'The Language of Synge', in M. Harmon, ed., *John M.
Synge: Centenary Papers, 1971* (Dolmen Press, Dublin, 1972), p.38: 'In Synge's
plays chronologically there is a progressive change of emphasis from syntax to
vocabulary. *The Playboy* in particular relies for its effect very largely on its exotic
vocabulary . . . '

22. James Joyce is only the most famous Irishman to be irritated by what he
sees as the unrealistic literariness of Synge's language. Mairi Nic Siublaigh and
W. G. Fay, both closely associated with the Abbey, Frank O'Connor, Oliver Gogarty
and many others agree that nobody in Ireland does speak as Synge's characters do;
though few reach the pitch of exasperation of Flann O'Brien: 'Nothing in the
whole galaxy of fake is comparable with Synge. It is not that Synge makes people
less worthy, or nastier, or even better than they are, but he brought forward
amusing clowns talking a sub-language of their own and bade us take them very
seriously' (cited in the *Times Literary Supplement*, 2 July 1971, p.749). Lurking
behind what animus there still is over Synge's language is native suspicion that the
Ascendancy man is simply exploiting the locals for colour, or worse, laughing at
them.

23. See, for example, Alan Bliss, 'The Language of Synge', and also 'A Synge
Glossary', S. Bushrui, ed., *Sunshine and the Moon's Delight: J. M. Synge 1871-
1909*, with a foreword by A.N. Jeffares (Smythe, Gerrards Cross, 1972), pp.297-
316; P. L. Henry, *An Anglo-Irish Dialect of North Roscommon* (University College,
Dublin, Department of English Publications, 1957); and Grene, *Synge* ch. 4.

24. See P. L. Henry, '*The Playboy of the Western World*', *Philologica Pragensis*,
vol.8 (1965), pp.189-204, who remarks: 'the primary cadence may be said to
relate to the mood (and manner) of the drama[tist] rather than to immediate
exigencies of context and character.'

25. Synge himself calls this the 'tense of habitude' when it occurs in expres-
sions like 'They do be driving', 'I do be thinking', etc. See *CW*, vol.3, p.275.

26. This quotation usefully confirms the point made above about the
uniformity of speech of Synge's characters, since it comes only a few lines after
the Widow Quin has scornfully rebuked a 'poetic' outburst from Christy on
Pegeen: 'There's poetry talk for a girl you'd see itching and scratching, and she
with a stale stink of poteen on her from selling in the shop.'

27. See Henry, *An Anglo-Irish Dialect of North Roscommon*, p.179: 'One
cannot fail to be struck with the strong consciousness of state as opposed to
action.' Henry gives examples which indicate the speaker's 'instability — or
indifference — with regard to the time relation and tense grading'.

28. Alan Price, *Synge and Anglo-Irish Drama* (Methuen, London, 1961), p.46:
'It is this felicitous and seemingly irresistible flow that gives to Synge's dialogue
something of that sense of ritual which all art must have while being linked to

recognizable everyday actualities . . . Synge's rhythms are similar enough to ordinary English speech for us to accept and understand them without undue effort, yet they are also dissimilar enough to give us a sense of novelty and freshness, to refurbish our words and to make us grasp them more fully and as if for the first time.'

29. Note the interesting suggestive passage from one of Synge's notebooks, on Aran dress: 'What has guided the women of grey-brown western Ireland to clothe them in red? The island without this simple red relief would be a nightmare fit to drive one to murder in order to gloat a while on the fresh red flow of blood . . .' (*CW*, vol.2, p.54).

30. See *CW*, vol.2, pp.151-2, 253-4, and the account on p.275 of a West Kerry fight after a day's horse-racing: '"There was great sport after you left," a man said to me in the cottage this evening. "They were all beating and cutting each other on the shore of the sea. Four men fought together in one place till the tide came up on them, and was like to drown them . . . Another man was left for dead on the road outside the lodges, and some gentleman found him and had him carried into his house, and got the doctor to put plasters on his head. Then there was a red-headed fellow had his finger bitten through, and the postman was destroyed for ever."'

31. Skelton, *J.M. Synge and His World*, p.57.

32. 'My story — in its *essence* — is probable given the psychic state of the locality.' Letter to Mackenna about *The Playboy*, *CW*, vol.4, p.xxiii.

33. Vivian Mercier, *'The Tinker's Wedding'*, in Bushrui, ed., *Sunshine and the Moon's Delight*, pp.75-89.

34. And, as Robin Skelton points out, 'it is important to recognize that the violent juxtaposition of literary with colloquial language also has a brutal effect' (*The Writings of J. M. Synge*, p.163). Skelton is referring to Synge's poems, but his point holds good for the plays. T. R. Henn in the introduction to his edition of *The Plays and Poems*, p.16, also notes Synge's 'fondness for violently colliding images'.

35. 'Synge's Poetic Use of Language', in M. Harmon, ed., *J. M. Synge: Centenary Papers*, p.132.

36. Henn, *The Plays and Poems of J. M. Synge*, p.15-16.

37. W. B. Yeats, 'Modern Ireland', in R. Skelton and D. R. Clark, eds., *Irish Renaissance* (Dolmen Press, Dublin, 1965), pp.18-20.

38. See A. N. Jeffares's foreword, p.12, to Bushrui, ed., *Sunshine and the Moon's Delight*.

39. Greene and Stephens, *J. M. Synge*, p.15. We may put alongside this the testimony of Jack B. Yeats, who travelled with Synge on the tour of Connemara in 1905: 'He loved mad scenes . . . all wild sights appealed to Synge, he did not care whether they were typical of anything else or had any symbolic meaning at all' (cited in E. H. Mikhail, ed., *J. M. Synge: Interviews and Recollections*, Macmillan, London, 1977, p.34).

40. Greene and Stephens, *J. M. Synge*, p.157.

41. See, e.g., Owen's speech to Deirdre: 'Stay here and rot with Naisi, or go to Conchubor in Emain. Conchubor's a swelling belly, and eyes falling downward from his shining crown, Naisi should be stale and weary; yet there are many roads, Deirdre, and I tell you I'd liefer be bleaching in a bog-hole than living on without a touch of kindness from your eyes and voice. It's a poor thing to be so lonesome you'd squeeze kisses on a cur dog's nose' (*CW*, vol.4, p.223).

42. Grene, *Synge*, p.174.

43. For further comment see Donald Davie, 'On the Poetic Diction of J. M. Synge', *Dublin Magazine*, vol.27 (new series, 1952), pp.32-8.

44. See Yeats's 'Coole Park and Ballylee, 1931'.

45. Mark Roberts, *The Tradition of Romantic Morality* (Macmillan, London, 1973).

46. Corkery, *Synge and Anglo-Irish Literature* pp.181 and 185.

47. Robert O'Driscoll ed., *Theatre and Nationalism in Twentieth Century Ireland* (Oxford University Press, London, 1971), p. 9.

48. Quoted in Lady Gregory, *Our Irish Theatre* (G. P. Putnam's Sons, New York, 1914), p.9.

49. 'The Poetry of Sir Samuel Ferguson', *Dublin University Review*, November 1886. Cited in *Uncollected Prose*, vol.1 (1970), p.100.

50. These sensibilities were whipped up by F. H. O'Donnell's pamphlet *Souls for Gold! Pseudo-Celtic Drama in Dublin* (London, 1904), which 'argued' that the play was heretical.

51. A full account of Yeats's revisions is given in Peter Ure's *Yeats the Playwright* (Routledge and Kegan Paul, London, 1963). My quotations from *The Countess Cathleen* are from the version given in Dublin in 1899, which may be found in vol.3 of the *Collected Works* of 1908.

52. Conor Cruise O'Brien, *States of Ireland*, p.60.

53. 'Another old man, the oldest on the island, is fond of telling me anecdotes – not folk-tales – of things that have happened here in his life-time. He often tells me about a Connaught man who killed his father with the blow of a spade when he was in passion, and then fled to this island and threw himself on the mercy of some of the natives with whom he was said to be related. They hid him in a hole – which the old man has shown me – and kept him safe for weeks, though the police came and searched for him, and he could hear their boots grinding on the stones over his head. In spite of a reward which was offered, the island was incorruptible, and after much trouble the man was safely shipped to America.

This impulse to protect the criminal is universal in the west. It seems partly due to the association between justice and the hated English jurisdiction, but more directly to the primitive feeling of these people, who are never criminals yet always capable of crime, that a man will not do wrong unless he is under the influence of a passion which is as irresponsible as a storm on the sea. If a man has killed his father, and is already sick and broken with remorse, they can see no reason why he should be dragged away and killed by the law.

Such a man, they say, will be quiet all the rest of his life, and if you suggest that punishment is needed as an example, they ask, 'Would any one kill his father if he was able to help it?''' (*CW*, vol.2, p.95). I quote the passage in full partly to demonstrate the radical changes in tone and emphasis to which Synge subjected the story in *The Playboy*.

54. And one might say that the forced marriage is also, despite the very different saga setting, a major element in *Deirdre of the Sorrows*, especially since, as has been pointed out, Synge attempts to impose a 'peasant' atmosphere on the saga world. Yeats's father had spelled out the implication of *The Shadow of the Glen* in a letter to the *United Irishman* in 1903: 'The outcry against Mr Synge's play seems to be largely dishonest, the real objection not being that it misrepresents Irishwomen, but that it is a very effective attack on loveless marriages – the most miserable institution so dear to our thrifty elders among the peasants and among their betters, by whom anything like impulse or passion is discredited, human nature coerced at every point and sincerity banished from the land' (cited Greene and Stephens, *J. M. Synge*, p.155).

55. See W. G. Fay and Catherine Carswell, *The Fays of the Abbey Theatre* (Rich and Cowan, London, 1935), p.211: 'He could not forgive the crass ignorance, the fatuity, the malevolence, with which *The Well of the Saints* had been received. He had given of his best in good faith, and offence had been taken where no offence had been intended. "Very well, then," he said to me bitterly one night,

"the next play I write I will make sure will annoy them." However, this anecdote may not be very reliable, having a touch of *arrière-pensée* about it.

56. A simple way of proving this is to compare the Yeats-Synge version of peasant life with that of a man who knew no other life, Tomás O Crohan's *The Islandman* (1929), translated from the Irish with an introduction, by Robin Flower (Chatto and Windus, London, 1934).

57. Padraic Colum, *The Road Round Ireland* (Macmillan, New York, 1926), p.368.

58. The biographer of Carleton and Mangan, D. J. O'Donoghue, referred in a letter to the *Freeman's Journal* to 'the continuous ferocity of the language in *The Playboy*'. (Greene and Stephens, *J. M. Synge* p.247).

59. Cited James Kilroy, *The 'Playboy' Riots* (Dolman Press, Dublin, 1971), p.38.

60. See above, p. 65. The 'childishness' and 'emotional volatility' of the Irish, tending to express itself in violence, was above all what made them unfit for Home Rule, in English eyes. The whole matter of violence as an impediment to the granting of Home Rule is examined fully in L. P. Curtis, *Anglo-Saxons and Celts*. Synge tended to sentimentalise things. In a letter of 19 February 1907 he writes: 'the wildness and, if you will, vices of the Irish peasantry are due, like their extraordinary good points of all kinds, to the *richness* of their nature – a thing that is priceless beyond words' (*CW*, vol.4, p.xxiii).

61. Kilroy, *The 'Playboy' Riots*, pp.9-10.

62. Conor Cruise O'Brien, *States of Ireland*, p.74.

63. In the case of *The Playboy*, the close reading approach, unchecked by any very lively sense of the play's origin in a specific culture at a specific time, has produced some ingenious but sterile readings. Most of these find suggestive analogies in Christy to Christ, or Oedipus, or Ossian, or Cuchulain, then proceed to work the analogy remorselessly through – to the detriment of genuine response to the play. Stanley Sultan's 'A Joycean Look at *The Playboy of the Western World*', in *The Celtic Master*, ed. M. Harmon (Dolmen Press, Dublin, 1969), pp.45-55, may be seen as definitive of this kind of Synge criticism: 'It is through his exploitation in *Playboy* of the ministry and crucifixion of Jesus that Synge crystallized the elements of the play into a coherent masterpiece.' At any rate, it's a good story, and Mr Sultan tells it lovely.

64. Una Ellis-Fermor, *The Irish Dramatic Movement*, p.176.

65. Letter to *The Irish Times* (30 Jan. 1907), cited *CW*, vol.4, p.364.

66. Kilroy, *The 'Playboy' Riots*, p.13.

67. Published in *The Irish Times*, 17 April 1971. The punning reference in 'Independent readers' is to the newspaper the *Irish Independent*, owned by Yeats's great enemy W. M. Murphy, and committed to the safe constitutional paths of the predominantly middle-class Irish party at Westminster.

68. *The Writings of J. M. Synge*, p.56.

69. See *CW*, vol.2, pp.70-2.

70. Corkery, *Synge and Anglo-Irish Literature*, pp.124, 129.

71. See *CW*, vol.3, pp.256-7.

72. Grene, *Synge*, pp.102-3.

73. See *CW*, vol.3, pp.265-7.

74. Greene and Stephens, *J. M. Synge*, pp.134-5.

75. Grene, *Synge*, p.110.

76. *Ibid.*, p.145.

77. *CW*, vol.4, pp.293-359.

78. See, e.g., J. L. Styan, *The Dark Comedy* (Cambridge University Press, London, 2nd edn 1968), p.131: 'The last sequence in the play . . . was a spit in the eye, or, to be more precise, three or four spits.'

79. Henn, *Plays and Poems of J. M. Synge*, p.27.

80. See F. M. Cornford, *The Origin of Attic Comedy* (Edward Arnold, London, 1914).

81. 'The Argument of Comedy', in *English Institute Essays* 1948, ed. D. A. Robertson, Jr (Columbia University Press, New York, 1949), pp. 58-73. See also Frye's *A Natural Perspective: The Development of Shakespearean Comedy and Romance* (Columbia University Press, New York, 1965), and R. W. Corrigan, *Comedy: Meaning and Form* (Chandler, San Francisco, 1965).

82. '*The Tinker's Wedding*', in Bushrui, ed., *Sunshine and the Moon's Delight*, p.81.

83. 'Synge and the Idea of a National Literature', in *J. M. Synge: Centenary Papers*, ed. M. Harmon, p.15.

84. Corkery, *Synge and Anglo-Irish Literature*, p.87.

85. *Ibid*., pp.27 and 87 (my italics).

Notes to Chapter 3

1. In 'Pages from a Diary in 1930', Yeats writes of his reactions to the portrait of him by Augustus John, that at first he (Yeats) saw the portrait as that of 'an unshaven, drunken bar-tender, and then I began to feel John had found something that he liked in me, something closer than character, and by that very transformation made it visible. He had found Anglo-Irish solitude, a solitude I have made for myself, an outlawed solitude' (*Explorations*, p.308).

2. Stephen Gwynn wrote: 'The effect of *Cathleen ni Houlihan* on me was that I went home asking myself if such plays should be produced unless one was prepared for people to go out to shoot and be shot' (cited A. N. Jeffares, *A Commentary on the Collected Poems of W. B. Yeats*, Macmillan, London, 1968, p.512). For the Republican revolutionary, P. S. O'Hegarty, the play was 'a sort of sacrament', and, writes Conor Cruise O'Brien, Constance Markievicz, sentenced to death for her part in the 1916 rising, recalled in prison that for her the play had been 'a sort of gospel' (*States of Ireland*, p. 70).

3. See Nicholas Mansergh, *The Irish Question 1840-1921*, esp. ch. 8, 'The Influence of the Romantic Ideal in Irish Politics', and W.I. Thompson, *The Imagination of an Insurrection: Dublin, Easter 1916*.

4. Probably the fullest, and certainly the most stimulating and provocative, account of Yeats's relationship to Irish politics is given by Conor Cruise O'Brien, 'Passion and Cunning: Notes on the Politics of Yeats', in A. N. Jeffares and K. G. W. Cross, eds., *In Excited Reverie: A Centenary Tribute to W. B. Yeats* (Macmillan, London, 1965) pp.207-78. As will be seen, however, I do not agree with the overall tone of Dr O'Brien's hugely entertaining essay.

5. In his essay of 1886, on Ferguson's poetry, Yeats writes: 'In these poems and the legends they contain lies the refutation of the calumnies of England and those amongst us who are false to their country. We are often told that we are men of infirm will and lavish lips, planning one thing and doing another, seeking this today and that tomorrow. But a widely different story do these legends tell. The mind of the Celt loves to linger on images of persistence; implacable hate, implacable love, on Conor and Deirdre, and Setanta watching by the door of Cullan.' (*Uncollected Prose*, vol.1, p.104).

6. A particularly clear example of Yeats's attitude is given in this passage, written in 1934: 'Even our best histories treat men as function. Why must I think the victorious cause the better? Why should Mommsen think the less of Cicero

because Caesar beat him? . . . I prefer that the defeated cause should be more vividly described than that which has the advertisement of victory.' (*Explorations*, p.398).

7. 'When I was a young lad all Ireland was organised under Parnell. Ireland then had great political power; she seemed on the verge of attaining great amelioration, and yet when we regret the breaking up of that power . . . we must remember that we paid for that power a very great price. The intellect of Ireland died under its shadow. Every other interest had to be put aside to attain it. I remember the *Freeman's Journal* publishing an article which contrasted the Parnell movement with the movement that had gone before it by saying: "The last movement was poetry plus cabbage garden" (meaning poetry and the failure of Smith O'Brien), "but this movement is going to be prose plus success". When that was written Ireland was ceasing to read her own poetry. Ireland was putting aside everything to attain her one political end.' From a speech on Robert Emmet – a spectacular example of heroic failure – in New York in 1904 (*Uncollected Prose*, vol.2, p.320).

8. See Donald Davie, 'The Young Yeats', in Conor Cruise O'Brien, ed., *The Shaping of Modern Ireland* (Routledge and Kegan Paul, London, 1960), p.143. p. 143.

9. F.S.L. Lyons, *Ireland since the Famine*, pp. 234-5.

10. Mansergh, *The Irish Question*, p.259.

11. The phrase is John Eglinton's, in an essay of 1902 in the *United Irishman* of 31 Mar. Thomas Davis (1814-45) had helped to found the 'Young Ireland' movement in the 1840s, and through its newspaper, *The Nation*, preached the religion of patriotism in verse which Yeats, like Eglinton, found hollow and rhetorical. Yet Yeats admired, always, Davis's idealism (see below, p. 100).

12. Cf. the directness of Padraic Pearse. Any boy entering his school, St Enda's, would find confronting him a fresco with the words attributed to Cuchulain emblazoned round it: 'I care not though I were to live but one day and one night, if only my fame and deeds live after me'. (Lyons, *Ireland since the Famine*, p. 332).

13. J.C. Beckett, *The Anglo-Irish Tradition*, p. 102.

14. Yeats wrote in 'The Celtic Element in Literature' (1897): 'When Matthew Arnold wrote [*On the Study of Celtic Literature*], it was not easy to know as much as we know now of folk-belief, and I do not think he understood that our "natural magic" is but the ancient religion of the world, the ancient worship of Nature' (*Essays and Introductions*, pp. 175-6). Frank Tuohy, *Yeats*, p. 33, makes the point that Yeats saw in theosophy an 'inclusiveness which might help him, unable as he was to accept Catholicism, to find a sense of belonging and community with his countrymen.

15. From the manifesto of the Irish Literary Theatre, quoted in Lady Gregory, *Our Irish Theatre*, p. 9.

16. 'The Message of the Folk-Lorist' (*Uncollected Prose*, vol.1, p.285).

17. 'To transmute the anti-English passion into a passion of hatred against the vulgarity and materialism whereon England has founded her worst life and the whole life that she sends us, has always been a dream of mine.' (*Autobiographies*, pp.431-2).

18. Cited Thompson, *The Imagination of an Insurrection*, pp.76-7.

19. Yeats knew this, as is demonstrated by his 1892 article, 'Hopes and Fears for Irish Literature', where he contrasts his literary aspirations with those of the members of the Rhymers' Club. (*Uncollected Prose*, vol.1, pp.247-50.)

20. As Yeats wrote in his diary for 1909: 'The need of a model of the nation, of some moral diagram, is as great as in the early nineteenth century, when national feeling was losing itself in a religious feud over tithes and emancipation. Neither

the grammars of the Gaelic League nor the industrialism of the *Leader*, nor the *Sinn Fein* attacks upon the Irish Party, give sensible images to the affections. Yet in the work of Lady Gregory, of Synge, of O'Grady, of Lionel Johnson, in my own work, a school of journalists with simple moral ideas could find right building material to create a historical and literary nationalism as powerful as the old and nobler. That done, they could bid the people love and not hate.' (*Autobiographies*, p.494).

21. Conor Cruise O'Brien, 'Notes on the Politics of Yeats', p.222.

22. Cited O'Brien, ed., *The Shaping of Modern Ireland*, p.111.

23. 'And we asked ourselves why our Willie Yeats should feel himself called upon to denounce his own class; millers and shipowners on one side, and on the other a portrait-painter of distinction; and we laughed, remembering AE's story, that one day whilst Yeats was crooning over his fire Yeats had said that if he had his rights he would be Duke of Ormonde. AE's answer was: I am afraid, Willie, you are overlooking your father – a detestable remark to make to a poet in search of an ancestry; and the addition: We both belong to the lower-middle classes, was in equally bad taste'. (*Hail and Farewell, A Trilogy*, vol.3, Heinemann, London, 1914, pp.160-1.)

24. See Harold Bloom, *Yeats* (Oxford University Press, New York, 1970), p.184: 'It is Yeats's highly individual contribution to the Romantic Sublime, this insistence that continued loss is crucial'.

25. This is a major theme in the great essay of 1917, 'Anima Hominis', where Yeats writes: 'The poet finds and makes his mask in disappointment, the hero in defeat.' (*Mythologies*, p.337).

26. Until, in fact, the kind of Ireland he had always dreaded – Catholic, middle-class, philistine, 'timid' – had come officially into being. Then the unmistakable and 'pure' Anglo-Irish tone emerges in poems like 'The Tower', 'Blood and the Moon' and 'The Seven Sages' (written in the period between 1925 and 1931), and in his famous speech during the Divorce Bill debate in the Senate in 1925: 'I think it is tragic that within three years of this country gaining its independence we should be discussing a measure which a minority of this nation considers grossly oppressive. I am proud to consider myself a typical man of that minority. We against whom you have done this thing are no petty people. We are one of the great stocks of Europe. We are the people of Burke; we are the people of Grattan; we are the people of Swift, the people of Emmet, the people of Parnell. We have created the most of the modern literature of this country. We have created the best of its political intelligence'. Cited in Donald R. Pearce, ed., *The Senate Speeches of W. B. Yeats* (Indiana University Press, Bloomington, 1960), p.99.

27. Alex Zwerdling, *Yeats and the Heroic Ideal* (Peter Owen, London, 1966).

28. Letter of 26 Sep. 1902. See Allan Wade, ed., *The Letters of W. B. Yeats* (Rupert Hart-Davis, London, 1954), p.379. There is a good discussion of Nietzsche's influence on Yeats in Denis Donoghue, *Yeats* (Fontana, London, 1971), pp.54 ff.

29. Cf. Yeats's 1930 diary entry: 'History is necessity until it takes fire in someone's head and becomes freedom or virtue'. (*Explorations*, p.336). The idea of creativity linked in flaming unity to destruction underlies Yeats's treatment of the poets of the 'Tragic Generation', in *Autobiographies*, pp.277-349. Perhaps Pater's famous phrase about burning 'with a hard gem-like flame' explains Yeats's fascination with the image. See Donoghue, *Yeats*, p.77.

30. From the introduction to 'Fighting the Waves' (1934) (*Explorations*, p.375).

31. 'The noble type of man . . . recognizes that it is he himself only that con-fers honour on things – he is *a creator of worth* . . . his morality is self-glorification', writes Nietzsche in *Beyond Good and Evil*. Cited from the translation in which Yeats first encountered Nietzsche: Thomas Common's compilation *Nietzsche as*

Critic, Philosopher, Poet and Prophet: Choice Selections from His Work (Unwin, London, 1902) p.110. And see Erich Heller, 'Yeats and Nietzsche: Reflections on a Poet's Marginal Notes', *Encounter*, vol.33 (December, 1969), pp.64-72.

32. In fact, Yeats originally thought his ancestors fought on the Jacobite side in 1690. The discovery that they had fought for William of Orange made no difference to him (beyond the alteration of a few lines) since, as I am arguing, the actualities of history Yeats tended to play down.

33. Brian Farrington, *Malachi-Stilt-Jack: A Study of W. B. Yeats and His Work* (Connolly Association pamphlet, London, 1965), p.9, makes the point forcefully.

34. *The Birth of Tragedy*, Common, pp.141-2.

35. See *Autobiographies*, p.395.

36. The 'sequence' which Harris argues for is Yeats's attempt to relate Coole firstly to Celtic Ireland, then to the Renaissance, and only finally to the eighteenth-century Anglo-Irish tradition (*Yeats: Coole Park and Ballylee*, The John Hopkins University Press, Baltimore, 1974, p.8). A useful article on Yeats's involvement with one aspect of the Renaissance is T. McAlindon, 'Yeats and the English Renaissance', *Publications of the Modern Language Association*, vol.82 (1967), pp.157-69.

37. See Lyons, *Ireland since the Famine*, pp.219, 289.

38. Harris, *Yeats: Coole Park and Ballylee*, p.60.

39. Major Robert Gregory, for example, is described in the noble elegy as 'our Sidney and our perfect man' (1918), and Yeats had begun earlier to see Lady Gregory as Castiglione's Duchess, as in his diary of 1909. (See *Autobiographies*, p.478). He continued to think of her in these terms.

40. Donoghue, *Yeats*, p.29.

41. See Zwerdling, p.81, and Harris, *passim*. Zwerdling speaks of Yeats's regard for 'the modern Irish aristocracy at its best', but exemplifies this only with reference to the Gregorys.

42. See Denis Donoghue's argument in *Yeats*, pp.120-2, that modern aesthetics are of their nature élitist, even authoritarian: 'The single article of faith which goes undisputed in the Babel of modern criticism is the primacy of the creative imagination . . . If you start with the imagination you propose an élite of exceptional men.'

43. In his 1901 essay, 'Magic' (*Essays and Introductions*, pp.28-52), Yeats explains that what he calls the Great Mind, or Great Memory – a kind of version of the collective or racial unconscious – can be evoked by symbols, and argues that 'imagination is always seeking to remake the world according to the impulses and the patterns in that Great Mind, and that Great Memory.' And see H. M. Block, 'Yeats's *The King's Threshold*: The Poet and Society', *Philological Quarterly*, vol. 34 (1955), pp.206-18; S. B. Bushrui, '*The King's Threshold*: A Defence of Poetry', *Review of English Literature*, vol.4 (1963), pp.81-94.

44. This is clearly a 'social' version of the 'personal' doctrine of the mask. See *Autobiographies*, pp.152, 463, and especially this, on pp.194-5: 'Nations, races and individual men are unified by an image, or bundle of related images, symbolical or evocative of the state of mind which is, of all states of mind not impossible, the most difficult to that man, race or nation; because only the greatest obstacle that can be contemplated without despair rouses the will to full intensity'. (Hence the importance of offering the aristocratic image to modern democratic and bourgeois Ireland.)

45. Dudley Young, *Out of Ireland: A Reading of Yeats's Poetry* (Carcanet Press, Cheadle, 1975) p.22.

46. 'Some will ask whether I believe in the actual existence of my circuits of sun and moon . . . I can but answer that if sometimes, overwhelmed by miracle as all men must be when in the midst of it, I have taken such periods literally, my reason has soon recovered, and now that the system stands out clearly in my

imagination I regard them as stylistic arrangements of experience comparable to the cubes in the drawing of Wyndham Lewis and to the ovoids in the sculpture of Brancusi' (*A Vision*, pp.24-5).

47. 'W. B. Yeats', *Horizon*, Jan. 1943. Reprinted in W. H. Pritchard, ed., *W. B. Yeats, A Critical Anthology* (Penguin, Harmondsworth, 1972), pp.190-1.

48. *The Identity of Yeats* (Macmillan, London, 1954), pp.260-3. While Ellmann admits that Yeats's stress is more on 'cyclical upheaval rather than future prosperity', the general tone of his analysis emphasises cyclical parallelisms. See also Jeffares, *Commentary*, p.289.

49. Ellmann, *Identity*; and T. R. Whitaker, *Swan and Shadow: Yeats's Dialogue with History* (University of North Carolina Press, Chapel Hill, 1964), pp.104-7. Whitaker's book is the most complete – and most arduous – attempt to relate Yeats's poems to the historical theories of *A Vision*, and is, generally and despite its obscurities, a most impressive critical work.

50. It is difficult to see why Whitaker, *Swan and Shadow*, p.105, speaks of the stanza as rendering the 'immediate sacred drama', when the emphasis seems to be on the human and time-bound response to the supernatural incursion.

51. 'The poems were written in 1926 with the exception of the latter stanza in II which was probably written in 1930-1931'. (Jeffares, *Commentary*, p.284).

52. Cf. the passage in *Autobiographies*, p.315, cited by Ellmann, *Identity*, p.262. 'Our love letters wear out our love; no school of painting outlasts its founders, every stroke of the brush exhausts the impulse'. Ellmann, despite this, does not feel that the last stanza follows very well from the rest of the poem, because he sees the whole as insisting chiefly on 'divine miracle'. He is particularly troubled by the last two lines.

53. In a letter of 1929 to T. Sturge Moore, Yeats wrote that Frobenius 'has confirmed a conception I have had for many years, a conception that has freed me from British liberalism and all its dreams. The one heroic sanction is that of the last battle of the Norse Gods, of a gay struggle without hope . . . The last kiss is given to the void' (cited Whitaker, *Swan and Shadow*, pp.112-13). The Nietzschean flavour here is also obvious.

54. This is the temptation so brilliantly described in Conrad's *Heart of Darkness*. Jung writes: 'Dionysus is the abyss of impassioned dissolution, where all human distinctions are merged in the animal divinity of the primordial psyche – a blissful and terrible experience. Humanity, huddling behind the walls of its culture, believes it has escaped this experience, until it succeeds in letting loose another orgy of bloodshed.' (Cited Whitaker, *Swan and Shadow*, pp.40-1).

55. See the superb lines in 'Meditations in Time of Civil War', VII, (*CP*, p.231):
'Vengeance upon the murderers', the cry goes up,
'Vengeance for Jacques Molay'. In cloud-pale rags, or in lace,
The rage-driven, rage-tormented, and rage-hungry troop,
Trooper belabouring trooper, biting at arm or at face,
Plunges towards nothing, arms and fingers spreading wide
For the embrace of nothing; and I, my wits astray
Because of all that senseless tumult, all but cried
For vengeance on the murderers of Jacques Molay.

56. This is the theme of 'Ancestral Houses', the first in the sequence of 'Meditations in Time of Civil War': 'O what if levelled lawns and gravelled ways . . . But take out greatness with our violence?'

57. Harvey Gross, *The Contrived Corridor: History and Fatality in Modern Literature* (University of Michigan Press, Ann Arbor, 1971), p.96.

58. See Helen H. Vendler, *Yeats's 'Vision' and the Later Plays* (Harvard University Press, Cambridge, Mass., 1963), p.106: 'Leda in the octave is "caught", but in the sextet she is "caught up"; there lies all the difference between captivity and rapture.'

59. For lines 11-12, Yeats originally wrote in draft 'Being so caught up/Did nothing pass before her in the air?' which suggests more clearly the possibilities of vision, though it is, compared to the final version, flaccid.

60. Compare words in a broadcast of 1936 on 'Modern Poetry': 'I think profound philosophy must come from terror. An abyss opens under our feet; inherited convictions, the pre-suppositions of our thoughts, those Fathers of the Church Lionel Johnson expounded, drop into the abyss. Whether we will or no we must ask the ancient questions: Is there reality anywhere? Is there a God? Is there a Soul? We cry with the Indian Sacred Book: "They have put a golden stopper into the neck of the bottle; pull it! Let out reality!"' (Yeats, *Essays and Introductions*, pp.502-3).

61. See Vendler, *Yeats's 'Vision' and the Later Plays*, p.152.

62. *Letters*, p.851.

63. Gross, *The Contrived Corridor*, pp.80-1.

64. *Letters*, p.741.

65. Vendler, *Yeats's 'Vision' and the Later Plays*, p.102. See 'Lapis Lazuli' (*CP*, pp.338-9), for a similar transposition of historical catastrophe into the terms of theatrical tragedy – 'All perform their tragic play . . . Black out; Heaven blazing into the head:/Tragedy wrought to its uttermost.'

66. 'Every time less than a pulsation of the artery/Is equal in its period and value to six thousand years./For in this period the poet's work is done, and all the great/Events of time start forth and are conceived in such a period,/Within a moment; a pulsation of the artery.' (Geoffrey Keynes, ed., Blake: *Complete Writings*, Oxford University Press, London, 1966, p.516.)

67. Bloom, *Yeats*, p.366.

68. Vendler, *Yeats's 'Vision' and the Later Plays*, p.99: '"The Second Coming" is a poem of intellectual acceptance and emotional retreat'. But, with Bloom, *Yeats*, p.321, I find in the poem emotional as well as intellectual acceptance.

69. Bloom, *Yeats*, p.324.

70. See the end of Yeats's essay on 'The Tragic Generation', *Autobiographies*, p.349.

71. See K. K. Ruthven, 'The Savage God: Conrad and Lawrence', *Critical Quarterly*, vol.10 (1968), p.39.

72. Julien Benda, *La Trahison des clercs* [*The Betrayal of the Intellectuals*], cited Fritz Stern, *The Politics of Cultural Despair: A Study in the Rise of the Germanic Ideology* (University of California Press, Berkeley, 1961), pp.xv and xvi.

73. Thomas Mann, *Friedrich und die grosse Koalition*, cited Ronald Gray, *The German Tradition in Literature, 1871-1945* (Cambridge University Press, London, 1965), p.39.

74. Gray, *The German Tradition in Literature*, p.52.

75. Thomas Mann, *Dr Faustus* (Penguin, Harmondsworth, 1968), pp.352-7.

76. Frank Kermode, *The Sense of An Ending: Studies in the Theory of Fiction* (Oxford University Press, New York, 1967), p.98.

77. Lionel Trilling, 'On the Teaching of Modern Literature', *Beyond Culture: Essays on Literature and Learning* (Secker and Warburg, London, 1966), p.3.

78. Yeats shared, in my view, this perverse excitement. In part – and this is an aspect of Yeats's complexity – behind his attitude lurks the old desire for 'unity of culture'. See two passages, both written in 1938: 'The danger is that there will be no war, that the skilled will attempt nothing, that the European civilisation, like those older civilisations that saw the triumph of their gangrel stocks, will accept decay . . . Love war because of its horror, that belief may be changed, civilisation renewed' (*Explorations*, p.425). And then: 'Desire some just war, that big house and hovel, college and public house, civil-servant – his Gaelic certificate in his pocket – and international bridge-playing woman, may know that they

belong to one nation' (*Explorations*, p.441).

79. An instructive comparison might be with Chekhov's dispassionate treatment of the passing of the cultured classes in *The Cherry Orchard*, where nostalgic and elegiac feelings are balanced by a clear-sighted view of their futility and irrelevance.

80. Standish O'Grady, *Selected Essays and Passages*, introduced by E. A. Boyd (Maunsel and Co., Dublin, n.d. [1918]), pp.180, 222. By contrast, Yeats, clearly familiar with O'Grady's essays, speaks of the Anglo-Irish Ascendancy thus in *Explorations*, p.350: 'Yet their genius did not die out; they sent everywhere administrators and military leaders, and now that their ruin has come . . . I would, remembering obscure ancestors that preached in their churches or fought beside their younger sons over half the world, and despite a famous passage of O'Grady's, gladly sing their song.'

Notes to Chapter 4

1. See Joyce's poem of 1904, 'The Holy Office', in *The Critical Writings of James Joyce*, eds. Ellsworth Mason and Richard Ellmann (Faber and Faber, London, 1959), p.152.

2. In a BBC Radio 3 broadcast in December, 1977.

3. Joyce, 'Ireland, Island of Saints and Sages', *Critical Writings*, p.171.

4. *Ibid.*, pp.162-3.

5. 'Fenianism. The Last Fenian', *ibid.*, p.190.

6. 'The Home Rule Comet', *ibid.*, p.213.

7. The hypothetical 'student of Trinity' is a neat and precise touch, since Trinity College was a bastion of English and Anglo-Irish values and attitudes. J. P. Mahaffy (1839-1919), a classics don and later Provost who had taught Wilde, embodied its snobbish arrogance; he would refer to 'my friend the King of Greece', but Queen Victoria was too bourgeois for him, 'having the manners of a badly-educated washerwoman'. (Cited in Ulick O'Connor's *Oliver St John Gogarty*, Jonathan Cape, London, 1964, p.17.)

8. Joyce, 'Ireland, Island of Saints and Sages', *Critical Writings*, p.170.

9. *Ibid.*, p.173.

10. *Ibid.*, p.243.

11. 'Oscar Wilde: the Poet of "Salomé"' (1909), *ibid.*, p.202.

12. 'Ireland, Island of Saints and Sages', *ibid.*, p.168.

13. *Ibid.*, p.70.

14. Frank Budgen, *James Joyce and the Making of 'Ulysses', and Other Writings*, with an introduction by Clive Hart (Oxford University Press, London, 1972 edn) (originally published in 1934), p.263.

15. See Joyce, 'The Soul of Ireland' (1903), *Critical Writings*, pp.102-5, a hostile review of Lady Gregory's anthology of folklore, *Poets and Dreamers*. Buck Mulligan says to Stephen: 'Longworth [the editor of the *Daily Express*] is awfully sick . . . after what you wrote about that old hake Gregory. O you inquisitional drunken jew jesuit! She gets you a job on the paper and then you go and slate her drivel to Jaysus' (*Ulysses*, p.204).

16. Joyce, 'Ireland, Island of Saints and Sages', *Critical Writings*, p.173.

17. Arthur Power, *Conversations with James Joyce*, ed. Clive Hart (Millington, London, 1974), p.33: '. . . in my experience the peasants in Ireland are a very different people from what he made them to be, a hard, crafty and matter-of-fact lot'.

18. Joyce, *Critical Writings*, p.44-5.

19. Joyce, *Stephen Hero*, p.83.

20. Joyce, *Critical Writings*, p.151.

21. J. P. Jakobsen, *Niels Lyhne* ('Siren Voices'), translated from the Danish by Ethel F. L. Robertson, with an introduction by Edmund Gosse (Heinemann, London, 1896), pp.xiv-xv.

22. *Ibid.*, p.138.

23. Letter of March, 1901, cited in Richard Ellmann, *James Joyce* (Oxford University Press, New York, 1959), pp.89-91. And see Joyce, *Stephen Hero*, p.45: 'the minds of the old Norse poet and of the perturbed young Celt met in a moment of radiant simultaneity'.

24. Joyce, *Critical Writings*, p.65.

25. Joyce, *Stephen Hero*, p.46.

26. Joyce, *Critical Writings*, p.42.

27. *Ibid.*, pp.54, 56.

28. Cited R. H. Deming, *James Joyce: The Critical Heritage* (2 vols., Routledge and Kegan Paul, London, 1970), vol.1, p.62.

29. John Gross, *Joyce* (Fontana/Collins, London, 1971), p.38.

30. Which was, indeed, the pseudonym Joyce used in the publication of the first story, 'The Sisters', in George Russell's *Irish Homestead* ('the pig's paper', as it is referred to in *Ulysses*).

31. *Letters of James Joyce*, eds. Stuart Gilbert and Richard Ellmann (3 vols., Faber and Faber, London, 1957, 1966), vol. 1, p. 55.

32. *Ibid.*, vol.2, p.134.

33. Joyce wrote to his publishers about 'the special odour of corruption which, I hope, floats over my stories' and about 'the odour of ashpits and old weeds and offal [which] hangs round my stories' (*Ibid.*, vol.2, p.123 and vol.1, p.64).

34. Peter K. Garrett, ed., *Twentieth Century Interpretations of 'Dubliners'*, Prentice-Hall, Englewood Cliffs, New Jersey, 1968), p.4.

35. Reprinted in Seon Givens, ed., *James Joyce: Two Decades of Criticism* (Vanguard Press, Inc., New York, 1948), pp.47-94.

36. *Ibid.*, p.76.

37. The whole question has been ably discussed by T. H. Gibbons, *'Dubliners* and the Critics', *Critical Quarterly*, vol. 9 (1967), pp. 179-87, who exposes the characteristic devices of analogical exegesis of Joyce's work: an illegitimate finding of similar forms of language and of parallel syntax being found to describe the two terms of the alleged analogy; a procedure involving highly selective use of evidence and an imprecise or 'sliding' use of terminology; and the use of parallel periphrases for unimportant elements, which then divert attention away from the more important differences.

38. 'The Unity of Joyce's *Dubliners*', *Accent*, vol.16 (1956), p.75. The article is reprinted in Garrett, ed., *Twentieth Century Interpretations of 'Dubliners'*, pp.57-85.

39. Garrett, *Twentieth Century Interpretations of 'Dubliners'*, p.61.

40. *Ibid.*, p.64.

41. Frank O'Connor, 'Work in Progress', from *The Lonely Voice: A Study of the Short Story* (Macmillan, London, 1963), pp.113-27.

42. Warren Beck, *Joyce's 'Dubliners': Substance, Vision and Art* (Duke University Press, Durham, N.C., 1969), p.15.

43. S. L. Goldberg, *James Joyce* (Oliver and Boyd Ltd., Edinburgh, 1962), p.38. One's disagreement with Goldberg's verb persists despite Joyce's praise of 'vivisection' as being the 'modern method' in art, in *Stephen Hero* (see above, p. 160). In the *Stephen Hero* context, there is no overtone of clinical and hostile dissection which Goldberg's use of the word implies.

44. Garrett, *Twentieth Century Interpretations of 'Dubliners'*, p.4.

45. *Ibid.*, p.4.

46. Joyce's own 'epiphanies' are collected and reprinted in Robert Scholes and Richard M. Kain, eds., *The Workshop of Daedalus* (Northwestern University Press, Evanston, 1965), pp.11-51.

47. Joyce's portrait of Mr Duffy in 'A Painful Case' is pertinent to my argument. For surely Mr Duffy, who 'wished to live as far as possible from the city of which he was a citizen', and whose rejection of any kind of human contact brings him to the bleak knowledge of his exile from life itself, embodies Joyce's critical comment on the self-defeating death-in-life of total detachment. The cost of severance from one's roots, whether willed or involuntary, is also a theme in the magnificent story 'The Dead', which has received so much and such excellent critical attention that I have not felt it necessary to discuss it here.

48. Beck, *Joyce's 'Dubliners'*, p.32.

49. Joyce, *Critical Writings*, p.45.

50. *Ibid.*, p.69.

51. *Ibid.*, p.152.

52. This may be said to be Joyce's secularised version of the theological concept of the *felix culpa*, or fortunate fall. The prevalence in modern literature of the notion of the artist as the man who courageously undertakes the exploration of hell has been discussed by Lionel Trilling in his essay 'On the Teaching of Modern Literature' in *Beyond Culture*.

53. Argued most persuasively, perhaps, in Hugh Kenner's *Dublin's Joyce* (Indiana University Press, Bloomington, 1956).

54. Gross, *Joyce*, p. 43.

55. Even here, Joyce indicates the rudiments of a saving sense of self-irony in Stephen, which will become more marked in *Ulysses*, for as sleep descends on his 'closely cowled head' Stephen 'seeing himself as he lay, smiled'.

56. Harry Levin, *James Joyce: A Critical Introduction* (Faber and Faber, London, 1944), p.42. See also Winston Weathers, 'A Portrait of the Broken Word', *James Joyce Quarterly*, vol.1 (1964), pp.27-40.

57. 'Fact / Has its proper plenitude'. Charles Tomlinson, *A Peopled Landscape* (Oxford University Press, London, 1963), p.14.

58. James H. Maddox, Jr, *Joyce's 'Ulysses' and the Assault upon Character* (The Harvester Press, Hassocks, Sussex, 1978), p.204. This book, which I found extremely stimulating, appeared after my work was already in manuscript; but I happily acknowledge that Mr Maddox had anticipated some of my own points.

59. C. H. Peake, *James Joyce: The Citizen and the Artist* (Edward Arnold, London, 1977), p.80.

60. Maddox, *Joyce's 'Ulysses'*, p.204.

61. *The Ordinary Universe: Soundings in Modern Literature* (Faber and Faber, London, 1968).

62. Goldberg, *The Classical Temper* (Chatto and Windus, London, 1961), pp. 41-65.

63. *Ibid.*, p.64.

64. Maddox, *Joyce's 'Ulysses'*, p.8.

65. Peake, *James Joyce*, p.65 (my italics).

66. Joyce, *Critical Writings*, p.43.

67. Budgen, *James Joyce*, p.107.

68. See, e.g., Goldberg, *The Classical Temper*, p.155.

69. A point made by Richard Ellmann, *The Consciousness of Joyce* (Faber and Faber, London, 1977), p.21.

70. 'Apart from parallel nocturnal settings, Joyce leaned upon Goethe's depiction of Mephistopheles for his own Mulligan. Mephistopheles is the spirit of

denial within the universe but also . . . within Faust's mind' (Ellmann, *The Consciousness of Joyce*, p.20).

71. Power, *Conversations with James Joyce*, p.98.

72. Johnson, *The History of Rasselas*, ch.32.

73. Geoffrey Keynes, ed., *Blake: Complete Writings* (Oxford University Press, London, 1966), p.604. Joyce had written, in his essay on Mangan in 1902, a passage full of echoes of Blake, which helps to illuminate the 'Nestor' episode: 'Poetry . . . as it is often found at war with its age, so it makes no account of history, which is fabled by the daughters of memory, but sets store by every time less than the pulsation of an artery, the time in which its intuitions start forth, holding it equal in its period and value to six thousand years. No doubt they are only men of letters who insist on the succession of the ages, and history or the denial of reality, for they are two names for one thing, may be said to be that which deceives the whole world.' (*Critical Writings*, p.81). E. L. Epstein discusses the problems and issues more fully, though I disagree with some of his conclusions, in *James Joyce's Ulysses: Critical Essays*, eds. Clive Hart and David Hayman (University of California Press, Berkeley, 1974).

74. Maddox, *Joyce's 'Ulysses'*, p.38.

75. Clive Hart makes the point in his *James Joyce's 'Ulysses'* (Sydney University Press, Sydney, 1968), p.53.

76. Ellmann, *The Consciousness of Joyce*, p.38.

77. Goldberg, *The Classical Temper*, p.66.

78. Budgen, *James Joyce and the Making of 'Ulysses'*, pp.17-18.

79. The reference here is to the Nameless One's characterisation of Bloom in the 'Cyclops' episode. 'Mister Knowall . . . old cod's eye . . . Gob, he'd have a soft hand under a hen' (pp.299-300).

80. This is true even of the Nameless One. 'You see', said Joyce, '"I" is really a great admirer of Bloom who, besides being a better man, is also more cunning, a better talker, and more fertile in expedients. If you reread *Troilus and Cressida* you will see that of all the heroes Thersites respects only Ulysses. Thersites admires Ulysses' (Budgen, *James Joyce and the Making of 'Ulysses'*, p.169).

81. If, as Mr Deasy says, the Englishman's proudest boast is 'I paid my way', the Irishman's might be 'I bought my round'. Backsliders from, or unbelievers in, this sacred principle are – as the unfortunate Bloom discovers – not favourably regarded.

82. Budgen, *James Joyce and the Making of 'Ulysses'*, pp.148-9.

83. *Ibid.*, p.262.

84. Goldberg, *The Classical Temper*, p.174.

85. Joyce was impressed by Verlaine's line 'Et tout le reste est littérature'. See *Critical Writings*, p.39.

86. Ellmann, *The Consciousness of Joyce*, p.13.

87. Joyce, *Letters*, vol.2, p.81.

88. V. S. Pritchett, 'The Comedian of Orgy', *New Statesman*, 15 Aug. 1969, p.205.

89. *Ibid.*

90. Eliot, '*Ulysses*, Order and Myth', *The Dial*, no.75 (1923), pp.480-3.

91. Arnold Kettle, *An Introduction to the English Novel* (2 vols., Hutchinson University Library, London, second edn, 1967), vol. 2, pp. 134-5.

92. Maddox, *Joyce's 'Ulysses'*, p.58.

93. Hart, *James Joyce's 'Ulysses'*, p.73.

94. From Litz's discussion of the 'Ithaca' chapter in Hart and Hayman, eds., *James Joyce's 'Ulysses': Critical Essays*, p.397.

95. '. . . if a writer were a free man and not a slave, if he could write what he chose, not what he must, if he could base his work upon his own feeling and not

upon convention, there would be no plot, no comedy, no tragedy, no love interest or catastrophe in the accepted style, and perhaps not a single button sewn on as the Bond Street tailors would have it.' ('Modern Fiction', *The Common Reader*: First Series, 1925; reprinted in *Collected Essays*, by Virginia Woolf, 4 vols., London, The Hogarth Press, 1966-7, vol.2, p.106.)

96. Power, *Conversations with James Joyce*, p.34. And see also pp.44-6 on Hardy.

97. Stanislaus Joyce, *My Brother's Keeper*, edited with an introduction by Richard Ellmann (Faber and Faber, London, 1958), p.106.

98. Anthony Cronin, *A Question of Modernity* (Secker and Warburg, London, 1966), p.71.

99. Maddox, *Joyce's 'Ulysses'*, p.177. He cites, among other examples, 'the disappointed bridge, the condition of almosting it, the Pisgah sight of Palestine, the life of Stephen's Shakespeare, "untaught by the wisdom he has written or by the laws he has revealed"'.

100. Goldberg, *The Classical Temper*, p.99.

101. T. S. Eliot (1919), reprinted in *The Sacred Wood* (Methuen, London, 1920), pp.47-59. Eliot writes: 'The progress of an artist is . . . a continued extinction of personality . . . the more perfect the artist, the more completely separate in him will be the man who suffers and the mind which creates'.

102. Ellmann, *James Joyce*, p.149.

103. *Ibid.*, p.275.

104. On 10 June 1919, Pound wrote to Joyce anent the 'Sirens' episode: 'In face of *mss* just arrived, I think . . . I may adjoin personal op. that you have once again gone "down where the asparagus grows" and gone down as far as the lector most bloody benevolens can be expected to respire' (*Pound/Joyce: The Letters of Ezra Pound to James Joyce, with Pound's Essays on Joyce*, ed. and with commentary by Forrest Read, Faber and Faber, London, 1968, p.157).

105. Stuart Gilbert, *James Joyce's 'Ulysses'* (Faber and Faber, London, revised edn 1952, originally published in 1930) stands probably at the head of the numerous critics who have devoted themselves to detailed study of the technical complexities of the novel. For him, every detail in *Ulysses* is significant, and with Joyce's apparent blessing, he argues the case for its highly schematic organisation with each episode being related not just to Homer, but to colours, organs of the body, particular arts, etc.

106. See Stanislaus Joyce, *My Brother's Keeper*, p.167: 'Surfeited with the tawdry melancholy of patriotic Irish poets, he [James] used to say that Ireland had contributed nothing but a whine to the literature of Europe'.

107. *Ibid.*, p.120: 'The interest that my brother always retained in the philosophy of the Catholic Church sprang from the fact that he considered Catholic philosophy to be the most coherent attempt to establish such an intellectual and material stability.'

108. See D. W. Jefferson, '*Tristram Shandy* and the Tradition of Learned Wit', *Essays in Criticism*, vol.1 (1951), pp.225-48, and Clive Hart, *James Joyce's 'Ulysses'*, p.88.

109. Power, *Conversations with James Joyce*, p.93.

110. See Vivian Mercier, *The Irish Comic Tradition* (Clarendon Press, Oxford, 1962).

111. Stanislaus Joyce, *My Brother's Keeper*, p.187. See also Hugh Kenner, *Flaubert, Joyce and Beckett: the Stoic Comedians* (W. H. Allen, London, 1964). Kenner calls Joyce 'the comedian of the inventory', and speaks of 'the comedy of exhaustion, comic precisely because exhaustive' (p.54); an idea I explore more fully below.

112. Hart, *James Joyce's 'Ulysses'*, pp.16-17.

113. Particularly useful on Joyce's attempts to solve this problem is A. Walton Litz, *The Art of James Joyce: Method and Design in 'Ulysses' and 'Finnegans Wake'* (Oxford University Press, London, 1961).

114. Forster's *Life of Charles Dickens*, cited W. J. Harvey, 'Chance and Design in *Bleak House*', in *Dickens and the Twentieth Century*, eds. John Gross and Gabriel Pearson (Routledge and Kegan Paul, London, 1962), pp.145-57.

115. A. W. Litz in Hart and Hayman, eds., *James Joyce's Ulysses: Critical Essays*, p.397: 'The relationship between objects and personality in Joyce's writing would seem to be much more complex than in Robbe-Grillet's. While "Ithaca" does resolve its human figures into their objective counterparts, at the same time the objective universe is suffused with their personalities'.

116. Litz, *The Art of James Joyce*, p.21.

117. Useful surveys of the critical argument may be found in Goldberg, *The Classical Temper*, and in W. M. Chace, ed., *Twentieth Century Views of Joyce* (Prentice-Hall, Englewood Cliffs, New Jersey, 1974).

118. Ellmann, *The Consciousness of Joyce*, pp.47-8.

119. As Kenner says in *Dublin's Joyce*, p.181: 'That the fundamental correspondence between Homer and *Ulysses* is not between incident and incident, but between situation and situation, has never gotten into the critical tradition'.

120. Stuart Gilbert, *James Joyce's 'Ulysses'*, p.266.

121. Joyce wrote to Budgen: 'Am working hard at *Oxen of the Sun*, the idea being the crime committed against fecundity by sterilizing the act of coition. Scene, lying-in hospital. Technique: a nine-parted episode without divisions introduced by a Sallustian-Tacitean prelude (the unfertilized ovum), then by way of earliest English alliterative and monosyllabic and Anglo-Saxon . . . then by way of Mandeville . . . then Malory's *Morte d'Arthur* . . . then the Elizabethan "chronicle style" . . . then a passage solemn, as of Milton, Taylor and Hooker, followed by a choppy Latin-gossipy bit, style of Burton-Browne, then a passage Bunyanesque . . . After a diarystyle bit Pepys-Evelyn . . . and so on through Defoe-Swift and Steele-Addison-Sterne and Landor-Pater-Newman until it ends in a frightful jumble of Pidgin English, Nigger English, Cockney, Irish, Bowery slang and broken doggerel. This procession is also linked back at each part subtly with some foregoing episode of the day and, besides this, with the natural stages of development in the embryo and the periods of faunal evolution in general. The double-thudding Anglo-Saxon motive recurs from time to time . . . to give the sense of the hoofs of oxen. Bloom is the spermatozoon, the hospital the womb, the nurse the ovum, Stephen the embryo. How's that for high?' (Cited Ellmann, *James Joyce*, pp.489-90).

122. I have not discussed Molly, for two reasons; one is that though full of an earthy vitality, and an important focus of Bloom's thoughts, she is not in herself an interesting or complex character. The Dublin of *Ulysses* is, as remarked earlier, a wholly male world; and Joyce is very Irish, as it seems to me, in the mixture of reverence and contempt with which he portrays women, especially Molly. Women are the life-givers, but let's keep them in the kitchen or – in Molly's case – the bed. Secondly, I agree with John Gross that – possibly as a result of Joyce's imperfect sympathy – the characterisation of Molly is flawed. There is too much strain between the attempt to present her as a naturalistic woman and the attempt to see her as an Earth-Goddess. (Gross, *Joyce*, pp. 71-2).

123. W.J. Harvey, 'Chance and Design in *Bleak House*', p. 146.

124. Eliot, *'Ulysses*, Order and Myth'.

125. The point is well made by T. Eagleton, *Exiles and Émigrés: Studies in Modern Literature* (Chatto and Windus, London, 1970), pp.171-2.

126. Gross, *Joyce*. pp. 63-4.

127. Budgen, *James Joyce and the Making of 'Ulysses'*, pp.69-71. Cf. Power, *Conversations with James Joyce*, p.97: 'cities are of primary interest nowadays,

said Joyce. This is the period of urban domination. The modern advance in techniques has made them so. − It is degeneration, I said. Joyce shrugged . . . − A writer's purpose is to describe the life of his day . . . and I chose Dublin because it is the focal point of the Ireland of today, its heart-beat you may say, and to ignore that would be affectation.'

128. Herring, 'Joyce's Politics', in *New Light on Joyce from the Dublin Symposium* ed. F. Senn, (Indiana University Press, Bloomington, 1972), pp. 3-14.

129. Conor Cruise O'Brien, ed., *The Shaping of Modern Ireland*, p. 14.

130. Budgen, *James Joyce and the Making of 'Ulysses'*, p.196. And see, *ibid.*, pp.339 and 345-6, where Budgen recants a much-quoted judgment of his: 'I must confess I was once guilty of helping to create the impression that Joyce was non-political. He was certainly non-party, but no man can be non-political who spends the greater part of his life in celebrating his native city'.

Notes to Chapter 5

1. David Krause, *Sean O'Casey: The Man and His Work* (MacGibbon and Kee, London, 1960) gives a very readable account of O'Casey's life; which is of course recounted by the author himself in lengthier and more colourful terms in the six volumes of autobiography. These appeared between 1939 and 1954. The six books were reprinted under the generic titles, *Mirror in My House* (2 vols. Macmillan, New York, 1956), and *Autobiographies* (2 vols. Macmillan, London, 1963).

2. Of O'Casey's third play to be rejected by the Abbey, *The Crimson and the Tri-Colour*, she remarked: 'I believe there is something in you and your strong point is characterization' (*Lady Gregory's Journals 1916-1930*, ed. Lennox Robinson, Macmillan, New York, 1947, p.73).

3. Ronald Ayling, ed., *Sean O'Casey: Modern Judgements* (Macmillan, London, 1969), p.11.

4. 'Illusion and Actuality in the Later O'Casey', in Ayling, *Modern Judgements*, p.145.

5. Krause, *Sean O'Casey*, p.69.

6. 'The Position of *The Plough and the Stars* in O'Casey's Dublin Trilogy', *James Joyce Quarterly*, vol.8 (1970), p.48.

7. Though many critics, like Kaufman in the article just cited, refer to O'Casey's three Dublin plays as a trilogy, this can be critically misleading. The differences between the plays are more interesting than their obvious and admitted similarities.

8. Krause, *Sean O'Casey*, p.86. He is taking issue with Ronald Peacock, *The Poet in the Theatre* (Harcourt, Brace, New York, 1946), pp.8-9, who states: '. . . in the present age, which is one of social disintegration . . . the individual is overshadowed by the conflict of impersonal forces . . . The tragic plays of O'Casey are symptomatic of this situation. His characters, vivid as some of them are, are not as important as the larger political tragedy of which they are fortuitous victims.' Both Peacock and Krause clearly see the *terms* of O'Casey's dramatic universe, but neither sees that, dramatically, the 'larger political tragedy' is something of a straw man. So Peacock gets the emphasis exactly the wrong way round, and Krause's assertion is pushing against an unresisting door.

9. Krause, *Sean O'Casey*, p.72.

10. Raymond Williams, *Drama from Ibsen to Brecht* (Chatto and Windus, London, 1968), p.148. Krause and Ayling both make much of the fact that

Williams's critique of O'Casey is headed (incautiously) 'A Note'. But there are seven pages, and whether or not one agrees with Williams, it is clear that he puts his finger on the central critical problems.

11. In Ayling, *Modern Judgements*, p.193.

12. First published 1949. Reprinted in *Autobiographies*, vol.2, p.9.

13. O'Casey's handling of the dynamics of crowd or party scenes, as here and in the pub scene of *The Plough*, has often been compared to Chekhov's mastery of the inappropriate or awkward festive celebration – one thinks of Mrs Ranevsky's decision to have a ball on the day of the auction of the cherry orchard.

14. Samuel Beckett has written enthusiastically of O'Casey as a poet of dis-integration. Reviewing O'Casey's *Windfalls*, a 1934 volume of verse, prose and 'two one-act knockabouts', Beckett sees these as the best things in it: 'Mr. O'Casey is a master of knockabout in this very serious and honourable sense – that he discerns the principle of disintegration in even the most complacent solidities, and activates it to their explosion. This is the energy of his theatre, the triumph of the principle of knockabout in situation, in all its elements and on all its planes, from the furniture to the higher centres. If *Juno and the Paycock*, as seems likely, is his best work so far, it is because it communicates most fully this dramatic dehiscence, mind and world come asunder in irreparable dissociation – "chassis".' From a review in *The Bookman*, vol.86 (1934), reprinted in Thomas Kilroy, ed., *Sean O'Casey: A Collection of Critical Essays* (Prentice-Hall, Englewood Cliffs, New Jersey, 1975), pp.167-8.

15. Seamus Deane, 'Irish Politics and O'Casey's Theatre', in Kilroy, *Critical Essays*, pp.149-58. I agree with much of what Mr Deane has to say; it may not be without significance that he, like the present writer, is of Northern Irish Catholic background and consequently the less impressed by O'Casey's dramatisation of Irish politics. See below, p.267.

16. 'Irish Politics', in Kilroy, *Critical Essays*, p.155.

17. Dion Boucicault (1820-1890), playwright, producer, actor, wrote or revamped many popular and highly theatrical plays, the most famous of which were 'Irish' – or stage-Irish: *The Colleen Bawn*, *The Shaughraun*, and *Arrah-Na-Pogue*.

18. Enid Welsford, *The Fool: His Social and Literary History* (Faber and Faber, London, 1935), p.317.

19. See Krause, ch.2, 'The Tragi-Comic Muse' and J. L. Styan, *The Dark Comedy*.

20. See W. Armstrong, 'Sources and Themes of *The Plough and the Stars*', *Modern Drama*, vol.4 (1961), pp.235-6.

21. 'A Dramatist of New-born Ireland', written 1927, reprinted in Ayling, *Modern Judgements*, p.65.

22. Krause, *Sean O'Casey*, p.39.

23. Kaufman, 'The Position of *The Plough and the Stars* in O'Casey's Dublin Trilogy', p.60.

24. Kilroy, *Critical Essays*, pp.6-7.

25. Williams, *Drama from Ibsen to Brecht*, p.149.

26. F. S. L. Lyons, *Ireland since the Famine*, p.275.

27. Williams, *Drama from Ibsen to Brecht*, p.149.

28. Eamonn McCann, *War and an Irish Town* (Penguin, Harmondsworth, 1974), p.119.

29. Reprinted in Robert Hogan, ed., *Feathers from the Green Crow: Sean O'Casey, 1905-1925* (Macmillan, London, 1963), p.88.

30. *Ibid.*, p.95.

31. A point made by Frank O'Connor, *The Backward Look*, p.217.

32. Seamus Deane, 'Irish Poetry and Irish Nationalism', in Douglas Dunn, ed.,

Two Decades of Irish Writing: A Critical Survey (Carcanet Press, Cheadle, 1975), p.8.

33. 'Sean O'Casey as a Socialist Artist', in Ayling, *Modern Judgements*, p.195.

34. To finish by arguing that *The Shadow of a Gunman* is O'Casey's most successful play may indeed be seen as falling victim to the dangers that Ayling sees lying on every side of the Irish critic in his approach to O'Casey (see above, p. 246). No; I enjoy parts of *Juno* and *The Plough* more than anything in *The Shadow of a Gunman*. My argument is, I hope, strictly in accord with literary principles: *The Shadow* is more consistent, unified, etc., than either of the other two. And it is extremely negative – so that I hope I cannot be accused of allowing nationalist sympathies to sway me. The two more famous plays seem to me, quite simply, and for all the local felicities, flawed as works of art.

35. Kilroy, *Critical Essays*, p.5.

SELECT BIBLIOGRAPHY

This bibliography makes no claim to be comprehensive. A complete bibliography of these four writers would be as long as the book itself. Further bibliographical information can be found in the following:

Finneran, R. J., ed. *Anglo-Irish Literature: A Review of Research* (The Modern Language Association of America, New York, 1976)

Deming, R. H. *A Bibliography of James Joyce Studies* (Kansas University Press, Kansas, 1964)

James Joyce Quarterly

Mikhail, E. H. *Sean O'Casey: A Bibliography of Criticism* (University of Washington Press, Seattle, 1972)

Levitt, Paul. *J. M. Synge: A Bibliography of Published Criticism* (Irish University Press, Dublin, 1974)

Mikhail, E. H. *J. M. Synge: A Bibliography of Criticism* (Macmillan, London, 1975)

Cross, K. G. W. and Dunlop, R. T. *A Bibliography of Yeats Criticism, 1887-1965* (Macmillan, London, 1971)

Stoll, J. E. *The Great Deluge: A Yeats Bibliography* (Whitston Publishing Co., Troy, New York, 1971)

The following is a list of works cited in the text:

Armstrong, W. 'Sources and Themes of *The Plough and the Stars*', *Modern Drama*, vol. 4 (1961), pp. 234-42.

Ayling, Ronald, ed. *Sean O'Casey: Modern Judgements* (Macmillan, London, 1969)

Beck, Warren. *Joyce's 'Dubliners': Substance, Vision and Art* (Duke University Press, Durham, North Carolina, 1969)

Beckett, J. C. *The Making of Modern Ireland, 1603-1923* (Faber and Faber, London, 1966)

—— *The Anglo-Irish Tradition* (Faber and Faber, London, 1976)

Blake, William. *Complete Writings*, ed. Geoffrey Keynes (Oxford University Press, London, 1966)

Block, H. M. 'Yeats's *The King's Threshold:* The Poet and Society', *Philological Quarterly*, vol. 34 (1955), pp. 206-18

Bloom, Harold. *Yeats* (Oxford University Press, New York, 1970)

Bowen, Elizabeth. *Bowen's Court* (Longmans, London, 1942)

Bowen, Elizabeth. *Seven Winters: Memories of a Dublin Childhood* (Longmans Green, 1943)

Boyce, D. G. *Englishmen and Irish Troubles* (Cape, London, 1972)

Brown, Malcolm. *The Politics of Irish Literature: From Thomas Davis to W. B. Yeats* (Allen and Unwin, London, 1972)

Budgen, Frank. *James Joyce and the Making of 'Ulysses', and Other Writings*, with an introduction by Clive Hart (Oxford University Press, 1972, originally published 1934)

Bushrui, S. *'The King's Threshold:* A Defence of Poetry', *Review of English Literature*, vol. 4 (1963), pp. 81-94

—— ed. *Sunshine and the Moon's Delight: J. M. Synge 1871-1909* (Smythe, Gerrards Cross, 1972)

Chace, W.M., ed. *Twentieth Century Views of Joyce* (Prentice-Hall, Englewood Cliffs, New Jersey, 1974)

Colum, Padraic. *The Road Round Ireland* (Macmillan, New York, 1926)

Common, Thomas. *Nietzsche as Critic, Philosopher, Poet and Prophet: Choice Selections from His Work* (Unwin, London, 1902)

Corkery, Daniel. *Synge and Anglo-Irish Literature* (Mercier Press, Cork, 1966. Originally published 1931)

Cornford, F. M. *The Origin of Attic Comedy* (Edward Arnold, London, 1914)

Corrigan, R. W. *Comedy: Meaning and Form* (Chandler, San Francisco, 1965)

Costello, Peter. *The Heart Grown Brutal: The Irish Revolution in Literature, from Parnell to the Death of Yeats, 1891-1939* (Gill and Macmillan, Dublin, 1977)

Cronin, Anthony. *A Question of Modernity* (Secker and Warburg, London, 1966)

Curtis, Edmund. *A History of Ireland* (Methuen, London, 1939, sixth edn 1950)

Curtis, Jr, L.P. *Anglo-Saxons and Celts: A Study of Anti-Irish Prejudice in Victorian England* (Bridgeport, Conn., 1968)

—— *Apes and Angels: The Irishman in Victorian Caricature* (David and Charles, Newton Abbot, 1971)

Davie, Donald. 'On the Poetic Diction of J. M. Synge', *Dublin Magazine*, vol. 27 (new series, 1952), pp. 32-8

Deming, R. H. *James Joyce: The Critical Heritage* (2 vols., Routledge and Kegan Paul, London, 1970)

Donoghue, Denis. *The Ordinary Universe: Soundings in Modern Literature* (Faber and Faber, London, 1968)

—— *Yeats* (Fontana, London, 1971)

Dunn, Douglas, ed. *Two Decades of Irish Writing: A Critical Survey* (Carcanet Press, Cheadle, 1975)

Eagleton, T. *Exiles and Emigrés: Studies in Modern Literature* (Chatto and Windus, London, 1970)

Edwards, R. Dudley. *A New History of Ireland* (Gill and Macmillan, Dublin, 1972)

Eliot, T. S. *The Sacred Wood* (Methuen, London, 1920)

—— 'Ulysses, Order and Myth', *The Dial*, no. 75 (1923), pp. 480-3

Ellis-Fermor, U. M. *The Irish Dramatic Movement* (Methuen, London, 1939)

Ellmann, Richard, ed. *The Artist as Critic: Critical Writings of Oscar Wilde* (W.H. Allen, London, 1970)

—— *The Consciousness of Joyce* (Faber and Faber, London, 1977)

—— and Ellsworth Mason, eds. *The Critical Writings of James Joyce* (Faber and Faber, London, 1959)

—— *The Identity of Yeats* (Macmillan, London, 1954)

—— *James Joyce* (Oxford University Press, New York, 1959)

—— and Stuart Gilbert, eds. *Letters of James Joyce* (3 vols., Faber and Faber, London, 1957, 1966)

Farrington, Brian. *Malachi-Stilt-Jack: A Study of W.B. Yeats and his Work* (Connolly Association, London, 1965)

—— 'Homage to J. M. Synge', *The Irish Times*, 17 April 1971

Fay, W. G. and Carswell, Catherine. *The Fays of the Abbey Theatre* (Rich and Cowan, London, 1935)

Flannery, James W. *W. B. Yeats and the Idea of a Theatre: The Early Abbey Theatre in Theory and Practice* (Yale University Press, New Haven and London, 1976)

Frye, N. 'The Argument of Comedy', in *English Institute Essays 1948*, ed. D. A. Robertson, Jr (Columbia University Press, New York, 1949)

—— *A Natural Perspective: The Development of Shakespearean Comedy and Romance* (Columbia University Press, New York, 1965)

Garrett, Peter K., ed. *Twentieth Century Interpretations of 'Dubliners'* (Prentice-Hall, Englewood Cliffs, New Jersey, 1968)

Gibbons, T. H. 'Dubliners and the Critics', *Critical Quarterly*, vol. 9 (1967), pp. 179-87

Gilbert, Stuart. *James Joyce's 'Ulysses'* (Faber and Faber, London, revised edn 1952, originally published 1930)

—— and Richard Ellmann, eds. *Letters of James Joyce* (3 vols., Faber and Faber, London, 1957, 1966)

Givens, Seon, ed. *James Joyce: Two Decades of Criticism* (Vanguard Press, New York, 1948)

Goldberg, S. L. *The Classical Temper* (Chatto and Windus, London, 1961)

—— *James Joyce* (Oliver and Boyd, Edingurgh, 1962)

Gray, Ronald. *The German Tradition in Literature, 1871-1945* (Cambridge University Press, London, 1965)

Greene, David H. and Stephens, Edward M. *J. M. Synge, 1871-1909* (Macmillan, New York, 1959)

Gregory, Lady Augusta, ed. *Ideals in Ireland* (At the Unicorn, London, 1901)

—— *Journals 1916-1930*, ed. Lennox Robinson (Macmillan, New York, 1947)

—— *Our Irish Theatre* (G. P. Putnam's Sons, New York, 1914)

Grene, N. *Synge: A Critical Study of the Plays* (Macmillan, London, 1975)

Griffin, Gerald. *The Wild Geese* (Jarrolds, London, 1938)

Gross, Harvey. *The Contrived Corridor: History and Fatality in Modern Literature* (University of Michigan Press, Ann Arbor, 1971)

Gross, John. *Joyce* (Fontana/Collins, London, 1971)

Harmon, M., ed. *The Celtic Master* (Dolmen Press, Dublin, 1969)

—— ed. *John M. Synge: Centenary Papers 1971* (Dolmen Press, Dublin, 1972)

Harris, Daniel. *Yeats: Coole Park and Ballylee* (The Johns Hopkins University Press, Baltimore, 1974)

Hart, Clive. *James Joyce's 'Ulysses'* (Sydney University Press, Sydney, 1968)

—— and David Hayman, eds. *James Joyce's 'Ulysses': Critical Essays* University of California Press, 1974)

Harvey, W. J. 'Chance and Design in *Bleak House*', in John Gross and Gabriel Pearson, eds., *Dickens and the Twentieth Century* (Routledge and Kegan Paul, London, 1962)

Heller, Erich. 'Yeats and Nietzsche: Reflections on a Poet's Marginal Notes', *Encounter*, vol. 33 (Dec. 1969), pp. 64-72

Henn, T. R., ed. *The Plays and Poems of J. M. Synge* (Methuen,London, 1963)

Henry, P. L. *An Anglo-Irish Dialect of North Roscommon* (University College Dublin publications, Dublin, 1957)

—— '*The Playboy of the Western World*', *Philologica Pragensis*, vol. 8 (1965), pp. 189-204

Hogan, Robert, ed. *Feathers from the Green Crow: Sean O'Casey, 1905-1925* (Macmillan, London, 1963)

Howarth, H. *The Irish Writers 1880-1940: Literature under Parnell's*

Star (Rockliff, London, 1958)

Humphreys, Alexander J. *New Dubliners: Urbanisation and the Irish Family* (Routledge and Kegan Paul, London, 1966)

Jakobsen, J.P. *Niels Lyhne [Siren Voices]*, translated from the Danish by Ethel F. L. Robertson, with an introduction by Edmund Gosse (Heinemann, London, 1896)

Jeffares, A. N. *A Commentary on the Collected Poems of W. B. Yeats* (Macmillan, London, 1968)

Jefferson, D. W. '*Tristram Shandy* and the Tradition of Learned Wit', *Essays in Criticism*, vol. 1 (1951), pp. 225-48

Joyce, Stanislaus. *My Brother's Keeper*, ed. with an introduction by Richard Ellmann (Faber and Faber, London, 1958)

Kaufman, M. 'The Position of *The Plough and the Stars* in O'Casey's Dublin Trilogy', *James Joyce Quarterly*, vol. 8 (1970), pp. 48-63

Kenner, Hugh. *Dublin's Joyce* (Indiana University Press, Bloomington, 1956)

—— *Flaubert, Joyce and Beckett: The Stoic Comedians* (W. H. Allen, London, 1964)

Kermode, Frank. *The Sense of An Ending: Studies in the Theory of Fiction* (Oxford University Press, New York, 1967)

Kettle, Arnold. *An Introduction to the English Novel* (2 vols., Hutchinson University Library, London, 2nd edn. 1967)

Kilroy, James. *The 'Playboy' Riots* (Dolmen Press, Dublin, 1971)

Kilroy, Thomas, ed. *Sean O'Casey: A Collection of Critical Essays* (Prentice-Hall, Englewood Cliffs, New Jersey, 1975)

Kinsella, Thomas. *Davis, Mangan, Ferguson? Tradition and the Irish Writer*. Writings by W. B. Yeats and by Thomas Kinsella (Dolmen Press, Dublin, 1970)

Krause, David. *Sean O'Casey: The Man and His Work* (MacGibbon and Kee, London, 1960)

Lee, Joseph. *The Modernisation of Irish Society, 1848-1918* (Gill and Macmillan, Dublin, 1973)

Levin, Harry. *James Joyce: A Critical Introduction* (Faber and Faber, London, 1944)

Litz, A. Walton. *The Art of James Joyce: Method and Design in 'Ulysses' and 'Finnegans Wake'* (Oxford University Press, London, 1961)

Loftus, R. *Nationalism in Modern Anglo-Irish Poetry* (Wisconsin University Press, Madison, 1964)

Lyons, F. S. L. *Ireland since the Famine* (Fontana, London, revised edn 1973)

McAlindon, T. 'Yeats and the English Renaissance', *Publications of the*

Modern Language Association of America, vol. 82 (1967), pp. 157-69

McCann, Eamonn. *War and an Irish Town* (Penguin, Harmondsworth, 1974)

Maddox Jr, James H. *Joyce's 'Ulysses' and the Assault upon Character* (Harvester Press, Hassocks, Sussex, 1978)

Mann, Thomas. *Dr Faustus* (Penguin, Harmondsworth, 1968)

Mansergh, Nicholas. *The Irish Question, 1840-1921* (George Allen and Unwin, London, 1965)

Mason, Ellsworth and Ellmann, Richard, eds. *The Critical Writings of James Joyce* (Faber and Faber, London, 1959)

—— *Beckett/Beckett* (Oxford University Press, New York, 1977)

Mercer, Vivian. *Beckett/Beckett* (Oxford University Press, New York, 1977)

—— *The Irish Comic Tradition* (Clarendon Press, Oxford, 1962) London, 1977)

Moore, George. *Hail and Farewell, A Trilogy* (3 vols., Heinemann, London, 1914)

—— *Parnell and His Island* (London, 1887)

O'Brien, Conor Cruise. 'Passion and Cunning: Notes on the Politics of Yeats', in A. N. Jeffares and K. G. W. Cross, eds., *In Excited Reverie: A Centenary Tribute to W. B. Yeats* (Macmillan, London, 1965)

—— ed. *The Shaping of Modern Ireland* (Routledge and Kegan Paul, 1960)

O'Casey, Sean. *Mirror in My House* (2 vols., Macmillan, New York, 1956)

O'Connor, Frank. *The Backward Look: A Survey of Irish Literature* (Macmillan, London, 1967)

—— *The Lonely Voice: A Study of the Short Story* (Macmillan, London, 1963)

O'Connor, Ulick. *Oliver St. John Gogarty* (Jonathan Cape, London, 1964)

O'Crohan, Tomas. *The Islandman* (1929), translated from the Irish with an introduction by Robin Flower (Chatto and Windus, London, 1934)

O'Driscoll, Robert, ed. *Theatre and Nationalism in Twentieth Century Ireland* (Oxford University Press, London, 1971)

O'Farrell, Patrick. *England and Ireland since 1800* (Oxford University Press, London, 1975)

O'Grady, Standish. *Selected Essays and Passages*, introduced by E. A. Boyd (Maunsel and Co., Dublin, n.d. [1918])

Peacock, Ronald. *The Poet in the Theatre* (Harcourt, Brace, New York, 1946)

Peake, C. H. *James Joyce: The Citizen and the Artist* (Edward Arnold, London, 1977)

Pearce, Donald R., ed. *The Senate Speeches of W. B. Yeats* (Indiana University Press, Bloomington, 1960)

Power, Authur. *Conversations with James Joyce*, ed. Clive Hart (Millington, London, 1974)

Price, Alan. *Synge and Anglo-Irish Drama* (Methuen, London, 1961)

Pritchard, W. H., ed. *W. B. Yeats, A Critical Anthology* (Penguin, Harmondsworth, 1972)

Pritchett, V. S. 'The Comedian of Orgy', *New Statesman*, 15 Aug. 1969, p. 205.

Read, Forrest, ed. *Pound/Joyce: The Letters of Ezra Pound to James Joyce, with Pound's Essays on Joyce*, with a commentary (Faber and Faber, London, 1968)

Roberts, Mark. *The Tradition of Romantic Morality* (Macmillan, London, 1973)

Ruthven, K. K. 'The Savage God: Conrad and Lawrence', *Critical Quarterly*, vol. 10 (1968), pp. 39-54

Scholes, Robert and Kain, Richard M., eds. *The Workshop of Daedalus* (Northwestern University Press, Evanston, 1965)

Senn, Fritz, ed. *New Light on Joyce from the Dublin Symposium* (Indiana University Press, Bloomington, 1972)

Sigerson, George, ed. *The Revival of Irish Literature: Addresses by Sir Charles Gavan Duffy, Dr. George Sigerson, and Dr. Douglas Hyde* (London, 1894)

Skelton, Robin. *J. M. Synge and His World* (Thames and Hudson, London, 1971)

—— *The Writings of J. M. Synge* (Thames and Hudson, London, 1971)

Smith, Howard. *Ireland: Some Episodes from Her Past* (BBC Publications, London, 1974)

Stern, Fritz. *The Politics of Cultural Despair: A Study in the Rise of the Germanic Ideology* (University of California Press, Berkeley, 1961)

Styan, J. L. *The Dark Comedy* (Cambridge University Press, London, 2nd edn 1968)

Tate, Allen, ed. *T. S. Eliot: The Man and His Work* (Chatto and Windus, London, 1967)

Thompson, W. I. *The Imagination of an Insurrection: Dublin, Easter 1916* (Oxford University Press, New York, 1967)

Tomlinson, Charles. *A Peopled Landscape* (Oxford University Press, London, 1963)

Trilling, Lionel. *Beyond Culture: Essays on Literature and Learning* (Secker and Warburg, London, 1966)

Tuohy, Frank. *Yeats* (Macmillan, London, 1976)

Ure, Peter. *Yeats the Playwright* (Routledge and Kegan Paul, London, 1963)

Vendler, Helen H. *Yeats's 'Vision' and the Later Plays* (Harvard University Press, Cambridge, Mass., 1963)

Wade, Allan, ed. *The Letters of W. B. Yeats* (Rupert Hart-Davies, London, 1954)

Weathers, Winston. 'A Portrait of the Broken Word', *James Joyce Quarterly*, vol. 1 (1964), pp. 27-40

Welsford, Enid. *The Fool: His Social and Literary History* (Faber and Faber, London, 1935)

Whitaker, T. R. *Swan and Shadow: Yeats's Dialogue with History* (University of North Carolina Press, Chapel Hill, 1964)

White, Terence de Vere. *The Anglo-Irish* (Gollancz, London, 1972)

Williams, Raymond. *Drama from Ibsen to Brecht* (Chatto and Windus, London, 1968)

—— *Keywords: A Vocabulary of Culture and Society* (Fontana, London, 1976)

Woolf, Virginia. *Collected Essays* (4 vols., The Hogarth Press, London, 1966-7)

Young, Dudley. *Out of Ireland: A Reading of Yeats's Poetry* (Carcanet Press, Cheadle, 1975)

Zwerdling, Alex. *Yeats and the Heroic Ideal* (Peter Owen, London, 1966)

INDEX

Abbey theatre 14, 33, 50n22, 59, 72,
  109, 245, 272, 274
Act of Union (1800) 27
Addison, Joseph 238n121
AE *see* Russell, George
Aeschylus 98
Allingham, William 99
D'Annunzio, Gabriele 229
Armstrong, W. 272n20
Arnold, Matthew 17, 96n14, 97
Ardilaun, Lord 118
Auden, W.H. 14
Ayling, Ronald 246, 247n4, 257n10,
  260n11, 273n21, 286n33, 287n34

Beardsley, Aubrey 190
Beardsley, Mabel 108
Beck, Warren 173, 178-9
Beckett, J.C. 15n2, 27, 28n32, 95
Beckett, Samuel 30, 262n14
Behan, Brendan 27
Benda, Julien 145
Bérard, Victor 236
Berkeley, Bishop George 30, 152
Black and Tans 134, 248-9, 251-4
Blake, William 31, 62, 96, 139, 144,
  203, 205
Blavatsky, Helena Petrovna 92, 96
Bliss, Alan J. 49n21, 50n23
Block, H.M. 123n43
Bloom, Harold 104n24, 145
Boucicault, Dion 268
Bowen, Elizabeth 19n12, 29
Boyce, D.G. 17n7
Brancusi, C. 129n46
Brandes, Georg 161
Brown, Malcolm 14n1
Browne, Sir Thomas 238n121
Budgen, Frank 158, 198, 211,
  212n80, 215-16, 238n121,
  239, 242-3
Bunyan, John 238n121; *The
  Pilgrim's Progress* 14, 170
Burke, Edmund 28, 106n26, 148,
  152
Burton, Robert 238n121
Bushrui, S. 50n23, 58n33, 59n38,
  83n82, 123n43

Carleton, William 72n58, 95
Carlyle, Thomas 16

Carswell, Catherine 70n55
Casement, Roger 87
Castiglione, Baldassare 118, 121n39
Catholic Emancipation Act (1829)
  27, 28n32
Cavalcanti, Guido 192
Chace, W.M. 235n117
Chaplin, Charlie 219
Chekhov, Anton 42n14, 149n79, 261n13
Clark, D.R. 59n37
Colum, Padraic 72
Common, Thomas 111n31
Congreve, William 152
Connolly, James 13, 113, 281
Conrad, Joseph 135n54, 145n71, 147,
  166
Corkery, Daniel 20-1, 42, 45, 48, 62, 71,
  77-8, 85-6
Cornford, F.M. 82n80
Corrigan, R.W. 83n81
Cosgrave, William 109, 221
Costello, Peter 14n1, 23n21, 26n27
Cronin, Anthony 226n98
Cross, K.G.W. 89n4
Curran, C.P. 167
Curtis, Edmund 27n30
Curtis Jr, L.P. 16n4, 17n6, 17n8, 18n9,
  72n60
Cusack, Michael 157

Dante 98, 207
Darwin, Charles 17n8, 37, 161
Davie, Donald 61n43, 91n8
Davis, Thomas 21n17, 22-3, 28, 70,
  93-4, 98-100
Davitt, Michael 22
Deane, Seamus 58, 262, 267, 285-6
Defoe, Daniel 238n121
Deming, R.H. 167n28
De Valera, Eamon 23, 33, 109, 242
Dickens, Charles 233, 239, 257
Dirane, Pat 77-8
Disestablishment Act (1869) 28n32
Disraeli, Benjamin 16
Donoghue, Denis 108n28, 110n29, 121-2,
  123n42, 152, 194
Dostoevski, Fyodor 147
Dublin Lockout (1913) 245, 259
Duffy, Sir Charles Gavan 19n13, 22
Dumas, Alexandre 188-9
Dunn, Douglas 286n32

320

Virgil 131, 188

Waugh, Evelyn 16, 106
Weathers, Winston 192n56
Wells, H.G. 219
Welsford, Enid 269-70
Whitaker, T.R. 131, 134n53, 135n54
White, Terence de Vere 30n36, 31n39
Wilde, Oscar 33, 152, 154n7, 156, 161
Williams, Raymond 25n26, 257, 280-1
Woolf, Virginia 226
Wordsworth, William 42-4

Yeats, Jack B. 39, 60n39
Yeats, John B. 69n54
Yeats, Lily 29
Yeats, William Butler 13-14, 17, 21, 23-8, 30-5, 38, 40-1, 44-6, 59-60, 62-5, 70-4, 83, 85-150 *passim*, 151-3, 158-60, 164, 189, 193, 199-200, 221-3, 229-32, 240, 242, 244, 246, 280, 282; 'Ancestral Houses' 177; 'Anima Hominis' 104n25; 'At Galway Races' 104; *Autobiographies* 38, 66, 87, 98n17, 100n20, 101, 103, 106-7, 110n29, 113, 116, 121n39, 124n46, 132n52, 139, 145n70; 'Beautiful Lofty Things' 109; 'Blood and the Moon' 106n26, 138; 'Byzantium' 142; *Cathleen ni Houlihan* 74, 87-9, 91-2, 94, 100-1; *The Celtic Twilight* 95; 'The Circus Animals' Desertion' 229; 'Coole Park, 1929' 127; 'Coole Park and Ballylee, 1931' 62n44, 116, 127-8, 149; *The Countess Cathleen* 25, 65-8, 101; 'Cuchulain's Fight with the Sea' 94; 'A Dialogue of Self and Soul' 135; 'Easter 1916' 91, 100, 111-13, 133; *Essays and Introductions* 31n40, 38n6, 41n12, 96n14, 99-100, 104, 107, 116, 123n43, 141n60, 145; *Explorations* 63, 65, 73, 86, 87n1, 89, 90n6, 110n29, 111n30, 114, 133, 141-3, 147n78, 150n80; *Fairy and Folk Tales of the Irish Peasantry* 95; 'Fallen Majesty' 150; 'Fergus and the Druid' 94; *The Green Helmet* 109, 114-15, 142; 'The Gyres' 129;

The Hour-Glass 140; 'In Memory of Major Robert Gregory' 110, 125; 'An Irish Airman Foresees His Death' 110-11; *The King's Threshold* 123-4, 137-8; 'The Lake Isle of Innisfree' 99; 'Lapis Lazuli' 135, 144n65; 'Leda and the Swan' 138, 140-5; 'The Madness of King Goll' 94; 'The Magi' 138-9; 'The Man and the Echo' 88; 'The Man Who Dreamed of Faeryland' 97; 'Meditations in Time of Civil War' 104, 117, 135n55, 136n56; *Memoirs* 91, 99; 'Meru' 139-40; 'The Municipal Gallery Revisited' 45n17, 117; 'My Descendants' 123; 'My Table' 135; *Mythologies* 104n25, 144; 'Nineteen Hundred and Nineteen' 134-8, 148; *On Baile's Strand* 133; 'On Those That Hated "The Playboy of the Western World", 1907' 63, 105; 'Pardon, old fathers' 103, 109, 111; 'Parnell's Funeral' 109, 221; 'The People' 121; *Per Amica Silentia Lunae* 144; 'Poetry and Tradition' 104-7, 115-16; 'A Prayer for My Daughter' 111, 125-6, 137; 'Remorse for Intemperate Speech' 244; *Representative Irish Tales* 95; *The Resurrection* 132, 141; 'The Rose Tree' 113; 'The Second Coming' 126-7, 133, 138, 142-5, 149, 223; 'September 1913' 87, 102-4, 108, 112; 'The Seven Sages' 106n26; *The Shadowy Waters* 60; 'Sixteen Dead Men' 74; 'The Stare's Nest by My Window' 221; 'The Statues' 124-5, 240; *Stories from Carleton* 95; 'Three Songs to the One Burden' 114; 'To A Friend Whose Work Has Come To Nothing' 107; 'To Be Carved on a Stone at Thoor Ballylee' 126; 'To Ireland in the Coming Times' 93; 'To a Wealthy Man Who Promised a Second Subscription to the Dublin Municipal Gallery If It Were Proved the People Wanted Pictures' 118-21; 'The Tower' 106n26, 148-9; 'Two Songs from a Play' 130-3, 135, 139; 'Under Ben Bulben' 96; *The Unicorn from the Stars* 138; 'Upon a Dying Lady' 108;